Lecture Notes in Computer Science 10470

Commenced Publication in 1973
Founding and Former Series Editors:
Gerhard Goos, Juris Hartmanis, and Jan van Leeuwen

More information about this series at http://www.springer.com/series/8379

Maciej Koutny · Jetty Kleijn
Wojciech Penczek (Eds.)

Transactions on
Petri Nets
and Other Models
of Concurrency XII

Editor-in-Chief

Maciej Koutny
Newcastle University
Newcastle upon Tyne
UK

Guest Editors

Jetty Kleijn
LIACS, Leiden University
Leiden
The Netherlands

Wojciech Penczek
Polish Academy of Sciences
Institute of Computer Science
Warsaw
Poland

ISSN 0302-9743   ISSN 1611-3349   (electronic)
Lecture Notes in Computer Science
ISSN 1867-7193   ISSN 1867-7746   (electronic)
Transactions on Petri Nets and Other Models of Concurrency
ISBN 978-3-662-55861-4   ISBN 978-3-662-55862-1   (eBook)
DOI 10.1007/978-3-662-55862-1

Library of Congress Control Number: 2008942189

Printed on acid-free paper

This Springer imprint is published by Springer Nature
The registered company is Springer-Verlag GmbH Germany
The registered company address is: Heidelberger Platz 3, 14197 Berlin, Germany

Preface by Editor-in-Chief

The 12th issue of LNCS *Transactions on Petri Nets and Other Models of Concurrency* (ToPNoC) contains revised and extended versions of a selection of the best papers from the workshops held at the 37th International Conference on Application and Theory of Petri Nets and Concurrency (Petri Nets 2016, Toruń, Poland, 19–24 June 2016), and the 16th International Conference on Application of Concurrency to System Design (ACSD 2016, Toruń, Poland, 19–24 June 2016). It also contains one paper submitted directly to ToPNoC.

I would like to thank the two guest editors of this special issue: Jetty Kleijn and Wojciech Penczek. Moreover, I would like to thank all authors, reviewers, and organizers of the Petri Nets 2016 and ACSD 2016 satellite workshops, without whom this issue of ToPNoC would not have been possible.

July 2017   Maciej Koutny

Preface by Editor-in-Chief

LNCS Transactions on Petri Nets and Other Models of Concurrency: Aims and Scope

ToPNoC aims to publish papers from all areas of Petri nets and other models of concurrency ranging from theoretical work to tool support and industrial applications. The foundations of Petri nets were laid by the pioneering work of Carl Adam Petri and his colleagues in the early 1960s. Since then, a huge volume of material has been developed and published in journals and books as well as presented at workshops and conferences.

The annual International Conference on Application and Theory of Petri Nets and Concurrency started in 1980. For more information on the international Petri net community, see: http://www.informatik.uni-hamburg.de/TGI/PetriNets/.

All issues of ToPNoC are LNCS volumes. Hence they appear in all main libraries and are also accessible on SpringerLink (electronically). It is possible to subscribe to ToPNoC without subscribing to the rest of LNCS.

ToPNoC contains:

- Revised versions of a selection of the best papers from workshops and tutorials concerned with Petri nets and concurrency
- Special issues related to particular subareas (similar to those published in the *Advances in Petri Nets* series)
- Other papers invited for publication in ToPNoC
- Papers submitted directly to ToPNoC by their authors

Like all other journals, ToPNoC has an Editorial Board, which is responsible for the quality of the journal. The members of the board assist in the reviewing of papers submitted or invited for publication in ToPNoC. Moreover, they may make recommendations concerning collections of papers for special issues. The Editorial Board consists of prominent researchers within the Petri net community and in related fields.

Topics

The topics covered include: system design and verification using nets; analysis and synthesis; structure and behavior of nets; relationships between net theory and other approaches; causality/partial order theory of concurrency; net-based semantical, logical and algebraic calculi; symbolic net representation (graphical or textual); computer tools for nets; experience with using nets, case studies; educational issues related to nets; higher level net models; timed and stochastic nets; and standardization of nets.

Also included are applications of nets to: biological systems; security systems; e-commerce and trading; embedded systems; environmental systems; flexible manufacturing systems; hardware structures; health and medical systems; office automation;

operations research; performance evaluation; programming languages; protocols and networks; railway networks; real-time systems; supervisory control; telecommunications; cyber physical systems; and workflow.

For more information about ToPNoC see: http://www.springer.com/gp/computer-science/lncs/lncs-transactions/petri-nets-and-other-models-of-concurrency-topnoc-/731240

Submission of Manuscripts

Manuscripts should follow LNCS formatting guidelines, and should be submitted as PDF or zipped PostScript files to ToPNoC@ncl.ac.uk. All queries should be addressed to the same e-mail address.

Preface by Guest Editors

This volume of ToPNoC contains revised versions of a selection of the strongest workshop papers presented at satellite events of the 37th International Conference on Application and Theory of Petri Nets and Other Models of Concurrency (Petri Nets 2016) and the 16th International Conference on Application of Concurrency to System Design (ACSD 2016).

As guest editors, we are indebted to the Program Committees of the workshops and in particular to their chairs. Without their enthusiastic support and assistance, this volume would not have been possible. The papers considered for this special issue were selected in close cooperation with the workshop chairs. Members of the Program Committees participated in reviewing the new versions of the papers eventually submitted.

We received suggestions for papers for this special issue from:

- ATAED 2016: Workshop on Algorithms & Theories for the Analysis of Event Data (chairs: Wil van der Aalst, Robin Bergenthum, and Josep Carmona),
- PNSE 2016: International Workshop on Petri Nets and Software Engineering (chairs: Lawrence Cabac, Lars Michael Kristensen, and Heiko Rölke).

The authors of these papers were invited to improve and extend their results where possible, based on the comments received before and during the workshops. Each resulting revised submission was reviewed by at least two referees. We followed the principle of asking for fresh reviews of the revised papers, also from referees not involved initially in the reviewing of the original workshop contributions. All papers went through the standard two-stage journal reviewing process, and eventually eight were accepted after rigorous reviewing and revising. In addition to these first eight papers, one paper was submitted directly to the Editor-in-Chief of the ToPNoC series through the regular submission track and handled by him as is usual for journal submissions.

The main purpose of the paper "Properties of Plain, Pure, and Safe Petri Nets" by Kamila Barylska, Eike Best, Uli Schlachter, and Valentin Spreckels, is to demonstrate that it is worthwile and useful to aim for a partial characterization of the state spaces of plain, pure, and safe Petri nets. It gives a set of necessary conditions for a Petri net to be plain, pure, and safe, and describes some applications of these conditions both in practice (for Petri net synthesis) and in theory (e.g., as part of a characterization of the reachability graphs of live and safe marked graphs).

The paper "Similarity-Based Approaches for Determining the Number of Trace Clusters in Process Discovery" by Pieter De Koninck and Jochen De Weerdt, considers trace clustering techniques used to partition an event log into subsets with a lower degree of variation. It presents approaches to determine the appropriate number of clusters in a trace clustering context. Two approaches built on similarity are proposed: a stability- and a separation-based method. Both approaches are tested on multiple real-life datasets to investigate the complementarity of the different components leading to results suggesting that both are successful in identifying an appropriate number of trace clusters.

Imposing access control onto workflows considerably reduces the set of users authorized to execute the workflow tasks. The paper "Log- and Model-Based Techniques for Security-Sensitive Tackling of Obstructed Workflow Executions" by Julius Holderer, Josep Carmona, Farbod Taymouri, and Günter Müller, envisages a new hybrid approach. The workflow and its authorizations into a Petri net are flattened and encode the obstruction with a corresponding 'obstruction marking'. Depending on whether a log is provided or not, different actions are taken.

Nowadays, distributed storage systems are ubiquitous, very often under the form of a hierarchy of multiple caches. In their paper "Formal Modelling and Analysis of Distributed Storage Systems", Jordan de la Houssaye, Franck Pommereau, and Philippe Deniel, propose a formal modelling framework to design distributed storage systems, with the innovating feature of separating the various concerns like data-model, operations, policy, consistency, topology, etc. They focus on performance analysis. The potential of the approach is illustrated by an example.

The integrated management of business processes and master data is a fundamental problem. The paper "DB-Nets: On The Marriage of Colored Petri Nets and Relational Databases", by Marco Montali and Andrey Rivkin, studies the foundations of the problem, arguing that contemporary approaches struggle to find a suitable equilibrium between data- and process-related aspects. The paper proposes a new formal model, called db-nets, that balances these two pillars through the marriage of colored Petri nets and relational databases.

Transition systems are a powerful formalism, which is widely used for process model representation from event logs. The paper "Transition Systems Reduction: Balancing between Precision and Simplicity" by Sergey A. Shershakov, Anna A. Kalenkova, and Irina A. Lomazova, proposes an original approach to discovering transition systems that perfectly fit event logs and whose size is adjustable depending on the user's need. The suggested approach allows the user to achieve the required balance between simple and precise models.

Partial order reduction is an important method for reducing state spaces. The paper "Stubborn Set Intuition Explained" by Antti Valmari and Henri Hansen, focuses on the differences between stubborn sets and other partial order methods. The deadlock-preserving stubborn set method is compared with the deadlock-preserving ample set and persistent set methods. Conditions to ensure that the reduced state space preserves the ordering of visible transitions are discussed and solutions to the ignoring problem are analyzed, both when only safety properties are to be preserved and when also liveness properties are relevant.

In the area of process mining, decomposed replay has been proposed to be able to deal with nets and logs containing many different activities. The paper "Decomposed Replay Using Hiding and Reduction as Abstraction", by H.M.W. Verbeek, shows an example net and log for which the decomposed replay may take much more time, and provides an explanation of why this is the case. To mitigate this problem, the paper proposes an alternative way to abstract the subnets from the single net, and shows that the decomposed replay using this alternative abstraction is faster than the monolithic replay.

Finally, the paper "Multiplicative Transition Systems" by Józef Winkowski was submitted directly to ToPNoC through the regular submission track. This article is concerned with algebras, called multiplicative transition systems, whose elements can be used to represent the runs of a system. The paper discusses how these algebras can represent discrete as well as continuous and partially continuous runs.

As guest editors, we would like to thank all authors and referees who contributed to this issue. The quality of this volume is the result of the high scientific value of their work. Moreover, we would like to acknowledge the excellent cooperation throughout the whole process that has made our work a pleasant task. We are also grateful to the Springer/ToPNoC team for the final production of this issue.

July 2017

Jetty Kleijn
Wojciech Penczek

Organization of This Issue

Guest Editors

Jetty Kleijn   Leiden University, The Netherlands
Wojciech Penczek   Polish Academy of Sciences, Poland

Workshop Co-chairs

Wil van der Aalst   Eindhoven University of Technology, The Netherlands
Robin Bergenthum   FernUniversität in Hagen, Germany
Lawrence Cabac   University of Hamburg, Germany
Josep Carmona   Universitat Politecnica de Catalunya, Spain
Lars Michael Kristensen   Bergen University College, Norway
Heiko Rölke   DIPF, Germany

Reviewers

Eric Badouel
Luca Bernardinello
Andrea Burattin
Lawrence Cabac
Josep Carmona
Claudio Di Ciccio
Jose Manuel Colom
Raymond Devillers
Dirk Fahland
Diogo R. Ferreira
Stefan Haar
Keijo Heljanko
Anna Kalenkova

Ekkart Kindler
Hanna Klaudel
Lars Kristensen
Benjamin Meis
Madhavan Mukund
Laure Petrucci
Marta Pietkiewicz-Koutny
Uli Schlachter
Natalia Sidorova
Eric Verbeek
Jan Martijn van der Werf
Karsten Wolf

Contents

Properties of Plain, Pure, and Safe Petri Nets 1
Kamila Barylska, Eike Best, Uli Schlachter, and Valentin Spreckels

Similarity-Based Approaches for Determining the Number
of Trace Clusters in Process Discovery 19
Pieter De Koninck and Jochen De Weerdt

Log- and Model-Based Techniques for Security-Sensitive Tackling
of Obstructed Workflow Executions 43
*Julius Holderer, Josep Carmona, Farbod Taymouri,
and Günter Müller*

Formal Modelling and Analysis of Distributed Storage Systems 70
Jordan de la Houssaye, Franck Pommereau, and Philippe Deniel

DB-Nets: On the Marriage of Colored Petri Nets
and Relational Databases 91
Marco Montali and Andrey Rivkin

Transition Systems Reduction: Balancing Between Precision
and Simplicity 119
*Sergey A. Shershakov, Anna A. Kalenkova,
and Irina A. Lomazova*

Stubborn Set Intuition Explained. 140
Antti Valmari and Henri Hansen

Decomposed Replay Using Hiding and Reduction as Abstraction 166
H.M.W. Verbeek

Multiplicative Transition Systems 187
Józef Winkowski

Author Index 217

Properties of Plain, Pure, and Safe Petri Nets

Kamila Barylska[1], Eike Best[2(✉)], Uli Schlachter[2], and Valentin Spreckels[2]

[1] Faculty of Mathematics and Computer Science, Nicolaus Copernicus University,
87-100 Toruń, Poland
kamila.barylska@mat.umk.pl
[2] Department of Computing Science, Carl von Ossietzky Universität Oldenburg,
26111 Oldenburg, Germany
{eike.best,schlachter,spreckels}@informatik.uni-oldenburg.de

Abstract. A set of necessary conditions for a Petri net to be plain, pure and safe is given. Some applications of these conditions both in practice (for Petri net synthesis), and in theory (e.g., as part of a characterisation of the reachability graphs of live and safe marked graphs) are described.

Keywords: Labelled transition systems · Marked graphs · Petri nets

1 Introduction

In this paper, we examine plain, pure and safe (pps) Petri nets. Such nets are intimately related to elementary Petri net systems, for which a substantial body of literature exists (e.g., [11–13,15,16]). Many interesting properties of pps nets are PSPACE-hard [8], and their synthesis problem is NP-hard [1]. The state spaces of pps nets are finite due to safeness,[1] but they are sufficiently complex in general, so that a full characterisation of them is presently out of reach.[2]

This complexity notwithstanding, the main purpose of this paper is to demonstrate that it is worthwile and useful to aim for a *partial* characterisation of pps Petri net state spaces. More specifically, our aim is to demonstrate that a strong set of properties can be delineated which are *necessarily* true in the reachability graphs of pps nets, and to hint at the use of such properties in the design of targetted synthesis [2,17], as well as for the easy recognition of transition systems which are not synthesisable into a pps Petri net.

The first part of this paper describes a collection of such necessary properties. We claim that they are useful in at least three ways: (i) for gaining some insight into the structure of pps net reachability graphs; (ii) for checking the

---

K. Barylska—Co-funded by project PO KL Information technologies: Research and their interdisciplinary applications, Agreement UDA-POKL.04.01.01-00-051/10-00 and by the Polish National Science Center (grant No.2013/09/D/ST6/03928).

U. Schlachter—Supported by DFG (German Research Foundation) through grant Be 1267/15-1 ARS (Algorithms for Reengineering and Synthesis).

[1] Unless infinite nets are considered, which we shall exclude in this paper.

[2] Characterisations have been obtained for more restricted classes, e.g. in [4].

© Springer-Verlag GmbH Germany 2017
M. Koutny et al. (Eds.): ToPNoC XII, LNCS 10470, pp. 1–18, 2017.
DOI: 10.1007/978-3-662-55862-1_1

non-synthesisability of such nets before or during synthesis; and (iii) for char-
acterising classes of pps nets. The results in the first part of this paper serve
to corroborate Claim (i), while Claims (ii) and (iii) will be substantiated in the
second part.

The organisation of the paper is as follows. Section 2 contains basic definitions
and a first example. In Sect. 3, we shall prove a set of properties which can be
seen as typical for plain, pure and safe Petri nets. Some of them apply to finite
transition systems in general, others do not. In Sect. 4, our results are applied in
two different ways. Section 4.1 describes a conjecture due to Edward Ochmański
[11], which relates to fairness and has (to our knowledge) not yet been resolved.
One of the properties derived in Sect. 3 will be used in order to show that a
tentative counterexample cannot be synthesised into a pps net. In Section 4.2,
we derive a simplification of a characterisation of the state spaces of live and
safe marked graphs [4,6], using one of the properties examined in Sect. 3. The
paper concludes with Sect. 5.

2 Labelled Transition Systems and Petri Nets

In accordance with Petri net synthesis theory [2], the basic objects of our study
are transition-unlabelled Petri nets and edge-labelled transition systems, where
the labels correspond to transitions, just like in the reachability graph of a net.

Definition 1. Labelled transition systems
A labelled transition system with initial state, abbreviated lts, is a quadruple
$TS = (S, \rightarrow, T, s_0)$ where S is a set of *states*, T is a set of *labels* with $S \cap T = \emptyset$,
$\rightarrow \subseteq (S \times T \times S)$ is the *transition relation*, and $s_0 \in S$ is an *initial state*.[3] A label
t is *enabled* in a state s, denoted by $s[t\rangle$, if there is some state $s' \in S$ such that
$(s, t, s') \in \rightarrow$, and *backward enabled* in s, denoted by $[t\rangle s$, if there is some state
$s'' \in S$ such that $(s'', t, s) \in \rightarrow$. For $s \in S$, let $s^\bullet = \{t \in T \mid s[t\rangle\}$. For $t \in T$,
$s[t\rangle s'$ iff $(s, t, s') \in \rightarrow$, meaning that s' is *reachable* from s through the execution
of t. The definitions of enabledness and of the reachability relation are extended
to sequences $\sigma \in T^*$:

$s[\varepsilon\rangle$ and $s[\varepsilon\rangle s$ are always true;
$s[\sigma t\rangle$ $(s[\sigma t\rangle s')$ iff there is some s'' with $s[\sigma\rangle s''$ and $s''[t\rangle$ $(s''[t\rangle s'$, respectively).

For any $s \in S$, $[s\rangle = \{s' \in S \mid \exists \sigma \in T^* : s[\sigma\rangle s'\}$ denotes the set of
states reachable from s. Two lts with the same label set, $(S, \rightarrow, T, s_0)$ and
$(S', \rightarrow', T, s'_0)$, will be called *isomorphic* if there is a bijection $\beta \colon S \rightarrow S'$ such
that $s'_0 = \beta(s_0)$ and $(r, t, s) \in \rightarrow$ iff $(\beta(r), t, \beta(s)) \in \rightarrow'$.

For a finite sequence $\sigma \in T^*$ of labels, the *Parikh vector* $\Psi(\sigma)$ is a T-vector
(i.e., a vector of natural numbers with index set T), where $\Psi(\sigma)(t)$ denotes the
number of occurrences of t in σ. A sequence $s[\sigma\rangle s$ is called a *cycle*, or more

---

[3] S can also be considered as a set of vertices and $\rightarrow$ as a set of edges of a directed
graph, labelled by letters from T.

precisely a *cycle at state* s. The cycle is *nontrivial* if $\sigma \neq \varepsilon$. An lts is called *acyclic* if it has no nontrivial cycles. A nontrivial cycle $s[\sigma\rangle s$ is called *small* if there is no nontrivial cycle $s'[\sigma'\rangle s'$ with $s' \in [s_0\rangle$ and $\Psi(\sigma') \lneqq \Psi(\sigma)$, where, by definition, $\lneqq$ equals $(\leq \cap \neq)$. An lts has property **P1** [4] if the Parikh vector of any small cycle in TS contains each transition exactly once.   □ 1

Definition 2. Basic properties of labelled transition systems
A labelled transition system $(S, \rightarrow, T, s_0)$ is called *totally reachable* if $[s_0\rangle = S$ (i.e., every state is reachable from s_0); *finite* if S and T (hence also $\rightarrow$) are finite sets; *deterministic*, if for any states $s, s', s'' \in [s_0\rangle$ and sequences $\sigma, \tau \in T^*$ with $\Psi(\sigma) = \Psi(\tau)$: $(s[\sigma\rangle s' \wedge s[\tau\rangle s'') \Rightarrow s' = s''$ and $(s'[\sigma\rangle s \wedge s''[\tau\rangle s) \Rightarrow s' = s''$ (i.e., from any one state, Parikh-equivalent sequences may not lead to two different successor states, nor come from two different predecessor states); *reversible* if $\forall s \in [s_0\rangle \colon s_0 \in [s\rangle$ (i.e., s_0 always remains reachable); *persistent* [9] if for all reachable states s, s', s'', and labels t, u, if $s[t\rangle s'$ and $s[u\rangle s''$ with $t \neq u$, then there is some (reachable) state $r \in S$ such that both $s'[u\rangle r$ and $s''[t\rangle r$ (i.e., once two different labels are both enabled, neither can disable the other, and executing both, in any order, leads to the same state); *backward persistent* if for all reachable states s, s', s'', and labels t, u, if $s'[t\rangle s$ and $s''[u\rangle s$ and $t \neq u$, then there is some reachable state $r \in S$ such that both $r[u\rangle s'$ and $r[t\rangle s''$ (i.e., persistence in backward direction).   □ 2

Definition 3. Petri nets
A (finite, initially marked, place-transition, arc-weighted) Petri net is a quadruple $N = (P, T, F, M_0)$ such that P is a finite set of *places*, T is a finite set of *transitions*, with $P \cap T = \emptyset$, F is a *flow* function $F \colon ((P \times T) \cup (T \times P)) \rightarrow \mathbb{N}$, and M_0 is the *initial marking*, where a *marking* is a mapping $M \colon P \rightarrow \mathbb{N}$. A transition $t \in T$ is *enabled by* a marking M, denoted by $M[t\rangle$, if for all places $p \in P$, $M(p) \geq F(p, t)$. If t is enabled at M, then t can *occur* (or *fire*) in M, leading to the marking M' defined by $M'(p) = M(p) - F(p, t) + F(t, p)$ (denoted by $M[t\rangle M'$). The set of markings reachable from M is denoted $[M\rangle$. The *reachability graph of* N, $RG(N)$, is the labelled transition system with the set of vertices $[M_0\rangle$ and set of edges $\{(M, t, M') \mid M, M' \in [M_0\rangle \wedge M[t\rangle M'\}$.   □ 3

Note that all notions defined for transition systems are carried over automatically to Petri nets through the fact that reachability graphs are transition systems.

Notes on notation: In all our propositions and examples, we shall use letters $a, b, c, \ldots \in T$ (but also $t \in T$) for the labels of a transition system (or, respectively, for the corresponding transitions of a Petri net); $u, v, w \in T^*$ or $\sigma, \tau \in T^*$ for sequences of transitions; p, q for the places of a net; and M, K, L for the markings of a net.

Definition 4. Basic structural properties of Petri nets
For a place p and a transition t of a Petri net $N = (P, T, F, M_0)$, let ${}^\bullet t = \{p \in P \mid F(p, t) > 0\}$ be the *preset of* t containing *pre-places*, $t^\bullet = \{p \in P \mid F(t, p) > 0\}$

its *postset* containing *post-places*, $^\bullet p = \{t \in T \mid F(t,p) > 0\}$ the *preset of* p, and $p^\bullet = \{t \in T \mid F(p,t) > 0\}$ its *postset*. N is called *connected* if it is weakly connected as a graph; *plain* if $cod(F) \subseteq \{0,1\}$; *pure* or *side-condition free* if $p^\bullet \cap {}^\bullet p = \emptyset$ for all places $p \in P$; and a *marked graph* if N is plain and $|p^\bullet| = 1$ and $|{}^\bullet p| = 1$ for all places $p \in P$.   □ 4

Definition 5. Basic behavioural properties of Petri nets
A Petri net $N = (P, T, F, M_0)$ is *k-bounded* for some $k \in \mathbb{N}$, if $\forall M \in [M_0\rangle \colon \forall p \in P \colon M(p) \leq k$ (i.e., the number of tokens on any place never exceeds k); *safe* if it is 1-bounded; *bounded* if $\exists k \in \mathbb{N} \colon N$ is k-bounded; *persistent* (*reversible*) if its reachability graph is persistent (reversible, respectively); and *live* if $\forall t \in T \colon \forall M \in [M_0\rangle \colon \exists M' \in [M\rangle \colon M[t\rangle$ (i.e., no transition can be made unfireable). Finally, N is called *pps* if it is plain, pure, and safe.   □ 5

The class of pps Petri nets is closely related to *elementary nets* [16], as follows. Elementary Petri nets have a strengthened firing rule: viz., t can occur if all its pre-places have exactly one token *and* all its post-places have exactly zero tokens. Every elementary net with this strengthened firing rule can be turned into an equivalent pps net with the usual firing rule, by adding appropriate complement places. Conversely, for pps nets, the two firing rules coincide. The next proposition, definition, and example, are designed to illustrate the relationship between transition systems and Petri nets.

Proposition 1. Properties of Petri net reachability graphs [14]
The reachability graph RG of a Petri net N is totally reachable and deterministic. N is bounded iff RG is finite.   □ 1

Pictorially, a transition system is represented as a directed graph whose nodes are states and whose edges are labelled with labels from the set T. As an example, consider the labelled transition system TS_0 shown on the left-hand side of Fig. 1. It has six states and five edges.

A Petri net, on the other hand, is represented by circle for places, tokens inside places to represent markings, squares for transitions, and directed arrows, inscribed by their weights, for arcs. For simplicity, arcs with weight zero are omitted altogether, and arcs with weight one are drawn without any explicit inscription.[4] As an example, the net N_0 shown on the right-hand side of Fig. 1 has six places, three transitions, 12 arcs with weight 1, and a marking comprising three tokens.

Definition 6. Solvability and pps-solvability
A Petri net N *solves* a transition system TS if $RG(N)$ and TS are isomorphic. A transition system is *pps-solvable* if there is a pps Petri net solving it.   □ 6

As an example, consider Fig. 1. N_0 solves TS_0.[5] Since N_0 is plain and safe, but not pure, this does not imply that TS_0 is pps-solvable. As we develop our set

---

[4] In this paper, no arc weights greater than 1 will be considered.
[5] This can be verified easily by playing the "token game" in the latter.

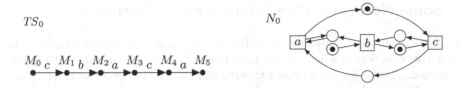

Fig. 1. A transition system TS_0 (l.h.s.) and a plain, safe Petri net N_0 solving it (r.h.s.).

of properties, we will eventually be in a position to verify that TS_0 can, in fact, *not* be pps-solved, i.e., that there is no pps Petri net whose reachability graph is isomorphic to TS_0; that is, the non-pureness around transition a is intrinsic.

Finally, we define the effect of a sequence of transitions on a given place. For pps nets, this notion generalises the notion of pre- and post-places of transitions introduced in Definition 4, and it turns out to be useful in proofs.

Definition 7. The effect of a transition sequence
Let $N = (P, T, F, M_0)$ be a Petri net. The *effect* of $w \in T^*$ on a place p is

$$ef_p(w) \;=\; \sum_{t \in {}^\bullet p} \Psi(w)(t) \;-\; \sum_{t \in p^\bullet} \Psi(w)(t)$$

This is the token difference w would generate on p if it were executed. For $w \in T^*$, define ${}^\bullet w = \{p \in P \mid ef_p(w) < 0\}$ and $w^\bullet = \{p \subset P \mid ef_p(w) > 0\}$. □ 7

Lemma 1. General properties of $^\bullet$ and the effect function
Let p be a place of a Petri net and let w, v etc. be sequences in T^*.

(a) ${}^\bullet \varepsilon = \emptyset = \varepsilon^\bullet$
(b) If $\Psi(w_1) = \Psi(w_2)$, then ${}^\bullet w_1 = {}^\bullet w_2$ and $w_1^\bullet = w_2^\bullet$.
(c) If $\Psi(w) = \Psi(w')$ and $\Psi(v) = \Psi(v')$ then $ef_p(wv) = ef_p(w') + ef_p(v')$.

Proof:
(a): The empty sequence ε acts neutrally on any place.
(b): For any place p, the number of transitions of ${}^\bullet p$ (and in $p^\bullet$) is the same in w_1 and in w_2.
(c): By (b) and by induction. □ 1

In the pps case, because of plainness and pureness, the $^\bullet$ notation for sequences is consistent with the pre- and postset notation introduced in Definition 4. That is, for any one-letter sequence $w = t \in T$, the dot notation introduced in Definition 7 reduces to the one introduced in Definition 4. Moreover, in a pps net, there are exactly three, mutually exclusive, possibilities for the effect of $w \in T^*$ on a given place p when there is a marking M with $M[w\rangle$: $ef_p(w) = -1$ (then $p \in {}^\bullet w$, and w removes a token from p if executed); $ef_p(w) = +1$ (then $p \in w^\bullet$, and w puts a token on p if executed); or $ef_p(w) = 0$ (then $p \notin ({}^\bullet w \cup w^\bullet)$, and the effect of w on p is neutral).

3   Some Necessary Conditions for pps Petri Nets

We distinguish two types of properties of Petri net reachability graphs. The distinctive criterion is whether sets mentioning $\bullet$ are used (or not) in their formalisations. In the former case, a property will be called *hybrid* (Sect. 3.1), since it refers both to the structure of a Petri net and to its behaviour in the shape of its reachability graph. In the latter case, a property will be called *dynamic* (Sect. 3.2), since it does not refer to a generating Petri net, but only to its behaviour, i.e., the reachability graph. Dynamic properties can be checked directly on any arbitrary transition system, while hybrid ones cannot. Section 3.3 focuses on the relationship between hybrid and dynamic properties, and on potential exploitation.

3.1   Hybrid Conditions for Plain, Pure, and Safe Petri Nets

Let us introduce, in this section, a number of properties related both to a transition system and a generating Petri net.

Proposition 2. Hybrid properties of pps nets
Let $N = (P, T, F, M_0)$ be a pps net, let a, b be (not necessarily different) transitions in T, let M, M_1, M_2, M_3 be reachable markings, and let $u, v, v_1, v_2, v_3, w,$ w_1, w_2, w_3 be sequences of transitions. Then

(H1) *If $M[wv\rangle$ or $M[vw\rangle$, then $\bullet w \cap \bullet v = \emptyset = w^\bullet \cap v^\bullet$.*

(H2) *If $M[v\rangle$ and $M[w\rangle$, then $v^\bullet \cap \bullet w = \emptyset = \bullet v \cap w^\bullet$.*

(H3) *If $[v\rangle M$ and $[w\rangle M$, then $v^\bullet \cap \bullet w = \emptyset = \bullet v \cap w^\bullet$.*

(H4) *If $M[awb\rangle$ then $(\bullet a \cap \bullet b) \subseteq w^\bullet$ and $(a^\bullet \cap b^\bullet) \subseteq \bullet w$.*

(H5) *– If $M_1[x_1w_1y_1\rangle$, $M_2[x_2w_2y_2\rangle$, and $M_3[x_3w_3y_3\rangle$*
  with $x_1, y_1, x_2, y_2, x_3, y_3 \in \{a, b\}$, and there exist v_1, v_2, v_3 such that
  $$\Psi(w_1) = \Psi(v_1) + \Psi(v_2), \ \Psi(w_2) = \Psi(v_2) + \Psi(v_3), \ \Psi(w_3) =$$
  $$\Psi(v_3) + \Psi(v_1),$$
  – then $\bullet a \cap \bullet b = \emptyset$ and $a^\bullet \cap b^\bullet = \emptyset$.

Proof:
(H1): Let us assume for a contradiction that $p \in (\bullet w \cap \bullet v) \cup (w^\bullet \cap v^\bullet)$. We have $ef_p(v) = ef_p(w) \neq 0$. Thus $ef_p(vw) = ef_p(wv) = 2 \cdot ef_p(v) \notin \{-1, 0, 1\}$. This contradicts $M[wv\rangle$ or $M[vw\rangle$.

(H2): Assume $p \in w^\bullet \cap \bullet v$. By the definition of effects, we have $p \notin \bullet w \cup v^\bullet$. This would lead to a contradiction if $w = v$, so $w \neq v$. By $p \in w^\bullet$ and safeness, we get $M(p) = 0$. By $p \in \bullet v$ and the Petri net firing rule, $M(p) \geq 1$. Contradiction.

(H3): The proof is similar to (H2).

(H4): Suppose that $M[a\rangle M_1[w\rangle M_2[b\rangle M'$ and that $p \in (\bullet a \cap \bullet b)$. Then $M(p) = 1$, $M_1(p) = 0$, $M_2(p) = 1$, and $M'(p) = 0$, so that w acts positively on p, that is, $p \in w^\bullet$. Similarly for $p \in (a^\bullet \cap b^\bullet)$: $M(p) = 0$, $M_1(p) = 1$, $M_2(p) = 0$ and $M'(p) = 1$ w acts negatively on p, that is, $p \in \bullet w$.

(H5): Assume for a contradiction that $p \in {}^\bullet a \cap {}^\bullet b$ exists.

Because of $M_1[x_1 w_1 y_1\rangle$, there is no token on p before w_1 and a token afterwards, i.e., $ef_p(w_1) = 1$. In a similar way, we can observe that $ef_p(w_2) = 1$ and $ef_p(w_3) = 1$. We can now write $ef_p(w_1) = ef_p(v_1 v_2) = ef_p(v_3 v_1) + ef_p(v_2 v_3) - 2ef_p(v_3) = ef_p(w_3) + ef_p(w_2) - 2ef_p(v_3)$. Inserting the previously computed values and solving for $ef_p(v_3)$ yields $ef_p(v_3) = \frac{1}{2}$, which is not possible in a Petri net.

Similarly, $p \in a^\bullet \cap b^\bullet$ leads to $ef_p(v_3) = -\frac{1}{2}$.   □ 2

Example: TS_0, as shown in Fig. 1, is not pps-solvable, because in any assumed plain, pure and safe solution, Property (H4) is violated. Indeed, from $M_2[aca\rangle$, we deduce, by (H4), that ${}^\bullet a \subseteq c^\bullet$ and $a^\bullet \subseteq {}^\bullet c$ in the purported pps solution, which implies that after each execution of c, every input place of a is marked and every output place of a is unmarked. Hence a is enabled at M_1 in any pps solution; but $\neg M_1[a\rangle$ in TS_0. Note that we cannot use this argument in an automatic verification of the non-pps-solvability of TS_0, since we would need to construct pps solutions in the first place.

3.2 Dynamic Conditions for Plain, Pure, and Safe Petri Nets

In order to eliminate the need for constructing solutions before properties can be checked, Proposition 3 below can be used. It describes a set of dynamic properties of pps-solvable transition systems which are independent of any generating net. These properties can smoothly be interpreted on any arbitrary labelled transition system, and hence tested directly on any such input.

Proposition 3. Dynamic properties of pps nets
Let $N = (P, T, F, M_0)$ be a pps net, let a, b, c be (not necessarily different) transitions in T, let $M, M', K, K_1, K_2, \ldots, L_0, L_1, \ldots$ be reachable markings, and let $u, v, v_1, v_2, \ldots, w, w_1, w_2, \ldots$ be sequences of transitions. Then

(D1) *If $M'[a\rangle M$ and $M''[b\rangle M$, then $[b\rangle M' \iff [a\rangle M''$.*

(D2) *If $M[ava\rangle$, $K[v'\rangle K'$ and $\Psi(v) = \Psi(v')$, then $K'[a\rangle$.*

(D3) *If $M[w\rangle M'$ and $M[a\rangle$ and $K'[w'\rangle K[a\rangle$ with $\Psi(w) = \Psi(w')$, then $M'[a\rangle$ and $K'[a\rangle$.*

(D4) *If $M[w\rangle M'$ and $M[a\rangle$ and $K[a\rangle K'[w'\rangle K''$ with $\Psi(w) = \Psi(w')$, then $M'[a\rangle$.*

(D5) – *If, for some $n \in \mathbb{N}$ and $v \in T^*$, $L_0[a\rangle$, $L_0[v_1\rangle L_1 \ldots [v_n\rangle L_n[a\rangle$ and $[w_i\rangle K_i[a\rangle$ or $[a\rangle K_i[w_i\rangle$ with $\Psi(w_i) = \Psi(vv_i)$ (for $1 \le i \le n$),*
   – *then $L_i[a\rangle$ for all $1 \le i < n$.*

(D6) – *If, for some $n \in \mathbb{N}$ and $v \in T^*$, $L_0[a\rangle$, $L_0[v_1\rangle L_1 \ldots [v_n\rangle L_n[a\rangle$ and $K_i[w_i\rangle \wedge K_i[a\rangle$ or $[w_i\rangle K_i \wedge [a\rangle K_i$ with $\Psi(w_i) = \Psi(vv_i)$ (for $1 \le i \le n$),*
   – *then $L_i[a\rangle$ for all $1 \le i < n$.*

(D7) – *If $L_1[x_1 w_1 y_1\rangle$, $L_2[x_2 w_2 y_2\rangle$, and $L_3[x_3 w_3 y_3\rangle$ with $x_1, y_1, x_2, y_2, x_3, y_3 \in \{a, b\}$, and there exist v_1, v_2, v_3 such that $\Psi(w_1) = \Psi(v_1) + \Psi(v_2)$, $\Psi(w_2) = \Psi(v_2) + \Psi(v_3)$, $\Psi(w_3) = \Psi(v_3) + \Psi(v_1)$, and $M[a\rangle$ and $M[b\rangle$,*

– then $M[ab\rangle$.

(D8) *If* $M[w\rangle M'[v\rangle M''$ *and* $\Psi(v) = \Psi(w)$, *then* $M = M' = M''$.

Proof:

(D1): Suppose that $K[b\rangle M'[a\rangle M$ and $M''[b\rangle M$, for some reachable K. We will show $[a\rangle M''$. By (H3), we get $^\bullet a \cap b^\bullet = \emptyset$. By (H1), we get $^\bullet a \cap {}^\bullet b = \emptyset$. By combining this, we get $^\bullet a \cap ({}^\bullet b \cup b^\bullet) = \emptyset$. Hence b cannot activate or deactivate a. Thus a is also enabled in K. Determinism (see Proposition 1) gives $K[a\rangle M''$. The other direction of the equivalence can be shown in the same way.

(D2): From (H4) and Lemma 1(b), we have $^\bullet a \subseteq v^\bullet = v'^\bullet$ and $a^\bullet \subseteq {}^\bullet v = {}^\bullet v'$; hence every time after v' a is enabled.

(D3): By (H2) and $M[w\rangle$, together with $M[a\rangle$, we get $^\bullet a \cap w^\bullet = \emptyset = a^\bullet \cap {}^\bullet w$. By (H1) and $K'[w'a\rangle$, we get $^\bullet a \cap {}^\bullet w' = \emptyset = a^\bullet \cap w'^\bullet$. Therefore, with Lemma 1(b), we get $({}^\bullet a \cup a^\bullet) \cap ({}^\bullet w \cup w^\bullet) = \emptyset = ({}^\bullet a \cup a^\bullet) \cap ({}^\bullet w' \cup w'^\bullet)$, i.e., w and w' are unable to enable or disable a. Thus, from $M[a\rangle$ and $K[a\rangle$, the conclusions follow.

(D4): Similarly to (D3), having $M[a\rangle$, $M[w\rangle$, $K[aw'\rangle$ and using (H1) and (H2), we show that w or w' cannot disable or enable a; hence $M'[a\rangle$.

(D5): Assume for a contradiction that there is some marking L_i ($1 \le i < n$) with $\neg L_i[a\rangle$. Assume that i is the minimal index with this property and let $p \in {}^\bullet a$ be a place which prevents a in L_i, i.e., satisfies $L_i(p) = 0$. This implies that $L_{i-1}(p) = 1$ (because of $L_{i-1}[a\rangle$). Thus, the effect of v_i on p is negative, i.e., $ef_p(v_i) = -1$. Since, by assumption, $L_n[a\rangle$, and thus $L_n(p) = 1$, there is also some sequence v_j, with $i < j \le n$, such that the effect of v_j on p is positive, i.e., $ef_p(v_j) = 1$. Since either $[w_i\rangle K_i[a\rangle$ or $[a\rangle K_i[w_i\rangle$, we have, by (H1), that $p \notin {}^\bullet w_i$, i.e., $ef_p(w_i) \ge 0$.

By $0 \le ef_p(w_i) = ef_p(vv_i)$ and $ef_p(v_i) = -1$, we get $ef_p(v) = 1$. Thus $ef_p(w_j) = ef_p(vv_j) = 1 + 1$, which contradicts the safeness of p. Hence the assumption that $\neg L_i[a\rangle$ for some i was wrong.

(D6): We can deduce, analogously to the proof of (D5), that $ef_p(v_i) = -1$ and $ef_p(v_j) = 1$. The changed conditions on the marking K_j give us $0 \ge ef_p(w_j)$. Therefore, we can now use $0 \ge ef_p(w_j) = ef_p(vv_j) = ef_p(v) + 1$ in order to derive $ef_p(v) = -1$. This gives us $ef_p(w_i) = ef_p(vv_i) = -1 - 1 = -2$, again a contradiction to safeness.

(D7): By (H5), we get $^\bullet a \cap {}^\bullet b = \emptyset = a^\bullet \cap b^\bullet$. Thus a and b are independent, and $M[a\rangle$ and $M[b\rangle$ yield $M[ab\rangle$.

(D8): Because of (H1), $^\bullet v \cap {}^\bullet w = \emptyset = v^\bullet \cap w^\bullet$. Because of $\Psi(v) = \Psi(w)$ and Lemma 1(b), $^\bullet w = {}^\bullet v$ and $w^\bullet = v^\bullet$. Combining this gives $^\bullet w = {}^\bullet v = \emptyset = w^\bullet = v^\bullet$. Thus firing w or v does not change the marking, i.e., $M = M' = M''$. □ 3

Example: The transition system TS_0 shown in Fig. 1 satisfies all hybrid properties defined so far, except (H4). TS_0 is solvable (even by a plain, safe net) but not pps-solvable. Now, instead of proving this fact indirectly through

Property (H4), we can do so more directly. Indeed, (D2) is not satisfied for TS_0 (setting $M = M_2$, $v = v' = c$, $K = M_0$ and $K' = M_1$) and thus, Part (D2) of Proposition 3 implies that TS_0 is not pps-solvable. Note that, as opposed to (H4), Property (D2) can be used in an automatic verification, since it can be tested directly on a given lts, without needing to construct a net first.

The properties defined in Proposition 3 are independent of each other, in the sense that none of them is implied by the rest. This is demonstrated by the examples displayed in Fig. 2. The following list shows how to choose transitions, sequences and markings in order to construct a violation:

(a) violates (D1), because of $[a\rangle M''$ and $\neg[b\rangle M'$.
(b) violates (D2) with $v = v' = x$, because of $\neg K'[a\rangle$.
(c) violates (D3) with $w = yx$, $w' = xy$.
(d) violates (D4) with $w = a$.
(e) violates (D5) with $v = e_1 e_2$, $v_1 = c_1 c_2$, $v_2 = d_1 d_2$, $w_1 = e_1 c_1 e_2 c_2$, and $w_2 = d_1 e_1 d_2 e_2$, and with $n = 2$, because of $L_0[a\rangle$ and $L_2[a\rangle$, but $\neg L_1[a\rangle$.
(f) violates (D6) with the same sequences as in (e).
(g) violates (D7) with $v_1 = c_1 c_2$, $v_2 = d_1 d_2$, $v_3 = e_1 e_2$, $w_1 = c_1 c_2 d_1 d_2$, $w_2 = d_1 e_1 d_2 e_2$, and $w_3 = e_1 c_1 e_2 c_2$, because of $\neg M[ab\rangle$.
(h) violates (D8) with $v = w = a$.

Due to the previous proposition, none of the transition systems depicted in Fig. 2 is pps-solvable. However, it turns out that all of them have a Petri net solution. APT [5] is useful in confirming this.

3.3   Relationship Between Hybrid and Dynamic Properties

In the preceding sections, we have concentrated on properties enjoyed by a pps solution for a given lts, if such a solution exists. The three properties – plainness, pureness and safeness – are strictly related to a possible solution (of course, together with its behaviour). That is why, on the one hand, we first introduced hybrid properties, as they constitute a natural answer to the question about the existence of a pps solution. On the other hand, it is not possible to check hybrid properties on a pre-synthesis level, i.e., without actually carrying out synthesis. For this reason, we introduced a set of dynamic properties as well. Dynamic properties may be checked in a pre-synthesis stage. As such, they may be useful for quick-fail purposes, since any lts not satisfying one of these properties may be rejected straight away in the context of pps synthesis.

The above proofs of dynamic properties already make use of hybrid properties; hence dynamic properties are consequences of the hybrid ones. From the proofs of these facts, every violation of a dynamic property allows us to draw conclusions about some violation of a particular hybrid one. For instance:

- if (D1) is violated, then (H1) and/or (H3) is/are violated;
- if (D2) is violated, then (H4) is violated;
- if (D3) or (D4) is violated, then (H1) and/or (H2) is/are violated;
- if (D5) or (D6) is violated, then (H1) is violated;

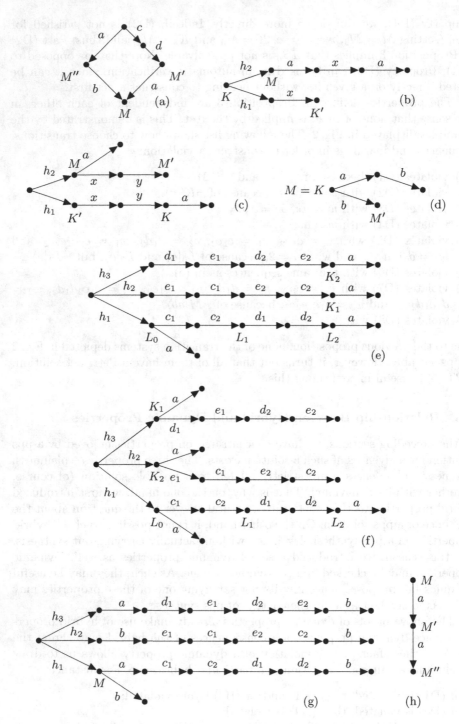

Fig. 2. Labelled transition systems violating only (Di), for $i \in \{1, \ldots, 8\}$.

- if (D7) is violated, then (H5) is violated;
- if (D8) is violated, then (H1) is violated.

In designing Properties (D1)–(D8), we took care to find a set which is both *strong* (in the sense of explaining as large as possible a set of non-pps-solvable lts) and *small* (in the sense of containing only mutually independent properties). These two aspects will next be discussed, in order.

First, we stress that (D1)–(D8) are by no means strong enough in order to guarantee the actual pps-solvability of a given labelled transition system. To see this, consider the lts shown in Fig. 3. It satisfies all dynamic properties of Proposition 3, but is still not pps-solvable. The problem is that transition a cannot be prevented at L_1. Assume for a contradiction that a is not enabled at L_1. Then there must be a place $p \in {}^\bullet a$ with $L_1(p) = 0$. Let us look at the effects of different firing sequences on p. Because of $L_0[a\rangle$ we know $L_0(p) = 1$ and can conclude from this and $L_0[c_1c_2\rangle$ that $ef_p(c_1c_2) = -1$. From $K_2[a\rangle$, we get $K_2(p) = 1$, which results, together with $[e_1c_1e_2c_2\rangle K_2$, in

$$0 \le ef_p(e_1c_1e_2c_2) = ef_p(c_1c_2) + ef_p(e_1e_2) = ef_p(e_1e_2) - 1$$

Therefore $ef_p(e_1e_2) = 1$. Similarly, we get $K_3(p) = 1$ from $K_3[a\rangle$. Together with $K_3[d_1e_1d_2e_2\rangle$, this results in

$$0 \ge ef_p(d_1e_1d_2e_2) = ef_p(d_1d_2) + ef_p(e_1e_2) = ef_p(d_1d_2) + 1$$

Hence $ef_p(d_1d_2) = -1$. By combining this with $L_1[d_1d_2\rangle L_2$, we get $L_2(p) = L_1(p) + ef_p(d_1d_2) = -1$. Thus such a place p cannot exist.

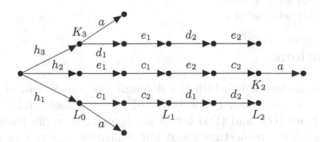

Fig. 3. An lts which satisfies all dynamic properties but is not pps-solvable.

Secondly, and to end this section, recall that (D1)–(D8) are independent of each other. In the implementation of a pps-oriented quick-fail mechanism which eliminates as many unsuitable lts as possible prior to synthesis, all of them should be incorporated. In practice, however, some of them are easier to test than others. For instance, Property (D1) would only need a single pass along the states of a transition system, while Properties (D2), (D3) and (D4) would also involve the examination of paths between them. Such paths could become quite long, leading to a considerable slow down. Properties (D5) and (D6) are even harder to check, since they involve the checking of a non-fixed number of paths. Therefore, for practical reasons, it may be reasonable to examine some simpler dynamic properties which do not involve too many paths and are, hopefully, computationally more amenable than, say, (D5/6). We offer a – slightly arbitrary but small – candidate list of such properties.

Proposition 4. More dynamic properties of pps nets
Let $N = (P, T, F, M_0)$ be a pps net, let a, b, c be (not necessarily different) transitions in T, let $M, M', K, \ldots$ be reachable markings, and let $w, v, u, \ldots$ be sequences of transitions. Then the following properties are true:

(D9) *If $M[aw\rangle$ and $M[v\rangle$ and $\Psi(w) = \Psi(v)$ then $M[va\rangle$.*
(D10) *If $M[a\rangle$ and $M[b\rangle$ and $K[ab\rangle$, then $M[ab\rangle$ and $M[ba\rangle$ and $K[ba\rangle$.*
(D11) *If $M[ava\rangle$ and $K[v\rangle K'$, then we have $K'[a\rangle$.*
(D12) *If $M_1[x_1 w_1 y_1\rangle$, $M_2[x_2 w_2 y_2\rangle$, $M_3[x_3 w_3 y_3\rangle$ for $x_1, y_1, x_2, x_3, y_2, y_3 \in \{a, b\}$, $\Psi(w_1) = \Psi(w_2) + \Psi(w_3)$, $M[a\rangle$, and $M[b\rangle$, then $M[ab\rangle$.*
(D13) *If $M[w\rangle M'[w\rangle M''$, then $M = M' = M''$.*
(D14) *If $M[w\rangle M'$ and $M[a\rangle$ and $K'[w\rangle K[a\rangle$, then $M'[a\rangle$ and $K'[a\rangle$.*
(D15) *If $M[w\rangle M'$ and $M[a\rangle$ and $K[a\rangle K'[w\rangle$, then $M'[a\rangle$.*

Proof *(Sketch).*

(D9) Follows from (D4) with $M = K$.
(D10) From (D3) and (D4).
(D11) From (D2) with $v = v'$.
(D12) From (D7) with $v_3 = \varepsilon$ (implying $\Psi(w_2) = \Psi(v_2)$ and $\Psi(w_3) = \Psi(v_1)$).
(D13) From (D8) with $v = w$.
(D14) From (D3) with $w' = w$.
(D15) From (D4) with $w' = w$.

4   Applications

We discuss two instances in which the dynamic properties defined in the previous section – in particular, Property (D10) – play a useful role. Notice that (D10) follows from (D3) and (D4) but is much easier to verify than the latter. Section 4.1 describes a conjecture about fair sequences, due to Ochmański [11], which applies to elementary Petri nets [15]. We use (D10) in order to show that a tentative counterexample fails to be pps-solvable. Section 4.2 describes how (D10) can be used in order to simplify an existing characterisation [4] of live and safe marked graph reachability graphs [6].

4.1   A Conjecture Relating to Fair Persistent Sequences

Ochmański's conjecture will be stated in terms of pps nets, rather than elementary nets as in [11]. This is actually a slightly strengthened version of the conjecture, since if it turns out to be true for pps nets, then it is also true for elementary nets (with an immediate proof). In order to be able to state the conjecture, we need to define persistent sequences and fair sequences. In the following, let $N = (P, T, F, M_0)$ be a Petri net and let T^∞ denote the set of finite or infinite sequences of transitions.

Definition 8. Persistence of firing sequences [11]
A finite or infinite firing sequence $M_0[t_1\rangle M_1[t_2\rangle \ldots$ is called *persistent* if for every $i > 0$ and $a \neq t_i$, if $M_{i-1}[a\rangle$ then also $M_i[a\rangle$.   □ 8

This means that no single step $M_{i-1}[t_i\rangle M_i$ may disable some transition $a \neq t_i$. We are interested in the case that firing sequences are permutation-equivalent to persistent firing sequences.

Definition 9. Permutation-equivalence of firing sequences [3]
The relation $\equiv_0$ between two firing sequences $M_0[\ldots\rangle$ is defined as follows:

$$M_0[\alpha t_i t_{i+1}\beta\rangle \quad \equiv_0 \quad M_0[\alpha t_{i+1} t_i \beta\rangle \quad \text{where } \alpha \in T^* \text{ and } \beta \in T^\infty$$

Let $\sigma_1, \sigma_2 \in T^\infty$. Define $M_0[\sigma_1\rangle \equiv M_0[\sigma_2\rangle$ if either $M_0[\sigma_1\rangle \equiv_0^* M_0[\sigma_2\rangle$, or for every $n \geq 0$ there are $M_0[\sigma_1'\rangle, M_0[\sigma_2'\rangle$ such that $M_0[\sigma_1\rangle \equiv_0^* M_0[\sigma_1'\rangle$ and σ_1' and σ_2 agree on the prefix of length n, as well as $M_0[\sigma_2\rangle \equiv_0^* M_0[\sigma_2'\rangle$ and σ_2' and σ_1 agree on the prefix of length n.   □ 9

The next definition uses modified existential and universal quantifiers: $\exists_i^\infty$ ("there are infinitely many i with ...") and $\forall_i^\infty$ ("for all but finitely many i, ...").

Definition 10. Fairness [10]
Finite sequences are fair. An infinite firing sequence $M_0[t_1\rangle M_1[t_2\rangle M_2[t_3\rangle M_3[t_4\rangle \ldots$ is *fair with respect to* $t \in T$ if

$$(\exists_i^\infty : (t = t_i)) \quad \vee \quad (\forall_i^\infty : \neg M_i[t\rangle)$$

and it is *fair* if it is fair with respect to every transition $t \in T$.   □ 10

Definition 11. Persistent permutation equivalents [11]
The net N is called SPE (S for "short") if every finite firing sequence starting from M_0 has a persistent equivalent, and FPE (F for "fair") if every fair firing sequence starting from M_0 has a persistent equivalent.   □ 11

Conjecture (based on [11]): Let a finite transition system be pps-solvable. Then it satisfies SPE if and only if it satisfies FPE.
Note first that the conjecture is well-formed because Definitions 8–11 apply equally well to transition systems as to Petri nets. Next, note that FPE $\Rightarrow$ SPE is immediate, since all finite sequences are fair by definition. It remains to investigate whether SPE $\Rightarrow$ FPE or not.
Figure 4 shows that the implication SPE $\Rightarrow$ FPE is not true in general. Indeed, any finite firing sequence can be permuted equivalently in such a way

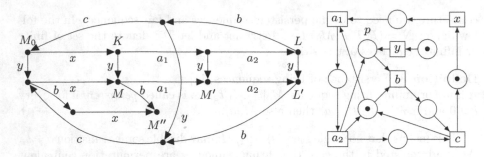

Fig. 4. An lts satisfying SPE but not FPE (l.h.s.) and a generating Petri net (r.h.s.).

that the last M' in it is reached via y rather than a_1, and M'' (which can occur at most once) is reached via x rather than b. Hence SPE is satisfied. However, consider the infinite firing sequence $M_0[y(xa_1a_2bc)^\infty\rangle$. This sequence is fair but has no persistent equivalent, since the marking M cannot be avoided and the firing $M[a_1\rangle M'$ is non-persistent (as M enables b but M' does not). Hence FPE is not satisfied.

Note that the Petri net shown on right-hand side of Fig. 4 solves this transition system. However, the net is not safe; indeed, at L', place p carries two tokens.[6] We use Property (D10) in order to show that there is no pps solution. At L, we have both $L[y\rangle$ and $L[b\rangle$, but at K (and also at M_0), only yb, but not by, is enabled. Therefore, (D10) does not hold, and as a consequence, the lts shown in Fig. 4 cannot be solved by a pps net.

4.2 The Reachability Graphs of Safe Marked Graphs

In this section, we present a novel characterisation of the reachability graphs of safe, connected and live marked graphs, based on (D10). We recall the main result of [4].

Theorem 1. Marked graph synthesis - Theorem 40 in [4]
An lts TS is isomorphic to the reachability graph of a bounded, connected and live marked graph $MG(TS)$ iff it is totally reachable, deterministic, persistent, backward persistent, reversible, finite, and satisfies **P1**.[7]   □ 1

A characterisation of the bound of $MG(TS)$ can also be found in [4]. However, this characterisation is somewhat complicated, because it relies on various technical notions. We outline the main ideas. Throughout the following (up to and including Proposition 5), assume $TS = (S, \rightarrow, T, s_0)$ to be a transition system which is finite, totally reachable, deterministic, persistent, backward persistent, reversible, and satisfies **P1**.

---

[6] Note that p is the only unsafe place (with bound 2), and that L' is the only non-safe reachable marking. In this sense, the example demonstrates that the conjecture is sharp. We also believe that it is the smallest example with this property.

[7] For **P1** and the other properties, see Definitions 1 and 2.

Definition 12. Short paths - Definition 24 in [4]
Let r, s be two states of TS. A path $r[\tau\rangle s$, with $\tau \in T^*$, is *short* if $|\tau| \leq |\tau'|$ for every path $r[\tau'\rangle s$, where $|\tau|$ denotes the length of τ.   □ 12

By Lemmata 26 and 28 of [4], there is a short path between any pair of reachable states of TS, and if $s[\tau\rangle s'$ and $s[\tau'\rangle s'$ are both short, then $\Psi(\tau) = \Psi(\tau')$. Hence the following definition is sound.

Definition 13. Distance - Definition 29 of [4]
Let s, s' be two states of TS, the Parikh vector of some short path from s to s' is called the *distance* between s and s', and denoted by $\Delta_{s,s'}$.   □ 13

By Proposition 31 of [4], for every $x \in T$, there is a unique state s_x enabling only x (and no other label). By Lemma 33 of [4], on any short path ending at state s_x, there is no label x (the proof uses **P1**). The set of states that do not enable x, but for which x is necessarily enabled after one further step, is defined as follows.

Definition 14. Sequentialising states - Definition 35 of [4]
For any $x \in T$, $Seq(x) = \{s \in S \mid \neg s[x\rangle \wedge (\forall a \in s^\bullet : s[ax\rangle)\}$.   □ 14

Now we can cite the characterisation of the bounds of $MG(TS)$:

Proposition 5. Exact bounds – Lemma 42 in [4]
The bound of $MG(TS)$ is $\max\{\Delta_{s_y,s_x}(y) \mid x, y \in T, s_y \in Seq(x)\}$.   □ 5

As an example, consider the transition system depicted in Fig. 5. It satisfies all the conditions given in Theorem 1, and can therefore be solved by a bounded and live marked graph. However, no safe marked graph is capable of doing this job. Let us check why the condition of Proposition 5 – for bound 1 – is violated.

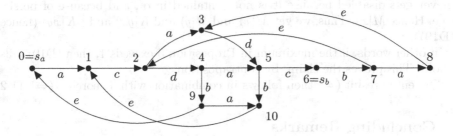

Fig. 5. An lts which has a 2-bounded but not a safe marked graph solution.

Consider the short path

$$6 = s_b\,[\,b\,\rangle\,7\,[\,e\,\rangle\,2\,[\,d\,\rangle\,4\,[\,b\,\rangle\,9\,[\,e\,\rangle\,s_a = 0$$

It contains b twice. Moreover, $s_b \in Seq(a)$. According to the proofs of Theorem 1 and Proposition 5 in [4], any marked graph Petri net solution must necessarily have a non-safe place with bound ≥ 2 leading from transition b to transition a.[8]

---

[8] Note that there is also a short path $s_a[a\rangle 1[c\rangle 2[d\rangle 4[a\rangle 5[c\rangle s_b$ containing a two times. However, this path is not indicative of an unsafe place from a to b, since $s_a \notin Seq(b)$.

This characterisation uses distances Δ, the special elements s_x and s_y associated with labels x and y, and sequentialising state sets. Our aim is to replace the characterisation given in Proposition 5 – in case the maximum is 1 – by a more direct one, using some suitable dynamic property. It turns out that (D10) can be used:

Theorem 2. Characterisation of safe marked graphs
A labelled transition system is isomorphic to the reachability graph of a safe, connected and live marked graph iff it is totally reachable, deterministic, persistent, backward persistent, reversible, finite, and satisfies **P1** *as well as* (D10).

As an illustration of this result, note how (D10) is violated in Fig. 5. Consider $x = a$, $y = b$, $K = 6$, and $M = 4$. We have $M[a\rangle$ and $M[b\rangle$, as well as $K[ba\rangle$. According to (D10), we should also have $K[ab\rangle$, but, by contrast, a is not enabled at state 6.

Proof:
($\Rightarrow$): All claimed properties (except (D10)) are established using Theorem 1 ($\Rightarrow$). (D10) follows with Proposition 4.
($\Leftarrow$): Suppose that a transition system TS is totally reachable, deterministic, persistent, backward persistent, reversible, finite, and satisfies Properties **P1** and (D10). We claim that the maximum in Proposition 5 does not exceed 1.

Consider a short path $s_y[y\rangle s[\alpha\rangle s_x$, with $s_y \in Seq(x)$, which contains another y in α (yielding a maximum ≥ 2). Consider the second y on such a path and a y-free prefix α' of α with $s_y[y\rangle s[\alpha'\rangle s'[y\rangle$. By Lemma 33 of [4] (explained just before Definition 14), α (and thus α') is x-free. Let $M = s'$ and $K = s_y$.

Because $K \in Seq(x)$, we get $\neg K[x\rangle$ as well as $K[yx\rangle$. Along α', transition x never gets disabled because it is not contained in α', and because of persistence. Hence $M[x\rangle$. Thus, we get $M[x\rangle$ and $M[y\rangle$ and $K[yx\rangle$ and $\neg K[xy\rangle$ (hence $\neg$(D10)).

In other words, if the maximum in Proposition 5 exceeds 1, then (D10) fails to hold. This proves the claim, by contraposition.

The entire result ($\Leftarrow$) then follows in combination with Theorem 1($\Leftarrow$). □ 2

5   Concluding Remarks

In the first part of this paper, we have derived a collection of properties of plain, pure and safe Petri nets. The ambition is that these properties encompass (or imply) many generally known properties of pps nets and – by proxy – elementary nets. Normally, in prior papers such as [13,15,16], far weaker necessary properties have been considered. We have made a distinction between hybrid properties (referring to a net and its reachability graph, viewed as a labelled transition system) and dynamic properties (referring only to a labelled transition system). The latter, but not the former, can be used in a pps net synthesis algorithm as a quick-fail mechanism. Amongst the dynamic properties, we have further identified a subset of properties which can – hopefully – relatively effectively be tested.

In the second part of the paper, we have shown how these properties can help checking a given labelled transition system for non-pps-solvability (Sect. 4.1), and how they can contribute to the characterisation of a class of pps-solvable transition systems (Sect. 4.2). It so happened that Property (D10) was instrumental in both cases, but this seems to be accidental.

The context of this paper is the *exact* synthesis of unlabelled Petri nets from labelled transition systems. If one allows transition labels, the synthesis problem changes. In unrestricted cases, it becomes trivial, because every finite lts can also be viewed as a labelled Petri net by identifying states with places, edges with transitions, and edge inscriptions with transition labels. To our knowledge, there are very few papers about the exact characterisation of the reachability graphs of classes of (pps) Petri nets (e.g., [4]), and also, very few papers about the exact synthesis of such classes (e.g., [1,17]). A more widely known approach is to weaken the exactness condition slightly by allowing partial transition labelling, through the splitting of transitions, such as, for instance, in the theory expounded in [7].

In this context, our hopes and aims for medium-term future work are twofold. It would be nice if the dynamic properties listed here could usefully be implemented in existing synthesis or pre-synthesis tools, to allow sophisticated input pruning. Also, it would be nice if they could help in yielding further insights into the structure of pps Petri net reachability graphs, e.g. by obtaining direct characterisations of the state spaces of net classes which are different from marked graphs, such as live and pps free-choice nets, or reversible, pps, persistent nets.

Acknowledgment. The authors are grateful to the reviewers for their helpful comments.

References

1. Badouel, É., Bernardinello, L., Darondeau, P.: The synthesis problem for elementary nets is NP-complete. Theor. Comput. Sci. **186**, 107–134 (1997)
2. Badouel, E., Bernardinello, L., Darondeau, P.: Petri Net Synthesis. Texts in Theoretical Computer Science. An EATCS Series, p. 339. Springer, Heidelberg (2015). doi:10.1007/978-3-662-47967-4
3. Best, E., Devillers, R.: Sequential and concurrent behaviour in Petri net theory. Theor. Comput. Sci. **55**(1), 87–136 (1987)
4. Best, E., Devillers, R.: Characterisation of the state spaces of marked graph Petri nets. In: Selected papers of LATA 2014, Information and Computation, vol. 253, Part 3, pp. 399–410 (2014). http://dx.doi.org/10.1016/j.ic.2016.06.006
5. Best, E., Schlachter, U.: Analysis of Petri nets and transition systems. In: Proceedings of 8th Interaction and Concurrency Experience, In: Knight, S., Lanese, I., Lafuente, A.L., Vieira, H.T. (eds.) 189 of Electronic Proceedings in Theoretical Computer Science, pp. 53–67, June 2015. http://eptcs.web.cse.unsw.edu.au/paper.cgi?ICE2015.6, https://github.com/CvO-Theory/apt
6. Commoner, F., Holt, A.W., Even, S., Pnueli, A.: Marked directed graphs. J. Comput. Syst. Sci. **5**(5), 511–523 (1971)

7. Cortadella, J., Kishinevsky, M., Lavagno, L., Yakovlev, A.: Deriving petri nets for finite transition systems. IEEE Trans. Comput. **47**(8), 859–882 (1998)
8. Esparza, J.: Decidability and complexity of Petri net problems — an introduction. In: Reisig, W., Rozenberg, G. (eds.) ACPN 1996. LNCS, vol. 1491, pp. 374–428. Springer, Heidelberg (1998). doi:10.1007/3-540-65306-6_20
9. Landweber, L.H., Robertson, E.L.: Properties of conflict-free and persistent Petri nets. JACM **25**(3), 352–364 (1978)
10. Lehmann, D., Pnueli, A., Stavi, J.: Impartiality, justice and fairness: the ethics of concurrent termination. In: Even, S., Kariv, O. (eds.) ICALP 1981. LNCS, vol. 115, pp. 264–277. Springer, Heidelberg (1981). doi:10.1007/3-540-10843-2_22
11. Ochmański, E.: On conflict-free executions of elementary nets. Systems Science, 27, Nr. 2, Wydawca Oficyna Wydawnicza Politechniki Wrocławskiej, 89–105. Also: Persistent Runs in Elementary Nets. FolCo Technical report, Nicol. Copernic. Univ. of Toruń, 2014 (2001)
12. Ochmański, E.: Occurrence traces: processes of elementary net systems. In: Rozenberg, G. (ed.) APN 1987. LNCS, vol. 340, pp. 331–342. Springer, Heidelberg (1988). doi:10.1007/3-540-50580-6_36
13. Pomello, L., Simone, C.: An algebraic characterisation of elementary net system (observable) state space. Formal Aspects Comput. **4**(6A), 612–637 (1992)
14. Reisig, W.: Petri Nets: An Introduction. Monographs in Theoretical Computer Science. An EATCS Series, vol. 4. Springer, Heidelberg (1985). doi:10.1007/978-3-642-69968-9
15. Rozenberg, G.: Behaviour of elementary net systems. In: Brauer, W., Reisig, W., Rozenberg, G. (eds.) ACPN 1986. LNCS, vol. 254, pp. 60–94. Springer, Heidelberg (1987). doi:10.1007/978-3-540-47919-2_4
16. Thiagarajan, P.S.: Elementary net systems. In: Brauer, W., Reisig, W., Rozenberg, G. (eds.) ACPN 1986. LNCS, vol. 254, pp. 26–59. Springer, Heidelberg (1987). doi:10.1007/978-3-540-47919-2_3
17. Schlachter, U.: Petri net synthesis for restricted classes of nets. In: Kordon, F., Moldt, D. (eds.) PETRI NETS 2016. LNCS, vol. 9698, pp. 79–97. Springer, Cham (2016). doi:10.1007/978-3-319-39086-4_6

Similarity-Based Approaches for Determining the Number of Trace Clusters in Process Discovery

Pieter De Koninck[✉] and Jochen De Weerdt

Research Center for Management Informatics,
Faculty of Economics and Business, KU Leuven, Leuven, Belgium
pieter.dekoninck@kuleuven.be

Abstract. Given the complexity of real-life event logs, several trace clustering techniques have been proposed to partition an event log into subsets with a lower degree of variation. In general, these techniques assume that the number of clusters is known in advance. However, this will rarely be the case in practice. Therefore, this paper presents approaches to determine the appropriate number of clusters in a trace clustering context. In order to fulfil the objective of identifying the most appropriate number of trace clusters, two approaches built on similarity are proposed: a stability- and a separation-based method. The stability-based method iteratively calculates the similarity between clustered versions of perturbed and unperturbed event logs. Alternatively, an approach based on between-cluster dissimilarity, or separation, is proposed. Regarding practical validation, both approaches are tested on multiple real-life datasets to investigate the complementarity of the different components. Our results suggest that both methods are successful in identifying an appropriate number of trace clusters.

Keywords: Stability · Trace clustering · Validity · Log perturbation · Process discovery · Separation

1 Introduction

Trace clustering is the partitioning of process instances into different groups, called trace clusters, based on their similarity. A wide variety of trace clustering techniques have been proposed, differentiated by their clustering methods and biases. The driving force behind these proposed techniques is the observation that real-life event logs are often quite complex and contain a large degree of variation. Since these event logs are often the basis for further analysis like process model discovery or compliance checking [29], partitioning dissimilar process instances into separate trace clusters is deemed appropriate. Although a wide array of techniques has been proposed, none of them makes any assertions on the correct number of clusters. Therefore, this paper is the first to propose a suitable approach for determining the most plausible number of clusters.

© Springer-Verlag GmbH Germany 2017
M. Koutny et al. (Eds.): ToPNoC XII, LNCS 10470, pp. 19–42, 2017.
DOI: 10.1007/978-3-662-55862-1_2

Since our approaches can be applied to any trace clustering technique, it raises the applicability of trace clustering techniques in general, and the validity of their trace clustering solutions.

Our first approach is based on the stability of trace clustering solutions. Intuitively, it can be expected that trace clustering solutions are more stable at the correct number of clusters. Therefore, we develop a general framework to assess the stability of trace clustering solutions. When repeatedly applied to an event log for a range of potential number of clusters, one can compare the stability scores obtained for each number of clusters. The result with the highest stability can be considered the most appropriate number. A number of elements are conceived to construct this approach: specifically, two approaches are proposed to resample event logs. Likewise, two methods are provided for calculating the similarity of clustering solutions. Finally, the concept of normalization and a calculation strategy are supplied. Each of these elements is thoroughly evaluated on four real-life event logs, resulting in the conclusion that the stability-based framework configured with model-based similarity metrics and a noise induction-based resampling strategy can lead to the correct identification of the appropriate number of clusters[1].

Our second approach is based on the concept of separation of a clustering solution. Conceptually, one prefers a clustering solution where the clusters are well separated, i.e. were the clusters are not too similar. For this, a component of the first stability-based approach, a method for calculating the similarity between trace clustering solutions, is leveraged to capture the separation of a clustering solution. Like the stability-based approach, it is evaluated on four real-life event logs.

The remainder of this article is structured as follows: in Sect. 2, the necessary background on the process mining domain is given, as well an overview of existing approaches for determining the number of clusters. Our stability-based approach is outlined in Sect. 3, while Sect. 4 details the separation-based approach. Finally, both approaches are evaluated in Sect. 5, before finishing with some concluding remarks in Sect. 6.

2   Background

This section contains the necessary background on the domain of process mining, as well as an overview of existing general approaches for determining the number of clusters in traditional clustering.

2.1   Event Logs, Process Discovery and Trace Clustering

Trace clustering, as it is considered in this paper, is a part of the process mining domain. Generally speaking, process mining consists of three distinct parts:

---

[1] This approach is implemented as an experimental ProM-plugin which can be found on http://www.processmining.be/clusterstability/.

process discovery, conformance checking, and process enhancement [1]. In process discovery, the starting point is an event log L, from which one wants to discover a corresponding process model M. Typically, this event log adheres to the IEEE eXtensible Event Stream (XES) standard[2]. In conformance checking, an event log L containing actual behaviour, and a process model M containing prescribed behaviour are compared to detect deviations between expected and observed behaviour. Finally, process enhancement is an umbrella term for techniques that aim to improve processes, for example by suggesting improvements to the as-is process-model.

One of the main problems surrounding the application of process discovery techniques to real-life datasets, however, is that they typically contain a wide variety of behaviour. Applying conventional process discovery techniques on event logs that contain such variation will most likely lead to sub-optimal results [8]. Therefore, a variety of authors [2,9,16] have proposed to apply clustering on event logs in order to improve the quality of the process models that can be mined from these event logs. Since an event log is a set of traces, this sub-discipline is called trace clustering.

2.2 Determining the Number of Clusters

In traditional clustering, numerous approaches have been suggested for assessing the adequate number of clusters. A taxonomy of approaches for determining the number of clusters has been presented in [26]. The most straightforward approach is to incorporate domain knowledge, either by directly adjusting your algorithm to suit the knowledge of a domain expert or by post-processing the results to adhere to this knowledge. In general, however, it is unlikely that such domain knowledge exists and is available for an event log. Creating an approach based on the specific generation of trace clusters will not be applicable for each existing trace clustering technique either. Therefore, we propose to adapt approaches based on the post-processing of partitions.

According to the taxonomy of [26], possible post-processing approaches can be based on variance, structure, consensus and resampling. The most commonly known variance-based method is probably the gap statistic [28], which is based on the within-cluster sum of squares using Euclidean distance. Likewise, structural approaches use indices to compare within-cluster cohesion to between-cluster separation [26]. It is clear that one would prefer a number of clusters where the within-cluster cohesion and the between-cluster separation are both large. As a third group of approaches, consensus clustering refers to choosing the number of clusters based on the agreement between different cluster solutions. These different solutions can be obtained by applying different clustering techniques, by applying the same clustering technique to perturbed versions of the same data set, or by randomly resetting initial centroids (in a centroid-based technique). Intuitively, the consensus between different clustering solutions should be higher at the true number of clusters. The final group of post-processing approaches

---

[2] For more info on the XES-standard, we refer to http://www.xes-standard.org/.

is based on resampling, and is related to consensus clustering in its intuition: a number of iterations are performed in which sub-sampled, bootstrapped or noisy versions of the original data set are clustered. The resulting partitions are then expected to be more similar at the appropriate number of clusters.

With regards to applicability for trace clustering, adapting variance- or structure-based approaches to trace clustering might not be straightforward, since a distance measure is needed. To calculate distances between traces, features would have to be derived from these traces. Considering that certain trace clustering techniques deliberately avoid 'featurizing' traces [9], this is not deemed an appropriate route for trace clustering. Rather than using direct trace similarity, a structure-based approach building on the concept of separation is presented in this paper. Consensus- and resampling-based approaches do not suffer from this issue as much. Therefore, a consensus- and resampling-based approach leveraging the concept of stability is described in this paper as well.

3   Stability of Trace Clustering Solutions

The approach proposed in this section is a resampling-based approach, inspired by a methodology for stability-based validation of clustering solutions in [22], which was adapted for biclustering solutions in [24]. In [22], it was shown to be an effective method for discovering the appropriate number of clusters on simulated and gene expression data. Furthermore, in [6], a similar stability-based approach is proposed to assess the quality of process discovery techniques.

In [22,24], resampling/perturbation strategies, learning algorithms, and solution similarity metrics are proposed that are specifically designed for general (bi)clustering problems. The general intuition is that clustering solutions should remain more stable at the true number of clusters that at others. As such, this paper contributes by proposing a stability-based approach for determining the correct number of trace clusters. Our approach leverages the so-called "log perturbation stability", which is the adaptation of general resampling to the process mining domain. In Fig. 1, our general stability approach is depicted. Tailoring the framework to trace clustering entails the configuration of three main components, i.e. the perturbation strategy (step 1), the solution similarity computation (step 3), a stability index calculation (step 4). In addition, a trace clustering technique should be chosen (step 2). This stability is then normalized with respect to the stability of a random clustering on the same perturbed event logs (step 5).

The steps of our approach thus become:

1. **Step 1:** Given an event log L, and a log perturbation function P, create n perturbed versions of the event log: P_1 to P_n.
2. **Step 2:** Create a clustered log CL by applying a trace clustering technique TC to the original event log: $CL = TC(L)$ and to the perturbed event logs: $CL_i = TC(P_i)$ with $i \in \{1..n\}$.
3. **Step 3:** Given a similarity index $I(CL_x, CL_y)$, quantify the similarity between the clustering of the original dataset and the clustering of the perturbed dataset as $I(CL, CL_i)$ for each $i \in \{1..n\}$.

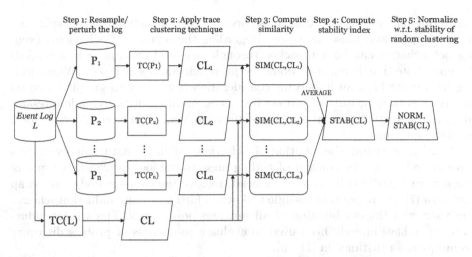

Fig. 1. A visualization of the proposed approach for calculating the stability of a clustered event log, based on a similar diagram in [24]. The normalized version of this stability is calculated at different numbers of clusters to determine the optimal number of clusters.

4. **Step 4:** Average these similarity measures to create a stability metric for event log L and trace clustering technique TC as

$$S^{TC} = \frac{1}{n} \sum_{i=1}^{n} I(CL, CL_i) \tag{1}$$

5. **Step 5**: Normalize with respect to the stability of a random clustering technique S^R over the same set of perturbed event logs:

$$\bar{S}^{TC} = \frac{S^{TC} - S^R}{1 - S^R} \tag{2}$$

Observe that a higher value for $\bar{S}^{TC}$ indicates a better stability of the solution. This metric should be evaluated at different numbers of clusters, at which point the best scoring number of clusters should be chosen. In the remainder of this section, we describe the three main components of our approach: possible perturbation strategies based on resampling and noise induction (Sect. 3.1), computation of solution similarity based on mutual information or process model similarity metrics (Sect. 3.3), calculation of the stability index based on a window-based approach (Sect. 3.4), and normalization of the stability with respect to random stability (Sect. 3.5).

3.1 Step 1: Log Perturbation Strategy

Perturbing event logs essentially boils down to three options: either some behaviour is removed, or some behaviour is added, or a combination of both. There are many different ways to do this, as argued in [26]: sub-sampling, data-splitting, bootstrapping and noise induction. Regarding the removal of behaviour, event log perturbation can be approached through case-level resampling in a random fashion. Note that here, cases would be process instances or traces. When dealing with event logs, an important consideration is whether to sample based on process instances or distinct process instances. An alternative to random resampling is systematic leave-one-out cross-validation, which can be considered a form of 'data-splitting'.

Finally, regarding the addition of behaviour, slightly perturbing event logs strongly relates to the concept of adding noise to the log. In [25], four types of noise were initially defined: remove head, remove tail, remove body, and swap tasks. In [7], the removal of a single task was added as a noise induction scheme, together with the combination of all previous noise types. These noise induction types have already been used to evaluate robustness of process discovery techniques, for instance in [11,19].

Taking these aspects into consideration, the log perturbation strategy underlying our stability assessment framework is as follows. First, behaviour can be removed through a resampling procedure, which is essentially sub-sampling at the level of distinct process instances. However, to make the resampling a bit less naive, the probability that a distinct process instance is removed, is inversely proportional to the frequency of this distinct process instance in the event log. Secondly, behaviour can be added through noise induction. Though several noise types were proposed in [25], we opt to include three types of noise: removing a single event, swapping two events, and adding a random single event (from the log activity alphabet) at a random place in the process instance. Example 1 presents the effects of noise induction on a single process instance. Noise induction is performed at the process instance level. For both removal of behaviour (sub-sampling at the distinct process instance level) and addition of behaviour (noise induction at the process instance level), a percentage of affected instances needs to be chosen.

Example 1. Given a process instance $ABBCD$, some potential effects of noise induction could be removal: $ABCD$, swapping: $AB\,CB\,D$, or addition: $ABBC\,C\,D$.

3.2   Step 2: Trace Clustering Technique

In the next step, a certain trace clustering algorithm is applied. An overview of existing trace clustering techniques is provided in Table 1. In general, trace clustering techniques can be classified according to three dimensions. Firstly, what they consider as input: a propositional representation or an event log. Secondly, which kind of clustering approach is used: for example k-means, hierarchical, model-driven. Thirdly and most importantly, the clustering bias they employ. Two broad categories exist: those that map traces onto a vector space model or quantify the similarity between two traces directly; and those that take the quality of the underlying process models into account.

Table 1. Existing trace clustering approaches with their data representation, clustering approaches and biases

Author	Data representation	Clustering technique	Clustering bias
Greco et al. [20]	Propositional	k-means	Instance similarity: alphabet k-grams
Song et al. [27]	Propositional	Various	Instance similarity: *profiles*
Ferreira et al. [16]	Event log	First order Markov mixture model	Maximum likelihood
Bose and van der Aalst [2,3]	Event log	Hierarchical clustering	Instance similarity metrics
Folino et al. [17]	Event log	Enhanced Markov cluster model	Maximum likelihood
De Weerdt et al. [9]	Event log	Model-driven clustering	Combined process model fitness (ICS)
Ekanayake et al. [14]	Propositional	Complexity-aware clustering	Instance similarity + repository complexity
Delias et al. [10]	Event log	Spectral	Robust instance similarity
Evermann et al. [15]	Event log	k-means	Instance similarity: alignment cost

3.3   Step 3: Solution Similarity Computation

In this section, two distinct approaches for computing the similarity between two clusterings will be described. One is inspired by information metrics from the consensus clustering domain, and one is inspired by similarity metrics from the process modelling domain.

On the one hand, we propose a consensus clustering-based metric. It is called the Normalized Mutual Information (NMI), and was proposed by [18]. It is a measure for the extent to which two clusterings contain the same information. Here, this mutual information is conceptually defined as the extent to which two process instances are clustered together in both clusterings. Let k_a be the number of clusters in clustering a, k_b the number of clusters in clustering b, n the total number of traces, n_i^a the number of elements in cluster i in clustering a, n_j^b, the number of elements in cluster j in clustering b, and n_{ij}^{ab} the number of elements present in both cluster i in clustering a and cluster j in clustering b. The NMI is then defined as:

$$I_{NMI}(a,b) = -2 \frac{\sum_{i=1}^{k_a} \sum_{j=1}^{k_b} n_{ij}^{ab} log(\frac{n_{ij}^{ab} n}{n_i^a n_j^b})}{\sum_{i=1}^{k_a} n_i^a log(\frac{n_i^a}{n}) + \sum_{j=1}^{k_b} n_j^b log(\frac{n_j^b}{n})} \tag{3}$$

On the other hand, we propose a metric based on the similarity between discovered process models. Rather than measuring the similarity by counting the number of elements that are included in the same cluster in both cluster solutions (i.e. measuring the consensus between both clusterings), each different cluster is used to discover a process model. Then, a process model similarity metric is used to measure the similarity between these discovered process models. This is represented conceptually in Fig. 2.

A plethora of process discovery techniques and process similarity metrics exist that could be leveraged for this purpose. With regards to process discovery techniques, an efficient and robust technique is preferred. Therefore, we propose the usage of Heuristics miner [31]. It mines a heuristic net, which is converted to a Petri net. This technique has demonstrated its efficacy on real-life datasets [8]. With regards to process model similarity, our preference goes out to the structural graph-edit distance (GED) similarity metric [12], though behavioural metrics such as causal footprints [13] or behavioural profiles [30] could be used as well. Graph-edit distance is a metric that reflects the distance between two models based on the insertion and deletion of places and transitions in a Petri net. Finally, our similarity metric for trace clustering solutions is summarized in Eq. 4, where n_i is the number of elements in cluster i of clustering a, and $sim_{HG}(i,j)$ is the graph-edit distance similarity between the converted heuristic net mined from cluster i of clustering a and the converted heuristic net mined from cluster j of clustering b.

$$I_{HG}(a,b) = \frac{\sum_{i \in a} n_i \max_{j \in b}(sim_{HG}(i,j))}{\sum_{i \in a} n_i} \qquad (4)$$

In [23], it is stated that a high-quality similarity index should have two characteristics: (1) it should take differences in cluster sizes into account, and (2) it should be symmetric. Note from Eq. 3 that these properties are fulfilled for $I_{NMI}(.,.)$. Likewise, from Eq. 4, it is clear that $I_{HG}(a,b)$ is weighted for the effects of different cluster sizes. However, it is not symmetric yet, i.e. $I_{HG}(a,b) \neq I_{HG}(b,a)$ due to the combination of weights and the max-operator. Therefore, we propose a final symmetric variant $\bar{I}_{HG}$:

$$\bar{I}_{HG}(a,b) = \frac{I_{HG}(a,b) + I_{HG}(b,a)}{2} \qquad (5)$$

Example 2. Figure 3 contains two clustering solutions, each consisting of 2 clusters. To calculate $I_{HG}(a,b)$ for each cluster in clustering A, the most similar cluster in cluster B is to be chosen, and then the corresponding similarities are weighted using Eq. 4. Both clusters are most similar to cluster 1 of clustering B, resulting in a $I_{HG}(a,b)$ of 0.9. Assuming that both clusters in clustering B contain an equal amount of traces, $I_{HG}(b,a)$ is equal to 0.83, and $\bar{I}_{HG}(a,b)$ is 0.87.

3.4   Step 4: Stability Index Computation

Next, in step 4 of our framework, the stability index is computed as an average over a number of iterations, as detailed in Algorithm 1 in the 'Stability'-function.

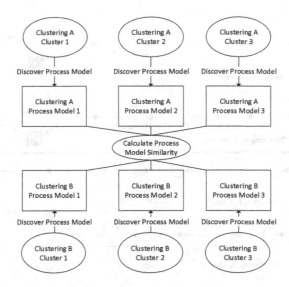

Fig. 2. Conceptual representation of the process model-based similarity metric, when two clusterings of three clusters each are under comparison.

Hereto, three extra input parameters are necessary: a minimal number of iterations r_{min}, a review window Δr and a maximal stability error ϵ_S. Typical values for these parameters are 20, 10, and 0.005 respectively. This iterative approach serves a double purpose: on the one hand, it ensures that the final stability is robust and sufficiently precise; on the other hand, it prevents unnecessary computation. The approach goes as follows (lines 2–8): for each of the number of clusters, the stability is calculated, as is the stability of a random clustering technique, which is then used to calculate the normalized stability. The number of clusters with the highest stability is returned. The stability (lines 10–22) is calculated by clustering the entire log to create a baseline clustered log. Then, the log is iteratively perturbed, clustered, and the similarity between this clustered log and the baseline clustered log is computed. The stability is calculated as the average of these similarities over the iterations. When the minimum amount of iterations (r_{min}) has passed, and the stability has not deviated more than the maximal error (ϵ_S) in the review window (last Δr iterations), the stability-function terminates.

3.5   Step 5: Normalization of the Stability

The final step is the normalization of the stability. This normalization is included to exclude unwanted information from entering the stability metric: if the random stability increases for higher cluster numbers, for example, then this is due to the inherent structure of the stability metric, rather than an actual improvement in the quality of the clustering. As provided in Algorithm 1, this is done as

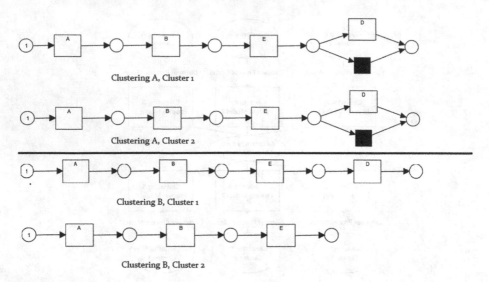

Fig. 3. Example of two clustering solutions and the process models corresponding to each cluster.

follows, where S_k is the stability of a certain clustering algorithm with k clusters, and S_k^R is the stability of randomly dividing the event log into clusters:

$$\bar{S}_k = \frac{S_k - S_k^R}{1 - S_k^R} \qquad (6)$$

Example 3. Given a hypothetical situation where one is determining whether 3 or 5 clusters is most appropriate, the normalization could have the effect illustrated in Table 2, reducing the preference for a number of clusters where even a random clustering is stable.

Table 2. Example of effect of the normalization.

Clusters	S_k	S_k^R	$\bar{S}_k$
3	0.6	0.5	0.2
5	0.6	0.4	0.33

Finally, we remark that a random clustering should cluster event logs based on their distinct process instances, not process instances. The underlying assumption is that any existing trace clustering technique should at least group those traces together that contain exactly the same behaviour, even a random clustering technique.

Algorithm 1. Stability evaluation

Input: L := Event log, TC := Trace clustering algorithm, P:= Perturbation strategy, I_s := similarity metric, k_{max}:= maximum number of clusters;
Input: r_{min} := 20, Δr := 10, ϵ_S := 0.005; % Configuration
Output: k := number of clusters for which the normalized stability is the highest
1: **function** NUMBEROFCLUSTERS(k_{max})
2:     $\bar{S}()$:= {} % List of normalized stability results per number of clusters
3:     **for** k := 2 ; $k <= k_{max}$ **do**
4:         S_k:= Stability(L, TC, P, I_s,r_{min}, Δr, ϵ_S) % Calculate stability
5:         S_k^R:= Stability(L, $Random$, P, I_s,r_{min}, Δr, ϵ_S) % Calculate random stability
6:         $\bar{S}_k$:= $\frac{S_k - S_k^R}{1 - S_k^R}$ % Normalize with regards to random stability
7:     **end for**
8:     **return** k := $\underset{k}{\mathrm{argmax}}(\bar{S}(k))$

9: **end function**

10: **function** STABILITY(L, TC, P, I_s,r_{min}, Δr, ϵ_S)
11:     r := 1 % Iteration
12:     CL := $TC(L)$ % Baseline clustered event log
13:     $u()$:= {} % List of similarity results per iteration
14:     $w()$:= {} % List of stability results per iteration
15:     **while** $(r < r_{min}) \vee [max_{p,q}|w(p) - w(q)| > \epsilon_S; \forall p, q : r - \Delta r < p < q \leq r)]$ **do**
16:         L_r := $P_r(L)$ % Perturb the log
17:         CL_r := $TC(L_r)$ % Cluster event log from perturbed log
18:         $u(r)$:= $I_s(CL, CL_r)$ % Calculate similarity with baseline clustered event log
19:         $w(r)$:= $\frac{(r-1)*w(r-1)+u(r)}{r}$ % Calculate stability
20:         r := $r + 1$
21:     **end while**
22:     **return** S := $w(r - 1)$
23: **end function**

4   A Cross-Cluster Separation-Based Approach

As detailed in Sect. 2.2, a wide array of different possible directions exist when it comes to assessing the number of clusters. In the previous section, an approach based on stability has been detailed. In this section, one of the constructs used to calculate this stability, $I_{HG}(a, b)$, is leveraged to create an alternative path for assessing an appropriate number of trace clusters.

Conceptually, cross-cluster separation represents how well the clusters in a partitioning are separated. Clearly, a quantification of separation can be used as a metric for the quality of a cluster solution. The most well-known separation metric is probably the Davies-Bouldin metric [4]. It can be considered a structural approach in the taxonomy of [26]. The main issue when it comes to defining such a metric in the trace clustering case, however, lies in the definition of the similarity between two traces. This can be done by incorporating a direct similarity between the traces, based on alignment or based on a mapping of the traces, however, clustering techniques exist that specifically aim to avoid such a mapping. Therefore, in this section, we propose a similarity metric based on the process models that represent each cluster, as in Sect. 3.3. Each different cluster is used to discover a process model. Then, a process model similarity metric is used to measure the similarity between these discovered process models. This similarity can then be used to calculate the separation of the clusters. While a number of process discovery techniques and process model similarity techniques exist which could be used for this task, we apply the Heuristics miner and the structural graph-edit distance, as before.

More specifically, we propose to use an internal version of the $I_{HG}(a, b)$ similarity index as a measure of cluster separation, where n_i is the number of elements in cluster i of clustering a, and $sim_{HG}(i, j)$ is the graph-edit distance similarity between the converted heuristic nets mined from clusters i and j of clustering a.

$$Sep_{HG}(a) = 1 - \frac{\sum_{i \in a} n_i \max_{(j \in a) \neq i}(sim_{HG}(i, j))}{\sum_{i \in a} n_i} \tag{7}$$

Three observations can be made regarding this weighted metric for inter-cluster separation based on the process model similarity of discovered process models. First, observe that it is inherently symmetrical, therefore no extra step is needed to render it symmetrical, in contrast to Eq. 5. Secondly, observe that this metric will be lower when inter-cluster separation is lower. Therefore, a higher value of the Sep_{HG} metric is preferable, and can be used as an indicator of an appropriate number of clusters.

Example 4. Figure 3 contains a comparison of 2 clustering solutions, both comprised of two clusters. In the top row, both clusters in the 2-cluster solution are represented by the same discovered process model. Therefore, the separation of this solution is 0. In the bottom row, the same set of traces is represented by two different discovered process models, with a separation of 0.16, assuming that both clusters contain an equal amount of process instances.

5   Experimental Evaluation

This evaluation serves multiple purposes: first, it is meant to show the general applicability of our techniques. Therefore, our approaches are tested on multiple real-life datasets in combination with a wide variety of trace clustering techniques. Furthermore, the purpose is to evaluate the different components of our stability framework: the underlying resampling strategies, the similarity metrics, and the normalization. Finally, the separation-based approach is demonstrated here as well, and its results are contrasted with those of the stability-based approach.

5.1   Setup

This section describes the different event logs and trace clustering techniques that are used, and the components of the stability-based approach: how the perturbation will be applied; which similarity indices will be used for measuring the similarity between the baseline clustering and the clusterings on the perturbed event logs.

General. Four real-life event logs [8] are subjected to our approach. The number of process instances, distinct process instances, number of distinct events and average number of events per process instance are listed in Table 3. Observe that no exact number of clusters is known upfront for these event logs: the starting point is that applying process mining methods such as process discovery techniques on the entire event log leads to undesirable results [8]. Hence, this evaluation shows how our stability measure and separation measure can be used to determine an appropriate number of clusters, or how they can be used to show that no appropriate number of clusters can be found.

With regards to trace clustering techniques, we have calculated the results using 7 different methods: 2 methods based on 'process-model aware' clustering techniques (*ActFreq* and *ActMRA*, [9]), and 5 'trace featurization' methods (*MR* and *MRA* [21]; *GED* an *LED* [3]; and *K-gram* [27]).[3]

Stability. With regards to the calculation of the stability, we have chosen to apply two strategies. On the one hand, a noise-induction perturbation strategy, where each process instance has a 10% chance of either having an event removed, two events swapped, or one event added from the existing activity alphabet. On the other hand, a sub-sampling approach, where 25% of the distinct process instances is removed. The probability of removal a distinct process instance is inversely proportional with its frequency in the event log.

Furthermore, both the Normalized Mutual Information similarity-metric (I_{NMI}) and the symmetrical discovered process model similarity metric based on Heuristics miner and graph-edit distance ($\bar{I}_{HG}$) will be employed, as described in Sect. 3.3. This allows for a comparison of the results of both similarity metrics.

Finally, the maximum number of clusters is set to 10. In addition, the evaluation strategy proposed in Algorithm 1 will deliberately not be used, to prevent randomization bias. Rather, a fixed number of 20 iterations will be used to calculate the stability, with appropriate seeding to prevent bias.

Table 3. Characteristics of the real-life event logs used for the evaluation: number of process instances (**#PI**), distinct process instances (**#DPI**), number of different events (**#EV**) and average number of events per process instance ($\frac{\#EV}{PI}$).

Log name	#PI	#DPI	#EV	$\frac{\#EV}{PI}$
KIM	1541	251	18	5.62
MCRM	956	212	22	11.73
MOA	2004	71	49	6.20
ICP	6407	155	18	5.99

Separation. With regards to separation, the non-normalized version of our proposed separation metric, Sep_{HG}, is used, as described in Sect. 4. This approach

---

[3] The first two methods are implemented in the ProM-framework for process mining in the *ActiTrac*-plugin. The latter five methods are implemented in the *GuideTree-Miner*-plugin.

is also tested on a number of clusters ranging from 2 to 10, on the same event logs and with the same clustering techniques as the stability-based approach.

5.2 Results of the Stability-Based Approach

The results are presented in Table 4, which contains the number of clusters with maximal stability for each combination of similarity metric and perturbation strategy; in Fig. 4, which visualises the results on the KIM-dataset; and Fig. 5, which visualises the results on the ICP-dataset. Since no clear cluster structures were found for the MCRM- and MOA-datasets, these Figures are not included here[4]. Note that this does not imply a shortcoming of our approach, these event logs most likely simply do not contain relevant trace clusters.

Table 4. Number of clusters for which the normalized stability is maximal. Two different similarity metrics, two different perturbation strategies and seven different clustering techniques were used, on four real-life datasets. The number of clusters for which the stability would have been maximal if no normalization had been applied is included between brackets.

Similarity	Technique	Noise induction				Sub-Sampling			
		KIM	MCRM	MOA	ICP	KIM	MCRM	MOA	ICP
I_{NMI}	ActFreq	4(5)	2(2)	2(10)	2(5)	4(4)	2(2)	4(10)	3(3)
I_{NMI}	ActMRA	2(4)	3(3)	7(7)	4(9)	4(9)	6(6)	3(10)	4(4)
I_{NMI}	GED	7(7)	3(3)	7(7)	3(3)	9(10)	2(4)	5(7)	3(3)
I_{NMI}	LED	4(10)	4(4)	2(2)	2(10)	7(8)	4(4)	3(9)	9(10)
I_{NMI}	MR	2(10)	2(2)	5(5)	10(10)	2(10)	2(2)	3(3)	10(10)
I_{NMI}	MRA	2(10)	2(2)	2(2)	4(5)	2(10)	2(2)	2(5)	4(5)
I_{NMI}	K-gram	2(10)	10(10)	2(9)	2(10)	2(10)	10(10)	2(10)	10(10)
$\bar{I}_{HG}$	ActFreq	3(7)	2(2)	10(2)	2(2)	4(4)	4(3)	9(10)	5(3)
$\bar{I}_{HG}$	ActMRA	3(3)	3(2)	7(2)	2(2)	4(4)	6(6)	10(10)	9(9)
$\bar{I}_{HG}$	GED	3(2)	2(2)	10(2)	6(2)	2(2)	10(2)	5(10)	10(10)
$\bar{I}_{HG}$	LED	3(2)	2(2)	3(2)	8(2)	4(2)	2(2)	9(10)	5(4)
$\bar{I}_{HG}$	MR	2(2)	2(2)	10(10)	6(2)	2(2)	2(2)	2(2)	10(10)
$\bar{I}_{HG}$	MRA	3(2)	2(2)	10(2)	5(5)	3(2)	4(2)	5(5)	2(2)
$\bar{I}_{HG}$	K-gram	3(2)	6(2)	6(2)	2(2)	4(2)	2(2)	2(2)	2(2)

Similarity Metrics. In Figs. 4 and 5, the I_{NMI}-metric is presented in the top row, while the $\bar{I}_{HG}$-metric is presented in the bottom row. For the KIM-dataset (Fig. 4), no clear peaks are apparent in the plots with the results of the

---

[4] The visual representations of the MCRM- and MOA-event logs are available on http://www.processmining.be/clusterstability/ToPNoCResults.

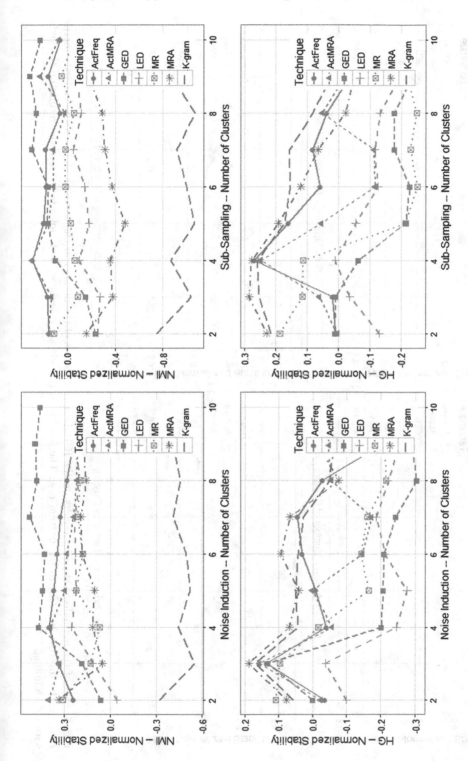

Fig. 4. Plot of the normalized stability results on the KIM-dataset in terms of the number of clusters, calculated with similarity metric I_{NMI} in the top row and $\bar{I}_{HG}$ in the bottom row. The results on the left are calculated with noise induction, the results on the right with sub-sampling.

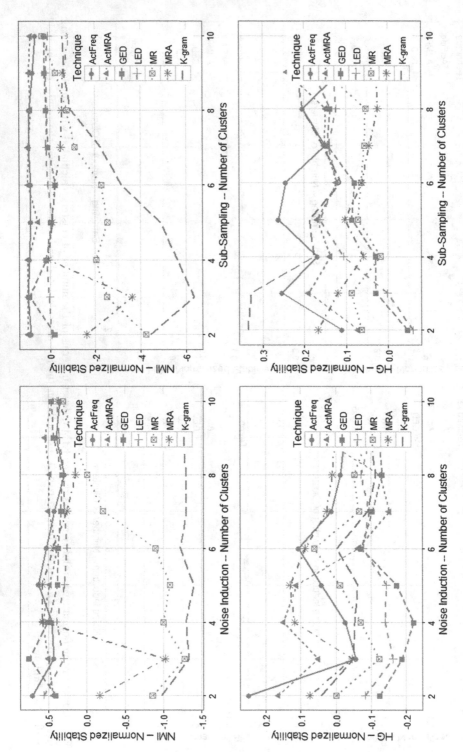

Fig. 5. Plot of the normalized stability results on the ICP-dataset in terms of the number of clusters, calculated with similarity metric I_{NMI} in the top row and $\bar{I}_{HG}$ in the bottom row. The results on the left are calculated with noise induction, the results on the right with sub-sampling.

I_{NMI}-metric. In the results of the $\bar{I}_{HG}$-metric, a peak appears to be present at a cluster number of 3 when applying a noise induction-perturbation. Similarly, there appears to be a consensus about 3 or 4 clusters when applying a sub-sampling perturbation strategy. The same observation holds for dataset ICP (Fig. 5): there appears to be a peak around 6 clusters when combining the $\bar{I}_{HG}$-metric with noise-induction, while no peaks are apparent for the I_{NMI}-metric. These findings are supported by Table 4.

Perturbation Strategy. With regards to perturbation strategy, similar results are found on the KIM-dataset (Fig. 4) regardless of whether noise induction or sub-sampling is applied. On the ICP-dataset (Fig. 5), the results seem to be in favour of a noise-induction approach.

Algorithmic Efficiency. In Fig. 6, the evolution of the stability before normalization over the iterations is visualised, calculated with similarity metric $\bar{I}_{HG}$ and noise induction, and using the K-gram clustering technique. This set-up is chosen as an example, with other configurations performing similarly. It is clear that the stability results converge rather quickly over the iterations, and that it was indeed appropriate to fix the number of iterations at 20 in the other evaluations in this section of the paper.

In Fig. 7, the evaluation of the computational time (in seconds) over the number of iterations is presented. These results where obtained in Java SE 8, on a device running Windows 10 Enterprise, with an Intel Core i7-4712HQ processor. The K-gram clustering technique is evaluated with similarity metric $\bar{I}_{HG}$ and noise induction. As expected, the runtime increases linearly over the number of iterations, with the slope depending on the number of clusters under scrutiny (the more clusters, the higher). Recall that these are real-life dataset, and that the ICP-event log is rather large, see Table 3. Nonetheless, even at 40 iterations, the algorithm terminates in under 4 min.

Normalization. Table 4 contains the number of clusters for which the normalized stability was maximal. The number of clusters for which the stability would have been maximal if no normalization had been applied is included between brackets. With regards to the stability without normalization, 16 of the 28 combinations combining noise induction with the $\bar{I}_{HG}$-metric would have had different best cluster numbers if no normalization had been applied. Likewise, 13 out of 28 results combining the I_{NMI}-metric with noise induction would have been different if no normalization had been applied. For sub-sampling, there would have been 11 and 15 differences with $\bar{I}_{HG}$ and I_{NMI}, respectively. The non-normalized application of $\bar{I}_{HG}$ generally leads to smaller cluster numbers, whereas the non-normalized application of I_{NMI} generally leads to higher cluster numbers. This validates the usefulness of the normalization: it prevents the results from favouring smaller (as with the $\bar{I}_{HG}$-metric) or larger numbers of clusters (as with the I_{NMI}-metric).

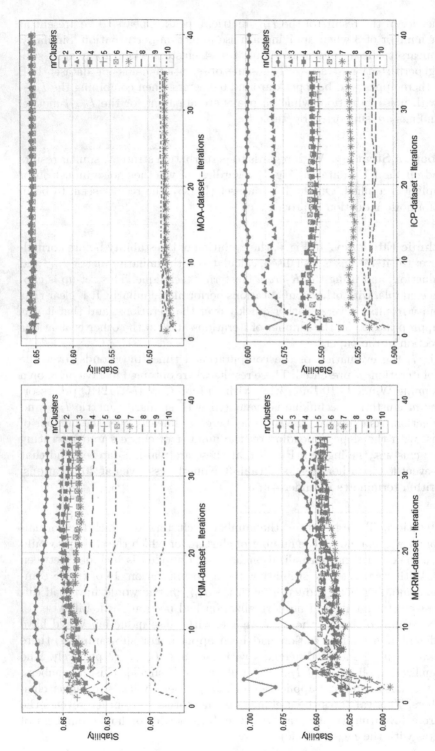

Fig. 6. Plot of the evolution of the stability results before normalization over the iterations on each dataset, calculated with similarity metric $\bar{I}_{HG}$ and noise induction, using the K-gram clustering technique.

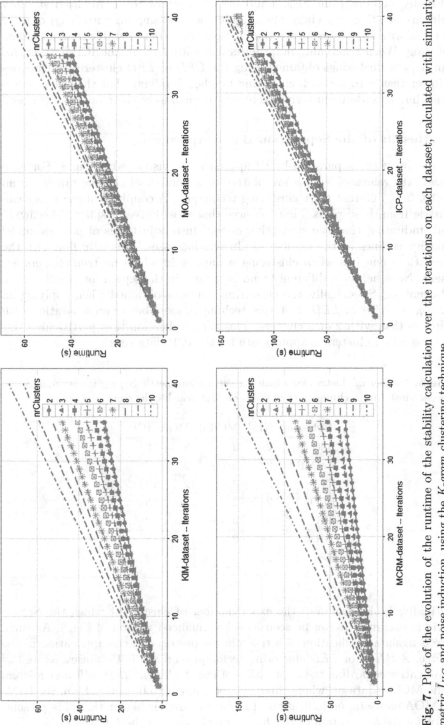

Fig. 7. Plot of the evolution of the runtime of the stability calculation over the iterations on each dataset, calculated with similarity metric $\bar{I}_{HG}$ and noise induction, using the *K-gram* clustering technique.

Finally, observe from Figs. 4 and 5 that a lot of the normalized stability results are negative, especially when combining sub-sampling with I_{NMI} or noise induction with $\bar{I}_{HG}$. This means that these results are less stable than a random clustering. When combining noise induction with $\bar{I}_{HG}$ on the ICP-dataset, for example, the clusterings obtained using the *GED* or *LED* clustering techniques are lower than zero for each clustering number, implying that they behave less stable than a random clustering technique regardless of the number of clusters.

5.3   Results of the Separation-Based Approach

The results of the separation-based approach are visualised in Fig. 8. For each dataset, the values of Sep_{HG} are plotted at a number of clusters ranging from 2 to 10, for 6 different trace clustering techniques. A couple of observations can be made from these plots. First, observe that most curves display a downward trend, indicating that the separation of the clusters in terms of process model similarity declines as the number of clusters increases. This is in line with the expectations one has when clustering a dataset in which no true clusters are present. Nonetheless, a different trend is present in the seperation results of the ICP-event log. Specifically, the clustering solutions obtained when applying an *ActFreq*, *ActMRA* or *LED* clustering technique, score better on separation with 4 clusters than with 2 or 3 clusters. This is an indication that partitioning this event log into 4 clusters is appropriate for the ICP-data set.

Table 5. Number of clusters for which the separation metric Sep_{HG} is maximal. Seven different clustering techniques were used, on four real-life datasets.

Technique	KIM	MCRM	MOA	ICP
ActFreq	2	2	2	8
ActMRA	2	3	2	4
GED	2	3	2	2
LED	2	2	2	5
MR	2	3	2	2
MRA	2	2	2	2
K-gram	2	3	3	2

Finally, Table 5 contains the exact number of clusters at which the Sep_{HG} metric is maximal. It can be seen as a less nuanced version of Fig. 8. As such, there is again an indication of a true cluster presence in the application of the *ActFreq*, *ActMRA* or *LED* clustering techniques on the ICP-dataset, as well as an indication regarding the application of the *ActMRA*, *GED*, *MR* and *K-gram* on the MCRM-dataset, where three clusters appear to be optimal. On the KIM- and MOA-datasets, no indication of a cluster number higher than 2 is present, except for the application of the *K-gram* technique on the MOA-set.

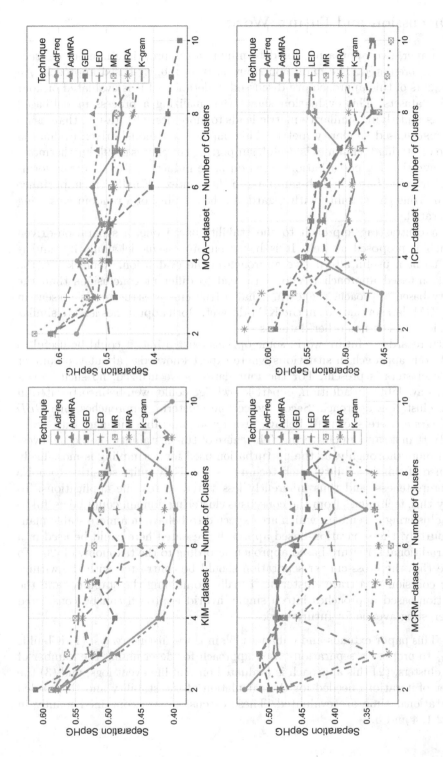

Fig. 8. The results of the separation-based approach on the four datasets.

6   Discussion and Future Work

In this paper, two approaches for determining an appropriate number of trace clusters is presented. The main contribution is a stability-based approach. All components of this approach are discussed in detail, and it is evaluated on four real-life datasets. This evaluation shows that utilizing a process model-based metric as underlying similarity metric leads to more desirable results than using a consensus-based similarity metric. This implies that model-driven evaluation of trace clustering techniques is useful, supporting the claims of [9]. Furthermore, it is shown that log-perturbation based on noise induction slightly outperforms log-perturbation based on sub-sampling in this context. Finally, the importance of normalizing the stability with regards to the stability of a random clustering is illustrated.

As a contrasting approach to the stability-based one, a separation-driven approach is proposed as well. It is based on process model-similarity, and is shown to be a useful alternative approach in the evaluation. Remarkably, the separation-based approach is shown to lead to different conclusions than the stability-based approach, suggesting that a true cluster structure is present in the MCRM-dataset and not in the KIM-dataset. Both approaches lead to similar conclusions on the two other datasets.

With regards to future work, some options exist. First, it could be useful to validate our approach in situations where expert knowledge about the number of trace clusters is present. For the four datasets we utilized, no such knowledge was available. In addition, expert knowledge could even be incorporated in a trace clustering approach. Secondly, certain clustering approaches, like *GED* and *K-Gram*, were shown to behave in a rather unstable manner, with lower stability than a random clustering. The cause of this instability should be investigated more thoroughly, as the perturbation used for resampling is most likely the cause of this instability: such techniques are likely quite sensitive to noise or incompleteness, and thus inherently less suited to real-life applications. To remedy this, techniques from the consensus clustering domain could be useful to create clustering ensembles, which are expected to behave in a more stable manner. Fourthly, the separation-based approach presented here could be used in a more traditional structure-based approach according to the taxonomy of [26]. To achieve this, the cross-cluster separation should be contrasted with the within-cluster cohesion of a trace clustering. Finally, combining the stability- and the separation-based approaches into a single, hybrid approach can be considered an interesting avenue for future work.

Note. This paper extends and enhances [5], in three distinct ways: (1) it builds on $\bar{I}_{HG}$ to propose a separation-based approach for determining the number of traces clusters, (2) this approach is evaluated on real-life event logs, and (3) the number of iterations needed for the calculation of the stability and the needed computational time are evaluated. These extensions are contained mainly in Sects. 2.1, 4 and 5.

References

1. van der Aalst, W.: Process Mining: Data Science in Action. Springer, Berlin (2016)
2. Bose, R.P.J.C., van der Aalst, W.M.P.: Trace clustering based on conserved patterns: towards achieving better process models. In: Rinderle-Ma, S., Sadiq, S., Leymann, F. (eds.) BPM 2009. LNBIP, vol. 43, pp. 170–181. Springer, Heidelberg (2010). doi:10.1007/978-3-642-12186-9_16
3. Bose, R., Aalst, W.V.D.: Context aware trace clustering: towards improving process mining results. In: SDM, pp. 401–412 (2009)
4. Davies, D.L., Bouldin, D.W.: A cluster separation measure. IEEE Trans. Pattern Anal. Mach. Intell. **2**, 224–227 (1979)
5. De Koninck, P., De Weerdt, J.: Determining the number of trace clusters: a stability-based approach. In: Proceedings of the International Workshop on Algorithms & Theories for the Analysis of Event Data (ATAED) 2016, vol. 1592, pp. 1–15. CEUR-ws Workshop Proceedings (2016)
6. De Koninck, P., De Weerdt, J.: A stability assessment framework for process discovery techniques. In: La Rosa, M., Loos, P., Pastor, O. (eds.) BPM 2016. LNCS, vol. 9850, pp. 57–72. Springer, Cham (2016). doi:10.1007/978-3-319-45348-4_4
7. De Medeiros, A.K.A., Weijters, A.J.M.M., Van Der Aalst, W.M.P.: Genetic process mining: an experimental evaluation. Data Min. Knowl. Discov. **14**(2), 245–304 (2007)
8. De Weerdt, J., De Backer, M., Vanthienen, J., Baesens, B.: A multi-dimensional quality assessment of state-of-the-art process discovery algorithms using real-life event logs. Inform. Syst. **37**(7), 654–676 (2012)
9. De Weerdt, J., Vanden Broucke, S., Vanthienen, J., Baesens, B.: Active trace clustering for improved process discovery. IEEE Trans. Knowl. Data Eng. **25**(12), 2708–2720 (2013)
10. Delias, P., Doumpos, M., Grigoroudis, E., Manolitzas, P., Matsatsinis, N.: Supporting healthcare management decisions via robust clustering of event logs. Knowledge-Based Syst. **84**, 203–213 (2015)
11. Di Ciccio, C., Mecella, M., Mendling, J.: The effect of noise on mined declarative constraints. In: Ceravolo, P., Accorsi, R., Cudre-Mauroux, P. (eds.) SIMPDA 2013. LNBIP, vol. 203, pp. 1–24. Springer, Heidelberg (2015). doi:10.1007/978-3-662-46436-6_1
12. Dijkman, R., Dumas, M., Van Dongen, B., Krik, R., Mendling, J.: Similarity of business process models: metrics and evaluation. Inform. Syst. **36**(2), 498–516 (2011)
13. van Dongen, B., Dijkman, R., Mendling, J.: Measuring similarity between business process models. In: Bellahsène, Z., Léonard, M. (eds.) CAiSE 2008. LNCS, vol. 5074, pp. 450–464. Springer, Heidelberg (2008). doi:10.1007/978-3-540-69534-9_34
14. Ekanayake, C.C., Dumas, M., García-Bañuelos, L., La Rosa, M.: Slice, mine and dice: complexity-aware automated discovery of business process models. In: Daniel, F., Wang, J., Weber, B. (eds.) BPM 2013. LNCS, vol. 8094, pp. 49–64. Springer, Heidelberg (2013). doi:10.1007/978-3-642-40176-3_6
15. Evermann, J., Thaler, T., Fettke, P.: Clustering traces using sequence alignment. In: Reichert, M., Reijers, H.A. (eds.) BPM 2015. LNBIP, vol. 256, pp. 179–190. Springer, Cham (2016). doi:10.1007/978-3-319-42887-1_15
16. Ferreira, D., Zacarias, M., Malheiros, M., Ferreira, P.: Approaching process mining with sequence clustering: experiments and findings. In: Alonso, G., Dadam, P., Rosemann, M. (eds.) BPM 2007. LNCS, vol. 4714, pp. 360–374. Springer, Heidelberg (2007). doi:10.1007/978-3-540-75183-0_26

17. Folino, F., Greco, G., Guzzo, A., Pontieri, L.: Editorial: mining usage scenarios in business processes: outlier-aware discovery and run-time prediction. Data Knowl. Eng. **70**, 1005–1029 (2011)
18. Fred, A., Lourenço, A.: Cluster ensemble methods: from single clusterings to combined solutions. Stud. Comput. Intell. **126**, 3–30 (2008)
19. Goedertier, S., Martens, D., Vanthienen, J., Baesens, B.: Robust process discovery with artificial negative events. J. Mach. Learn. Res. **10**, 1305–1340 (2009)
20. Greco, G., Guzzo, A., Pontieri, L., Saccà, D.: Discovering expressive process models by clustering log traces. IEEE Trans. Knowl. Data Eng. **18**(8), 1010–1027 (2006)
21. Jagadeesh Chandra Bose, R.P., van der Aalst, W.M.P.: Abstractions in process mining: a taxonomy of patterns. In: Dayal, U., Eder, J., Koehler, J., Reijers, H.A. (eds.) BPM 2009. LNCS, vol. 5701, pp. 159–175. Springer, Heidelberg (2009). doi:10.1007/978-3-642-03848-8_12
22. Lange, T., Roth, V., Braun, M.L., Buhmann, J.M.: Stability-based validation of clustering solutions. Neural Comput. **16**(6), 1299–1323 (2004)
23. Lee, Y., Lee, J.H., Jun, C.H.: Validation measures of bicluster solutions. Ind. Eng. Manag. Syst. **8**(2), 101–108 (2009)
24. Lee, Y., Lee, J., Jun, C.H.: Stability-based validation of bicluster solutions. Pattern Recognit. **44**(2), 252–264 (2011)
25. Maruster, L.: A machine learning approach to understand business processes. Eindhoven University of Technology (2003)
26. Mirkin, B.: Choosing the number of clusters. Wiley Interdiscip. Rev. Data Min. Knowl. Discov. **1**, 252–260 (2011)
27. Song, M., Günther, C.W., van der Aalst, W.M.P.: Trace clustering in process mining. In: Ardagna, D., Mecella, M., Yang, J. (eds.) BPM 2008. LNBIP, vol. 17, pp. 109–120. Springer, Heidelberg (2009). doi:10.1007/978-3-642-00328-8_11
28. Tibshirani, R., Walther, G., Hastie, T.: Estimating the number of clusters in a data set via the gap statistic. J. R. Stat. Soc. Ser. B (Statistical Methodol.) **63**, 411–423 (2001)
29. Van der Aalst, W., Adriansyah, A., Van Dongen, B.: Replaying history on process models for conformance checking and performance analysis. Wiley Interdiscip. Rev. Data Min. Knowl. Discov. **2**(2), 182–192 (2012)
30. Weidlich, M., Polyvyanyy, A., Desai, N., Mendling, J., Weske, M.: Process compliance analysis based on behavioural profiles. Inform. Syst. **36**(7), 1009–1025 (2011)
31. Weijters, A.J.M.M., van der Aalst, W.: Rediscovering workflow models from event-based data using little thumb. Integr. Comput. Eng. **10**, 151–162 (2003)

Log- and Model-Based Techniques for Security-Sensitive Tackling of Obstructed Workflow Executions

Julius Holderer[1]([⊠]), Josep Carmona[2]([⊠]), Farbod Taymouri[2], and Günter Müller[1]

[1] University of Freiburg, Freiburg im Breisgau, Germany
{holderer,mueller}@iig.uni-freiburg.de
[2] Universitat Politècnica de Catalunya, Barcelona, Spain
jcarmona@cs.upc.edu, taymouri@lsi.upc.edu

Abstract. Imposing access control onto workflows considerably reduces the set of users authorized to execute the workflow tasks. Further constraints (e.g. Separation of Duties) as well as unexpected unavailability of users may finally obstruct the successful workflow execution. To still complete the execution of an obstructed workflow, we envisage a hybrid approach. We first flatten the workflow and its authorizations into a Petri net and analyse for or encode the obstruction with a corresponding "obstruction marking". If a log is provided, we partition its traces into "successful" or "obstructed" by replaying the log on the flattened net. An obstruction should then be solved by finding its nearest match from the list of successful traces. If no log is provided, the structural theory of Petri nets shall be used to provide a minimized Parikh vector, that may violate given firing rules, but reach a complete marking and by that, complete the workflow.

Keywords: Workflow satisfiability · Authorization · Obstruction · Petri nets

1 Introduction

From the Société Générale scandal with loss of nearly five billion Euro caused by shuffling transactions [8] to more recent scandals, for instance in the automotive industry (e.g. the "Dieselgate" [23]) — the increasing number of corporate fraud cases underline the growing demand for security and control in enterprises and their corresponding information systems. Such systems increasingly adapt to a process-oriented view to reach the intended business goals. These so called process-aware information systems (PAIS) [18] can help to mitigate such fraudulent behaviour by enhancing workflows with authorization constraints. In this respect security in business processes gains more and more importance [1,28]. Classic computer security [4] usually follows the CIA triad, trying to achieve or sustain confidentiality, integrity and availability, or simply "keeping bad things

© Springer-Verlag GmbH Germany 2017
M. Koutny et al. (Eds.): ToPNoC XII, LNCS 10470, pp. 43–69, 2017.
DOI: 10.1007/978-3-662-55862-1_3

from happening". Security in business processes, however, should also consider to "make good things happen" by reaching the intended business goals in completing corresponding processes.

The interplay of security in business processes and this notion of process availability can be shown by analysing the impact of introducing authorization in PAIS to achieve confidentiality and integrity. First, access control policies are added on top of users contributing in the process, controlling who is authorized to perform which task. On top of that, further constraints are defined, for instance "separation of duties" (SoD) constraints [5] or contrary "binding of duties" (BoD) constraints. Moreover, users can be on vacation or become ill. In this way, the set of authorized users to execute tasks in a process is drastically reduced and can result in a state where no user can be found to execute the given task at hand, obstructing the workflow execution.

In this setting, an obstruction describes a state of a workflow instance where the enforcement of the authorization policy conflicts with the business objectives. In the control-flow level, the business objectives can be achieved by executing a task t, but in the task-execution level there is no user who is authorized to execute t without violating the given authorization policy [2].

1.1 Running Example

Figure 1 illustrates a simplified payment workflow and a user-task assignment. Now, we add an SoD constraint for t_1 and t_2, meaning that the preparation of payment needs to be done by a different user than the one who approves the payment. Given the user-task assignment in Fig. 1(b), if u_2 executes t_1, t_2 can be performed by u_1. If u_1 executes t_1, she can not execute t_2 due to the imposed SoD constraint, although she basically is authorized to perform this task. u_2 can neither execute t_2, since he is not authorized at all. This situation indicates an *obstruction* of the workflow resulting from given authorization constraints [2,3,16].

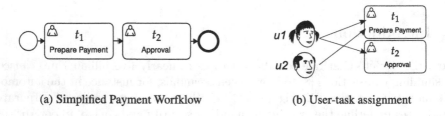

(a) Simplified Payment Worfklow   (b) User-task assignment

Fig. 1. Simplified payment workflow based on [6].

1.2 Related Work

Literature regarding satisfiability of authorization constrained workflows mainly offers theoretical approaches so far [16]. In particular, research related to the so called workflow satisfiability problem (WSP) (see Sect. 2) shows that (under the assumption that $P \neq NP$) the NP-complete WSP is efficiently solvable for a growing number of constraint types. Regarding access control systems in general, there mainly exist two approaches for the case when no user is available to access a certain object [11]: either alternative constraints are defined ("Break-the-Glass") or another user is empowered to access the object by use of delegation. However, classic delegation requires the delegator to be available to perform the delegation and involves the danger that delegation capabilities are misused (e.g. collusion [27]). Considering these deficits, the approach of Crampton et al. given in [11] suggests the concept of auto-delegation, in which qualifications are introduced that indicate a potential delegatee. Examples on how the qualification hierarchy may be computed based on an access control model are reported in [11]. However, the auto-delegation mechanism only exists as a first concept so far, which seems promising for the use in PAIS. In summary, the state of the art on workflow satisfiability only scarcely solves the consequent practical problems in terms of obstructions in workflow executions at runtime. Therefore, we envisage to develop an approach that caters for the detection of obstructions *and* policy-wise sound workarounds that allow their execution.

1.3   Structure

We first state Petri nets, events logs, authorization and structural theory formally and introduce the corresponding terminology in Sect. 2. To tackle an obstructed state in a workflow, we envisage a hybrid approach, depending on the existence of historical information. The basis for the subsequent approaches builds the flattening of a workflow and its authorization data into a Petri net, which is presented in Sect. 3. In case no historical information is provided, we propose a model-based exploration approach in Sect. 4 that suggests the minimal amount of resources to be added into the model to escape from an obstructed state. When historical information is provided in form of an event log, the method presented in Sect. 5 could be used, which simply detects the most similar historical successful trace. In both approaches the solutions propose which users shall be assigned to which tasks to resolve the obstructions with least security violations. The experimental evaluation at the end of each section show specific solutions to given obstructions. We conclude in Sect. 6, draw the potential practical applications of the presented work and show further research steps on the topic.

2   Preliminaries

We first give the definition of a Petri net to model workflows with a clear execution semantics. Then, we introduce users, user-task authorization and define SoD and BoD constraints. In this way, we are able to grasp unsatisfiability in workflows formally, leading us to introduce structural theory as a way to encounter this (see Sect. 4.1).

2.1 Petri Nets and Event Logs

Definition 1 (Petri net). *A Petri net [19] is a 4-tuple* $N = \langle P, T, \mathcal{F}, m_0 \rangle$, *where* P *is the set of places,* T *is the set of transitions, satisfying* $P \cap T = \emptyset$ *and* $\mathcal{F} : (P \times T) \cup (T \times P) \to \{0, 1\}$ *is the flow relation, and* m_0 *is the initial marking. A marking is an assignment of a non-negative integer to each place. If* k *is assigned to place* p *by marking* m *(denoted* $m(p) = k$), *we say that* p *is marked with* k *tokens. Given a node* $x \in P \cup T$, *its pre-set* $\{y | \langle y, x \rangle \in \mathcal{F}\}$ *and post-set* $\{y | \langle x, y \rangle \in \mathcal{F}\}$ *are denoted by* $\bullet x$ *and* $x^\bullet$ *respectively. A transition* t *is enabled in a marking* m *when all places in* $\bullet t$ *are marked. When a transition* t *is enabled, it can* fire *by removing a token from each place in* $\bullet t$ *and putting a token to each place in* $t^\bullet$. *A marking* m' *is reachable from* m *if there is a sequence of firings* $t_1 t_2 \ldots t_n$ *that transforms* m *into* m', *denoted by* $m[t_1 t_2 \ldots t_n\rangle m'$. *A sequence of transitions* $t_1 t_2 \ldots t_n$ *is a feasible sequence if it is firable from* m_0.

Workflow processes can be represented in a simple way by using workflow nets (WF-nets) [24]. A WF-net is a Petri net with a place *start* (denoting the initial state of the system) with no incoming arcs and a place *end* (denoting the final state of the system) with no outgoing arcs, and every other node is within a path between *start* and *end*. The transitions in a WF-net represent tasks. For the sake of simplicity, the techniques of this paper assume that models are specified with WF-nets.

Definition 2 (System net, full firing sequences). *A system net defines a set of sequences, each one starting from the initial marking and ending in the final marking. A system net is a tuple* $SN = (N, m_{start}, m_{end})$, *where* N *is a WF-net and the two last elements define the initial and final marking of the net, respectively. The set* $\{\sigma \mid (N, m_{start})[\sigma\rangle(N, m_{end})\}$ *denotes all the full firing sequences of* SN.

Definition 3 (Trace, event log, Parikh vector). *Given an alphabet of events* $T = \{t_1, \ldots, t_n\}$, *a trace is a word* $\sigma \in T^*$ *that represents a finite sequence of events. An* event log $L \in \mathcal{B}(T^*)$ *is a multiset of traces.* $|\sigma|_a$ *represents the number of occurrences of* a *in* σ. *The Parikh vector of a sequence of events is a function* $\widehat{\ } : T^* \to \mathbb{N}^n$ *defined as* $\widehat{\sigma} = (|\sigma|_{t_1}, \ldots, |\sigma|_{t_n})$. *For simplicity, we will also represent* $|\sigma|_{t_i}$ *as* $\widehat{\sigma}(t_i)$. *The support of a Parikh vector* $\widehat{\sigma}$, *denoted by* $supp(\widehat{\sigma})$ *is the set* $\{t_i | \widehat{\sigma}(t_i) > 0\}$.

Analogous to full firing sequences, full traces indicate a sequence of events that are fully replayable on a WF-net, taking the net from the initial to the end marking. Further, we adapt and extend the sequence definitions from [25]:

Definition 4 (Sequence to set operation, concatenation, set of log events). *For any sequence* $\sigma = \langle t_1, t_2, ..., t_n \rangle$ *over* T, $\partial_{set}(\sigma) = \{t_1, t_2, ..., t_n\}$. ∂_{set} *converts a sequence into a set, e.g.,* $\partial_{set}\langle d, a, a, a, a, a, a, d \rangle = \{a, d\}$. a *is an element of* σ, *denoted as* $a \in \sigma$, *if and only if* $a \in \partial_{set}(\sigma)$. $\sigma \bigoplus t' = \langle t_1, ..., t_n, t' \rangle$ *is the sequence with element* t' *appended at the end. Similarly,* $\sigma_1 \bigoplus \sigma_2$ *appends sequence* σ_2 *to* σ_1 *resulting a sequence of length* $|\sigma_1| + |\sigma_2|$.

For any log $L = \{\sigma_1, \sigma_2, ..., \sigma_n\}$, $L_{\oplus} = \sigma_1 \oplus \sigma_2 \oplus ... \oplus \sigma_n$ concatenates all traces in one sequence of length $|\sigma_1| + |\sigma_2| + |...| + |\sigma_n|$. Hence, $\partial_{set}(L_{\oplus})$ gives the set of all events that occur in all sequences contained in the log.

2.2 Security in Workflows

To connect WF-nets with users and authorization, we adapt the definitions from [26]. Further constraints regarding workflow satisfiability analysis have already been investigated [10]. However, in this paper we focus on the SoD/BoD related binary constraints, which are sufficient to reach an obstructed state.

Definition 5 (Authorization). *A configuration is given by a tuple $\langle U, B \rangle$, where $U \subseteq \mathcal{U}$ is a set of users and $B = \{\rho_1, \cdots, \rho_m\} \subseteq \mathcal{B}$ is a set of binary relations such that $\rho_i \subseteq U \times U (i \in [1, m])$. Furthermore, we assume that B contains two predefined binary relations $=$ and $\neq$, which denote equality (for BoD) and inequality (for SoD), respectively. A configuration $\langle U, B \rangle$ defines the environment in which a workflow is to be run.*

A workflow is represented as a tuple $\langle N, TA, C \rangle$, where N is a WF-net, $TA \subseteq \mathcal{U} \times T$ is the user-task authorization where $(u, t) \in TA$ indicates that a user u is authorized to perform task t, and C is a set of constraints, that is explained below.

Definition 6 (Constraints). *Each of the constraints takes one of the following forms:*

1. *$\langle \rho(t_1, t_2) \rangle$: the user who performs t_1 and the user who perform t_2 must satisfy the binary relation ρ.*
2. *$\langle \rho(\exists X, t) \rangle$: there exists a task $t' \in X$ such that $\langle \rho(t', t) \rangle$ holds, i.e., the user who performs t' and the user who performs t satisfy ρ.*
3. *$\langle \rho(t, \exists X) \rangle$: there exists a task $t' \in X$ such that $\langle \rho(t, t') \rangle$ holds.*
4. *$\langle \rho(\forall X, t) \rangle$: for each task $t' \in X, \langle \rho(t', t) \rangle$ must hold.*
5. *$\langle \rho(t, \forall X) \rangle$: for each task $t' \in X, \langle \rho(t, t') \rangle$ must hold.*

Consider the simplified payment workflow in Fig. 1a. Let $t1_{prepare}, t2_{approve}$ denote the two tasks in the workflow. The SoD constraint of the workflow can be represented in tuple-based specification $\langle \neq (t1_{prepare}, t2_{approve}) \rangle$.

A plan Pl for workflow $W = \langle N, TA, C \rangle$ is a subset of $\mathcal{U} \times T$ such that, for every task $t_i \in T$, there is exactly one tuple (u_a, t_i) in Pl, where $u_a \in \mathcal{U}$. Intuitively, a plan assigns exactly one user to every task in a workflow.

Given a workflow $W = \langle N, TA, C \rangle$ and a configuration $\Gamma = \langle U, B \rangle$, we say that a plan Pl *is valid for* W under Γ if and only if for every $(u, t) \in Pl, u$ is an authorized user of t and no constraint in C is violated. We say that W is *satisfiable* under Γ if and only if there exists a plan Pl that is valid for W under Γ.

The *workflow satisfiability problem* (WSP) checks whether a workflow W is satisfiable under a configuration Γ. Given configuration $\langle U, B \rangle$, checking whether W is satisfiable under Γ is equivalent to checking whether there is a valid plan for W under Γ. Note that there can be multiple valid plans for a workflow W under a configuration. In fact, it is the existence of multiple valid plans that makes it possible for W to be completed even if a number of users are absent. Therefore, the notion of *resilience* in workflows is introduced [26]: Given a workflow W and an integer $n \geq 0$, a configuration $\langle U, B \rangle$ is *resilient* for W up to n absent users if and only if for every size-n subset U' of U, W is satisfiable under $\langle (U - U'), B \rangle$. In our example, the absence of either u_1 or u_2 would result in an unsatisfiable workflow therefore it is not resilient for $n > 0$ absent users. We show how we capture the aforementioned obstructions based on a WF-net with an "obstruction marking" in Sect. 3.

2.3   Structural Theory of Petri Nets

Let $N = \langle P, T, \mathcal{F}, m_0 \rangle$ be a Petri net. Given a feasible sequence $m_0 \xrightarrow{\sigma} m$, the number of tokens for a place p in m is equal to the tokens of p in m_0 plus the tokens added by the input transitions of p in σ minus the tokens removed by the output transitions of p in σ:

$$m(p) = m_0(p) + \sum_{t \in {}^\bullet p} |\sigma|_t \, \mathcal{F}(t, p) - \sum_{t \in p^\bullet} |\sigma|_t \, \mathcal{F}(p, t)$$

The marking equations for all the places in the net can be written in the following matrix form (see Fig. 2(c) as an example): $m = m_0 + \mathbf{N} \cdot \widehat{\sigma}$, where $\mathbf{N} \in \mathbb{Z}^{P \times T}$ is the *incidence matrix* of the net: $\mathbf{N}(p, t) = \mathcal{F}(t, p) - \mathcal{F}(p, t)$.

If a marking m is reachable from m_0, there exists a sequence σ such that $m_0 \xrightarrow{\sigma} m$ and the following system of equations has at least the solution $X = \widehat{\sigma}$

$$m = m_0 + \mathbf{N} \cdot X \tag{1}$$

If (1) is infeasible, m is not reachable from m_0. The inverse does not hold in general: there are markings satisfying (1) which are not reachable. Those markings are said to be *spurious* [22]. Figures 2(a)–(c) present an example of a net with spurious markings: the Parikh vector $\widehat{\sigma} = (2, 1, 0, 0, 1, 0)$ and the marking $m = (0, 0, 1, 1, 0)$ are a solution to the marking equation, as shown in Fig. 2(c). However, m is not reachable by any feasible sequence. Figure 2(b) depicts the graph containing the reachable markings and the spurious markings (shadowed). The numbers inside the states represent the tokens at each place $(p_1, \ldots, p_5)$. This graph is called the *potential reachability graph*. The initial marking is represented by the state $(1, 0, 0, 0, 0)$. The marking $(0, 0, 1, 1, 0)$ is only reachable from the initial state by visiting a negative marking through the sequence $t_1 t_2 t_5 t_1$, as shown in Fig. 2(b). Therefore, Eq. (1) provides only a sufficient condition for reachability of a marking.

For well-structured Petri nets, e.g. when the net is *free-choice* [19], *live*, *bounded* and *reversible*, Eq. (1) together with a collection of sets of places (called *traps invariants*) of the system completely characterizes reachability [12]. For the rest of cases, the problem of the spurious solutions can be palliated by the use of trap invariants [14], or by the addition of some special places named *cutting*

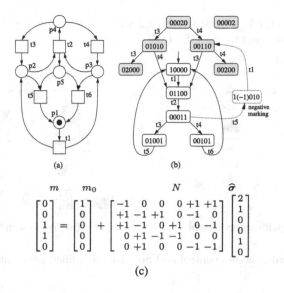

(a)   (b)

$$
\begin{bmatrix} 0 \\ 0 \\ 1 \\ 1 \\ 0 \end{bmatrix} = \begin{bmatrix} 1 \\ 0 \\ 0 \\ 0 \\ 0 \end{bmatrix} + \begin{bmatrix} -1 & 0 & 0 & 0 & +1 & +1 \\ +1 & -1 & +1 & 0 & -1 & 0 \\ +1 & -1 & 0 & +1 & 0 & -1 \\ 0 & +1 & -1 & -1 & 0 & 0 \\ 0 & +1 & 0 & 0 & -1 & -1 \end{bmatrix} \begin{bmatrix} 2 \\ 1 \\ 0 \\ 0 \\ 1 \\ 0 \end{bmatrix}
$$

where the columns are labeled m, m_0, N, $\hat{\sigma}$.

(c)

Fig. 2. (a) Petri net, (b) Potential reachability graph, (c) Marking equation.

implicit places [22] to the original Petri net that remove spurious solutions from the original marking equation.

3   Flattening of Authorization Data

We first flatten the workflow and the corresponding authorization data into one net, which builds the basis for the model and the log-based approach we will present in Sects. 4 and 5. We start with an example to explain the flattening of the different types of authorization/users constraints. For the sake of simplicity and efficiency, we then first describe the generalized encoding on acyclic nets. Then we proceed with nets containing cycles, which have a more complex encoding, but preserves the idea of the encoding described in the acyclic case.

Given the example workflow in Fig. 1(a), we flatten the authorization and constraints into a WF-net step by step. First, because of the absence of ambiguous gateways in the model in Fig. 1(a), we can easily transform the workflow into the Petri net in Fig. 3.

Fig. 3. Simplified payment workflow as WF-net with initial marking.

To model access control, we assume the simple access control model without roles from Fig. 1(b). The user-task allocation is noted by the corresponding transitions (e.g. *u1t1* in Fig. 4(a)). Firing *u1t1* for instance represents the decision of who shall execute a specific task.

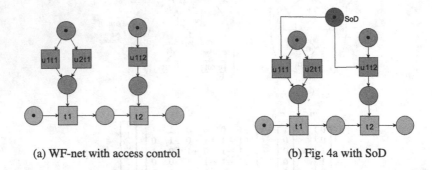

(a) WF-net with access control   (b) Fig. 4a with SoD

Fig. 4. Flattening access control and SoD into simplified payment workflow.

3.1 Generalizing Flattening

Given a workflow with authorization $W = \langle N, TA, C \rangle$, our aim is to flatten the user-task authorization TA and the set of constraints C into a net N' to be able to encode an obstructed marking directly into the net N'.

We first take the user-task authorization TA and encode it into the net N_{TA}. Afterwards, we flatten further SoD and BoD constraints into the net N_{TA+SoD} and N_{TA+BoD}.

Flattening of User-Task Assignment: The user-task assignment is flattened with the intuition that for every possible user-task assignment, we introduce a transition denoted by user and transition name (e.g. u1t1), that consumes a token from one single place for the regarded transition to execute. By that, it is guaranteed, that the transition can only be executed once by a specific user.

Definition 7 (Flattening user-task assignment). *Given a workflow with authorization $W = \langle N, TA, C \rangle$, flattening the user-task authorization TA into N is as follows:*

1. *For each transition t_i in N, create a place p_{t_i-} and a place p_{t_i+} representing the state that no user is assigned (−) or a user was assigned (+) to execute t_i respectively, and mark each of the p_{t_i-} places with one token.*
2. *For each user-task authorization $(u_j, t_i) \in TA$, create a transition $t_{u_j t_i}$.*
3. *For every place p_{t_i-} and its corresponding transition(s) $t_{u_j t_i}$, create an arc $\langle p_{t_i-}, t_{u_j t_i} \rangle$.*
4. *For every transition $t_{u_j t_i}$ and its corresponding place p_{t_i+}, create an arc $\langle t_{u_j t_i}, p_{t_i+} \rangle$.*
5. *For every place p_{t_i+} and its dedicated transition t_i, create an arc $\langle p_{t_i+}, t_i \rangle$.*

After performing these steps, we obtain the net $N_{TA} = \langle P_{TA}, T_{TA}, \mathcal{F}_{TA}, m_{TA_0} \rangle$, *where* $P_{TA} = P \cup \{p_{t_1-}, p_{t_2-}, \dots, p_{t_i-}\} \cup \{p_{t_1+}, p_{t_2+}, \dots, p_{t_i+}\}$, $T_{TA} = T \cup \{t_{u_1t_1}, t_{u_1t_2}, t_{u_2t_1}, t_{u_2t_2}, \dots, t_{u_jt_i}\}$, $F_{TA} = F \cup \{\langle p_{t_1-}, t_{u_1t_1}\rangle, \langle p_{t_2-}, t_{u_1t_2}\rangle, \langle p_{t_1-}, t_{u_2t_1}\rangle, \langle p_{t_2-}, t_{u_2t_2}\rangle, \dots, p_{t_i-}, t_{u_jt_i}\rangle\} \cup \{\langle t_{u_1t_1}, p_{t_1+}\rangle, \langle t_{u_1t_2}, p_{t_2+}\rangle, \langle t_{u_2t_1}, p_{t_1+}\rangle, \langle t_{u_2t_2}, p_{t_2+}\rangle, \dots, t_{u_jt_i}, p_{t_i+}\rangle\} \cup \{\langle p_{t_1+}, t_1\rangle, \langle p_{t_2+}, t_2\rangle, \dots, \langle p_{t_i+}, t_i\rangle\}$ *and the marking* $m_{TA_0} = \langle 1,0,0,\dots,0,1,0,1,0,\dots,1,0\rangle$ *with* m_{TA_0} *according to the order* $p_1, p_2, \dots, p_i, p_{t_1-}, p_{t_1+}, p_{t_2-}, p_{t_2+}, \dots, p_{t_i-}, p_{t_i+}$.

For example, we apply these five steps from Definition 7 to our running example based on the net N and the user-task authorization: First, for the transitions t1 and t2 we create the places p_{t_1-}, p_{t_1+}, p_{t_2-}, and p_{t_2+} and mark p_{t_1-} and p_{t_2-} with one token. Secondly, we create the user-task transitions $t_{u_1t_1}$, $t_{u_2t_1}$, and $t_{u_1t_2}$, based on the user-task authorization. Thirdly, for p_{t_1-} and its corresponding transitions $t_{u_1t_1}$ and $t_{u_2t_1}$ we create the arcs $\langle p_{t_1-}, t_{u_1t_1}\rangle$ and $\langle p_{t_1-}, t_{u_2t_1}\rangle$; for p_{t_2-} and its corresponding transition $t_{u_1t_2}$ we create the arc $\langle p_{t_2-}, t_{u_1t_2}\rangle$. Fourthly, for transitions $t_{u_1t_1}$ and $t_{u_2t_1}$ and its corresponding place p_{t_1+} we create the arcs $\langle t_{u_1t_1}, p_{t_1+}\rangle$ and $\langle t_{u_2t_1}, p_{t_1+}\rangle$; for $t_{u_1t_2}$ and its corresponding place p_{t_2+} we create the arc $\langle t_{u_1t_2}, p_{t_2+}\rangle$. The fifth and last step is then to connect all the created Petri net parts with the initial net, which is realized by adding arcs from $\langle p_{t_1+}, t_2\rangle$ to $\langle p_{t_2+}, t_2\rangle$.

By this we finally merge N and TA of the running example into N_{TA}, where $P = \{p_1, p_2, p_3, p_{t_1-}, p_{t_1+}, p_{t_2-}, p_{t_2+}\}$, $T = \{t_1, t_2, t_{u_1t_1}, t_{u_2t_1}, t_{u_1t_2}\}$, $F = \{\langle p_1, t_1\rangle, \langle p_1, t_2\rangle \langle t_2, p_3\rangle \langle p_{t_1-}, t_{u_1t_1}\rangle, \langle p_{t_1-}, t_{u_2t_1}\rangle, \langle p_{t_2-}, t_{u_1t_2}\rangle, \langle t_{u_1t_1}, p_{t_1+}\rangle, \langle t_{u_2t_1}, p_{t_1+}\rangle, \langle t_{u_1t_2}, p_{t_2+}\rangle\}$ and the marking $m_{TA_0} = \langle 1,0,0,1,0,1,0\rangle$ with m_{TA_0} according to the order $p_1, p_2, p_3, p_{t_1-}, p_{t_1+}, p_{t_2-}, p_{t_2+}$.

Flattening of SoD Constraints: In a further step, we model the SoD constraint by introducing a choice place for all users authorized for both tasks (see Fig. 4(b)). A generalized way to model SoD is depicted in Fig. 5a.

Note that only for user-task assignments that are in conflict with each other a SoD choice place is introduced (see SoD_{u1} and SoD_{u2}). Notice that the restriction on the sequential execution of ti and tj can be dropped, e.g. ti and tj can be concurrent (as shown in Fig. 5a).

Definition 8 (Flattening SoD constraints). *Given a workflow with authorization* $W = \langle N, TA, C\rangle$, *after transforming the user-task authorization* TA *into* N *resulting in* N_{TA}, *flattening of SoD constraints* $c_{SoD} \in C$ *of the form* $\langle \neq (t_k, t_l)\rangle$ *into* N_{TA} *is as follows:*

1. *For each pair of user-task transitions* $t_{u_jt_k}$ *and* $t_{u_jt_l}$ *of each transition* t_k *and* t_l *of each SoD constraint* $\langle \neq (t_k, t_l)\rangle$, *create a place* $SoD_{u_jt_kt_l}$ *and mark it with one token.*
2. *For every created place* $SoD_{u_jt_kt_l}$ *and its corresponding user-task transitions* $t_{u_jt_k}$ *and* $t_{u_jt_l}$, *create the arcs* $\langle SoD_{u_jt_kt_l}, t_{u_jt_k}\rangle$ *and* $\langle SoD_{u_jt_kt_l}, t_{u_jt_l}\rangle$.

After performing these steps, we get the net N_{TA+SoD}, *which can be written down similarly to* N_{TA}, *but is avoided here for the sake of space.*

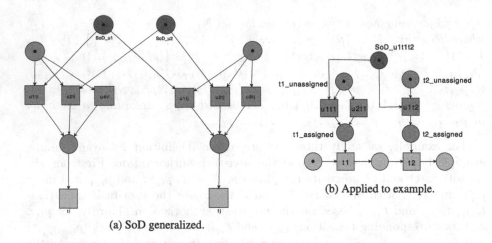

(a) SoD generalized.

(b) Applied to example.

Fig. 5. Generalized SoD with application to simplified payment workflow.

Given the SoD Constraint from the running example $\langle \neq (t_1, t_2)\rangle$, we apply these two steps. First, we create an SoD place $SoD_{u_1t_1t_2}$ for the user-task-transition pair $t_{u_1t_1}$ and $t_{u_1t_2}$ and add one token to it. Secondly, we create the arcs $\langle SoD_{u_1t_1t_2}, t_{u_1t_1}\rangle$ and $\langle SoD_{u_1t_1t_1}, t_{u_1t_2}\rangle$ to make the SoD place act as a choice place (see Fig. 4b).

By this we finally merge N_{TA} of the running example into N_{TA+SoD}, where $P = \{p_1, p_2, p_3, p_{t_1-}, p_{t_1+}, p_{t_2-}, p_{t_2+}, SoD_{u_1t_1t_2}\}$, $T = \{t_1, t_2, t_{u_1t_1}, t_{u_2t_1}, t_{u_1t_2}\}$, $F = \{\langle p_1, t_1\rangle, \langle p_1, t_2\rangle \langle t_2, p_3\rangle\langle p_{t_1-}, t_{u_1t_1}\rangle, \langle p_{t_1-}, t_{u_2t_1}\rangle, \langle p_{t_2-}, t_{u_1t_2}\rangle, \langle t_{u_1t_1}, p_{t_1+}\rangle, \langle t_{u_2t_1}, p_{t_1+}\rangle, \langle t_{u_1t_2}, p_{t_2+}\rangle\langle SoD_{u_1t_1t_2}, t_{u_1t_1}\rangle, \langle SoD_{u_1t_1t_1}, t_{u_1t_2}\rangle\}$ and the marking $m_{TA+SoD_0} = \langle 1, 0, 0, 1, 0, 1, 0, 1\rangle$ with m_{TA+SoD_0} according to the order p_1, $p_2, p_3, p_{t_1-}, p_{t_1+}, p_{t_2-}, p_{t_2+}, SoD_{u_1t_1t_2}$. Figure 5b depicts this net, which is basically the net of Fig. 4a with additional place annotations.

Flattening of BoD Constraints: Figure 6a depicts how we encode BoD constraints. Here, also choice places are added, however the arcs are connected differently. Every choice place aims to prevent firing of a user-task transition containing another user than the one first started with. Therefore, for each user-task transition for one task a choice place is introduced and this place is connected to the respective transition. Then, from each choice place, arcs are added to every user-task transition for the other task, that does not contain the user for which the choice place has been introduced. Notice that, just like in SoD flattening, ti and tj can be concurrent.

Definition 9 (Flattening BoD constraints). *Given a workflow with authorization* $W = \langle N, TA, C\rangle$, *after transforming the user-task authorization* TA *into* N *resulting in* N_{TA}, *flattening of BoD constraints* $c_{BoD} \in C$ *of the form* $\langle = (t_k, t_l)\rangle$ *into* N_{TA} *is as follows:*

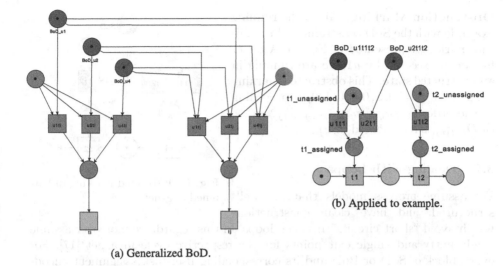

(a) Generalized BoD.

(b) Applied to example.

Fig. 6. Generalized BoD with application to simplified payment workflow.

1. *For each user-task transition $t_{u_j t_k}$ or $t_{u_j t_l}$ of each transition t_k and t_l of each BoD constraint $\langle = (t_k, \ t_l) \rangle$, create a place $BoD_{u_j t_k t_l}$ and mark it with one token. If the respected user-task transition is already connected to a BoD place regarding the respective constraint, proceed to the next user-task transition or terminate if there are none left.*

2. *For every created place $BoD_{u_j t_k t_l}$ and its corresponding user-task transition $t_{u_j t_k}$ create an arc $\langle BoD_{u_j t_k t_l}, t_{u_j t_k} \rangle$. For every user-task transition for t_l except $t_{u_j t_l}$ create an arc $\langle BoD_{u_j t_k t_l}, t_{u_x t_l} \rangle$.*

After performing these steps, we obtain the net N_{TA+BoD}, which can be written down similarly to N_{TA}, but is avoided here for the sake of space.

The running example does not contain an SoD constraint, however, we could replace the SoD constraint with the BoD constraint $\langle = (t_{1_{prepare}}, \ t_{2_{approve}}) \rangle$. Applying the first step of Definition 9 then creates the place $BoD_{u_1 t_1 t_2}$ for the user-task transition $t_{u_1 t_1}$, and $BoD_{u_2 t_1 t_2}$ for $t_{u_2 t_1}$. Secondly, we create the arcs $\langle BoD_{u_1 t_k 1_1}, t_{u_1 t_1} \rangle$, here we can not create the second arc because of no other user-task transitions for t2 than $t_{u_1 t_2}$. Then we create the arcs $\langle BoD_{u_2 t_k 1_1}, t_{u_2 t_1} \rangle$ and $\langle BoD_{u_2 t_k 1_1}, t_{u_1 t_2} \rangle$.

This finally results in the net N_{TA+BoD}, where $P = \{p_1, p_2, p_3, p_{t_1-}, p_{t_1+}, p_{t_2-}, p_{t_2+}, BoD_{u_1 t_1 t_2}, BoD_{u_2 t_1 t_2}\}$, $T = \{t_1, t_2, t_{u_1 t_1}, t_{u_2 t_1}, t_{u_1 t_2}\}$, $F = \{\langle p_1, t_1 \rangle, \langle p_1, t_2 \rangle \ \langle t_2, p_3 \rangle \ \langle p_{t_1-}, t_{u_1 t_1} \rangle, \langle p_{t_1-}, t_{u_2 t_1} \rangle, \langle p_{t_2-}, t_{u_1 t_2} \rangle, \langle t_{u_1 t_1}, p_{t_1+} \rangle, \langle t_{u_2 t_1}, p_{t_1+} \rangle, \langle t_{u_1 t_2}, p_{t_2+} \rangle \ \langle BoD_{u_1 t_1 t_2}, t_{u_1 t_1} \rangle, \langle BoD_{u_2 t_1 t_2}, t_{u_2 t_1} \rangle, \langle BoD_{u_2 t_1 t_2}, t_{u_1 t_2} \rangle\}$ and the marking $m_{TA+BoD_0} = \langle 1, 0, 0, 1, 0, 1, 0, 1, 1 \rangle$ with m_{TA+BoD_0} according to the order $p_1, p_2, p_3, \ p_{t_1-}, \ p_{t_1+}, \ p_{t_2-}, \ p_{t_2+}, \ BoD_{u_1 t_1 t_2}, \ BoD_{u_2 t_1 t_2}$. Figure 6b depicts this net graphically.

Obstruction Marking: Given the running example with the SoD constraint and the initial marking represented in Fig. 5b. After $t1$ has been executed by $u1$, we are running in an obstructed state. This obstructed marking $m_{TA+SoD_{obs}} = \langle 0, 1, 0, 0, 0, 1, 0, 0 \rangle$ according to the order p_1, p_2, p_3, p_{t_1-}, p_{t_1+}, p_{t_2-}, p_{t_2+}, $SoD_{u_1 t_1 t_2}$ is represented in Fig. 7.

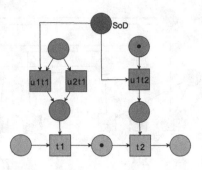

Fig. 7. Obstructed marking in flattened WF-net.

3.2 Dealing with Loops

We assume process models that are well-structured, and have clean constructions which avoid "short circuits" between loops. In this regard, we moreover assume single entry and single exit points for the respective cycle in a net [17]. For every block of SoD or BoD and its corresponding user-task assignment encoding, we "recharge" the corresponding SoD/BoD and (un)assignment places, i.e. we produce tokens into all these places, when a loop involving them is entered.

The cyan part in Fig. 8 shows how we implement this "charging". We first introduce a transition "enter_charging" that produces a token into the

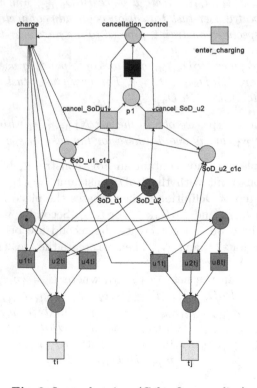

Fig. 8. Loop charging. (Color figure online)

place "cancellation_control". From there, we add for every SoD/BoD and (un)assignment place a transition that is able to consume leftover tokens in them ("cancel-transitions"). After all leftover tokens in regarded places are erased, the "charge" transition can be fired to put one token back in each of them. To control that this "charging" can only be performed when all corresponding SoD/BoD and (un)assignment places are empty, we need to bound their capacity to 1. Based on the "complementary-place transformation" that can be found in [19], we introduce complementary places for this, labelled with the place it is complementing followed by "_c1c" ("capacity 1 complement"). Further, we add arcs to the transitions which are connected to the regarded places, so that the sum of tokens for each pair of place and its place-complement equals always the capacity (which is 1 in our case) before and after executing the regarded transitions.

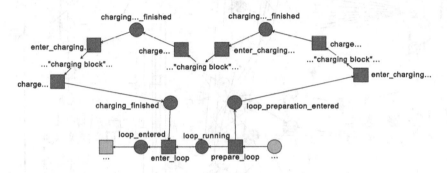

Fig. 9. Connecting charging elements into a given loop.

Figure 9 illustrates how to connect the "recharging" into a given loop. For this, we add a transition "prepare_loop" after the loop entry-point, which produces a token into a further place that is connected to "enter_charging". Now, all "charging blocks" that are involved with the transitions of the regarded loop can be concatenated. When the final charging transition is executed, a token is produced into a newly introduced place that indicates that "charging_finished".

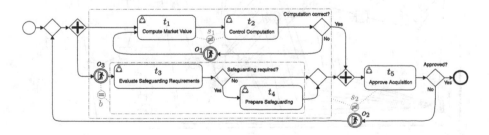

Fig. 10. Collateral evaluation workflow from [2].

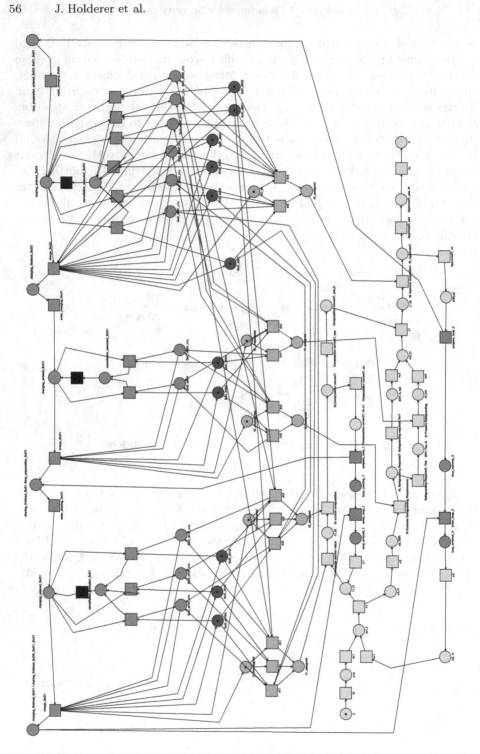

Fig. 11. Collateral evaluation workflow (blue) with the user-task flattening (green), the SoD or BoD flattening (red) and loop-recharging (cyan). (Color figure online)

Finally, this place is connected to the "enter_loop" transition, that can only be fired if the "enter_charging" transition has been executed before producing a token into the "loop_running" place.

3.3 Comprehensive Example

To show the applicability of our generalization, we now introduce an example based on the IBM Information Framework for collateral evaluation workflow which has been modelled in BPMN in [2]. It is executed by a financial institution to evaluate, accept, and prepare the safeguarding of the collateral that a borrower pledges in return for a secured loan.

Here, the SoD and BoD constraints are noted right in the BPMN model. Therefore, the authors in [2] also introduced the concept of release points (see o_1, o_2, o_3) to be able to look at SoD/BoD constraints in the scope of each loop separately. To show the applicability of our flattening to different models, our intention was to leave the model as it is, although release points are not necessary for our encoding of SoD or BoD. Besides, we have the user-task assignment shown in Fig. 12.

According to [13] we first transform the BPMN model into a P/T-Net. Then, we flatten the user-task assignment, the two SoD constraints and one BoD constraint into the net according to our presented theory. Finally we add the charging for loops. Figure 11 depicts the resulting net, with colours highlighting the different parts of the net. This net also contains obstructions, for which we will provide solutions in the experimental evaluation. in the subsequent sections, that present the approaches to solve obstructions based on the presented flattening.

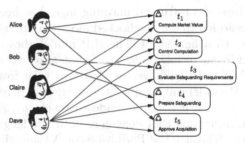

Fig. 12. User-task assignment.

4 Model-Based Obstruction Solving

If only the model of a workflow with its authorizations and constraints are given, we intend to solve an obstructed state not by changing the semantics of the model (cf. [3]), but by finding the best path with minimal violation. Importantly, by flattening the workflow with its authorizations and users into a Petri net according to Sect. 3, we can regard obstruction states as deadlocked markings. Hence, encoding the obstruction with a corresponding marking, the marking equation can be used to provide a minimized Parikh vector to reach a completed marking, which if it is fired from the obstruction state will violate the firing rules. We now explain the use of the structural theory of Petri nets [22] to provide a solution.

4.1   Approach Using the Marking Equation

Given an obstruction marking m_{obs} and a final marking m_{end}, we use the marking equation $m = m_0 + \mathbf{N} \cdot X$ to find the Parikh vector X, indicating which transitions has to be fired to reach the final marking. To enable the transitions proposed by X, first, a live marking has to be reached by adding tokens from variable Δ to the obstructed marking. With the help of a cost function $cost(X, \Delta)$ considering trace length, the amount of tokens, and user-defined costs (e.g. for security violations), the optimized solution with minimal cost for X and Δ shall be proposed. The integer linear programming (ILP) [7] model below sketches our approach for using the marking equation:

ILP model for completing an obstruction state m_{obs}

Min $cost(X, \Delta)$ subject to:
$$m_{live} = m_{obs} + \Delta$$
$$m_{end} = m_{live} + \mathbf{N} \cdot X$$
$$X, \Delta \geq \mathbf{0} \quad X \in \mathbb{N}^{|T|} \quad \Delta \in \mathbb{N}^{|P|}$$

After an obstructed marking m_{obs} has been reached, the necessary tokens will be added to the deadlocked model in order to take the current obstructed marking to a final state. The ILP model above has two sets of variables[1]: Δ is the addition of tokens to m_{obs} that takes to an unobstructed marking m_{live}, and X is the Parikh vector that will take from m_{live} to m_{end}. A solution to the ILP model will then jointly decide the necessary amount of tokens and the consequent firings to be made to reach m_{end}. Remarkably, the cost function is a minimization that considers both the length of the trace completing the workflow (through the Parikh vector X) and the amount of tokens needed to escape from the obstruction marking (the variables Δ), thus globally optimizing these two decisions. We consider the cost as a user-defined function, since different costs could be assigned depending on the context, e.g., if a shortest path is preferred independently of the violations performed then one can set cost to 0 (or significantly less than X variables) to Δ variables. On the other hand, if the amount of violations should be reduced, the opposite cost can be set. Also, the cost for variables in the X vector may differ, e.g., if the firing of certain activities should be incentivized or avoided. The same holds for the Δ variables.

For instance, for the Petri net in Fig. 7, the given ILP model (assigning unitary costs to both X and Δ) will find the solution $\Delta = (0, 0, 0, 1, 0, 0, 0, 0)$, i.e., putting a token in the SoD place, and $X = (0, 1, 0, 0, 1)$, with X according to the order $t1$, $t2$, $u1t1$, $u2t1$, $u1t2$.

Clearly, the assignment on Δ and X variables defines the violations to make in order to complete the workflow. Assessing the impact and meaning of these violations for the authorization, constraints and users is a further challenge here, representing a next step in our research dealing with security.

---

[1] m_{live} can be computed from m_{obs} and Δ.

4.2   Model-Based Obstruction Solving Experiments

The theory presented in Sect. 4.1 was implemented and conducted on the inputs given from the net in Fig. 11.

Implementation: The tool for model-based obstruction solving has been developed under Python 2.7, and Gurobi [15] was used as ILP solver. All the implementations were run on a Microsoft Windows 7 machine with 6 GB of RAM and an Intel Core i7 2.6 GHZ CPU. The tool accepts the input files in PNML standard format and returns the optimal solution as a list which contains an encoding of the Δ and X vectors.

To assign costs in the implementation, we extended the Petri net type definition (PNTD) of Place/Transition nets with the optional adding of costs to places or transitions, resulting in P/T cost Petri nets (P/TCost-nets)[2]. This PNTD redefines the value of P/T-nets with costs for places and transitions and inherits the marking and annotations from the official PNML P/T-net definition.

Remarks on Cost and Results: Note that, no matter how costly, there may be places (e.g. the SoD place from the simple payment workflow) to which a token **must** be added to reach the final marking constraint. If there is a choice between multiple transitions or places (e.g. SoD places to violate) to reach the final marking, different costs assigned are crucial. The implementation can handle both, unitary and differing costs. The optimal solution is obtained when the constraint regarding the final marking is satisfied. Solutions provided in the experiments are not unique. It is possible to have many optimal solutions and all of them are correct.

Experiment Preparation: To facilitate for the tool to detect the final marking as a unique place holding a token, we needed to introduce further cancellation transitions at the end of the process, consuming of all the remaining tokens in the places that were put on top of the initial workflow before the flattening, i.e. (un)assignment, SoD/BoD, and their corresponding capacity-1-complement places. Therefore, similar to the introduction of new elements to deal with loops, we inserted the following construct right before the end place: a transition "reach_end", that produces a token into a place to which all cancellation transitions are connected, similar to the cancellation in the "loop-charging" (see Fig. 8). However, the 1-boundedness restriction is not necessary here, because no tokens have to be added to the respected places again. This construct allows the cancellation of remaining tokens if needed. In this way, we were able to simply change the obstruction marking without the need to consider changes in the final marking (i.e. changes in the marking for the places resulting from the flattening).

---

[2] https://github.com/iig-uni-freiburg/SEPIA/blob/ptcnet/res/pntd/ptcnet.pntd.

Experiment Setting and Solution: Based on the net in Fig. 11 with unitary costs assigned (cost = 1.0 for each place and transition), given an arbitrary obstruction marking and a final marking to reach, our tool was able to provide a solution. To demonstrate this, we show an interesting obstruction markings which was reached after executing the following trace:

$\sigma_{obs} = \langle ts, m1, f1, dt1, t1_{compute\_market\_value}, at2, t2_{control\_computation},$
$Computation\_correct?_{yes}, o3, bt3, t3_{Evaluate\_Safeguarding\_Requirements},$
$Safeguarding\_Required?_{yes}, bt4, t4_{Prepare\_Safeguarding}, m2, j1 \rangle$

The obstruction marking resulting from this trace is shown below, listing only places which contain $m(p) > 0$. For reasons of clarity and understandability, the marked places were categorized:

Workflow places (with $m(p) = 1$) = $P_{j1,t5}$

SoD places with (with $m(p) = 1$) = $SoD_{ct1t2}, SoD_{at5t1}, SoD_{dt5t3}, SoD_{dt5t4},$ SoD_{dt5t2}

C1C places with (with $m(p) = 1$) = $SoD_{at1t2\_c1c}, SoD_{dt1t2\_c1c}, BoD_{bt3t4\_c1c},$ $BoD_{dt3t4\_c1c}, SoD_{at5t2\_c1c}, SoD_{dt5t1\_c1c}$

The solution provided required to put one token into SoD_{at5t2} (Δ) and provided the Parikh vector X containing the following transitions: $Approved?_{yes}, reach\_end, at5, Approve\_Acquisition, te^3$. However, running the tool again on the same obstruction marking and net provided a different optimal solution, adding one token into SoD_{dt5t1} and with the Parikh vector X containing the following transitions: $Approved?_{yes}, reach\_end, dt5, Approve\_Acquisition, te$. Hence there are multiple correct solutions obtained by our approach. The replayability for both of the Parikh vectors on the net was checked with an extension to the same tool.

Experiments with Bigger Nets: We then stepwise concatenated the same net (again with equal costs) up to 6 times (see Fig. 14 for the 6th concatenation) and encoded the upper obstruction marking into it. For all cases, the solution proposed the addition of one token into SoD_{at5t2} or SoD_{dt5t1}.

The obstruction marking was always encoded in the first of the concatenated nets. Therefore, the solutions assigning values to the X vector to reach the final marking increased. Table 1 represents some statistics of the ILP which we solved. Gurobi also computed the corresponding costs. Note here that some transitions in the computed solution happened more than one time because of the loops in the net. Figure 13 represents a perfect linear relationship (i.e., $R^2 = 99\%$) between the required execution time and the size of the problem.

Replayability: Since the solutions provided by the X vector do not provide the real ordering of transition executions, we explored all the possible linearizations to assess whereas a solution obtained denoted (in some of its possible linearizations) a real trace. We could only do this checking for the first four experiments

---

^{3} We omit the cancellation transitions here for the sake of clarity.

Table 1. ILP statistics.

Places	Transitions	Variables	ILP-Constraints	Runtime	Size of $supp(\Delta)$	$supp(X)$	Total cost
69	82	151	220	0.117	1	17	30
138	165	303	441	0.269	1	51	74
207	248	455	662	0.352	1	85	118
276	331	607	883	0.440	1	119	162
345	414	759	1104	0.564	1	153	206
414	497	911	1325	0.643	1	187	250

(since for the rest, the exploration of possible solutions was very large). It is remarkable that for these four models, the solutions obtained represented a real trace, i.e., there was a linearization replayable in the model.

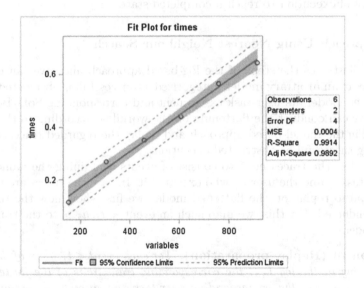

Fig. 13. Runtime of experiments.

Obstruction Position and Differing Costs: To check, whether the position of the obstruction in the net has an impact on runtime, we also implemented an obstruction in the last of the concatenated nets for the 6th concatenation (cf. Fig. 14). The regarded net with 911 variables took 0.725 s to be solved, although the solution contained only 18 instead of 188 variables. Hence, there were no significant runtime differences to the same net with same size but different position of obstruction marking. Obviously, the position of the obstruction has no impact on the tools runtime.

In a further experiment we assigned different costs to SoD_{dt5t1} (cost = 3.0) and SoD_{at5t2} (cost = 5.0) to the net from the first experiment (with 151 Variables). Consequently, now, the second solution containing SoD_{dt5t1} became the only one, resulting in a total cost of 32.0. Hence, the solution with least cost, i.e. least violations was proposed.

5   Log-Based Obstruction Solving

If there is historical information of the process, i.e. an event log, we exploit this information and divide the cases of the log into successful and obstructed ones, based on the analysis of obstructions with the given model. Given such partition of cases in the log, we intend to take an obstructed trace and find its nearest match to the successfully executed traces by applying a k-nearest neighbour (kNN) algorithm [9]. The nearest match would then propose the partial sequence for the rest of execution to reach a completed state.

5.1   Approach Using Nearest Neighbour Search

Figure 15 illustrates the steps of the log-based approach and gives an example with traces of an arbitrary model, categorized as successful or obstructed. Based on the given model, its user-task assignment and corresponding SoD/BoD constraints, we can conduct the flattening on the workflow according to the theory presented in the model-based approach and replay the regarded traces, thereby identifying successful or obstructed executions.

To do this, the traces need to consist of events containing the name of the executed task t_i and the user u_j who executed it. In case the traces are not easy to map and to replay on the flattened model, we first show how the replaying can be conducted. For this, we map such an event $< t_i, u_j >$ to the transitions of the model:

Definition 10 (Replay preparation). *For each event $< t_i, u_j >$ of the traces σ_{tu} occurring in the log L_{tu}, the corresponding transitions of the flattened net $N_{TA+SoD+BoD}$, i.e. the corresponding user-task transition $t_{u_j t_i}$ assigning the user to its task, and the transition t_i indicating the task itself afterwards are mapped to each other. By doing this, each event $< t_i, u_j >$ of the trace σ_{tu} is transformed to the sequence $\langle t_{u_j t_i}, t_i \rangle$. The resulting trace is notated as σ_{utt}, indicating the event order of the transformed events. Analogously, the log is denoted as L_{utt}.*

Replay Analysis: To replay the resulting traces σ_{utt}, we use the *log replay* algorithm [21]. The transformation from the BPMN model into a P/T-Net [13] and the conducted flattening introduces transitions, which are not visible in the log. Such invisible tasks are considered to be lazy, i.e., they might fire to enable one of their succeeding visible tasks, in our regard the tasks from the BPMN model (t_i) or the user-task transitions $(t_{u_j t_i})$, but will never be fired directly in

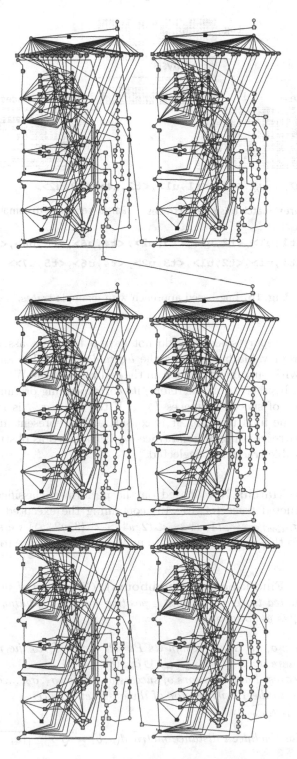

Fig. 14. Concatenated net.

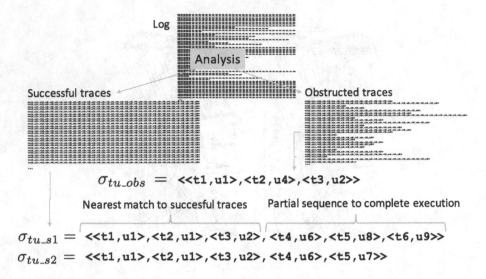

$$\sigma_{tu\_obs} = \texttt{<<t1,u1>,<t2,u4>,<t3,u2>>}$$

Nearest match to succesful traces   Partial sequence to complete execution

$$\sigma_{tu\_s1} = \texttt{<<t1,u1>,<t2,u1>,<t3,u2>,<t4,u6>,<t5,u8>,<t6,u9>>}$$
$$\sigma_{tu\_s2} = \texttt{<<t1,u1>,<t2,u1>,<t3,u2>, <t4,u6>,<t5,u7>>}$$

Fig. 15. Log-based approach with example traces.

the course of log replay since they do not have a log event associated [21]. If a trace σ_{utt} is replayable by applying the *log replay* algorithm and reaches the final marking (with only one token left in the end place of the WF-net) the trace is considered to be *successful*. Therefore, its corresponding original trace σ_{tu} is added to the set of successful traces L_{tu_s}. If the trace σ_{utt} is replayable but does not reach the final marking, it is considered to represent an *obstruction*. Therefore, its corresponding original trace σ_{tu} is classified as obstructed σ_{tu_obs}. Not fully replayable traces are neglected.

Find Nearest Match: Now, based on the performed classification of logs, given the obstructed trace (cf. Fig. 15) containing the executed tasks and its executor (e.g. $\sigma_{tu\_obs} = \langle < t1, u1 >, < t2, u4 >, < t3, u2 > \rangle$) we search for the nearest match to the successful traces, to find a partial sequence to complete the execution.

Definition 11 (Find k-nearest neighbours). *Given a set of successful traces L_{tu_s}, an obstructed trace σ_{tu_obs} and a positive integer k, finding the k nearest traces to σ_{tu_obs} is as follows:*

1. *For each trace σ_i in L_{tu_s}, assign its Parikh vector $\widehat{\sigma}_i$ to the n-dimensional space $\mathcal{R}^n$, where $n = |\{\partial_{set}(L_{tu\_s} \oplus) \cup \partial_{set}(\sigma_{tu\_obs})\}|$.*
2. *Find the k nearest Parikh vectors of successful traces $\{\widehat{\sigma}_1, \widehat{\sigma}_2, ..., \widehat{\sigma}_k\}$ with minimal distance to the Parikh vector of the obstructed trace*
   $$\min_{\widehat{\sigma}_i \in L_{tu\_s} \oplus}^{k} d(\widehat{\sigma}_i, \widehat{\sigma_{tu\_obs}}),$$
   where d is the Euclidean distance metric $d(a, b) = \sqrt{\sum_{i=1}^{n}(a_i - b_i)^2}$.

Given $\{\widehat{\sigma_1}, \widehat{\sigma_2}, ..., \widehat{\sigma_k}\}$, *the partial sequences of the corresponding traces* $\{\sigma_{1|\sigma_{tu\_obs}|}, \sigma_{2|\sigma_{tu\_obs}|}, ..., \sigma_{k|\sigma_{tu\_obs}|}\}$ *contain all the events after the* $|\sigma_{tu\_obs}|$-*th position of the trace, presenting k potential sequences to complete from* σ_{tu_obs}.

If we find more than one candidate, we need to select one of them by an objective function considering the length of the partial sequence to complete or the number of violations taken into account. For instance, the two successful candidates $\sigma_{tu\_s1} = \langle< t1, u1 >, < t2, u1 >, < t3, u2 >, < t4, u6 >, < t5, u8 >, < t6, u9 >\rangle$ and $\sigma_{tu\_s2} = \langle< t1, u1 >, < t2, u1 >, < t3, u2 >, < t4, u6 >, < t5, u7 >\rangle$ are chosen as the nearest match, both having the same first three events $< t1, u1 >$, $< t2, u1 >, < t3, u2 >$ in which only the executor of $t2$ ($u1$) differs to the executor of $t2$ in the obstructed trace ($u4$). Then the potential partial sequences to complete the execution $\sigma_{tu\_s1|\sigma_{tu\_obs}|} = \langle< t4, u6 >, < t5, u8 >, < t6, u9 >\rangle$ and $\sigma_{tu\_s2|\sigma_{tu\_obs}|} = \langle< t4, u6 >, < t5, u7 >\rangle$ are compared by the objective function. If we would like to minimize the length of the partial sequence, we would choose $\sigma_{tu\_s2\_part}$ to complete σ_{tu_obs}. Implications from choosing the closest trace regarding security violations need further investigation.

5.2   Log-Based Obstruction Solving Experiments

We implemented the log-based approach and conducted experiments on the basis of the comprehensive example presented in Fig. 10.

Implementation: The implementation of the log-based obstruction solving approach was done in Java 8, using the Apache Commons math library to calculate the Euclidean distance for the kNN algorithm. The tool takes two CSV files for the successful and the obstructed traces as input plus a positive integer value of k, which encodes the vicinity to look at when finding the closest matches to a given obstructed trace. The experiments were conducted on a MacBook Pro OS X El Capitan V 10.11.2 Machine, with 8 GB RAM and an Intel Core i7 3 Ghz CPU.

Getting Traces: In Sect. 5.1 we presented how to classify traces into successful or obstructed ones by replaying them on a flattened model. Since we did not have real traces with a corresponding model and all the authorization data required to perform the described analysis, we generated successful and obstructed traces by playing the flattened Petri net from Fig. 11 (i.e. stepwise firing of enabled transitions until an obstructed or a final marking is reached). By this, both evaluations build upon the same model, allowing us to compare the results. After generating the traces, we mapped the events of the traces to the users who executed them according to the flattened user-task assignment and filtered only the relevant user-task events (in a real log, such event would contain the task name with a user/originator who executed it (cf. Definition 10)). In this way, we generated successful and obstructed traces conforming to the user-task assignment and SoD/BoD constraints. For each trace σ, the corresponding Parikh vector $\widehat{\sigma}$

Table 2. Encoding of successful traces in 12-dimensional space

at1	ct1	dt1	at2	ct2	dt2	bt3	dt3	bt4	dt4	at5	dt5
0	0	1	0	1	0	0	1	0	1	1	0
1	0	0	0	1	0	1	0	1	0	0	1
0	1	0	1	0	0	1	0	0	0	0	1
0	1	0	0	0	1	0	1	0	1	1	0
0	1	0	0	0	1	0	1	0	0	1	0
0	1	0	0	0	1	1	0	1	0	1	0
0	0	1	0	1	0	1	0	0	0	1	0
0	1	0	1	0	0	1	0	1	0	0	1
0	0	1	0	1	0	0	1	0	0	1	0
1	0	0	0	1	0	1	0	0	0	0	1
1	0	0	0	0	1	1	0	0	0	0	1

was build and assigned to the n-dimensional space. Table 2 displays the successful traces which are assigned to a 12-dimensional space, based on all possible user-task assignments.

Experiment Setting and Solution: Based on the Euclidean distance measure, we then computed the nearest-neighbour of the successful traces to the regarded obstructed trace. For comparability, we chose the obstructed trace σ_{obs} from the model-based experiments (encoded as $(0, 0, 1, 1, 0, 0, 1, 0, 1, 0, 0, 0)$). The solution for $k = 5$ is depicted in Table 3.

Table 3. Solution for k = 5 with highlighted partial sequence.

Distance	Closest vector	Related trace
1.732	0,1,0,1,0,0,1,0,1,0,0,1	$\langle < t1, c >, < t2, a >, < t3, b >, < t4, b >, \boldsymbol{< t5, d >} \rangle$
2.0	0,1,0,1,0,0,1,0,0,0,0,1	$\langle < t1, c >, < t2, a >, < t3, b >, \boldsymbol{< t5, d >} \rangle$
2.0	0,0,1,0,1,0,1,0,0,0,1,0	$\langle < t1, d >, < t2, c >, < t3, b >, \boldsymbol{< t5, a >} \rangle$
2.236	1,0,0,0,1,0,1,0,1,0,0,1	$\langle < t1, a >, < t2, c >, < t3, b >, < t4, b >, \boldsymbol{< t5, d >} \rangle$
2.236	0,1,0,0,0,1,1,0,1,0,1,0	$\langle < t1, c >, < t2, d >, < t3, b >, < t4, b >, \boldsymbol{< t5, a >} \rangle$

Clearly, if $k = 1$ there would be no need to make a decision which partial sequence to choose (interestingly $< t5, d >$ would then be proposed, although the majority of successful traces for $k = 5$ in Table 2 ends with $< t5, a >$). Aside from the Euclidean distance, the $k = 5$ solution requires an objective function to be able to choose a partial trace that considers security violations or the minimal length of the partial trace. However, because of the same length of all partial traces the latter measure was neglected. To assess the security violations, the obstructed trace was checked against the different solutions and their impact on given SoD and BoD constraints. Similarly to the model based approach, both solutions violate one SoD constraint so that either $< t5, a >$ or $< t5, d >$ can be chosen. However, looking onto the set of partial sequences provided in Table 3, there is a majority for $< t5, d >$.

Experiment Outlook: The investigation of these and further factors to be considered in the objective function is subject to future work. Moreover, the features in the space of the kNN algorithm could be connected to the weight of executing certain places or transitions, which could also be derived from a corresponding P/TCost-net. Besides, different distance measures like the edit distance could be implemented as well. Eventually, we want to conduct the tool on real logs to show its applicability. For this, we tested the tools performance and conducted it also on a bigger data set with 65-dimensional space and 247192 traces. Finding the 5 nearest neighbours for one trace took only 0.31 s. Therefore, we are confident that the tool can handle big log files.

6   Conclusion and Future Work

Our work is located in the tension between security controls on the one hand and maintaining flexibility in terms of process availability on the other. The intention is to take a certain degree of violation into account to still succeed the workflow. The presented approach provides a range of practical applications. For example, it could be used to recommend who shall perform which tasks, for example in a break glass situation, or as an assisted delegation, showing potential best delegates (with least violation) to the delegator. The core idea behind the approach however is to enable automated delegation. Moreover, obstruction analysis techniques and the visualization of authorizations and workflow in one model could also help policy designers to better understand and improve their policies.

Regarding the presented model-based approach there is the limitation that the Parikh vector does not describe the execution order of the transitions. In this regard, results need to be investigated further which can trade efficiency by precision, i.e., incorporating ordering constraints in the marking equation. Moreover, to better assess the violations taken into account, future work will also aim to use profiling techniques based on logs.

Another line of research would be devoted to estimate resilience by using structural theory of Petri nets: by estimating the minimal amount of users needed to successfully complete a workflow, we will be able to provide an insight on the resilience of the workflow.

Finally, we want to integrate the presented tools into the Security Workflow Analysis Toolkit (SWAT) [20] to provide more specific evidence on how a reliable solution in an organizational software system should be constituted.

Acknowledgments. This work has been partially supported by funds from the Spanish Ministry for Economy and Competitiveness (MINECO), the European Union (FEDER funds) under grant COMMAS (ref. TIN2013-46181-C2-1-R).

References

1. Accorsi, R.: Sicherheit im Prozessmanagement. digma Zeitschrift für Datenrecht und Informationssicherheit (2013)
2. Basin, D.A., Burri, S.J., Karjoth, G.: Obstruction-free authorization enforcement: aligning security with business objectives. In: CSF, pp. 99–113. IEEE Computer Society (2011)
3. Basin, D.A., Burri, S.J., Karjoth, G.: Optimal workflow-aware authorizations. In: Atluri, V., Vaidya, J., Kern, A., Kantarcioglu, M. (eds.) SACMAT, pp. 93–102. ACM (2012)
4. Bishop, M.: Introduction to Computer Security. Addison-Wesley Professional, Reading (2004)
5. Botha, R., Eloff, J.: Separation of duties for access control enforcement in workflow environments. IBM Syst. J. **40**(3), 666–682 (2001)
6. Burri, S.J.: Modeling and enforcing workflow authorizations. Ph.D. thesis, ETH, Zürich (2012)
7. Carmona, J., Colom, J.M., Cortadella, J., García-Vallés, F.: Synthesis of asynchronous controllers using integer linear programming. IEEE Trans. CAD Integr. Circuits Syst. **25**(9), 1637–1651 (2006)
8. Clark, N., Jolly, D.: Societe generale loses $7 billion in trading fraud (2008)
9. Cover, T., Hart, P.: Nearest neighbor pattern classification. IEEE Trans. Inform. Theory **13**(1), 21–27 (1967)
10. Crampton, J., Gutin, G.: Constraint expressions and workflow satisfiability. In: Conti, M., Vaidya, J., Schaad, A. (eds.) SACMAT, pp. 73–84. ACM (2013)
11. Crampton, J., Morisset, C.: An auto-delegation mechanism for access control systems. In: Cuellar, J., Lopez, J., Barthe, G., Pretschner, A. (eds.) STM 2010. LNCS, vol. 6710, pp. 1–16. Springer, Heidelberg (2011). doi:10.1007/978-3-642-22444-7_1
12. Desel, J., Esparza, J.: Reachability in cyclic extended free-choice systems. TCS 114, Elsevier Science Publishers B.V. (1993)
13. Dijkman, R.M., Dumas, M., Ouyang, C.: Semantics and analysis of business process models in BPMN. Inf. Softw. Technol. **50**(12), 1281–1294 (2008)
14. Esparza, J., Melzer, S.: Verification of safety properties using integer programming: beyond the state equation. Formal Methods Syst. Des. **16**, 159–189 (2000)
15. Inc. Gurobi Optimization. Gurobi optimizer reference manual (2016)
16. Holderer, J., Accorsi, R., Müller, G.: When four-eyes become too much: a survey on the interplay of authorization constraints and workflow resilience. In: Wainwright, R.L., Corchado, J.M., Bechini, A., Hong, J. (eds.) Proceedings of the 30th Annual ACM Symposium on Applied Computing, Salamanca, Spain, 13–17 April 2015, pp. 1245–1248. ACM (2015)
17. Hopcroft, J.E., Tarjan, R.E.: Dividing a graph into triconnected components. SIAM J. Comput. **2**(3), 135–158 (1973)
18. Leitner, M., Rinderle-Ma, S.: A systematic review on security in process-aware information systems - constitution, challenges, and future directions. Inform. Softw. Technol. **56**(3), 273–293 (2014)
19. Murata, T.: Petri nets: properties, analysis and applications. Proc. IEEE **77**(4), 541–574 (1989)

20. Accorsi, R., Holderer, J., Stocker, T., Zahoransky, R.M.: Security workflow analysis toolkit. In: Katzenbeisser, S., Lotz, V., Weippl, E.R. (eds.) Sicherheit 2014: Sicherheit, Schutz und Zuverlässigkeit, Beiträge der 7. Jahrestagung des Fachbereichs Sicherheit der Gesellschaft für Informatik e.V. (GI), 19–21 März 2014, Wien, Österreich, vol. 228. LNI, pp. 433–442. GI (2014)

21. Rozinat, A., van der Aalst, W.M.P.: Conformance checking of processes based on monitoring real behavior. Inform. Syst. **33**(1), 64–95 (2008)

22. Silva, M., Terue, E., Colom, J.M.: Linear algebraic and linear programming techniques for the analysis of place/transition net systems. In: Reisig, W., Rozenberg, G. (eds.) ACPN 1996. LNCS, vol. 1491, pp. 309–373. Springer, Heidelberg (1998). doi:10.1007/3-540-65306-6_19

23. Trope, R.L., Ressler, E.K.: Mettle fatigue: Vw's single-point-of-failure ethics. IEEE Secur. Priv. **14**(1), 12–30 (2016)

24. van der Aalst, W.M.P.: The application of Petri nets to workflow management. J. Circuits Syst. Comput. **8**(1), 21–66 (1998)

25. van der Aalst, W.M.P.: Process Mining - Discovery Conformance and Enhancement of Business Processes. Springer, Berlin (2011)

26. Wang, Q., Li, N.: Satisfiability and resiliency in workflow authorization systems. ACM Trans. Inform. Syst. Secur. **13**(4), 40:1–40:35 (2010)

27. Wang, Q., Li, N., Chen, H.: On the security of delegation in access control systems. In: Jajodia, S., Lopez, J. (eds.) ESORICS 2008. LNCS, vol. 5283, pp. 317–332. Springer, Heidelberg (2008). doi:10.1007/978-3-540-88313-5_21

28. Wolter, C., Menzel, M., Meinel, C.: Modelling security goals in business processes. In: Kühne, T., Reisig, W., Steimann, F. (eds.) Modellierung 2008, 12–14 März 2008, Berlin, vol. 127. LNI, pp. 197–212. GI (2008)

Formal Modelling and Analysis of Distributed Storage Systems

Jordan de la Houssaye[1], Franck Pommereau[1(✉)], and Philippe Deniel[2]

[1] IBISC, Univ. Évry, IBGBI, 23 bd de France, 91000 Évry, France
{jordan.delahoussaye,franck.pommereau}@ibisc.fr
[2] CEA, DAM, DIF, 91297 Arpajon, France
philippe.deniel@cea.fr

Abstract. Distributed storage systems are nowadays ubiquitous, very often under the form of a hierarchy of multiple caches. While a lot of effort has been dedicated to design, implement and optimise such systems, there exists to the best of our knowledge no attempt to use formal modelling and analysis in this field. This paper proposes a formal modelling framework to design distributed storage systems, with the innovating feature to separate the various concerns they involve like data-model, operations, policy, consistency, topology, etc. A model can then be analysed through model-checking to prove properties, or through simulation to assess its performance. In this paper, we define the framework and focus on performance analysis. We illustrate this on a simple yet realistic example, a LRU cache (*least recently used*, possibly the most known cache algorithm), showing that our proposal has the potential to be used to make design decisions before the real system is implemented.

1 Introduction

Nowadays technologies make intensive use of distributed storage systems. A particular and prominent form of such systems is caches. They can be found embedded in almost every piece of hardware or software system that involves information storage at some point. This results in overwhelmingly complex systems in which we cannot even be sure that caches actually improve the global performance. One reason for this situation is the lack of tools to analyse such systems during their design stages. In particular, to the best of our knowledge, there exists no attempt to formally model and analyse distributed storage systems.

Our main contribution in this paper is thus to propose a modelling framework that can be applied to design distributed storage systems. Moreover, the overall performance depends on a very large number of intricate aspects that cannot easily be considered separately from each other in most implementations. An important and innovative part of our contribution is to provide a clear separation of various concerns with an explicit link between them:

- a generic *data model* is defined, allowing to consider a variety of operations applicable to data;

M. Koutny et al. (Eds.): ToPNoC XII, LNCS 10470, pp. 70–90, 2017.
DOI: 10.1007/978-3-662-55862-1_4

- *topology* is defined independently, describing how states are arranged in the distributed system and how its nodes communicate;
- *policy*-related questions like placement strategy, organisation of nodes (typically hierarchically), collaboration between nodes, interpretation of the distributed state as a global state, etc., are considered and defined separately;
- *properties* like data consistency (*e.g.* cache coherence), correctness and termination of operations, deadlock-freeness, worst/best/mean-time execution, etc., can be studied separately on the modelled systems.

The next section starts by defining the static aspects of the framework, including: data model, operations on data, topology model, communication between nodes, interpretation of the distributed data as a global state and policy. This is then enriched in Sect. 2.5 by defining the processes executed on each node, in particular the actors that generate activity yielding executions (for instance, a CPU in a memory hierarchy is an actor). Section 3 illustrates this on a three levels cache hierarchy, showing how it can be modelled and how its performance can be analysed. The last section concludes and gives perspectives, together with a survey of related work. Finally, Appendix A describes the Petri nets that implement the processes presented in Sect. 2.5.

2   The Modelling Framework

From a static point of view, a model consists of three aspects: (1) a *data model* that defines states and operations on them; (2) a *topology model* that defines a notion of nodes storing data, together with a communication model between nodes. This leads to a notion of interpretation of a distributed state into a global state; (3) a *policy* that decides how to manage the storage on nodes and where each piece of state has to be located.

Each of these aspects is described in a dedicated subsection below; two more subsections describe the dynamic aspects of the framework: (1) the *management of jobs* (*i.e.* tasks) that each node has to execute in order to perform the expected operations; (2) the *processes* run on each node in order to actually execute the jobs. We shall distinguish particular nodes called *actors* that initiate all the activity in a distributed storage, while other nodes are reacting to their requests.

2.1   Data

We consider three pairwise disjoint nonempty sets: K is the set of *keys* that can be thought of as addresses; V is the set of *values* stored at these addresses; L is the set of *labels* used to relate keys. For instance, for a Unix filesystem, K would be the inodes addresses, V their content and L could model relations like directory membership. For a memory model, V would hold all the possible memory blocks whose addresses would be in K, and L would not be used.

Definition 1. *A state σ is a pair $(\sigma.h, \sigma.r)$ such that $\sigma.h \in 2^{K \times V}$ and $\sigma.r \in 2^{L \times 2^K \times 2^K}$. We note by $\Sigma_{K,V,L}$ the set of all states, and define $\mathsf{dom}(\sigma.h) \stackrel{\mathrm{df}}{=} \{k \mid$*

$\exists v \in V, (k, v) \in \sigma.h\}$. *A state* $\sigma \in \Sigma_{K,V,L}$ *is* well-formed *iff it satisfies the following conditions:*

- $\sigma.h$ *is a map:* $\forall k \in \mathsf{dom}(\sigma.h)$, $|\{(k,v) \in \sigma.h\}| = 1$;
- *all the keys in* $\sigma.r$ *are mapped by* $\sigma.h$: $\bigcup_{(l, K_1, K_2) \in \sigma.r} K_1 \cup K_2 \subseteq \mathsf{dom}(\sigma.h)$.

Such a state σ shall be depicted vertically as: $\left(\begin{smallmatrix} \sigma.h \\ \sigma.r \end{smallmatrix}\right)$. Intuitively, a state is a map from related keys to the corresponding data. For instance, consider an extremely simplified filesystem containing the following objects: the root directory "/", sub-directories "/bin", "/usr" with nested sub-directory "/usr/bin", and files "/bin/sh" and "/usr/bin/sh". These objects could be represented as a state σ as follows:

$$\sigma.h \stackrel{\mathrm{df}}{=} \big\{ (0, /),\ (1, \mathsf{bin}),\ (2, \mathsf{usr}),\ (3, \mathsf{sh}),\ (4, \mathsf{bin}),\ (5, \mathsf{sh}) \big\}$$
$$\sigma.r \stackrel{\mathrm{df}}{=} \big\{ (\mathsf{root}, \{0\}, \emptyset),\ (\mathsf{dir}, \{0\}, \{1\}),\ (\mathsf{dir}, \{0\}, \{2\}),\ (\mathsf{dir}, \{2\}, \{4\}),$$
$$(\mathsf{file}, \{1\}, \{3\}),\ (\mathsf{file}, \{4\}, \{5\}) \big\}$$

where $\sigma.h$ stores the identifiers of the filesystem objects associating them to their names, and $\sigma.r$ stores links between the objects, allowing to identify a root directory (root label) and the children of each directory, which may be directories themselves (dir label) or files (file label).

States are equipped with various compositions and operations. For $\sigma_a, \sigma_b \in \Sigma_{K,V,L}$, we define union ($\cup$), intersection ($\cap$) and difference ($\backslash$) as componentwise extensions of their sets counterparts. For instance, we have $\sigma_a \cup \sigma_b \stackrel{\mathrm{df}}{=} (\sigma_a.h \cup \sigma_b.h,\ \sigma_a.r \cup \sigma_b.r)$. For $k \in K$, $\sigma \in \Sigma_{K,V,L}$, we note by σ/k the restriction of σ from which any element involving k has been removed.

Prior to the definition of operations, we define an *effect* as a pair of states $[e.plus, e.minus] \in \Sigma_{K,V,L}^2$. It is interpreted as a patch (*i.e.* a collection of additions and removals) that can be applied to a state in order to obtain a new state. This application is a called a *projection*, noted $\gg$ (or $\ll$ is used the other way round), and is defined for $e \in \Sigma_{K,V,L}^2$ and $\sigma \in \Sigma_{k,V,L}$ as $e \gg \sigma \stackrel{\mathrm{df}}{=} (\sigma \backslash e.minus) \cup e.plus$. We also extend states restriction/component-wise on effects.

In order to compose effects (and by consequence, operations), we introduce operator $\mathbin{\fatsemi}$ (sequence). Let σ, e, f be respectively a state, and two effects, we define: $(e \mathbin{\fatsemi} f) \stackrel{\mathrm{df}}{=} [(e.plus \backslash f.minus) \cup f.plus,\ e.minus \cup f.minus]$. So that it is easy to show we have: $(e \mathbin{\fatsemi} f) \gg \sigma = f \gg (e \gg \sigma)$.

We can now associate a state with an effect as a pair (σ, e). These kind of historicised states are needed to model distributed storage. Consider indeed a simple case where a cache lies between a process and a storage. If the process requests to delete the resource associated with a key k, this may be made in the cache only. But just dropping the information associated with k in the cache is not correct. Indeed, by definition, the cache holds only a subset of the information that the storage holds. The absence of k in the cache is thus not a sufficient information to know that k has to be deleted in the storage too, it may as well mean that k has never been stored in the cache. Moreover, if later k is allocated again, the cache may store the new value associated with k and forget about the fact that k has been deleted previously. So, a history allows a cache to hide operations to the storage, which is exactly what one wants from a cache.

Projection is used to compute the effect of operations on states. Consider for instance our example of a simplified filesystem presented above, and take an initial state where only "/" and "/bin" exist. The creation of "/usr" can be computed through a projection as follows:

$$
\left(
\begin{array}{c}
\{(0, /), (1, \texttt{bin})\} \\
\{(\texttt{root}, \{0\}, \emptyset), (\texttt{dir}, \{0\}, \{1\})\}
\end{array}
\right)
\ll
\left[
\begin{array}{cc}
\{(2, \texttt{usr})\} & \{\} \\
\{(\texttt{dir}, \{0\}, \{2\})\} & \{\}
\end{array}
\right]
$$

$$
=
\left(
\begin{array}{c}
\{(0, /), (1, \texttt{bin}), (2, \texttt{usr})\} \\
\{(\texttt{root}, \{0\}, \emptyset), (\texttt{dir}, \{0\}, \{1\}), (\texttt{dir}, \{0\}, \{2\})\}
\end{array}
\right)
$$

Operations. An operation is a request a user of the storage system might perform. So a system definition includes the definition of its available operations. We want any operation to have a parametrised effect (possibly neutral) and a result. To apply an operation, one provides a valuation in $K \cup V \cup L$ of the input parameters, which we call a *binding*, then the result is a binding of the output parameters. If no output parameters can be found, the operation fails. Otherwise, the actual effect of the operation is computed by binding its parameters and applying the result onto the state. A *binding* is a mapping from variables to values, usually noted by β, possibly with subscripts or superscripts. We note by $\text{keys}(\beta) \overset{\text{df}}{=} \text{img}(\beta) \cap K$ the set of keys referenced in β, where img is the image (or codomain) of the binding.

Definition 2. *Let* $\text{vars}(e)$ *be the set of variables involved in an expression e. An operation is a 4-tuple* $op \overset{\text{df}}{=} (op.name, op.guard, op.effect, op.params)$ *such that:*

- *$op.name$ is a name used to refer to the operation (any string);*
- *$op.guard$ is a Boolean expression that guards the application of op;*
- *$op.effect$ is an expression that can be evaluated to an effect;*
- *$op.params$ is a set of (input) variables such that $op.params \subseteq \text{vars}(op)$, where $\text{vars}(op) \overset{\text{df}}{=} \text{vars}(op.guard) \cup \text{vars}(op.effect)$;*
- *we have $\text{vars}(op.effect) \subseteq op.params \cup \text{vars}(op.guard)$;*
- *there exists at least one binding such that both $op.effect$ and $op.guard$ can be actually evaluated (i.e. both are actually computable together).*

We note by $\mathcal{OPS}$ the set of all operations.

The role of the guard is to prevent operations to be applied on incompatible states (*e.g.* one cannot read from an unallocated address). Thus the guard is always evaluated on the state on which the operation is meant to be applied for a given binding of the input parameters. Then, if the guard is true and output parameters can be computed, the effect is evaluated and projected onto the state. Given an operation op, we note by:

- $\mathcal{B}_{op,K,V,L}$ the set of all bindings $\beta : \text{vars}(op) \to K \cup V \cup L$;

– $\mathcal{B}^{in}_{op,K,V,L}$ the set of all bindings $\beta : op.params \to K \cup V \cup L$;
– $\mathcal{B}^{out}_{op,K,V,L}$ the set of all bindings $\beta : \mathsf{vars}(op) \setminus op.params \to K \cup V \cup L$.

It should be stressed that we intentionally avoid to define a precise syntax for expressions because we do not want to fix K, V and L, nor do we want to restrict the scope of our definitions. The last item in Definition 2 is sufficient to ensure that a concrete implementation of the framework has to provide a concrete syntax (possibly a typing) for expressions as well as an effective way to evaluate them.

For two bindings $\beta_a, \beta_b \in \mathcal{B}_{op,K,V,L}$ such that $\mathsf{dom}(\beta_a) \cap \mathsf{dom}(\beta_b) = \emptyset$, we define their composition $\beta \overset{\mathrm{df}}{=} \beta_a + \beta_b : \mathsf{dom}(\beta_a) \cup \mathsf{dom}(\beta_b) \to K \cup V \cup L$ as follows:

$$\forall x \in \mathsf{dom}(\beta), \beta(x) \overset{\mathrm{df}}{=} \begin{cases} \beta_a(x) & \text{if } x \in \mathsf{dom}(\beta_a), \\ \beta_b(x) & \text{otherwise, } i.e. \text{ if } x \in \mathsf{dom}(\beta_b) \end{cases}$$

For convenience, we introduce some more notations. Let $\sigma_{in} \in \Sigma_{K,V,L}$, $op \in \mathcal{OPS}$, and $\beta_{in} \in \mathcal{B}^{in}_{op,K,V,L}$, we define:

– $op.guard(\sigma_{in}, \beta)$ is the evaluation of $op.guard$ through $\beta + \{\sigma \mapsto \sigma_{in}\}$ (i.e., β extended with name σ being bound to σ_{in}), where σ refers to the input state and can be used to access it from the guard;
– $op.effect(\beta)$ is the evaluation of $op.effect$ through a binding β;
– $op.candidates(\sigma_{in}, \beta_{in}) \overset{\mathrm{df}}{=} \{\beta_{out} \in \mathcal{B}^{out}_{op,K,V,L} \mid op.guard(\sigma_{in}, \beta_{in} + \beta_{out}) \wedge op.effect(\beta_{in} + \beta_{out}) \in \Sigma^2_{K,V,L}\}$ is the set of possible output bindings that, combined with β_{in}, allow to validate the guard and to fully evaluate the effect to a pair of valid states;
– op is called *elligible* for σ_{in} and β_{in} iff $op.candidates(\sigma_{in}, \beta_{in}) \neq \emptyset$.

Then, when op is elligible for some input state and input binding, the set of output states and output bindings is computed by applying op with every possible candidate binding, which is made using a projection as follows.

Definition 3. *The application of operation $op \in \mathcal{OPS}$ onto input state $\sigma_{in} \in \Sigma_{K,V,L}$ given an input binding $\beta_{in} \in \mathcal{B}^{in}_{op,K,V,L}$ results in the subset of $\mathcal{B}^{out}_{op,K,V,L} \times \Sigma_{K,V,L}$ defined by $op(\sigma_{in}, \beta_{in}) \overset{\mathrm{df}}{=} \{(\beta_{out}, op.effect(\beta_{in} + \beta_{out}) \gg \sigma_{in}) \mid \beta_{out} \in op.candidates(\sigma_{in}, \beta_{in})\}$.*

The part of the model defined so far can be used on its own to study the data model itself. For instance, one can check the correctness of operations, or sequences of operations, on a chosen set of states and input bindings.

2.2 Topology

A distributed storage consists of a set of *nodes* that communicate through *buses* and store local states as state-effect pair $(\sigma, e) \in \Sigma_{K,V,L} \times \Sigma^2_{K,V,L}$. This topology of nodes with states, and buses is formalised as an hypergraph as follows.

Definition 4. *Let N be a set of* nodes, *a topology T on N is a pair $T \overset{\text{df}}{=}$ $(T.nodes, T.buses)$ where $T.nodes \overset{\text{df}}{=} N$ is the set of nodes and $T.buses \subseteq 2^N \setminus \emptyset$ is the set of hyperedges. For $i, j \in T.nodes$, we define $T[i, j] \overset{\text{df}}{=} \{b \in T.buses \mid \{i, j\} \subseteq b\}$.*

The (historicised) state of a topology is a function $T.nodes \rightarrow \Sigma_{K,V,L} \times \Sigma^2_{K,V,L} = \Sigma^3_{K,V,L}$ that maps each node to its (historicised) local state.

Given a topology T, nodes in $T.nodes$ are allowed to communicate by exchanging *frames* over the buses in $T.buses$. We assume that a bus can transmit only one message at a time, *i.e.* a sender is blocked until a previously sent message has been received. Moreover reading on a bus is a blocking operation, *i.e.* a receiver attempting to get a message is blocked until a message is actually sent for it. A non-limitative list of possible frames is presented in Fig. 1; other may be considered, in particular non-blocking requests as in [7–9] that we omitted here for the sake of simplicity. Each frame is a 4-tuple formed with the bus on which the communication is made, the sender and recipient nodes identities, and the message itself that can be of two types:

- `block` this type of message transmits a ⟨request⟩. It is blocking in that there can be no further message between source and destination until the destination has responded with a `return` message holding the expected ⟨response⟩;
- `return` this type of message transmits a ⟨response⟩ to a ⟨request⟩, which comes as a pair (return, ⟨response⟩).

We present here only one type of ⟨request⟩, but others can be easily considered. A request $req \overset{\text{df}}{=}$ (operate, op, β) is parametrised by an operation $req.op$ and an input binding $req.\beta$ for this operation. The corresponding answer is a ⟨response⟩ that can be a `success` or a `failure`. In the former case, it comes with the output binding (noted $resp.\beta$) chosen by the system; in the latter case, it comes with a message to explain the failure.

Interpretations and integration. As soon as states are distributed over a topology, we need to define how to compose these local states into a unique global state. This must be user-defined together with the topology. Moreover we must define how a node integrates the information about states it can deduce from its exchanges with other nodes. For instance, consider a memory hierarchy with a cache that receives a request to read a block a. If it forwards the request to the

$$
\begin{aligned}
\langle \mathtt{frame} \rangle &::= (bus, source, destination, \langle \mathtt{message} \rangle) \\
\langle \mathtt{message} \rangle &::= (\mathtt{block}, \langle \mathtt{request} \rangle) \mid (\mathtt{return}, \langle \mathtt{response} \rangle) \\
\langle \mathtt{request} \rangle &::= (\mathtt{operate}, op, \beta_{in}) \\
\langle \mathtt{response} \rangle &::= (\mathtt{success}, \beta_{out}) \mid (\mathtt{failure}, text)
\end{aligned}
$$

Fig. 1. The frames exchanged between the nodes of a topology T, where $bus \in T.buses$, $source, destination \in T.nodes$, $op \in \mathcal{OPS}$, $\beta_{in} \in \mathcal{B}^{in}_{op,K,V,L}$, $\beta_{out} \in \mathcal{B}^{out}_{op,K,V,L}$ and $text$ is a string. Special typesettings denote ⟨**non terminals**⟩ and **symbols** (*i.e.* constants).

next level in the hierarchy and eventually receives the value v in the response, it knows that (a, v) could be added to its local state. More generally, because of the way operations are defined, knowing the operation together with the input and output bindings is enough to evaluate *op.effect*. The latter may be composed with the local historicised state. How this composition must be made (or avoided) is dependent on how the distributed state is interpreted and must be user-defined as well.

Definition 5. *An* interpretation I_T *of a topology* T *is a pair of functions:*

$$I_T \stackrel{\mathrm{df}}{=} \begin{cases} globalview : (T.nodes \to \Sigma^3_{K,V,L}) \to \Sigma^3_{K,V,L} \\ integrate : \quad T.nodes \times T.nodes \to (\Sigma^5_{K,V,L} \to \Sigma^3_{K,V,L}) \end{cases}$$

In this definition, *globalview* is responsible for computing a single pair (σ, e) from the distributed historicised state. Function *integrate* is more complex: it takes a pair of nodes (a, b) and returns another function $(\Sigma_{K,V,L} \times \Sigma^2_{K,V,L}) \times \Sigma^2_{K,V,L} \to \Sigma_{K,V,L} \times \Sigma^2_{K,V,L}$. This one takes a historicised state (σ_a, e_a) and an effect e_b and combines them into a single historicised state (σ'_a, e'_a) that can be understood as the integration on a of the effect e_b on the state σ_a, for an operation that was actually computed on node b.

2.3   Job Management

We have described a notion of request, transporting operations to be applied by a node on its local state (according to its local policy as shown below). This implies a way for a given node to keep track of these requests.

Therefore, at the core of each node is the *job manager*: when a ⟨request⟩ is received by a node, it is first stored in the job manager and associated with a handler from a set $\mathcal{H}$; then it is kept there until it is fully processed. Dependencies can occur between requests: two requests r_1 and r_2 are dependent iff keys$(r_1.\beta) \cap$ keys$(r_2.\beta) \neq \emptyset$, otherwise they are independent. The job manager handles these dependencies and provides the following methods:

last $(key \in K) \to \mathcal{H} \uplus \{\mathbf{✗}\}$

Returns the handler of the last request added with a domain including *key* if any, or a dummy value ✗ if no request is associated with *key*.

add $(request \in \langle\mathtt{request}\rangle) \to \mathcal{H}$

Adds *request* into the manager and returns a fresh handler for it. The added request is recorded as dependent on the lastly added request for every key in keys(*request*). We assume that $\mathcal{H}$ is large enough (*e.g.* infinite) to assign a unique handler for every request added.

next $() \to \langle\mathtt{request}\rangle \times \mathcal{H}$

Returns a pair (*request, handler*) that is ready to be proceeded (no pending dependencies). The caller is blocked until such a job is actually available.

deps $(handler \in \mathcal{H}) \to (\langle\mathtt{request}\rangle \times \mathcal{H})^*$

Returns the list of pairs (r, h) corresponding to all the requests r and handler h

the request $r_{handler}$ associated with *handler* it depends on. This list is ordered consistently with dependencies, its last item being $(r_{handler}, handler)$, and it is computed deterministically.

done $(handler \in \mathcal{H})$

Marks every information associated with *handler* as disposable (*i.e.* not needed anymore) and clears from the job manager any such information.

2.4 Policy

A major challenge for our framework is to allow to define policy independently of a particular data model and of a particular topology as well. This is addressed in two ways: (1) the policy may consider only the presence or absence of the data, as well as its internal relations, and (2) it may consider only a particular interpretation I_T, and not a specific topology.

The policy's duties for a given node are to answer to the received requests and to manage the available space. It may resort to a number of different strategies and procedures to do so, including but not limited to: searching for a local solution, searching for a remote solution (*i.e.* sending new requests to other nodes), recording in its local state a solution that has been found (locally or remotely), freeing storage space locally (*i.e.* making room).

Let us assume a variable *me*, global to each node, that is the identity of this node. Its policy $P_{I_T}^{me}$ for an interpretation I_T is provided as a set of methods:

space $(keys \subseteq K, \sigma_{in} \in \Sigma_{K,V,L}) \rightarrow \mathbb{N}$

Returns the number of values currently stored on node *me* that need to be deleted in order to be able to store locally the values associated with *keys*.

update $(keys \subseteq K, handler \in \mathcal{H})$

This method does not return any value but is called on node *me* whenever a request identified by *handler* has just been received. It is used to update the current knowledge about the situation that may be maintained by the policy. For instance it may update the MRU (*most recently used*) keys in a LRU (*least recently used*) cache. Notice that the set $\mathcal{H}$ is exactly the same set of handlers as used by the job manager described above.

purge $() \rightarrow K$

Returns a resource currently stored on node *me*, which should be chosen as the one which is the least useful when purge is called. For instance, a LRU cache will precisely chose the least recently used key.

close $(handler \in \mathcal{H}, outcome \in \{\texttt{success}, \texttt{failure}\})$

This method is called to commit (on a **success**) or cancel (on a **failure**) the changes that occurred when update has been called.

trigger $(string) \rightarrow (req \in \langle \texttt{request} \rangle, handler \in \mathcal{H}) \rightarrow resp \in \langle \texttt{response} \rangle$

This method returns a procedure associated with an event name. This procedure takes a request and its handler and returns the response. In this paper, only event **operate** is considered, it corresponds to the processing of an **operate** request. Other events and the corresponding procedures are considered in [7], which leads to significantly more complex definitions as also discussed in the appendix.

Methods update and close work together: calling update allows to advertise about an incoming processing of some keys, then calling close allows to commit or cancel the possible changes made by update . The reason for such a mechanism is that many operations on a node cannot be realised atomically and in particular may require to communicate with other nodes. During this process, the node may receive and proceed other requests, some of which may be completed locally. So we cannot rely on a mechanism that would lock the whole node during the processing of a request. Instead, we have this notion of transactions that we can commit or rollback.

Note that several methods are expected to have side effects on the node, both on its state and on meta-data it may maintain. For instance, a LRU cache has to maintain a LRU-to-MRU ordered list of keys, which needs to be updated typically on update .

2.5   Processes

We present now how our framework exploits all the objects presented so far to actually model a distributed storage. To do so, each node executes a process and we distinguish two kind of nodes: those that model the distributed storage itself and that all run a copy of the same process (but not necessarily with the same policy), and those that exploit the distributed storage and run a specific process to model a particular user behaviour. The latter nodes are called *actors* and we discuss them at the end of this subsection.

Node process are currently specified as code that generates a coloured Petri net according to the policy. Appendix A shows the fixed parts of this net. Here, we provide pseudo-code that describes in a more generic fashion how every such generated net will work. Let us consider the following objects:

- me is the node on which the current process instance is executed;
- $jobs_{me}$ is the job manager for node me;
- T and I_T are respectively the topology and its interpretation, they are shared by all nodes;
- $P_{I_T}^{me}$ is the policy and is specific to the node;
- (σ_{me}, e_{me}) is the historicised state (*i.e.* a state and an effect) for node me.

Moreover, keyword atomic denotes a section of code that is executed atomically and is actually implemented by a single Petri net transition.

Communications. We will use communication channel, like chan, that correspond to Petri net places, in which we can produce, consume, or check for the presence of messages, which is blocking until the expected message arrives. These operations are noted respectively by chan.put (msg) (produce a message implemented as a Petri net token), chan.get (msg) (consumes a message), and chan.wait (msg) (both consumes and reproduces the same message). We note by chan$_{me}$ a channel that is local to node me, otherwise it is a global channel.

Let io and buses be two channels, respectively holding $\emptyset$ and $T.buses$ initially. Figure 2 shows how communications are modelled. Procedures SND and

procedure SND($b, me, n, \langle$msg$\rangle$) :
| # send $\langle$msg$\rangle$ from me to n on bus b
| buses.get (b)
| io.put$((b, me, n, \langle$msg$\rangle))$

procedure RCV($b, n, me, \langle$msg$\rangle$) :
| # receive $\langle$msg$\rangle$ from n to me on b
| io.get$((b, n, me, \langle$msg$\rangle))$
| buses.put (b)

procedure *receiveRequest()* :
| **atomic** :
|| RCV($b, n, me,$ (block, req))
|| idle$_{me}$.get (n)
| **atomic** :
|| $h \leftarrow jobs_{me}$.add (req)
|| waiter$_{me}$.put (h, n, b)
|| $P_{I_T}^{me}$.update ($keys(req.\beta), h, req$)

procedure *sendResponse(resp, h)* :
| **atomic** :
|| idle$_{me}$.put (n)
|| waiter$_{me}$.get (h, n, b)
|| SND($b, me, n,$ (return, $resp$))

procedure *sendRequest(b, n, req, h* :
| **atomic** :
|| idle$_{me}$.get (n)
|| SND($b, me, n,$ (block, req))
|| waiter$_{me}$.put (h, n)

procedure *receiveResponse(h)* :
| **atomic** :
|| waiter$_{me}$.get (h, n)
|| idle$_{me}$.put (n)
|| RCV($b, n, me,$ (return, $resp$))
| return *resp*

Fig. 2. Messages passing between nodes.

processus *listener* :
| io.wait ($bus, src, me,$ (block, req))
| *receiveRequest()*
| returns$_{me}$.get ($resp, h$)
| *sendResponse(resp, h)*

processus *dispatcher* :
| $req, h \leftarrow jobs_{me}$.next ()
| $resp \leftarrow P_{I_T}^{me}$.trigger ($req.type$)($req, h$)
| **atomic** :
|| $P_{I_T}^{me}$.close ($h, resp[0]$)
|| $jobs_{me}$.done (h)
| returns$_{me}$.put ($resp, h$)

Fig. 3. Main processes on generic nodes.

RCV at the top ensure that only one message *msg* transits on a bus b at once. Then, to implement blocking communications we introduce a channel idle$_{me}$ and a channel waiter$_{me}$ for each node of T. We initialise idle$_{me}$ with $\{n \in T.nodes \mid T[me, n] \neq \emptyset\}$ and waiter$_{me}$ with $\emptyset$. Note that SND and RCV defined above are only used here and thus, always in the context of an atomic block. Note also that *sendRequest* and *receiveResponse* will be used only in the next section within nodes policies.

Node processes. Figure 3 defines two processes: *listener* and *dispatcher*. The former waits for the arrival of a new request to activate procedure *receiveRequest* that adds it to the job manager and notifies the policy. The latter takes a request from the job manager, selects the procedure to apply using the policy, applies it, notifies the policy and the job manager of the result, and returns the response to *listener* through a local channel returns$_{me}$. Noting by $p!$ the infinite parallel replication of a process p, each node runs a process consisting of two such replications composed in parallel *listener*! ‖ *dispatcher*!, which is executed in a context that provides the previously defined global variables.

Actors. To produce activity, we need to introduce dedicated nodes, called *actors*, whose only role is to send messages and receive the corresponding answers. For instance, a processor is the actor in a memory hierarchy. It could behave in many different ways depending on what kind of programs it is supposed to execute. As an illustration, we design in the next section an actor that models a CPU with a LRU-friendly activity. The process executed by an actor is based on that for generic nodes and complemented with an additional component that runs in parallel to inject requests into the job manager, simulating the particular profile of activity of the considered actor.

3   Application Example

3.1   A Simple Hierarchical System with a LRU Cache

To illustrate our framework, we model now a simple hierarchical system: an actor A requests memory blocks to a storage S through a LRU cache C. These nodes are arranged on topology $T \overset{\mathrm{df}}{=} (\{A, C, S\}, \{\{A, C\}, \{C, S\}\})$ and, assuming that the set of keys K is $\{k_1, \ldots, k_{sz_K}\}$, their initial states are:

$$(\sigma_A, e_A) \overset{\mathrm{df}}{=} (\sigma_C, e_C) \overset{\mathrm{df}}{=} \left(\begin{pmatrix} \emptyset \\ \emptyset \end{pmatrix}, \begin{bmatrix} \emptyset \\ \emptyset, \emptyset \end{bmatrix} \right), \quad \text{and} \quad (\sigma_S, e_S) \overset{\mathrm{df}}{=} \left(\begin{pmatrix} \alpha \\ \emptyset \end{pmatrix}, \begin{bmatrix} \emptyset \\ \emptyset, \emptyset \end{bmatrix} \right),$$

where $\alpha \overset{\mathrm{df}}{=} \{k_i \to v_i \mid k_i \in K\}$ is randomly generated. Note that sz_K is here a parameter to control the size of the system, *i.e.* its number of key/value pairs. This system uses two operations defined as follows:

Name	Guard	Effect	Params
read	$(k, v) \in \sigma.h$	$\begin{matrix} (k,v) \\ \emptyset \end{matrix}, \begin{matrix} \emptyset \\ \emptyset \end{matrix}$	$\{k\}$
write	$(k, v_1) \in \sigma.h$	$\begin{matrix} (k,v_2) \\ \emptyset \end{matrix}, \begin{matrix} (k,v_1) \\ \emptyset \end{matrix}$	$\{k, v_2\}$

Operation **read** gets the value v associated with a given key k. Operation **write** replaces the value v_1 associated with key k with value v_2 also passed as argument.

We have here a hierarchical system in which state interpretation is straightforward: the global state is obtained by projecting effects top-down and integration projects an observed state onto the local state (except for A that maintains an empty local state). Thus, interpretation I_T is defined as follows:

$$\begin{aligned}
globalview \quad & \{(A, \sigma_A, e_A), (C, \sigma_C, e_C), (S, \sigma_S, e_S)\} \mapsto (e_A \gg e_C) \gg \sigma_S \\
integrate \quad & me, pos \mapsto \begin{cases} \sigma_{me}, e_{pos} \mapsto \sigma_{me} & \text{if } me = A, \\ \sigma_{me}, e_{pos} \mapsto e_{pos} \gg \sigma_{me} & \text{otherwise.} \end{cases}
\end{aligned}$$

Modelling storage S. The policy P_S for S is basically to answer the requests itself, *i.e.* apply the **operate** it receives and return the result. This is detailed in Fig. 4, where **nop** is a procedure that does nothing.

space $(keys, \sigma_{in}) \to 0$

update $(keys, handler) \overset{\mathrm{df}}{=}$ nop

close $(handler, outcome) \overset{\mathrm{df}}{=}$ nop

purge $() \to \emptyset$

trigger $(event)$

$$\to \begin{cases} tryLF & \text{if } event = \text{operate} \\ \times & \text{otherwise} \end{cases}$$

procedure $tryLF(req, h)$:
  $c \leftarrow req.op.candidates(\sigma_{me}, req.\beta_{in})$
  if $c = []$:
  $\mid$ $resp \leftarrow$ (failure, "no solution")
  else :
  $\mid$ $e \leftarrow req.op.effect(req.\beta_{in}, c[0])$
  $\mid$ $\sigma_{me} \leftarrow I_T.integrate(me, me)(\sigma_{me}, e)$
  $\mid$ $e_{me} \leftarrow e_{me} \,\substack{o\\ 9}\, e$
  $\mid$ $resp \leftarrow$ (success, $c[0]$)
  $jobs_{me}.$done (h)
  return $resp$

Fig. 4. Policy P_S for storage S. Name $tryLF$ stands for *"try locally else fail"*.

space $(keys, \sigma_{in}) \to 0$

update $(keys, handler) \overset{\mathrm{df}}{=}$ nop

close $(handler, outcome) \overset{\mathrm{df}}{=}$ nop

purge $() \to \emptyset$

trigger (str)

$$\to \begin{cases} tryTF & \text{if } event = \text{operate} \\ \times & \text{otherwise} \end{cases}$$

procedure $tryTF(req, h)$:
  $l \leftarrow jobs_{me}.$deps (h)
  $last, i \leftarrow SyncOperate(l, h)$
  $jobs_{me}.$done (h)
  return $last$

procedure $SyncOperate(l, h)$:
  $i \leftarrow NextNode()$
  for $req, h_2 \in l$:
  $\mid$ atomic :
  $\mid$ $\mid$ choose $b \in T[i, me]$
  $\mid$ $\mid$ $sendRequest(b, i, req, h_2)$
  $\mid$ $last \leftarrow receiveResponse(h_2)$
  return $last, i$

procedure $NextNode()$:
  if $me = A$:
  $\mid$ return C
  elif $me = C$:
  $\mid$ return S
  else :
  $\mid$ return $\times$

Fig. 5. Policy P_A for actor A. Name $tryTF$ stands for *"try to transfer else fail"*.

Modelling actor A. To observe the impact of cache C, we have to design an actor that generates requests in a LRU-friendly way. It maintains a MRU-to-LRU ordered list of $sz_A < sz_K$ recently used keys and randomly generates requests following an exponential law such that MRU keys are more likely to be chosen, and a key that is not in the list may be chosen with a probability P_ν. Moreover, **read** requests are randomly chosen with a probability P_r and **write** requests with a probability $1 - P_r$. Policy P_A for A amounts to keep its state empty and to forward all its requests to the cache. This is detailed in Fig. 5.

Modelling cache C. We call $sz_C < sz_K$ the capacity of cache C, and assume that C maintains a MRU-to-LRU ordered list ℓ of the keys it has most recently used. Let a and b be two lists, we define the following notations: $a[-1]$ is the last element of a; $a \setminus b$ is the list a from which all the elements also present in b have been removed; $|a|$ is the length of a; $a \oplus b$ is the list a extended by $b \setminus a$. The cache policy is detailed in Fig. 6.

space $(keys, \sigma_{in})$
$$\rightarrow \max(0, |keys \oplus \ell| - sz_C)$$

update $(keys, handler) \stackrel{\mathrm{df}}{=} UpdateLRU$

close $(handler, outcome) \stackrel{\mathrm{df}}{=} \mathbf{nop}$

purge $() \rightarrow \ell[-1]$

trigger $(\mathbf{str})$
$$\rightarrow \begin{cases} tryLT & \text{if } event = \mathbf{operate} \\ \textbf{✗} & \text{otherwise} \end{cases}$$

procedure $tryLT(req, h)$:
$\quad resp \leftarrow tryLF(req, h)$
$\quad$ **if** $resp.type \neq$ **success** :
$\quad\quad resp \leftarrow tryTF(req, h)$
$\quad\quad$ **if** $resp.type =$ **success** :
$\quad\quad\quad i \leftarrow NextNode()$
$\quad\quad\quad \sigma_{me} \leftarrow I_T.integrate(me, i)(\sigma_{me}, req.op.effect(req.\beta_{in}, resp.\beta_{out}))$
$\quad\quad\quad e_{me} \leftarrow e_{me} \,\text{\fontsize{6}{6}\selectfont;}\, e$
$\quad$ **return** $resp$

procedure $UpdateLRU(keys, handler)$
$\quad \ell \leftarrow keys \oplus \ell$
$\quad n \leftarrow P_{I_T}^{me}.\text{space}(keys, \sigma_{me})$
$\quad$ **while** $n > 0$:
$\quad\quad$ **atomic** :
$\quad\quad\quad least \leftarrow P_{I_T}^{me}.\text{purge}()$
$\quad\quad\quad h_2 \leftarrow jobs_{me}.\text{last}(least)$
$\quad\quad\quad l \leftarrow jobs_{me}.\text{deps}(h_2)$
$\quad\quad\quad last, i \leftarrow SyncOperate(l, h_2)$
$\quad\quad$ **atomic** :
$\quad\quad\quad \sigma_{me} \leftarrow \sigma_{me}/least$
$\quad\quad\quad e_{me} \leftarrow e_{me}/least$
$\quad\quad\quad jobs_{me}.\text{done}(h_2)$
$\quad\quad\quad \ell \leftarrow \ell \setminus [least]$
$\quad\quad\quad n \leftarrow n - 1$

Fig. 6. Policy P_C for cache C. Name $tryLT$ stands for *"try locally else transfer"*.

3.2   Analysis of the Example

To validate our model, we have created a reference implementation of our case study, *i.e.* we have built a program that could be instrumented to observe its execution. This allowed to compare the behaviour of the model with that of the reference implementation. The result of this comparison is shown in Fig. 7.

From these plots we can observe that the model and the reference implementation have exactly the same hit ratio, and transfer almost exactly the same amount of requests to the storage. The small difference on the latter measure is due to our simulation that did not exclude some runs that perform correct

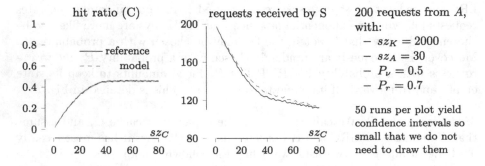

Fig. 7. Comparison of the modelled cache and the reference implementation.

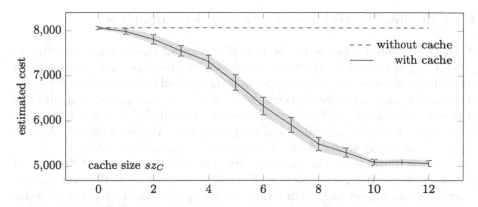

Fig. 8. Estimated cost of a request (lower is better) with respect to cache size; 95% confidence intervals are depicted as vertical segments (and the gray zone).

but unnecessary actions (in particular, synchronising cached blocks with the storage). It is interesting to have such behaviour in the model for correctness analysis, but they introduce bias in performances simulations, fortunately with a very limited effects as shown by our example. Future works should investigate how to avoid such undesirable runs during performances simulations.

Then, choosing $sz_K = 10$, we have run 100 executions of the model for every $sz_C \in \{0, \ldots, 12\}$. For each run we have measured its duration by weighting events as follows: communication events cost 0 on A, 40 on C and 400 on S; other events cost 0 on A, 1 on C and S. Figure 8 shows the mean value of these runs durations (estimated cost) with respect to the size of the cache. Because the actor is LRU friendly, costs decrease with the cache size, until sz_K where we reach the number of available keys. This closely matches the shape of curves one can obtain from exercising a real LRU like our reference implementation. However, comparing both costs would have required a tedious fine tuning of the events weighting while it would have not provided more information. Note finally that curves obtained with larger values of sz_K are closely similar as well.

This example shows how easy it is to use simulations of modelled systems to analyse the impact of various parameters on the timed performance of the system. We have considered here a simple system with a simple analysis, but it is easy to see that we could have considered many other analyses of the already numerous parameters of this system. A more complex case study can be found in [7, chap. 4] where the *demote* distributed cache protocol (see below) is analysed. Both these studies are done within a prototype implementation of the framework presented in this paper. Using the SNAKES toolkit [13], it defines all the classes and methods that correspond to the definitions as well as those necessary to build the Petri net actually used to compute runs or state spaces. In particular, the LRU case study presented in this section requires about 120 straightforward lines of Python to be implemented.

4   Conclusion, Related Work and Perspectives

We have presented what is, to the best of our knowledge, the first attempt to provide a generic modelling framework for distributed storage systems, and in particular cache systems. Our proposal has the original feature to allow for a separation of usually intricate concerns. Moreover, it can be applied to qualitative or quantitative analysis. We have illustrated on a simple yet realistic example how a system can be modelled and its performance can be analysed. A more complex case study with a detailed analysis is proposed in [7, Chap. 4].

We have thoroughly surveyed the literature about caches and distributed storage systems and found no work directly related to ours. However, among others, several papers are worth citing. [1] is probably the first paper to introduce the notion of cache (not yet named this way) using a FIFO eviction algorithm. Later, in [4], LRU (*least recently used*) is introduced, which is further generalised in [15] that considers a hierarchy of caches. A recent evolution is ARC, defined in [12], that is a sophisticated dynamic eviction algorithm which adapts with respect to frequently or recently used blocks. Regarding analysis aspects, [15] presents a simulation driven design of an efficient cache algorithm (called *demote*). However, it is not implemented because it involves extensions of existing low-level APIs of storage. This work also introduces the idea of distributed storage by partitioning the key domain across the caches in a hierarchy. Another proposal is [6] that defines *promote* to fix costs problems of *demote*. An interesting contribution is to introduce a notion of optimality of a cache algorithm, showing that *promote* approaches it. Moreover, this work introduces ideas to address multi-path hierarchies. [11] explores the idea of exploiting the relations between resources, which are discovered through statistical analysis of accesses. Our proposal makes these relations explicitly available in $\sigma.r$. Finally, an interesting paper is [3] that surveys majors multi-level cache systems, with a classification with respect to collaboration between levels, eviction algorithm and local optimisation strategies. It also shows an analysis of the algorithm through simulation and actual implementation of widely used benchmarks. These benchmarks could be rendered as dedicated actors in our proposal.

Future work will be dedicated to explore performance analysis directly on the state space, instead of resorting to simulated traces. It may be more accurate than our current simulation-based method in the presence of rare but dramatically slow runs. But it will be also less efficient if non trivial actors are considered (leading to larger state spaces). To cope with this, we shall consider symbolic techniques to reduce the cost of model-checking on models in our framework. In particular, symmetries reductions on keys like in [5] and finite abstraction of values on infinite domain like in [2] should be easy to adapt to our case and would allow to consider realistic storage sizes. Combining both is a more challenging problem that we would like to address on the long term. Note however that this is needed for state-space analysis only, indeed, traces are always fast to compute, even with large number of keys as we have experienced using varied parameters of the case study presented in Sect. 3. Moreover, we observed that usually few traces are required in order to obtain smooth curves and small confidence intervals like that of Fig. 8. Another perspective would be to experiment with evaluating runs duration using non-fixed costs functions when to take into account some variability, in particular in communications. Finally, we consider to replace direct Petri nets usage with a modelling language like ABCD [14]. Indeed, we have used quite complex programs to generate our nets at a higher level of abstraction, which is the purpose of languages like ABCD. But our programs are not easily readable while ABCD code is way more readable and could be presented itself, not necessarily through the Petri nets it allows to generate.

A   Petri Nets Implementation

To allow their actual execution, the processes presented above are implemented as coloured Petri nets. We present them here to illustrate their complexity but we lack space to give fully detailed explanations and refer to [7] for such details. We have used the SNAKES toolkit [13] to generate Petri nets for the various processes and assemble them into a single net, then to run traces for performance analysis and comparison with the reference implementation.

A.1   Notations

The Petri net modelling a complete system is split into sub-nets with shared places that are merged later on. Figure 10 shows the most important sub-nets. We depict shared places with thick borders and give them names; non-shared places are depicted with thin borders and are unnamed. For the sake of readability, we do not draw all the places. Instead we introduce some notations. For instance, the policies are stored in a place *Policy* as pairs $(me, P_{I_T}^{me})$ for each node me. This place and the arcs to read and write back these pairs are not depicted; possibly an updated value of $P_{I_T}^{me}$ is wrote back if we have called a method with a side effect. We also use assignment on transitions guards to denote the computation of a value that we bound to a variable to reuse it in the guard or on the output arcs.

In the model, handlers for new requests are created by the job manager. Our implementation makes use a feature of the SNAKES framework: dynamic process identifiers. This feature has initially been created to handle systems that can dynamically start/stop processes, see [5, 10]. We use here the same notations as in these papers to create requests handlers while being able to record by which node each was created: each node is identified by me that is implemented as a pid (process identifier); given a pid p, $\nu(p)$ creates a new pid that has a parent-child relation with p, and $\chi(p)$ destroys pid p from the system.

A.2   Implementing Communications

Communications are modelled with two shared places used together: *io* and *buses*. Every sent message is produced as a token in place *io*, from where it will be consumed by a transition of the destination node. When a message is sent on a bus b, the token b is also consumed by the sender from place *buses* and it is produced back by the receiver of the message. This way, only one message can transit at a time on a bus. To further simplify the pictures, Fig. 9 also introduces a notation for communications. Communications are implemented in such a way that they could be replaced with variants without changing the rest of the model. To do so, we define four shared places (see Fig. 10):

- *reqs* is the starting point of messages to be sent, it stores the requests to be sent, its source and destination, and the bus to be used;
- *resps* is similar to *reqs* for the responses;
- *pend* stores received requests awaiting to be processed on the node;
- finally, when a response is received, it is placed into *rets*.

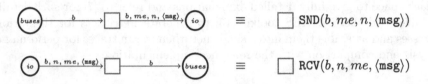

Fig. 9. Graphical notations for communications.

Process *listener* is implemented by the sub-net around transition $B1$ that (with $C1$) corresponds to procedure *receiveRequest* and transition $B2$ that corresponds to *sendResponse*. Place *idle* is used to prevent node me from communicating with another node n while a response has not been received, implementing the channels $\texttt{idle}_{me}$. It is initialised with all the pairs corresponding to the buses starting from me: $\{(me, n) \mid me, n \in T \wedge T[me, n] \neq \emptyset\}$. Channels $\texttt{waiter}_{me}$ are implemented by the unnamed places below the two copies of *idle*. Similarly, transitions $A1$ and $A2$ correspond to procedure *sendRequest* and *receiveResponse* respectively.

The infinite replication of *listener* is obtained by the concurrency within this sub-net: each message in *reqs* is processed concurrently to the others as long as the corresponding buses are all available.

A.3   Implementing Processes

Place *pend* is filled either when a request is received by *listener* firing $B1$, or directly by an actor (this is how activity is injected in its job manager).

A node starts its activity with transition $C1$ that picks a task in *pend* and adds it to the job manager, from which transition $C2$ (first instruction of *dispatcher*) picks jobs, then asks the policy to select the appropriate processing through place $i(onreq)$ (abstracted by the call to a trigger procedure) and waits for the result on transition $C3$ (atomic block in *dispatcher*). The latter puts back the result in *rets* so that it is retrieved by *listener* with transition $B2$.

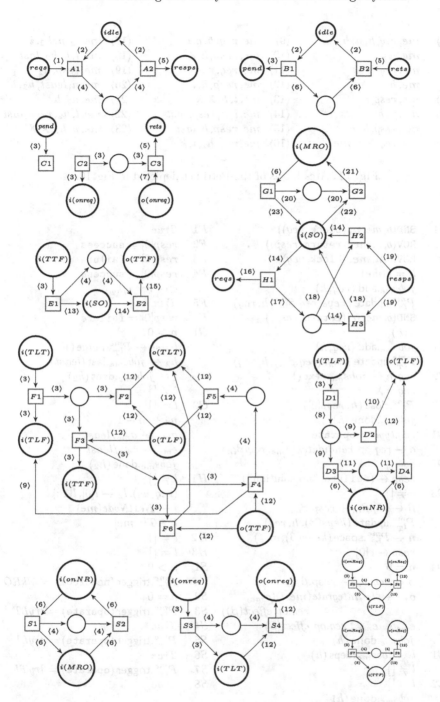

Fig. 10. Petri net implementation of the processes. The two nets at the bottom right are similar to that at the bottom center with $S1/S2/i(LTL)$ being replaced by $S3/S4/i(TLF)$ (top net) and $S5/S6/i(TTF)$ (bottom net) respectively. Arcs and transitions labels are defined in Figs. 11 and 12 respectively.

$\langle 1 \rangle$ me, req, h, n, b	$\langle 9 \rangle$ me, req, h, c, i	$\langle 17 \rangle$ me, l_2, h, h_2, i
$\langle 2 \rangle$ me, n	$\langle 10 \rangle$ $me, resp, h, ✗$	$\langle 18 \rangle$ $me, l, h, h_2, last$
$\langle 3 \rangle$ me, req, h	$\langle 11 \rangle$ $me, req, resp, h, i$	$\langle 19 \rangle$ $me, resp, h_2$
$\langle 4 \rangle$ me, h	$\langle 12 \rangle$ $me, resp, h, i$	$\langle 20 \rangle$ $me, n, least, h_2, h$
$\langle 5 \rangle$ $me, resp, h$	$\langle 13 \rangle$ $me, l, h, ✗, ✗$	$\langle 21 \rangle$ me, n_2, h
$\langle 6 \rangle$ me, n, h	$\langle 14 \rangle$ $me, l, h, resp, last$	$\langle 22 \rangle$ $me, l, h_2, resp, last$
$\langle 7 \rangle$ $me, resp, h, n$	$\langle 15 \rangle$ $me, resp, h, last$	$\langle 23 \rangle$ $me, n, h_2, ✗, ✗$
$\langle 8 \rangle$ me, req, h, c, me	$\langle 16 \rangle$ me, req, h_2, i, k	

Fig. 11. Arcs labels of the Petri net depicted in Fig. 10.

$A1$ $\text{SND}(b, me, n, (\text{block}, req))$

$A2$ $\text{RCV}(b, n, me, (\text{return}, resp))$

$B1$ $\text{RCV}(b, n, me, (\text{block}, req))$
$h = \nu(me)$
$jobs_{me}.\text{add}(req, h)$
$P^{me}_{I_T}.\text{update}(keys(req.\beta_{in}), h, req)$

$B2$ $\text{SND}(b, me, n, (\text{return}, resp))$
$\chi(h)$

$C1$ $jobs_{me}.\text{add}(req, h)$
$P^{me}_{I_T}.\text{update}(keys(req.\beta_{in}), h, req)$

$C2$ $req, h \leftarrow jobs_{me}.\text{next}()$
$req \neq ✗$

$C3$ $P^{me}_{I_T}.\text{close}(h, resp[0])$
$jobs_{me}.\text{done}(h)$

$D1$ $req.type = \textbf{operate}$
$c \leftarrow req.op.candidates(\sigma_{me}, req.\beta_{in})$

$D2$ $c = []$
$resp \leftarrow (\textbf{failure}, \text{"no solution"})$

$D3$ $c \neq []$
$\beta \leftarrow req.\beta_{in} + resp.\beta_{out}$
$P^{me}_{I_T}.\text{update}(keys(\beta), h, req)$
$n \leftarrow P^{me}_{I_T}.\text{space}(keys(\beta), \sigma_{me})$
$resp \leftarrow c[0]$

$D4$ $n = 0$
$\beta \leftarrow req.\beta_{in} + resp.\beta_{out}$
$\sigma_{me} \leftarrow I_T.integrate(me, i)(\sigma_{me}, req.op.effect(\beta))$
$e_{me} \leftarrow e_{me} \,\text{⨾}\, req.op.effect(\beta)$
$jobs_{me}.\text{done}(h)$

$E1$ $l \leftarrow jobs_{me}.\text{deps}(h)$
$l \neq []$

$E2$ $l = []$
$jobs_{me}.\text{done}(h)$

$F1$ $True$

$F2$ $resp[0] = \textbf{success}$

$F3$ $resp[0] = \textbf{failure}$

$F4$ $resp[0] = \textbf{success}$
$c \leftarrow resp.\beta_{out}$

$F5$ $True$

$F6$ $resp[0] = \textbf{failure}$

$G1$ $n > 0$
$least \leftarrow P^{me}_{I_T}.\text{purge}()$
$h_2 \leftarrow jobs_{me}.\text{last}(least)$
$l \leftarrow jobs_{me}.\text{deps}(h_2)$
$l \neq []$

$G2$ $l = []$
$n_2 \leftarrow n - 1$
$\sigma_{me} \leftarrow \sigma_{me}/least$
$e_{me} \leftarrow e_{me}/least$
$jobs_{me}.\text{done}(h_2)$

$H1$ $l \neq []$
$(req, h_2), l_2 \leftarrow l[0], l[1:]$
$i \leftarrow NextNode(me)$
$k \in T[i, me]$

$H2$ $l \neq []$

$H3$ $l = []$

$S1$ $n > 0$
$P^{me}_{I_T}.\text{trigger}(\textbf{needroom}) = MkRO$

$S2$ $n = 0$

$S3$ $P^{me}_{I_T}.\text{trigger}(\textbf{operate}) = tryLT$

$S4$ $True$

$S5$ $P^{me}_{I_T}.\text{trigger}(\textbf{operate}) = tryLF$

$S6$ $True$

$S7$ $P^{me}_{I_T}.\text{trigger}(\textbf{operate}) = tryTF$

$S8$ $True$

Fig. 12. Transitions labels of the Petri net depicted in Fig. 10.

The mechanism with **trigger** procedures presented above is similar to the late binding of method calls in object programming langages. A procedure is chosen dynamically and called with the appropriate arguments by putting its name in $i(onreq)$ and its result is awaited for in $o(onreq)$. The sub-nets that perform this dynamic call are generated from the events specification, we have presented above only event **operate** but others exist, in particular for internal use. Look in particular to the sub-net around transitions $S3$ and $S4$: the former picks in $i(onreq)$ a call to $tryLT$ and puts in $i(TLT)$ the appropriate arguments to execute this procedure (req and h). Its result is retrieved by $S4$ ($resp$, h, and i, where i is the node that actually performed the operation) and sent back to *dispatcher* through place $o(onreq)$.

Each procedure is implemented by its own sub-net and all the calls are handled similarly. Procedure $tryLF$ (*try locally else fail*) is implemented by the sub-net around transitions $D\star$ and called through the sub-net around $S5$ and $S6$. Procedure $tryTF$ (*try to transfer else fail*) is implemented by the sub-net around transitions $E\star$ and called through $S7$ and $S8$. Moreover, the while loop in *UpdateLRU* is actually implemented by a **needroom** event that triggers a procedure *makeRoomOperate* implemented by the sub-net around $G1$ and $G2$ through $S1$, we can observe in particular how the call to *syncOperate* that occurs in the middle of the loop is implemented by $G1$ putting a token in $i(SO)$ to trigger the sub-net around transitions $H\star$ which corresponds to the execution of *syncOperate*.

As we have seen, the pseudo-code presented earlier on in the paper specifies processes that are intrinsically sequential, and concurrency has been rendered using an infinite parallel replication. But the Petri net implementation handles concurrency through multiple tokens identified by node identifiers (me) and tasks handlers (h).

References

1. Belady, L.A.: A study of replacement algorithms for a virtual-storage computer. IBM Syst. J. **5**, 78–101 (1966)
2. Belardinelli, F., Lomuscio, A., Patrizi, F.: Verification of agent-based artifact systems. ArXiv:1301.2678 [cs.MA] (2013)
3. Chen, Z., Zhang, Y., Zhou, Y., Scott, H., Schiefer, B.: Empirical evaluation of multi-level buffer cache collaboration for storage systems. In: SIGMETRICS 2005. ACM (2005)
4. Denning, P.J.: The working set model for program behavior. Commun. ACM **11**, 323–333 (1968)
5. Fronc, Ł.: Effective marking equivalence checking in systems with dynamic process creation. In: INFINITY 2012. ENTCS, Elsevier (2012)
6. Gill, B.S.: On multi-level exclusive caching: offline optimality and why promotions are better than demotions. In: FAST 2008. USENIX Association (2008)
7. de la Houssaye, J.: Modles de stockages distribus appliqus aux caches hirarchiques. Ph.D. thesis, University of Évry, July 2015
8. de la Houssaye, J., Pommereau, F., Deniel, P.: Formal modelling and analysis of distributed storage systems. Technical report, IBISC, Univ. Évry (2014)

9. de la Houssaye, J., Pommereau, F., Deniel, P.: Formal modelling and analysis of distributed storage systems. In: Proceeding of PNSE 2016. vol. 1591. CEUR-WS (2016)
10. Klaudel, H., Koutny, M., Pelz, E., Pommereau, F.: State space reduction for dynamic process creation. Sci. Ann. Comput. Sci. **20**, 131–157 (2010)
11. Li, Z., Chen, Z., Srinivasan, S.M., Zhou, Y.: C-miner: mining block correlations in storage systems. In: FAST 2004. USENIX Association (2004)
12. Megiddo, N., Modha, D.S.: ARC: a self-tuning, low overhead replacement cache. In: FAST 2003. USENIX Association (2003)
13. Pommereau, F.: SNAKES: a flexible high-level petri nets library (tool paper). In: Devillers, R., Valmari, A. (eds.) PETRI NETS 2015. LNCS, vol. 9115, pp. 254–265. Springer, Cham (2015). doi:10.1007/978-3-319-19488-2_13
14. Pommereau, F.: ABCD: a user-friendly language for formal modelling and analysis. In: Kordon, F., Moldt, D. (eds.) PETRI NETS 2016. LNCS, vol. 9698, pp. 176–195. Springer, Cham (2016). doi:10.1007/978-3-319-39086-4_12
15. Wong, T.M., Wilkes, J.: My cache or yours? Making storage more exclusive. In: FAST 2002. USENIX Association (2002)

DB-Nets: On the Marriage of Colored Petri Nets and Relational Databases

Marco Montali[✉] and Andrey Rivkin

Free University of Bozen-Bolzano, Piazza Domenicani 3, 39100 Bolzano, Italy
{montali,rivkin}@inf.unibz.it

Abstract. The integrated management of business processes and master data is being increasingly considered as a fundamental problem, by both the academia and the industry. In this position paper, we focus on the foundations of the problem, arguing that contemporary approaches struggle to find a suitable equilibrium between data- and process-related aspects. We then propose a new formal model, called db-nets, that balances such two pillars through the marriage of colored Petri nets and relational databases. We invite the research community to build on this new model, discussing in particular its potential in conceptual modeling, formal verification, and simulation.

1 Introduction

In contemporary organizations, the integrated management of business processes (BPs) and master data is being increasingly considered as a fundamental problem, both by academia and the industry. From the practical point of view, it has been widely recognized that the traditional isolation between process and data management induces fragmentation and redundancies in the organizational structure and its underlying IT solutions, with experts and tools solely centered around data, and others only focusing on process management [19,30,31]. This isolation falls short, especially when it comes to knowledge-intensive and human-empowered processes [4,21,23].

State-of-the-art BP management systems (BPMSs), such as Bizagi BPM, Bonita BPM, Activiti, Camunda, and YAWL[1], actually provide clean conceptualizations for the process control flow as well as the "touching joints" between control flow and data: *(i)* process instances (also called cases) carry local data, *(ii)* a database backend is typically used to store global, persistent data, *(iii)* the decision logic queries local and persistent data to choose which path to select among multiple alternatives, *(iv)* the task logic dictates how to update local and persistent data. However, as argued in [17], no well-established approach exists to express the decision and task logic, which is in fact handled in an ad-hoc way, usually combining tool-specific languages with general purpose programming languages such as Java. The result is that the interaction of the process and its data becomes a sort of "procedural attachment" that is exploited during

---

[1] bizagi.com, bonitasoft.com, activiti.org, camunda.com, yawlfoundation.org.

© Springer-Verlag GmbH Germany 2017
M. Koutny et al. (Eds.): ToPNoC XII, LNCS 10470, pp. 91–118, 2017.
DOI: 10.1007/978-3-662-55862-1_5

the process enactment, but that is not conceptually well-understood [11]. As an effect, the verification tasks offered by such systems become either disabled when data are present, or produce misleading answers, since they do not take into account that the presence of data subtly affects the behaviors described by the process [17]. For example, seemingly concurrent behavior in the process may be in fact sequenced due to the presence of data constraints, which implicitly induce an order on the allowed data updates. More generally, non-executable paths and deadlocks may emerge only when the interplay between the process and its data is considered.

Foundational research has also witnessed a similar separation, with non-interacting areas of research either focused on data management or dynamic concurrent systems, with database theory and Petri net theory being the two most prominent representatives of each field. Over the years, both fields actually entered into the problem of combining data and processes, with quite complementary approaches. A first series of approaches stem from Petri nets, the reference formalism to represent the control-flow of BPs. All such models are more or less directly inspired by Colored Petri nets (CPNs) [3, 22], where colors abstractly account for data types, and where the control threads (i.e., tokens) traversing the net carry data conforming to colors. Verification in this setting is tackled by severely restricting the contribution of data. This is done by requiring colors to have a finite domain, thus realizing a form of a-priori propositionalization of the data, or by limiting the way tokens can carry data. This latter approach has led to the identification of several CPN fragments that are amenable to formal analysis even in the case of infinite color domains, ranging from nets where tokens carry single data values (as in data- and ν-nets [25, 32]), to nets where tokens are associated to more complex data structures such as nested relations [20], nested terms [34], or XML documents [8]. However, the common limitation of all such approaches is that data are still subsidiary to the control-flow dimension: data elements are "locally" attached to tokens, while no native support for global, persistent relational data is provided. In this light, CPNs naturally support cases and case data through the abstraction of colored tokens [33]. However, they do not lend themselves to modeling, querying, updating, and ultimately reasoning on persistent, relational data, like those typically maintained inside an enterprise information system. For this reason, they are unable to impact contemporary BPMSs, which, as argued above, all support the explicit linkage of BPs and an underlying persistent relational layer [17].

The second group of foundational approaches to data-aware processes has emerged at the intersection of database theory, formal methods and conceptual modeling, and specularly mirrors the advantages and lacks of CPN-based solutions. Such proposals go under the umbrella term of data-centric approaches [11], and gained momentum during the last decade, in particular due to the development of the business artifact paradigm [15], which also lead to concrete languages and implementations [16, 23]. The common denominator of all such approaches is that processes are centered around an explicit, persistent data component maintaining information about the domain of interest, and possibly capturing also its semantics in terms of classes, relations, and constraints. Atomic tasks induce CRUD (create-ready-update-delete) operations over the data component, in turn supporting the evolution of the master data maintained therein. Proposals then differ in terms of the adopted data model (e.g., relational, tree-shaped, graph-structured), and on the nature of information (e.g., whether it is complete or not). For example, [9,18] focus on relational databases, while [7] on XML and tree-shaped data models. The main downside of data-centric process models is that they disregard an explicit representation of how tasks have to be sequenced over time, only implicitly representing the control flow via (event-)condition-action rules [9,16,18]. Hence, they are too distant from contemporary BPMSs, which all rely on Petri net-inspired languages to define the process control flow.

We believe that this lack of equilibrium is a major obstacle towards the adoption of such foundational results into contemporary BPMSs, and that a more balanced formal model will pave the way towards simulation, verification, monitoring, and mining techniques that more effectively reflect, and exploit, the main abstractions offered by contemporary BPMSs, and their interrelationships. Technically, this in turn calls for the development of a formal model that natively establishes intimate, synergic connections between CPNs and data-centric approaches. To the best of our knowledge, the only existing proposal that makes an effort in this direction is [17]. However, it employs workflow nets [1] for capturing the process control flow, without leveraging the sophistication of CPNs. Taking inspiration from [17], we then propose *db-nets*, a new, balanced formal model for data-aware processes, rooted in CPNs and relational databases. We rigorously describe the abstractions offered by the model, and formalize its execution semantics. We finally invite the research community to build on this new model, discussing its potential impact on modeling, verification, and simulation. In particular, although preliminary, the verification results here presented introduce conditions that could not be singled out in previous formal models.

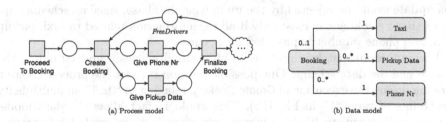

Fig. 1. A Petri net (a) and an informal diagram (b) respectively capturing the process and the data for our taxi booking example

2   The DB-Net Model: A Gentle Introduction

We discuss a concise, yet meaningful example that serves a twofold purpose: illustrating the issues arising when separating data and process modeling, and providing a gentle introduction to our proposal.

An airport website offers a door-to-door taxi shuttle service that can be booked on-line without any registration. To book a taxi, one only needs to leave a phone number, a pickup address and a desired pickup time. Once all the necessary data have been provided, the client confirms the booking and a free taxi driver is assigned to execute the order. In a typical industrial setting where business process experts and master data managers operate within separate silos [12,31], capturing this scenario would require to independently gather process and data requirements about the booking process. The *process expert* uses Petri nets (see Fig. 1(a)) to capture the process requirements as the basis for the construction of a web application. The application consists of the following steps. Whenever a client enters a taxi booking page, a booking is created, by nondeterministically picking a free taxi driver that will serve the booking (this is done by consuming a token from the resource place *FreeDrivers*). The process then demands the user to provide the relevant booking data (phone number and pickup data). After that, the booking is finalized, entering into the phase of the process where the booking is actually served, eventually leading to free the taxi driver (this is modeled by feeding a token back to the *FreeDrivers* place).

On the other hand, the *master data expert* typically gathers requirement about relevant data in the domain, and how to structure them in terms of classes, relationships, and constraints that must hold in each system snapshot. This creates the basis for building a corresponding database schema. Figure 1(b) sketches the resulting diagram informally, showing that a booking requires a combination of taxi, pickup data, and phone number, while, on the other hand, at any moment a taxi may be associated to one or no booking (i.e., busy or free).

Both models are reasonable in their respective contexts. However, their combination may lead to an overall faulty solution. For example, once the process in Fig. 1(a) is deployed on top of the database obtained from the diagram in Fig. 1(b), the process expert may be tempted to program the task logic underlying **Create Booking** by actually creating a new instance of class *Booking*. However, this update would be rejected by the underlying database, since its schema stipulates that a booking can exist only if all the information related to taxi, pickup data, and phone number is provided all at once.

Fixing this mismatch is possible only by simultaneously understanding the process and the data schema. One possible solution is to let the process create a booking during the execution of **Create Booking**, relaxing to "0...1" all multiplicity constraints of type "1" in Fig. 1(b). This would in fact allow the data model to store an incomplete booking where only some booking-related information is known. Another possible solution would instead require to change the task logic of the process, for example introducing local data variables to keep track of the reserved taxi, provided phone number, and provided pickup data, then creating a booking entry in the underlying database during the execution of the **Finalize Booking** task.

To enable this form of integrated modeling and analysis, we propose db-nets. The main idea is to maintain both the data and the process model intact, and to enrich them with an interface that conceptually interconnects them. This three-layered approach, applied to the booking example, may lead to the solution

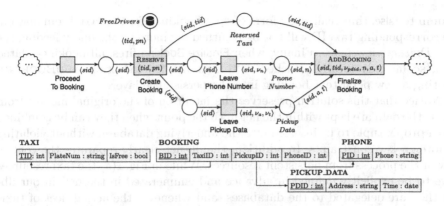

Fig. 2. A db-net representing the taxi booking process

shown in Fig. 2. The first layer, shown at the bottom, is the *persistence layer*, a full-fledged relational database with constraints (in the figure, primary and foreign keys) that faithfully mirrors the data model of Fig. 1(b). The second layer, shown at the top, is the *control layer*, which captures the process logic using a sophisticated variant of a CPN, which supports: *(i)* typing of tokens, so as to account for local variables attached to execution threads; *(ii)* injection of possibly fresh data values via special so-called ν-variables (leveraging the ν-PN model [32]); *(iii)* accessing the content of the underlying data layer via special *view-places*; *(iv)* updating the underlying data layer by attaching a database update logic to its transitions.

Intuitively, *sid* – a variable used to manage booking sessions (resembling the classical notion of "case id" in BPM) – will have a type **int**, while the *PickupData* place will host tokens carrying data of type **int** × **string** × **date**. The only view-place *FreeDrivers* accesses the underlying data layer to know which free taxies do exist when the **Create Booking** transition is fired. The connection between the view place and the transition is a read arc: to realize a clean update logic for the data, tuples obtained from the data layer are not consumed at the level of the net, but are manipulated via the update logic attached to the net transitions.

Such query and update functionalities are offered by a third, intermediate layer in our framework, called *data logic layer*. On the one hand, view places exploit the data logic layer to query the underlying data layer. E.g., the *Free Drivers* place exploits a query that returns the IDs of taxis whose *isFree* column is true. This realizes the fact that **Create Booking** cannot fire if no ID of this kind exists. On the other hand, the two transitions **Create Booking** and **Finalize Booking** exploit the data logic layer to update the persistent data depending on the current state of the net, the data locally carried by tokens, and additional data obtained from the external world via additional variables. Using this information, the transitions call corresponding parametric actions that are exposed by the data logic layer, and that encapsulate the update logic. In our example, whenever **Create Booking** fires, action RESERVE will update selected taxi setting its *isFree* column to false, thus realizing a form of "pre-booking" for the taxi. From now on, the corresponding taxi ID will not be returned anymore by the query feeding the *Free Drivers* view place. Finally, when Finalize Booking fires, all booking-related data, so far only locally attached to tokens, are fed to action ADDBOOKING, creating a new persistent booking into the persistence layer.

Notice that this solution preserves the intention of the original models from Fig. 1: the data are kept within the net until the point when they can be combined into a proper tuple to be inserted into the underlying database, without violating its foreign key constraints. In addition, the db-net clearly separates the control flow of the process from persistent resources. While in Fig. 1(a) the taxi resources have to be explicitly defined in advance and enumerated in the net, in our db-net they are delegated to the databases, and whenever the actual fleet of taxis changes, this change will be simply recorded in the data layer.

3   The db-net Formal Model

In this section, we formalize db-nets going through the three layers informally introduced in Sect. 2: persistence layer, data logic layer, and control layer.

3.1   Persistence Layer

The persistence layer maintains the relevant data in the domain of interest. To this end, we rely on standard relational databases equipped with constraints, in the spirit of [9]. First-order (FO) constraints allow for the formalization of conventional database constraints, such as keys and functional dependencies, as well as semantic constraints reflecting the domain of interest. Differently from [9], though, we also consider data types, on the one hand resembling concrete logical schemas of relational databases (where table columns are typed), and on the other reconciling the persistence layer with the notion of "color" in CPNs.

Definition 1. A *data type* $\mathcal{D}$ is a pair $\langle \Delta_{\mathcal{D}}, \Gamma_{\mathcal{D}} \rangle$, where $\Delta_{\mathcal{D}}$ is a *value domain*, and $\Gamma_{\mathcal{D}}$ is a finite set of *predicate symbols*. Each predicate symbol $S \in \Gamma_{\mathcal{D}}$ comes with an arity n_S and an n-ary predicate $S^{\mathcal{D}} \subseteq \Delta_{\mathcal{D}}^n$ that rigidly defines its semantics. A *type domain* is a finite set of data types.   □

In the following, we use $\mathfrak{D}$ to denote a type domain of interest, assuming that types in $\mathfrak{D}$ are pairwise disjoint, that is, their domains do not intersect, and their predicate symbols are syntactically distinguished. This guarantees that a predicate symbol S defined in some type of $\mathfrak{D}$, is defined only in that type, which can be then unambiguously denoted, with slight abuse of notation, by $\text{type}(S)$. We also employ $\Delta_{\mathfrak{D}} = \bigcup_{\mathcal{D} \in \mathfrak{D}} \Delta_{\mathcal{D}}$. Examples of data types are:

- **string** : $\langle \mathbb{S}, \{=_s\} \rangle$, strings with the equality predicate;
- **real** : $\langle \mathbb{R}, \{=_r, <_r\} \rangle$, real numbers with the usual comparison operators;
- **int** : $\langle \mathbb{Z}, \{=_{int}, <_{int}, succ\} \rangle$, integers with the usual comparison operators, as well as the successor predicate.

Definition 2. A $\mathfrak{D}$-*typed relation schema* is a pair $\langle R, \vec{\mathcal{D}} \rangle$, where R is a relation name, and $\vec{\mathcal{D}}$ is a tuple of elements from $\mathfrak{D}$, indicating the data types associated to each component of R. A $\mathfrak{D}$-*typed database schema* $\mathcal{R}$ is a finite set of $\mathfrak{D}$-typed relation schemas. □

For compactness, we represent a typed relation schema $\langle R, \langle \mathcal{D}_1, \ldots, \mathcal{D}_n \rangle \rangle$ using notation $R(\mathcal{D}_1, \ldots, \mathcal{D}_n)$.

Definition 3. Given a $\mathfrak{D}$-typed database schema $\mathcal{R}$, a $\mathfrak{D}$-*typed database instance* $\mathcal{I}$ *over* $\mathcal{R}$ is a *finite* set of facts of the form $R(o_1, \ldots, o_n)$, such that (i) $R(\mathcal{D}_1, \ldots, \mathcal{D}_n) \in \mathcal{R}$ and (ii) $o_i \in \Delta_{\mathcal{D}_i}$, for each $i \in \{1, \ldots, n\}$. Given a type $\mathcal{D} \in \mathfrak{D}$, the $\mathcal{D}$-*active domain of* $\mathcal{I}$, written $Adom_{\mathcal{D}}(\mathcal{I})$, is the set of values in $\Delta_{\mathcal{D}}$ such that $o \in Adom_{\mathcal{D}}(\mathcal{I})$ if and only if $o \in \Delta_{\mathcal{D}}$ and o occurs in $\mathcal{I}$. We also define $Adom_{\mathfrak{D}}(\mathcal{I}) = \bigcup_{\mathcal{D} \in \mathfrak{D}} Adom_{\mathcal{D}}(\mathcal{I})$. □

Example 1. The relation schema for a taxi in Fig. 1 is $Taxi(\textbf{int}, \textbf{string}, \textbf{bool})$. Then, $Taxi(1, 123AB, \textbf{false})$ is a fact for $Taxi$ denoting that taxi number 1 has plate number 123AB and is currently busy. ■

We now turn to queries. As query language, we resort to standard first-order logic (FOL), interpreted under the active domain semantics [26]. This means that quantifiers are relativized to the active domain of the database instance of interest, guaranteeing that queries are domain-independent (actually, safe-range): their evaluation only depends on the values explicitly appearing in the database instance over which they are applied. Recall that this query language is equivalent to the well-known SQL standard [6]. Since the relational structures we consider are typed, the logic is typed as well.

Given a type domain $\mathfrak{D}$, we fix a countably infinite set $\mathcal{V}_{\mathfrak{D}}$ of variables. Each variable is typed. To this end, we introduce a *variable typing function* **type** : $\mathcal{V}_{\mathfrak{D}} \rightarrow \mathfrak{D}$ mapping variables to their types. The typing function prescribes that x may be substituted only by values taken from $\Delta_{\textbf{type}(x)}$. For compactness, the variable type may be explicitly shown using a colon notation $x:\textbf{type}(x)$.

Definition 4. A *(well-typed)* $\text{FO}(\mathfrak{D})$ *query* over a $\mathfrak{D}$-typed database schema $\mathcal{R}$ is a formula of the form:

$$Q ::= S(\vec{y}) \mid R(\vec{z}) \mid \neg Q \mid Q_1 \wedge Q_2 \mid \exists x.Q, \text{ where}$$

- for $\vec{y} = \langle y_1, \ldots, y_n \rangle$, we have that S/n is a predicate defined in $\Gamma_{\mathcal{D}}$ for some $\mathcal{D} \in \mathfrak{D}$, and for each $i \in \{1, \ldots, n\}$, we have that y_i is either a value $o \in \Delta_{\mathcal{D}}$, or a variable $x \in \mathcal{V}_{\mathfrak{D}}$ with $\textbf{type}(x) = \mathcal{D}$;
- for $\vec{z} = \langle z_1, \ldots, z_m \rangle$, we have that $R(\mathcal{D}_1, \ldots, \mathcal{D}_m)$ is a relation defined in $\mathcal{R}$, and for each $i \in \{1, \ldots, m\}$, we have that z_i is either a value $o \in \Delta_{\mathcal{D}_i}$, or a variable $x \in \mathcal{V}_{\mathfrak{D}}$ with $\textbf{type}(x) = \mathcal{D}_i$.

We use standard abbreviations $Q_1 \vee Q_2 = \neg(\neg Q_1 \wedge \neg Q_2)$, and $\forall x.Q = \neg \exists x.\neg Q$. □

Definition 5. A variable $x \in V_{\mathfrak{D}}$ is *free* in a $\mathsf{FO}(\mathfrak{D})$ query Q, if x occurs in Q but is not in the scope of any quantifier. By $\mathit{Free}(Q)$ we denote the set of variables occurring free in Q. A *boolean query* is a query without free variables. □

Given a query Q such that $\mathit{Free}(Q) = \{x_1, \ldots, x_n\}$, we employ notation $Q_{\mathtt{name}}(x_1, \ldots, x_n)\text{:-}\, Q$ to emphasize the free variables of Q, and to fix a natural ordering over them.

Example 2. Consider the *Taxi* relation schema of Example 1. Query $Q_{\mathtt{FreeTaxiId}}(x)\text{:-}\, \exists p.\, \mathit{Taxi}(x, p, \mathsf{true})$ returns the set of ids associated to free taxies. ∎

As usual, queries are used to extract answers from a database instance.

Definition 6. Given a set $X = \{x_1, \ldots, x_n\}$ of typed variables, a *substitution* for X is a function $\theta : X \to \Delta_{\mathfrak{D}}$ mapping variables from X into values, such that for every $x \in X$, we have $\theta(x) \in \Delta_{\mathtt{type}(x)}$. A *substitution θ for a $\mathsf{FO}(\mathfrak{D})$ query Q* is a substitution for the free variables of Q. □

As customary, we may view a substitution θ for a query Q simply as a tuple of values, assuming the natural ordering over the free variables of Q. We denote by $Q\theta$ the boolean query obtained from Q by replacing each free variable $x \in \mathit{Free}(Q)$ with the corresponding value $\theta(x)$. In the following, we apply substitutions to any structure containing variables. Substitutions are the basis for capturing the semantics of query answers, which we tackle next.

Definition 7. Given a $\mathfrak{D}$-typed database schema $\mathcal{R}$, a $\mathfrak{D}$-typed instance $\mathcal{I}$ over $\mathcal{R}$, A $\mathsf{FO}(\mathfrak{D})$ query Q over $\mathcal{R}$, and a substitution θ for Q, we inductively define relation $\mathcal{I}$ entails Q under θ with active domain semantics, written $\mathcal{I}, \theta \models Q$, as:

$$
\begin{aligned}
&\mathcal{I}, \theta \models R(y_1, \ldots, y_n) && \text{if } R(y_1, \ldots, y_n)\theta \in \mathcal{I} \\
&\mathcal{I}, \theta \models S(y_1, \ldots, y_n) && \text{if } S(y_1, \ldots, y_n)\theta \in S^{\mathtt{type}(S)} \\
&\mathcal{I}, \theta \models \neg Q && \text{if } \mathcal{I}, \theta \not\models Q \\
&\mathcal{I}, \theta \models Q_1 \wedge Q_2 && \text{if } \mathcal{I}, \theta \models Q_1 \text{ and } \mathcal{I}, \theta \models Q_2 \\
&\mathcal{I}, \theta \models \exists x.Q && \text{if } \text{there exists } \mathsf{o} \in \mathit{Adom}_{\mathtt{type}(x)}(\mathcal{I}) \text{ such that } \mathcal{I}, \theta[x/\mathsf{o}] \models Q
\end{aligned}
$$

where $\theta[x/\mathsf{o}]$ denotes the substitution obtained from θ by assigning o to x.[2] □

Definition 8. Given a $\mathfrak{D}$-typed database schema $\mathcal{R}$, a $\mathfrak{D}$-typed instance $\mathcal{I}$ over $\mathcal{R}$, and a $\mathsf{FO}(\mathfrak{D})$ query $Q(x_1, \ldots, x_n)$ over $\mathcal{R}$, the set of *answers to Q in $\mathcal{I}$*, written $\mathit{ans}(Q, \mathcal{I})$, is the set of substitutions θ from the free variables of Q to the active domain of $\mathcal{I}$, such that Q holds in $\mathcal{I}$ under θ:

$$
\mathit{ans}(Q, \mathcal{I}) = \{\text{substitution } \theta : \mathit{Free}(Q) \to \mathit{Adom}_{\mathfrak{D}}(\mathcal{I}) \mid \mathcal{I}, \theta \models Q\}
$$

□

---

[2] If $\theta(x)$ is defined, its value is replaced by o, otherwise θ is extended so that $\theta(x) = \mathsf{o}$.

When Q is boolean, we write $ans(Q, \mathcal{I}) \equiv$ true if $\langle \rangle \in ans(Q, \mathcal{I})$, or $ans(Q, \mathcal{I}) \equiv$ false if $ans(Q, \mathcal{I}) = \emptyset$.

Example 3.
Let $\mathcal{I}_t = \{Taxi(1, 123\text{AB}, \text{false}), Taxi(2, 432\text{CD}, \text{true}), Taxi(3, 456\text{DA}, \text{true})\}$ be a database instance for taxies, and consider query $\mathbb{Q}_{\text{FreeTaxi}}(x, y):\text{-}\ Taxi(x, y, \text{true})$, which extracts the id and plate number of all free taxies. We then have $ans(\mathbb{Q}_{\text{FreeTaxi}}(x, y), \mathcal{I}_t) = \{\{x \mapsto 2, y \mapsto 432CD\}, \{x \mapsto 3, y \mapsto 456DA\}\}$. ∎

We are finally ready to define the persistence layer.

Definition 9. A $\mathfrak{D}$-typed *persistence layer* is a pair $\langle \mathcal{R}, \mathcal{E} \rangle$ where: *(i)* $\mathcal{R}$ is a $\mathfrak{D}$-typed database schema; *(ii)* $\mathcal{E}$ is a finite set $\{\Phi_1, ..., \Phi_k\}$ of boolean $\text{FO}(\mathfrak{D})$ queries over $\mathcal{R}$, modeling *constraints over* $\mathcal{R}$. □

Example 4. Boolean query $\forall x, y_1, y_2, z_1, z_2.\ Taxi(x, y_1, z_1) \wedge Taxi(x, y_2, z_2) \rightarrow y_1 = y_2 \wedge z_1 = z_2$ expresses that the first component of $Taxi$ (i.e., the taxi id) is a key for the $Taxi$ relation schema. ∎

The presence of constraints calls for a definition of which database instances are compliant by a given persistence layer, i.e., satisfy its constraints.

Definition 10. Given a $\mathfrak{D}$-typed persistence layer $\mathcal{P} = \langle \mathcal{R}, \mathcal{E} \rangle$ and a $\mathfrak{D}$-typed database instance $\mathcal{I}$, we say that $\mathcal{I}$ *complies with* $\mathcal{P}$ if: *(i)* $\mathcal{I}$ is defined over $\mathcal{R}$; *(ii)* $\mathcal{I}$ satisfies all constraints in $\mathcal{E}$, that is, $ans(\bigwedge_{\Phi \in \mathcal{E}} \Phi, \mathcal{I}) \equiv$ true. □

Example 5. The persistence layer $\mathcal{P} = \langle \mathcal{R}, \mathcal{E} \rangle$ is a fragment of an information system used by a company to handle the submission of tickets, and their management by employees. $\mathcal{R}$ employs types **string** and **int** to define the following relation schemas:

- $Emp(\textbf{string})$ lists employee (names);
- $Ticket(\textbf{int}, \textbf{string})$ models ticket (ids) and their description;
- $Resp(\textbf{string}, \textbf{int})$ models which employees handle which tickets: $Resp(\text{e}, 1)$ indicates that the employee named e is responsible for ticket number 1.
- $Log(\textbf{int}, \textbf{string}, \textbf{string})$ represents a log table storing information about all the tickets processed so far, also listing their responsible employees and their description.

The persistence layer is also equipped with a set of constraints over $\mathcal{R}$, expressing (primary) keys, foreign keys, functional dependencies, and multiplicity constraints. E.g., the ticket number provides the primary key for $Ticket$, the second component of $Resp$ references the primary key of $Ticket$, and *each employee can handle at most one ticket at a time*. It is well-known that such constraints can be formalized in FO [6]. E.g., the latter constraint may be formalized as: $\forall e, t_1, t_2.\ Resp(e, t_1) \wedge Resp(e, t_2) \rightarrow t_1 = t_2$. ∎

3.2 Data Logic Layer

The data logic layer provides a bidirectional "interface" to interact with a database instance complying with a persistence layer of interest. On the one hand, the data logic allows one to *extract* data from the database instance using queries. On the other hand, it allows one to *update* the database instance, adding and deleting possibly multiple facts at once, with a *transactional* semantics: if the new database instance obtained after the update is still compliant with the persistence layer, the update is *committed*, otherwise it is *rolled back*. This approach is in line with how database management systems operate in practice.

To query the database instance, we use $\text{FO}(\mathfrak{D})$ queries as in Definition 4. To update the database instance, we instead resort to the literature on data-centric processes [11, 35], where *actions* are typically used to apply CRUD (create-read-update-delete) operations over a relational database. Specifically, we adopt a minimalistic approach, keeping the actions as simple as possible. The approach is inspired by the well-known STRIPS language for planning, which has been adopted also in for data-centric processes [5]. More sophisticated forms of actions, as those in [9], can be seamlessly introduced.

Definition 11. A *(parameterized) action* over a $\mathfrak{D}$-typed persistence layer $\langle \mathcal{R}, \mathcal{E} \rangle$ is a tuple $\langle \mathrm{n}, \vec{p}, F^+, F^- \rangle$, where: *(i)* n is the *action name*; *(ii)* $\vec{p}$ is a tuple of pairwise distinct typed variables from $\mathcal{V}_{\mathfrak{D}}$, denoting the *action (formal) parameters*. *(iii)* F^+ and F^- respectively represent a finite set of $\mathcal{R}$-facts over $\vec{p}$, to be *added* to and *deleted* from the current database instance. Given a typed relation $R(\mathcal{D}_1, \ldots, \mathcal{D}_n) \in \mathcal{R}$, an R-fact over $\vec{p}$ has the form $R(y_1, \ldots, y_n)$, such that for every $i \in \{1, \ldots, n\}$, y_i is either a value $\mathrm{o} \in \Delta_{\mathcal{D}_i}$, or a variable $x \in \vec{p}$ with $\mathrm{type}(x) = \mathcal{D}_i$. An $\mathcal{R}$-fact is an R-fact for some relation R from $\mathcal{R}$. □

To access the different components of an action $\alpha = \langle \mathrm{n}, \vec{p}, F^+, F^- \rangle$, we use a dot notation: $\alpha \cdot \mathtt{name} = \mathrm{n}$, $\alpha \cdot \mathtt{params} = \vec{p}$, $\alpha \cdot \mathtt{add} = F^+$, and $\alpha \cdot \mathtt{del} = F^-$.

Example 6. Consider the RESERVE action from Fig. 1. It takes as input two parameters, respectively denoting a taxi id and its plate number, and has the effect of switching its status from free to busy. This is modeled as follows:

$$\text{RESERVE·}\mathtt{params} = \langle id, pn \rangle \quad \text{RESERVE·}\mathtt{del} = \{ Taxi(id, pn, \mathsf{true}) \}$$
$$\text{RESERVE·}\mathtt{add} = \{ Taxi(id, pn, \mathsf{false}) \} \quad ∎$$

We now turn to the semantics of actions. Actions are executed by grounding their parameters to values. Given an action α and a (parameter) substitution θ for α, we call *action instance* $\alpha\theta$ the (ground) action resulting from α by substituting its parameters with corresponding values, as specified by θ.

Definition 12. Let $\mathcal{P} = \langle \mathcal{R}, \mathcal{E} \rangle$ be a $\mathfrak{D}$-typed persistence layer, $\mathcal{I}$ be a $\mathfrak{D}$-typed database instance $\mathcal{I}$ compliant with $\mathfrak{D}$, α be an action over $\mathcal{P}$, and θ be a substitution for *action*·$\mathtt{params}$. The *application* of $\alpha\theta$ on $\mathcal{I}$, written $\mathtt{apply}(\alpha\theta, \mathcal{I})$, is a database instance over $\mathcal{R}$ obtained as $(\mathcal{I} \setminus F_{\alpha\theta}^-) \cup F_{\alpha\theta}^+$, where: *(i)* $F_{\alpha\theta}^- = \bigcup_{R(\vec{y}) \in \alpha \cdot \mathtt{del}} R(\vec{y})\theta$; *(ii)* $F_{\alpha\theta}^+ = \bigcup_{R(\vec{y}) \in \alpha \cdot \mathtt{add}} R(\vec{y})\theta$. We say that $\alpha\theta$ can be *successfully applied* to $\mathcal{I}$ if $\mathtt{apply}(\alpha\theta, \mathcal{I})$ complies with $\mathcal{P}$. □

The application of an action instance amounts to ground all the facts contained in the definition of the action as specified by the given substitution, then applying the update on the given database instance, giving priority to additions over deletions (this is a standard approach, which unambiguously handles the situation in which the same fact is asserted to be added and deleted).

Example 7. Consider the data layer shown in Fig. 2, the database instance $\mathcal{I}_t$ from Example 3, and action RESERVE from Example 6. The application of $\text{RESERVE}[id/2, pn/432\text{CD}]$ is *successful*, and leads to the new database instance $\mathcal{I}'_t = \{\, Taxi(1, 123\text{AB}, \text{false}),\ Taxi(2, 432\text{CD}, \text{false}),\ Taxi(3, 456\text{DA}, \text{true})\,\}$, where taxi number 2 is in fact busy.   ∎

The data logic simply exposes a set of queries and a set of actions that can be used by the control layer to obtain data from the persistence layer, and to induce updates on the persistence layer.

Definition 13. Given a $\mathfrak{D}$-typed persistence layer $\mathcal{P}$, a $\mathfrak{D}$-*typed data logic layer over* $\mathcal{P}$ is a pair $\langle \mathcal{Q}, \mathcal{A} \rangle$, where: *(i)* $\mathcal{Q}$ is a finite set of $\text{FO}(\mathfrak{D})$ queries over $\mathcal{P}$; *(ii)* $\mathcal{A}$ is a finite set of actions over $\mathcal{P}$.   □

Example 8. We make the scenario of Example 5 operational, introducing a data logic layer $\mathcal{L}$ over $\mathcal{P}$. $\mathcal{L}$ exposes two queries to inspect the persistence layer:

- $Q_e(e) :\text{-} Emp(e) \wedge \neg \exists t. Resp(e, t)$, to extract *idle* employees;
- $Q_t(t, d) :\text{-} Ticket(t, d)$, to extract tickets and their description.

In addition, $\mathcal{L}$ provides three main functionalities to manipulate tickets in the persistence layer: ticket registration, assignment/release, and logging. Such functionalities are realized through four actions (where, for simplicity, we blur the distinction between an action and its name). The registration of a new ticket is managed by an action REG that, given an integer t, and two strings e and d, (REG·**params** $= \langle t, e, d \rangle$), simultaneously creates a ticket identified by t and described by d into the persistence layer, and assigns the employee identified by e to such ticket (thus making her *busy*):

$$\text{REG·}\textbf{del} = \{Emp(e)\} \qquad \text{REG·}\textbf{add} = \{\, Ticket(t, d), Resp(e, t)\,\}$$

Two specular actions ASSIGN and RELEASE assign or release a ticket to/from an employee, making her busy or idle. Both actions take as input a string for the employee name and an integer for a ticket it (ASSIGN·**params** $=$ RELEASE·**params** $= \langle e, t \rangle$), and update e by removing or adding that e is responsible of t:

$$\text{RELEASE·}\textbf{del} = \text{ASSIGN·}\textbf{add} = \{Resp(e, t)\} \qquad \text{RELEASE·}\textbf{add} = \text{ASSIGN·}\textbf{del} = \emptyset$$

Finally, action LOG with LOG·**params** $= \langle t, e, d \rangle$ is used to flush all the information of a ticket into a log table. The action erases all information about the ticket, and logs that it has been processed, also recalling its employee and description:

$$\text{LOG·}\textbf{del} = \{\, Ticket(t, d), Resp(e, t)\,\} \qquad \text{LOG·}\textbf{add} = \{Log(t, e, d)\}$$

∎

3.3   Control Layer

The control layer employs a variant of CPNs to capture the process control flow, and how it interacts with an underlying persistence layer through the functionalities provided by the data logic. The spirit is to conceptually ground CPNs by adopting a data-oriented approach. This is done by introducing dedicated constructs exploiting such functionalities, as well as simple, declarative patterns to capture the typical token consumption/creation mechanism of CPNs.

Before introducing the different constitutive elements of the control layer together with their graphical appearance, we fix some preliminary notions. We consider the standard notion of a *multiset*. Given a set A, the *set of multisets* over A, written $A^\oplus$, is the set of mappings of the form $m : A \to \mathbb{N}$. Given a multiset $S \in A^\oplus$ and an element $a \in A$, $S(a) \in \mathbb{N}$ denotes the number of times a appears in S. Given $a \in A$ and $n \in \mathbb{N}$, we write $a^n \in S$ if $S(a) = n$. We also consider the usual operations on multisets. Given $S_1, S_2 \in A^\oplus$: *(i)* $S_1 \subseteq S_2$ (resp., $S_1 \subset S_2$) if $S_1(a) \leq S_2(a)$ (resp., $S_1(a) < S_2(a)$) for each $a \in A$; *(ii)* $S_1 + S_2 = \{a^n \mid a \in A \text{ and } n = S_1(a) + S_2(a)\}$; *(iii)* if $S_1 \subseteq S_2$, $S_2 - S_1 = \{a^n \mid a \in A \text{ and } n = S_2(a) - S_1(a)\}$; *(iv)* given a number $k \in \mathbb{N}$, $k \cdot S_1 = \{a^{kn} \mid a^n \in S_1\}$.[3]

Places. The control layer contains a finite set P of places, which in turn are classified in two groups. On the one hand, so-called *control places* play the role of standard places in classical Petri nets: they represent conditions/states of a dynamic system. On the other hand, so-called *view places* are used as an interface to the underlying persistence layer, so as to make the persistent data available to the control layer. We then have $P = P_c \uplus P_v$, where P_c and P_v respectively denote the set of control and view places.

In the spirit of CPNs, the control layer assigns to each place a color, which in turn combines one or more data types from a type domain $\mathfrak{D}$. Formally, a $\mathfrak{D}$-*color* is a cartesian product $\mathcal{D}_1 \times \ldots \times \mathcal{D}_m$, where for each $i \in \{1, \ldots, m\}$, we have $\mathcal{D}_i \in \mathfrak{D}$. We denote by Σ the set of all possible $\mathfrak{D}$-colors.

Definition 14. A $\mathfrak{D}$-*color assignment* over places P is a function $\mathtt{color} : P \to \Sigma$ mapping each place $p \in P$ to a corresponding $\mathfrak{D}$-color.   □

As for control places, it is well-known that the coloring mechanism can be exploited to realize a plethora of conceptual abstractions on top of the control flow. We mention here the two most important abstractions in our setting: *(i)* cases and their data, and *(ii)* resource. A *case* represents a specific process instance, and its *case data* [33] are local data whose scope is the case itself, and that are used to store important information for the progression of the case. Such data may be either extracted from the underlying persistence layer, or obtained by interacting with the external environment (e.g., human users, external services, or data generators). *Resources* represent actors able to handle the execution of tasks. They are also typically associated to data attributes (e.g., id, role, group). Tasks typically consume (certain kinds of) resources when

---

[3] Hence, given a multiset S, we have $0 \cdot S = \emptyset$.

executed, and this implicitly affect the degree of concurrency in the progression of cases, as well as the possibility of spawning new cases.

The fact that control places are colored implies that whenever a token is assigned to a control place, it must carry a data tuple whose types match component-wise the place color. It is worth noting that a colored place may be interchangeably considered as a specific state/condition within the control layer, or as a special relation schema used to enrich the persistence layer with control-related information. Similarly, a token distributed over a place may be interchangeably seen as a thread of control located in that state, or as a tuple assigned to the relation schema represented by that place.

As discussed above, control places host tokens carrying local data. Obviously, the control layer also requires to query persistent data, using them to decide how to route tokens when it comes to business decisions, or to assign them to case data. We want to support both possibilities, but clearly separating the data retrieved from the persistence layer, from those carried by tokens. This is why we distinguish view places from control places. Each view place exposes to the control layer a portion of the data stored in the persistence layer. Formally, this is done by equipping the view place with a query defined in the data logic layer.

Definition 15. Given a data logic layer $\mathcal{L} = \langle \mathcal{Q}, \mathcal{A} \rangle$, a *query assignment* from view places P_v to queries $\mathcal{Q}$ is a function $\texttt{query} : P_v \to \mathcal{Q}$ mapping each view place $p \in P_v$ with $\texttt{color}(p) = \mathcal{D}_1 \times \ldots \times \mathcal{D}_n$ to a query $Q(x_1, \ldots, x_n)$ from $\mathcal{Q}$, such that the color of p component-wise matches with the types of the free variables in Q: for each $i \in \{1, \ldots, n\}$, we have $\mathcal{D}_i = \texttt{type}(x_i)$. $\qquad\square$

A view place may be seen as a normal place, whose color is implicitly obtained by the types of the free variables of the query, considered with their natural ordering. However, tokens are not arbitrarily attached to it: at a given time, the tokens it contains represent the answers to the query it is associated to. All such tokens are only "virtually" present in the control layer, and in fact they cannot be consumed within the control layer itself, but only accessed in a read-only way. Notice, however, that the content of the view place is not immutable: it changes whenever the data it fetches from the persistence layer are updated.

Example 9. Consider the db-net of Fig. 2. Place *FreeDrivers* is a view place, connected to the query $\texttt{Q}_{\texttt{FreeTaxi}}$ shown in Example 3. At a given time, such a place "inspects" the content of the underlying persistence layer and retrieves all pairs $\langle tid, pn \rangle$, where tid is the id of a free taxi, and pn is its plate number. Such pairs are seen as tokens "virtually" present in the view place. Place *ReservedTaxi* is a normal, control place, used to store session ids together with their corresponding reserved taxi id. $\qquad\blacksquare$

Transitions. As customary, in our model transitions represent atomic units of work within the control layer, thus providing the fundamental building block to describe the dynamics of a process. In our setting, they simultaneously account for three different aspects: the token consumption/production mechanism of

CPNs, the injection of possibly fresh data from the external environment a là ν-Petri nets [32], and the impact on the underlying persistence layer.

We start with the consumption of tokens. This is modeled through input arcs connecting places to transitions, together with inscriptions that declaratively match tokens and their data. To this end, we build on the approach adopted in variants of data nets [5,25,32]: an inscription is just a multiset of tuples over a given set of typed variables. Each tuple nondeterministically matches a token from the input place, and the variables therein are bound, component-wise, to the data carried by that token. Upon firing, the token is consumed if the input place is a control place, whereas it is *only inspected* if the place is a view place.

The overall consumption/inspection of tokens and the data they carry along all arcs incoming into a transition constitutes a *firing mode* for that transition. In the context of a transition definition, we call *inscription* a tuple of typed variables (and, possibly, values). We denote the set of all possible inscriptions over set $\mathcal{Y}$ as $\Omega_{\mathcal{Y}}$, and the set of variables appearing inside an inscription $\omega \in \Omega_{\mathcal{Y}}$ as $Vars(\omega)$, extending such notation to sets and multisets of inscriptions.

Definition 16. An *input flow* from places P to transitions T is a function $F_{in} : P \times T \to \Omega_{\mathcal{V}_{\mathfrak{D}}}^{\oplus}$ assigning multisets of inscriptions (over variables $\mathcal{V}_{\mathfrak{D}}$) to input arcs, such that all such inscriptions are compatible with their input places. An inscription $\langle x_1, \ldots, x_m \rangle$ is *compatible* with a place p if $\texttt{color}(p) = \mathcal{D}_1 \times \ldots \times \mathcal{D}_m$, such that for every $i \in \{1, \ldots, m\}$, we have $\texttt{type}(x_i) = \mathcal{D}_i$. $\qquad\square$

Graphically, we do not depict input arcs whose inscription is $\emptyset$. We define the *input variables* of t, written $InVars(t)$ as the set of all variables occurring on input arc inscriptions for t:

$$InVars(t) = \{x \in \mathcal{V}_{\mathfrak{D}} \mid \text{there exists } p \in P \text{ such that } x \in Vars(F_{in}(\langle p, t \rangle))\}.$$

The set $InVars(t)$ gives an indication about which input data elements are accessed when a transition fires. The multiple usage of the same variable in an inscription, or in inscriptions attached to different arcs incident to a transition, captures the requirement of *matching* the same data object in different tokens, allowing the transition to fire only if the accessed tokens carry the *same* data value. This mirrors the notion of join used when querying relational data. In general, though, the modeler may require to specify additional constraints over such input data to allow firing the transition. To this end, we introduce guards.

Definition 17. A $\mathfrak{D}$-typed *guard* is a formula of the form:

$$\varphi ::= \texttt{true} \mid S(\vec{y}) \mid \neg\varphi \mid \varphi_1 \wedge \varphi_2$$

where, for $\vec{y} = \langle y_1, \ldots, y_n \rangle \subseteq \mathcal{V}_{\mathfrak{D}}$, we have that S/n is a predicate defined in $\Gamma_{\mathcal{D}}$ for some $\mathcal{D} \in \mathfrak{D}$, and for each $i \in \{1, \ldots, n\}$, we have that y_i is either a value $\texttt{o} \in \Delta_{\mathcal{D}}$, or a variable $x_i \in \mathcal{V}_{\mathfrak{D}}$ with $\texttt{type}(x_i) = \mathcal{D}$. $\qquad\square$

We denote by $\mathbb{F}_{\mathfrak{D}}$ the set of all possible $\mathfrak{D}$-typed guards. Additionally, with a slight abuse of notation, given guard φ we denote by $Vars(\varphi)$ the set of variables occurring in φ. Guards may be seen as the quantifier- and relation-free fragment of $FO(\mathfrak{D})$ queries (cf. Definition 4). Consequently, their semantics is inherited from Definition 7 (considering the empty database instance). Guards are attached to transitions, and defined over their input variables, thus being an additional filter on the data that can be matched to the input inscriptions.

Definition 18. A $\mathfrak{D}$-typed *transition guard assignment* over transitions T is a function $\mathsf{guard} : T \to \mathbb{F}_\mathfrak{D}$ assigning to each transition $t \in T$ a $\mathfrak{D}$-typed guard φ, such that $Vars(\varphi) \subseteq InVars(t)$. $\qquad\square$

We now concentrate on the effect of firing a transition, which may simultaneously impact the control layer and the underlying persistence layer. Such an effect is tuned by the input variables attached to the transition, as well as additional data obtained from the external environment. Injection of external data is crucial for two reasons [5,11,28]. First, during the execution of a case, input data may be dynamically acquired from human users or external services, and used later on; this is, e.g., what happens when a user form needs to be filled before continuing with the case execution, then deciding how to route the case depending on the inserted data. Second, fresh ids may be injected into the system, e.g., to explicitly distinguish tokens via certain data attributes, or to insert a new tuple in the underlying database instance (which typically requires to create a distinctive primary key for that tuple). We call these two types of external inputs *arbitrary external inputs* and *fresh external inputs*. To account for arbitrary external inputs in the context of a transition, we just employ "normal" variables distinct from those used in the input inscriptions. To account for fresh external inputs, we employ the well-known mechanism adopted in ν-Petri nets [29,32]. In particular, we introduce a countably infinite set $\Upsilon_\mathfrak{D}$ of $\mathfrak{D}$-typed *fresh variables*. To guarantee an unlimited provisioning of fresh values, we impose that for every variable $\nu \in \Upsilon_\mathfrak{D}$, we have that $\Delta_{\mathsf{type}(\nu)}$ is countably infinite.

From now on, we fix a countably infinite set of $\mathfrak{D}$-typed variable $\mathcal{X}_\mathfrak{D}$, obtained as the disjoint union of "normal" variables $\mathcal{V}_\mathfrak{D}$ and fresh variables $\Upsilon_\mathfrak{D}$. In formulae, $\mathcal{X}_\mathfrak{D} = \mathcal{V}_\mathfrak{D} \uplus \Upsilon_\mathfrak{D}$. Let us first focus on the impact of transition firing on the underlying persistence layer. This is, again, mediated by the data logic, exploiting in particular the actions it exposes. Specifically, a transition can bind to an action, using variables from $\mathcal{X}_\mathfrak{D}$ as "actual" parameters. In this light, data passing from the control to the persistence layer is captured by re-using the same variable inside an input inscription and an action binding for the same transition. When the transition fires, actual parameters are substituted with concrete data values, instanating the action and allowing for its further invocation.

Definition 19. Given a data logic layer $\mathcal{L} = \langle \mathcal{Q}, \mathcal{A} \rangle$, an *action assignment* from transitions T to actions $\mathcal{A}$ is a partial function $\mathsf{act} : T \to \mathcal{A} \times \Omega_{\mathcal{X}_\mathfrak{D} \cup \Delta_\mathfrak{D}}$, where $\mathsf{act}(t)$ maps t to an action $\alpha \in \mathcal{A}$ together with a (binding) inscription compatible with α. An inscription $\langle y_1, \ldots, y_m \rangle$ is compatible with α if $\alpha \cdot \mathsf{params} = \langle z_1, \ldots, z_m \rangle$ and, for each $i \in \{1, \ldots, m\}$, we have $\mathsf{type}(y_i) = \mathsf{type}(z_i)$ if y_i is a variable from $\mathcal{X}_\mathfrak{D}$, or $y_i \in \Delta_{\mathsf{type}(z_i)}$ if y_i is a value from $\Delta_\mathfrak{D}$. $\qquad\square$

The action assignment provides a distinctive feature of our model, namely the ability of the control layer to invoke an action applied to the underlying persistence layer. This, however, does not in general guarantee that the action invocation will actually turn into an update over the persistence layer. Recall in fact that an action instance is applied transactionally: if it produces a new database instance that is compliant with the persistence layer, the action instance *succeeds* and the update is committed; if, instead, some constraints is violated, the action instance *fails* and the update does not take place.

Lastly, we consider the effect of transitions on the control layer itself, defining which tokens have to produced, together with the data they will carry, and to which places such tokens have to be assigned. This is done by mirroring the definition of input flow (cf. Definition 16), with two distinctions. First, output arcs connect transitions to control places only, as view places cannot be explicitly modified within the control layer. Second, the inscriptions attached to output arcs may mention not only input variables, but also: *(i)* values, allowing for constructing tokens that carry explicitly specified data; *(ii)* fresh variables, allowing for constructing tokens that carry data not already present in the net, nor in the underlying database instance.

Definition 20. An *output flow* from transitions T to control places P_c is a function $F_{out} : T \times P_c \to \Omega^\oplus_{\mathcal{X}_\mathfrak{D} \cup \Delta_\mathfrak{D}}$ assigning multisets of inscriptions to output arcs, such that all such inscriptions are compatible with their output places (as defined in Definition 16). □

We do not depict output arcs graphically when their inscription is $\emptyset$. We define the *output variables* of t, written $OutVars(t)$, as the set of variables occurring in the action assignment for t (if any), and in its output arc inscriptions:

$$OutVars(t) = \quad \{x \in \mathcal{X}_\mathfrak{D} \mid \mathtt{act}(t) \text{ is defined as } \langle \alpha, \omega \rangle, \text{ and } x \in Vars(\omega)\}$$
$$\cup \{x \in \mathcal{X}_\mathfrak{D} \mid \text{there exists } p \in P \text{ such that } x \in Vars(F_{out}(\langle t, p \rangle))\}.$$

With this notion at hand, we can obtain the *external variables* of transition t as $OutVars(t) \setminus InVars(t)$. Each such variable x is not bound by any input inscription, and can consequently be assigned arbitrarily (if $x \in \mathcal{V}_\mathfrak{D}$), or to a fresh value (if $x \in \Upsilon_\mathfrak{D}$). Among such variables, we explicitly refer to the fresh variables attached to t, using notation $FreshVars(t)$. Mathematically, $FreshVars(t) = OutVars(t) \cap \Upsilon_\mathfrak{D}$.

Example 10. Consider the *FinalizeBooking* transition in Fig. 2. It has three input arcs, used to consume three tokens respectively belonging to three places *ReservedTaxi*, *PhoneNumber*, and *PickupData*. The inscriptions on the input arcs indicate that whenever three tokens from such places are consumed, they have to agree on their first data component, i.e., they must belong to the same session. This realizes a sort of join, and ensures that only tokens produced within the same session are considered upon firing. The so-obtained data are then fed to the ADDBOOKING action, which uses the session id *sid*, the reserved taxi id *tid*, the phone number n, the address a and the time t to create a new booking. However, since the creation of a new booking also requires to provide a fresh id for a new tuple to be inserted in the *Pickup_Data* relation schema, an additional fresh variable ν_{pdid} is also used when invoking that action. ∎

As discussed before, firing a transition may incur in the instantiation and invocation of an action from the data logic layer, and the so-obtained action instance may or not result in an actual update. To raise awareness of the control layer about these two radically different outcomes, we introduce two separate output flows: a normal output flow, capturing the actual effect of a transition on the control flow when its attached action succeeds, and a *rollback flow*, capturing the actual effect of a transition on the control flow when its attached action fails. With this distinction, the control layer can fine-tune its own behavior in accordance with the transactional semantics of the persistence layer, e.g., taking a standard or a compensation route depending on the outcome of the action. To graphically distinguish *normal output arcs* from *rollback output arcs*, we proceed as follows. We depict the former as usual: □——O. Instead, we decorate the latter with an "x": □x——O.

Definition 21. A $\mathfrak{D}$-typed *control layer* over a data logic layer $\mathcal{L} = \langle \mathcal{Q}, \mathcal{A} \rangle$ is a tuple $\langle P, T, F_{in}, F_{out}, F_{rb}, \texttt{color}, \texttt{query}, \texttt{guard}, \texttt{act} \rangle$, where:

- $P = P_c \uplus P_v$ is a finite set of control places constituted by control places P_c and view places P_v;
- T is a finite set of transitions, such that $T \cap P = \emptyset$;
- F_{in} is an input flow from P to T (cf. Definition 16);
- F_{out} and F_{rb} are two output flows from T to P_c (cf. Definition 20), respectively called *normal output flow* and *rollback flow*;
- $\texttt{color}$ is a color assignment over P (cf. Definition 14);
- $\texttt{query}$ is a query assignment from P_v to $\mathcal{Q}$ (cf. Definition 15);
- $\texttt{guard}$ is a transition guard assignment over T (cf. Definition 18);
- $\texttt{act}$ is an action assignment from T to $\mathcal{A}$ (cf. Definition 19).   □

3.4 DB-nets

We now put the three layers together, providing a formal definition for db-nets.

Definition 22. A *db-net* is a tuple $\langle \mathfrak{D}, \mathcal{P}, \mathcal{L}, \mathcal{N} \rangle$, where:

- $\mathfrak{D}$ is a type domain (cf. Definition 1);
- $\mathcal{P}$ is a $\mathfrak{D}$-typed persistence layer (cf. Definition 9);
- $\mathcal{L}$ is a $\mathfrak{D}$-typed data logic layer over $\mathcal{P}$ (cf. Definition 13);
- $\mathcal{N}$ is a $\mathfrak{D}$-typed control layer over $\mathcal{L}$ (cf. Definition 21).   □

Example 11. Figure 3 shows the control layer of a db-net $\mathcal{B}$, using the persistence layer $\mathcal{P}$ defined in Example 5 and the data logic layer $\mathcal{L}$ defined in Example 8. The control layer realizes a simple ticket processing workflow, where tickets are created, manipulated, and finally resolved. In spite of its simplicity, $\mathcal{B}$ already shows many distinctive features of our model. We intuitively describe the control layer moving from left to right and from top to bottom. Each case of this process is constituted by a ticket and its responsible employee. A ticket is created by the **Create Ticket** transition, which requires the presence of an idle

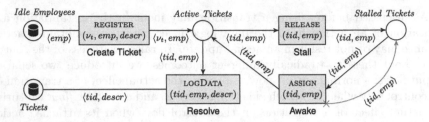

Fig. 3. The control layer of a db-net for ticket management. In CreateTicket, ν_t is a fresh input variable, and *descr* is an arbitrary input variable.

employee to be fired. Since this condition needs to inspect the persistence layer so as to retrieve idle employees, we model it through a view place associated to query Q_e from $\mathcal{L}$. Notice that if no employee is currently idle, then **Create Ticket** is not enabled. Upon firing **Create Ticket** for a given idle employee, a fresh ticket id is generated using fresh variable ν_t, and a ticket description is obtained through the "external" input variable *descr*. All such data are bound to action REGISTER, which is applied when the transition fires. Among the effects of REGISTER, there is one asserting that the selected employee becomes responsible for the newly created ticket. This indirectly implies that such an employee is not present anymore in the view place for idle employees. The ticket id, together with its responsible employee, represent the case and its data. The two control places *Active Tickets* and *Stalled Tickets* have color **int** × **string**, and model two distinct states in which tickets may be. Such states are important only within the evolution of cases, and are therefore not propagated to the underlying persistence layer. An active ticket may be "stalled" if the employee is currently unable to resolve it. Executing the **Stall** transition has a twofold effect. Within the control layer, the ticket is moved from active to stalled. Within the persistence layer, its responsible employee is released. Interestingly, the relation of responsibility is now only recalled within the control layer. A stalled ticket may be revived, by inserting such a relation back into the persistence layer. This is captured by the **Awake** transition, which mirrors the effect of the **Stall** transition. However, there is a particularly interesting aspect here. When a ticket t_1 is stalled, its responsible employee e is released and becomes idle. She may be then selected as responsible of a newly created ticket t_2. Due to the constraints present in $\mathcal{P}$, the indirect effect of this situation is that t_1 cannot be awaken unless t_2 is either stalled or resolved. In fact, awakening t_1 in a situation where t_2 is active would violate the requirement that e is responsible of at most one ticket. For this reason, we enrich the **Awake** transition with a rollback output arc, which brings back the ticket to the stalled state if it is awaken in the "wrong" moment. For example, if t_1 is awaken while t_2 is active, the application of ASSIGN applied to $\langle t_1, e \rangle$ will fail, consequently bringing t_1 back to stalled. Finally, an active ticket may be resolved. This has a twofold effect. On the one hand, the token carrying the ticket and its responsible employee is removed from the net. On the other hand, the case information is logged into the persistence layer. However, logging also requires to retrieve the description of the ticket. To this end, we employ a second view place accessing tickets and their description by exploiting Q_t from $\mathcal{L}$. By using the same variable tid in the two input inscriptions of the Resolve transition, we realize a join, thus inspecting the view place and extracting the description of tid.

4 Execution Semantics

The execution semantics of a db-net simultaneously accounts for the progression of a database instance compliant with the persistence layer of the net, and for the evolution of a marking over the control layer of the net. Such two information sources affect each other via the data logic layer: the database instance exposes its own data through view places, influencing the current marking and the enabled transitions; the marking over the control layer determines which transitions may be fired, in turn triggering updates the database instance. As customary in process analysis, the execution semantics considers the db-net of interest in *isolation*, hence assuming that the persistence layer of the db-net is updated only through its associated control layer, without any form of interference from external, unpredictable updates. Notice that external updates can be simulated in the db-net by means of additional, always enabled transitions, which may nondeterministically fire and modify the content of the persistence layer.

We start by formalizing the notion of marking over the control layer of the db-net. A marking distributes tokens over the places of the net, so that each token carries data that are compatible with the color of the place in which that token resides. In this light, tokens are nothing else than tuples of values over the place colors. In addition, the marking of a view place must correspond to the answers obtained by issuing its associated query over the underlying database instance.

Definition 23. A *marking* of a $\mathfrak{D}$-typed control layer $\mathcal{N} = \langle P, T, F_{in}, F_{out}, F_{rb},$ color, query, guard, act$\rangle$ is a function $m : P \to \Omega_{\mathfrak{D}}^{\oplus}$ mapping each place $p \in P$ to a corresponding multiset of p-compatible tuples using data values from $\mathfrak{D}$. A tuple $\langle o_1, \ldots, o_n \rangle$ is p-compatible if color(p) is of the form $\langle \mathcal{D}_1, \ldots, \mathcal{D}_n \rangle$, and for every $i \in \{1, \ldots, n\}$, we have $o_i \in \Delta_{\mathcal{D}_i}$. Given a database instance $\mathcal{I}$, we say that m is *aligned* to $\mathcal{I}$ via query if the tuples it assigns to view places exactly correspond to the answers of their corresponding queries over $\mathcal{I}$: for every view place $v \in P$ and every v-compatible tuple $\vec{o}$, we have that $\vec{o} \in m(v)$ if and only if $\vec{o} \in ans(query(v), \mathcal{I})$. $\qquad \square$

We mirror the notion of active domain as provided in Definition 3 to the case of markings. Given a type $\mathcal{D} \in \mathfrak{D}$, the $\mathcal{D}$-*active domain* of a marking m, written $Adom_{\mathcal{D}}(m)$, is the set of values in $\Delta_{\mathcal{D}}$ such that $o \in Adom_{\mathcal{D}}(m)$ if and only if there exists p such that o occurs in $m(p)$. From the practical point of view, one may consider the marking of control places to be initially defined by the modeler, and then evolved by the control layer, while the marking of view places computed on-the-fly from the underlying database instance when needed.

In db-nets, then, both the persistence layer and the control layer are stateful: during the execution, the persistence layer is associated to a database instance, while the control layer to a marking aligned with that database instance.

Definition 24. A *snapshot* of a db-net $\mathcal{B} = \langle \mathfrak{D}, \mathcal{P}, \mathcal{L}, \mathcal{N} \rangle$ (also called $\mathcal{B}$-*snapshot*) is a pair $\langle \mathcal{I}, m \rangle$, where $\mathcal{I}$ is a database instance compliant with $\mathcal{P}$, and m is a marking of $\mathcal{N}$ aligned to $\mathcal{I}$ via query. $\qquad \square$

As customary for CPNs, the firing of a transition t in a snapshot is defined w.r.t. a so-called *binding* for t, that is, a substitution $\sigma : \mathit{Vars}(t) \to \Delta_{\mathfrak{D}}$, where $\mathit{Vars}(t) = \mathit{InVars}(t) \cup \mathit{OutVars}(t)$. However, to properly enable the firing of t, the binding σ must guarantee a number of properties:

1. agreement with the distribution of tokens over the places, in accordance with the inscriptions on the corresponding input arcs;
2. satisfaction of the guard attached to t;
3. proper treatment of fresh variables, guaranteeing that they are substituted with values that are pairwise distinct, and also distinct from all the values present in the current marking, as well as in the current database instance.

To formalize these conditions, we need a notion of *inscription binding*. Given an inscription (i.e., multiset of tuples of variables) $\omega \in \Omega^{\oplus}_{\mathcal{X}_{\mathfrak{D}} \cup \Delta_{\mathfrak{D}}}$, and a substitution θ over a set X of variables containing all variables from ω, the *inscription binding* of ω under θ is a multiset $\theta^{\oplus}(\omega)$ from $\Omega^{\oplus}_{\mathfrak{D}}$ defined as follows: $\langle \mathsf{o_1}, \ldots, \mathsf{o_n} \rangle^m \in \theta^{\oplus}(\omega)$ if and only if $\langle y_1, \ldots, y_n \rangle^m \in \omega$, such that for every $i \in \{1, \ldots, n\}$, we have $\mathsf{o_i} = y_i$ if $y_i \in \Delta_{\mathfrak{D}}$, or $\mathsf{o_i} = \theta(y_i)$ if $y_i \in \mathcal{X}_{\mathfrak{D}}$. For example, given $\omega = \{\langle x, y \rangle^2, \langle x, 1 \rangle\}$ and $\theta = \{x \mapsto 1, y \mapsto 2\}$, we have $\theta^{\oplus}(\omega) = \{\langle 1, 2 \rangle^2, \langle 1, 1 \rangle\}$.

Definition 25. Let $\mathcal{B}$ be a db-net with control layer $\langle P, T, F_{in}, F_{out}, F_{rb},$ color, query, guard, act$\rangle$. A transition $t \in T$ is *enabled* in a $\mathcal{B}$-snapshot $\langle \mathcal{I}, m \rangle$, written $\langle \mathcal{I}, m \rangle [t, \sigma \rangle$, if:

1. for every place $p \in P$, $m(p)$ provides enough tokens matching those required by inscription $\omega = F_{in}(\langle p, t \rangle)$ once ω is bound by σ, i.e., $\sigma^{\oplus}(\omega) \subseteq m(p)$;
2. guard$(t)\sigma$ is true;
3. σ is injective over $\mathit{FreshVars}(t)$, thus guaranteeing that fresh variables are assigned to pairwise distinct values by σ, and for every fresh variable $\nu \in \mathit{FreshVars}(t)$, $\sigma(\nu) \notin (\mathit{Adom}_{\mathsf{type}(\nu)}(\mathcal{I}) \cup \mathit{Adom}_{\mathsf{type}(\nu)}(m))$. $\qquad \square$

Definition 26. Let $\mathcal{N} = \langle P, T, F_{in}, F_{out}, F_{rb},$ color, query, guard, act$\rangle$ be a $\mathfrak{D}$-typed control layer, and let $t \in T$ be a transition of $\mathcal{N}$ such that act$(t) = \langle \alpha, \omega \rangle$, with α·params $= \langle x_1, \ldots, x_n \rangle$ and $\omega = \langle y_1, \ldots, y_n \rangle$. The *action instance induced by transition* $t \in T$ under binding σ, written act$_\sigma(t)$, is the action instance $\alpha \sigma'$, where $\sigma' : \alpha$·params $\to \Delta_{\mathfrak{D}}$ is a substitution for the formal parameters of α, defined as: for every $i \in \{1, \ldots, n\}$, if $y_i \in \Delta_{\mathfrak{D}}$, then $\sigma'(x_i) = y_i$; if instead $y_i \in \mathcal{X}_{\mathfrak{D}}$, then $\sigma'(x_i) = \theta(y_i)$. $\qquad \square$

The firing of an enabled transition under some mode has then a threefold effect. First, all tokens present in control places that are used to match the input inscriptions are consumed. Second, the action instance induced by the firing is applied on the current database instance. If the application is successful, the database instance is updated (*commit*); if not, it is kept unaltered (*rollback*). Third, tokens built from the inscriptions on output arcs are produced and put into target places, considering either normal output arcs or rollback arcs depending on whether the action instance has been committed or rolled back.

Definition 27. Let $\mathcal{B} = \langle \mathfrak{D}, \mathcal{P}, \mathcal{L}, \mathcal{N} \rangle$ be a db-net with $\mathcal{N} = \langle P, T, F_{in}, F_{out}, F_{rb}, \mathtt{color}, \mathtt{query}, \mathtt{guard}, \mathtt{act} \rangle$, and $s_1 = \langle \mathcal{I}_1, m_1 \rangle$, $s_2 = \langle \mathcal{I}_2, m_2 \rangle$ be two $\mathcal{B}$-snapshots. Let $t \in T$ be a transition of $\mathcal{N}$, and σ be a binding for t, such that $s_1[t, \sigma\rangle$. We say that t *fires* in s_1 with binding σ producing s_2, written $s_1[t, \sigma\rangle s_2$, if the following conditions hold: given $\mathcal{I}_3 = \mathtt{apply}(\mathtt{act}_\sigma(t), \mathcal{I}_1)$,

- if $\mathcal{I}_3$ is compliant with $\mathcal{P}$, then $\mathcal{I}_2 = \mathcal{I}_3$, otherwise $\mathcal{I}_2 = \mathcal{I}_1$;
- For every control place $p \in P$, given $\omega_{in} = F_{in}(\langle p, t \rangle)$, $\omega_{out} = F_{out}(\langle t, p \rangle)$, and $\omega_{rb} = F_{rb}(\langle t, p \rangle)$, we have

$$m_2(p) = (m_1(p) - \sigma^\oplus(\omega_{in})) + k_{out} \cdot \sigma^\oplus(\omega_{out}) + (1 - k_{out}) \cdot \sigma^\oplus(\omega_{rb}),$$

where $k_{out} = 1$ if $\mathcal{I}_3$ is compliant with $\mathcal{P}$, and $k_{out} = 0$ otherwise.   □

The execution semantics of a db-net is captured by a possibly *infinite-state labeled transition system* (LTS) that accounts for all possible executions of the control layer starting from an initial snapshot. States of this transition systems are db-net snapshots, and transitions model the effect of firing db-net transitions under given bindings. Formally, given a db-net $\mathcal{B} = \langle \mathfrak{D}, \mathcal{P}, \mathcal{L}, \mathcal{N} \rangle$ with $\mathcal{N} = \langle P, T, F_{in}, F_{out}, F_{rb}, \mathtt{color}, \mathtt{query}, \mathtt{guard}, \mathtt{act} \rangle$, and given a snapshot s_0 over $\mathcal{B}$ (called the *initial $\mathcal{B}$-snapshot*), the *execution semantics* of $\mathcal{B}$ starting from s_0 is given by the LTS $\Gamma^\mathcal{B}_{s_0} = \langle S, s_0, \rightarrow \rangle$, where:

- S is a possibly infinite set of $\mathcal{B}$-snapshots;
- $\rightarrow \subseteq S \times T \times S$ is a *transition relation* over states, labeled by transitions T;
- S and $\rightarrow$ are defined by simultaneous induction as the smallest sets such that: (i) $s_0 \in S$; (ii) given a $\mathcal{B}$-snapshot $s \in S$, for every transition $t \in T$, binding σ, and $\mathcal{B}$-snapshot s', if $s[t, \sigma\rangle s'$ then $s' \in S$ and $s \xrightarrow{t} s'$.

Example 12. Consider the db-net $\mathcal{B}$ in Fig. 3, with the initial $\mathcal{B}$-snapshot s_1 that contains two idle employees Paul and Jane. Figure 4 shows a possible, finite execution of $\mathcal{B}$ starting from s_1, which actually corresponds to a portion of the LTS $\Gamma^\mathcal{B}_{s_1}$. For example, to reach s_2 from s_1, Create Ticket has to be fired with binding $\sigma = \{\nu_t \mapsto 12, emp \mapsto \text{Jane}, descr \mapsto ☎\}$. The resulting snapshot contains the generated ticket, and is such that Jane is not idle anymore. Notably, along the run we encounter a situation that concretely demonstrates the rollback semantics. This is the case of snapshot s_4, where Jane is responsible of an active, but also associated to a currently stalled ticket. Due to the constraints present

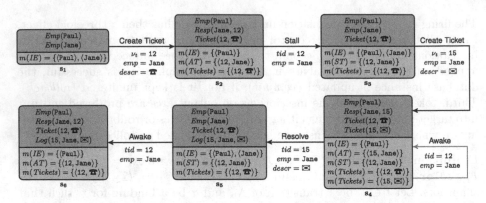

Fig. 4. A finite execution of the db-net from Example 11. Here we use the following abbreviations: $AT = Active\,Tickets$, $IE = Idle\,Employees$, $ST = Stalled\,Tickets$.

in the persistence layer of $\mathcal{B}$, this implies that Jane cannot awake the stalled ticket unless the active one is either stalled or resolved. Hence, if Jane chooses to awake the stalled ticket, the system ends up into an inconsistent state due to the violation of the database constraint imposting that an employee can be responsible of at most one ticket (cf. Example 5). This leads to the rollback of ASSIGN, and to the consequent activation of the corresponding rollback arc (marked in red in Fig. 4). In this specific example, the rollback arc has the effect of bringing the consumed ticket back to the stalled state, thus concretely realizing a simultaneous rollback for the persistence and the control layers.

5   Modeling and Verification

We discuss some key features of db-nets, considering the problem of modeling data-aware business processes, and that of verification, where we provide some initial results on the boundaries of decidability for the formal analysis of db-nets.

5.1   Modeling

From the modeling point of view, db-nets incorporate all typical abstractions needed in data-aware business processes, reconstructing all the distinctive features of various Petri net classes enriched with data, as well as those of data-centric processes. More formally, in terms of expressiveness, we observe the following correspondences. First of all, db-nets subsume ν-PNs [32], and become expressively equivalent to ν-PNs when: *(i)* there is only one unary color assigning places to the only one unordered countably infinite data type, *(ii)* the data logic layer is empty. With such a restrictions, the only modeling construct not natively provided by ν-PNs is that of arbitrary external input, which can be however simulated using ν-PNs by following the strategy defined in [5]. Second, db-nets are expressively equivalent to recently introduced formal models for data-centric business processes, like DCDSs [9] and DMSs [5]. To transform those models into a db-net, it is sufficient to realize a control layer that simulates the application of condition-action rules. The translation of a db-net into those models, instead, is more convoluted, but can be attacked by leveraging the technique introduced in [29] to encode ν-PNs into DCDSs, with the only difference that while the transformation from ν-PNs into DCDSs requires the introduction of binary relations for places (keeping track of token ids and their pure names), in the case of db-nets the arity of place relations depend on the place colors.

Since DCDSs and DMSs are expressively equivalent to the richest models for business artifacts, such a correspondence paves the way towards the study of CPN-based business artifacts, making approaches like that of [27] data-aware. We also stress that db-nets go beyond the aforementioned approaches, since they conceptually componentize the different aspects of a dynamic system, giving first-class citizenships to relations, constraints, queries, database access points in the process, database updates triggered by the process, external inputs, and so on. This creates the basis for studying db-nets from the conceptual and methodological point of view, and exploit them to formalize concrete process-aware information systems like Bizagi, Bonita, and Camunda, in the style of [17].

5.2 Formal Verification

Formal verification of db-nets is obviously of utmost importance. As usual, verification may range from the analysis of fundamental properties such as *reachability*, to model checking temporal logics.

In the case of data-aware dynamic systems, such formal properties have also to incorporate a "first-order" component, consequently allowing one to inspect the data present in the system, and express properties about the (un)desired evolutions of such data [11, 29]. We consider here a very pristine form of reachability, namely *reachability of a nonempty place*. Formally, this decision problem is defined as follows:

Input: A db-net $\mathcal{B}$, an initial $\mathcal{B}$-snapshot s_0, and a control place p from $\mathcal{B}$
Question: starting from s_0, is it possible to reach a $\mathcal{B}$-snapshot where p has at least one token? Formally, given the LTS $\Gamma_{s_0}^{\mathcal{B}} = \langle S, s_0, \rightarrow \rangle$, does there exist a finite sequence of $\mathcal{B}$-snapshots of the form $s_0 \rightarrow \ldots \rightarrow s_n = \langle \mathcal{I}_n, m_n \rangle$, such that $|m_n(p)| \geq 1$?

We show next that, as expected, db-nets are Turing-powerful even when the different layers are severely restricted, basic verification tasks such as reachability of a nonempty place remain undecidable.

Theorem 1. *Reachability of a nonempty place is undecidable:*

1. *for db-nets whose control layer only employs unary, string types, and whose data logic and persistence layers are empty;*
2. *for db-nets whose control layer consists of a state machine, and whose persistence layer contains only two unary relations.*

Proof (sketch). The first case corresponds to reachability in ν-PNs, which is undecidable [32]. The second case can be proved by reducing into the state reachability problem for deterministic two-counter automata. In fact, it is sufficient to show how to simulate an increment transition and a conditional decrement transition of a two-counter automaton. Figure 5 shows two fragments of a db-net whose control layer is a simple state machine, respectively simulating increment and conditional decrement transitions for a counter. We assume that the underlying persistence layer contains two initially empty unary relations C_1 and C_2 of type **string**. The size of such relations (i.e., the number of string values they contain) simulates the value of the two corresponding counters. In this light, incrementing the first counter amounts to inserting a fresh string into C_1; this is done by the action INSERT1. As for conditional decrement, we proceed as follows. We create two view places for the first counter. The first view place is called *NonEmptyC$_1$* and used to retrieve the values contained in relation C_1. If there is at least one such value, it means that the counter is positive. The second view place, called *EmptyC$_1$*, is a boolean view place associated to a query that tests whether relation C_1 does not contain any value. So, if there is a token in such a view place, it means that the first counter is zero. The conditional decrement transition is then easily realized by choosing which transition to take depending on the content of such view places. In the case of decrement, one value from C_1 is nondeterministically picked and passed as parameter to the REMOVE1 action, which removes it from C_1. This two fragments are simply replicated to handle increment and conditional decrement using relation C_2.   □

To contrast this undecidability proof, we consider the case where the "size" of information maintained by the control layer and the persistence layer is suitably controlled.

Definition 28. Let $\mathcal{B}$ be a db-net, s_0 a $\mathcal{B}$-snapshot, and $\Gamma_{s_0}^{\mathcal{B}} = \langle S, s_0, \rightarrow \rangle$ the corresponding LTS. We say that $\mathcal{B}$ is *bounded w.r.t.* s_0 if

- $\mathcal{B}$ is *width-bounded*, i.e., there exists $b_1 \in \mathbb{N}$ such that for every $\mathcal{B}$-snapshot $\langle \mathcal{I}, m \rangle$ reachable from s_0 through $\rightarrow$, the number of distinct values assigned by m to the places of $\mathcal{B}$ is bounded by b_1:
- $\mathcal{B}$ is *depth-bounded*, i.e., there exists $b_2 \in \mathbb{N}$ such that for every $\mathcal{B}$-snapshot $\langle \mathcal{I}, m \rangle$ reachable from s_0 through $\rightarrow$, the number of tokens (possibly with the same values) assigned by m to the places of $\mathcal{B}$ is bounded by b_2.
- $\mathcal{B}$ is *state-bounded*, i.e., there exists $b_3 \in \mathbb{N}$ such that for every $\mathcal{B}$-snapshot $\langle \mathcal{I}, m \rangle$ reachable from s_0 through $\rightarrow$, we have $|\bigcup_{\mathcal{D} \in \mathfrak{D}} Adom_{\mathcal{D}}(\mathcal{I})| \leq b_3$.   □

The first two conditions lift the two notions of boundedness introduced in [32] to the case of db-nets, while the third one is borrowed from the notion of state-boundedness in DCDSs [9]. Notice that a bounded $\mathcal{B}$ may still give raise to an infinite-state LTS, due to the insertion of fresh values into the boundedly many information slots available, and the fact that no restriction is imposed on the size of the type domains, from which external inputs are borrowed. In spite of this infinity, we are able to prove the following key result.

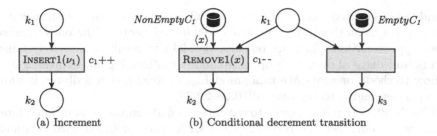

(a) Increment   (b) Conditional decrement transition

Fig. 5. Simulation of an increment and conditional decrement transition of a two-counter machine using db-nets

Theorem 2. *Reachability of a nonempty place is decidable for bounded db-nets using* **string** *and* **real** *types.*

Proof (sketch). The proof is obtained by reconstructing, step-by-step, the translation technique proposed in [29], which encodes a ν-PN into a corresponding DCDS [9]. On the one hand, the translation has to be generalized to the case of tokens carrying tuples of data, and on the other hand, it has to merge the DCDS resulting from the translation, with the one natively provided by the data logic layer of the db-net of interest. In [29], it is shown that the translation does not only preserve the execution semantics of the original net, but also guarantees that if the input ν-PN is width- and depth-bounded, then the corresponding DCDS is state-bounded. This holds also in our setting, and consequently we inherit the decidability result for model checking first-order μ-calculus properties as considered in [29], which are clearly able to express reachability properties. Finally, the case of reals is handled as shown in [13], extending the abstraction technique of [9,29] so as to deal with dense orders.   □

Interestingly, decidability holds not only for reachability, but also for the variant of first-order μ-calculus considered in [29], thus allowing one to check data-aware soundness [29] over db-nets. In addition, we conjecture that decidability can be strengthened to the case where the db-net of interest is width- and state-bounded, but not depth-bounded (the first two notions being essential towards decidability, as a consequence of Theorem 1).

Such initial undecidability and decidability results pave the way towards a refine analysis of the boundaries of decidability for the formal analysis of db-nets, taking advantage from the fact that the different sources of complexity are clearly separated in our model. For example, decidability could be studied by restricting the query language used in the data logic layer, or by leveraging recent dychotomic results on the analysis of data-aware extensions of Petri nets with ordered vs. unordered data types, and in presence or absence of (globally) fresh inputs, which are intimately connected to the boundaries of decidability for reachability [25]. In this light, it is important to notice that the technique mentioned in the proof sketch of Theorem 2 cannot be lifted to the case of integers, for which reachability turns out to be undecidable when the db-net is bounded (as a consequence of the undecidability result for orders with successor shown in [13]). Another interesting line could be to leverage techniques based on under-approximations [5]. Since our first decidability result is intimately linked with boundedness of db-nets, it opens up another interesting line of investigation on how to check, or guarantee using modeling strategies, that a db-net is state-bounded, leveraging recent results [10,28,29,32].

Finally, db-nets pave the way towards the formal analysis of additional properties, which only become relevant when CPNs are combined with relational databases. We mention in particular two families of properties. The first is related to *rollbacks*, so as to check whether it is always (or never) the case that a transition induces a failing action. The second is related to the *true concurrency* present in a db-net, which may contain transitions that appear to be concurrent by considering the control layer in isolation, but have instead to be sequenced due to the interplay with the persistence layer (and its constraints).

6   Conclusion

We have introduced a formal model for data-aware business processes that, for the first time, combines an approach based on colored Petri nets with the standard relational model and transactional updates over it. We hope that db-nets will attract attention of researchers interested in the formal analysis of data-aware dynamic systems, as well as that of those interested in providing strong foundations for process-aware information systems and their concrete languages. We close by mentioning a further area of research that we consider of particular relevance for the database community. Since the control layer of db-nets is grounded on CPNs, all simulation techniques developed for CPNs can be seamlessly lifted to our setting. The result of a db-net simulation produces, as a by-product, a final database instance, populated through the execution of the control layer. The so-obtained database instance implicitly reflects the footprint of the control layer, which inserts data as the result of the execution of a process. This makes the obtained database instance much more intriguing than one synthetically generated without considering how data are produced over time. In this light, simulation of db-nets has the potential of providing novel insights into the problem of data benchmarking [24], especially in the context of data preparation for process mining [2,14].

Acknowledgements. This research has been partially supported by the Euregio IPN12 *"KAOS: Knowledge-Aware Operational Support"* project, which is funded by the "European Region Tyrol-South Tyrol-Trentino" (EGTC) under the first call for basic research projects, and by the UNIBZ internal project *"KENDO (Knowledge-driven ENterprise Distributed cOmputing)"*.

References

1. Aalst, W.M.P.: Verification of workflow nets. In: Azéma, P., Balbo, G. (eds.) ICATPN 1997. LNCS, vol. 1248, pp. 407–426. Springer, Heidelberg (1997). doi:10.1007/3-540-63139-9_48

2. Aalst, W.M.P.: Process cubes: slicing, dicing, rolling up and drilling down event data for process mining. In: Song, M., Wynn, M.T., Liu, J. (eds.) AP-BPM 2013. LNBIP, vol. 159, pp. 1–22. Springer, Cham (2013). doi:10.1007/978-3-319-02922-1_1

3. van der Aalst, W.M.P., Stahl, C.: Modeling Business Processes - A Petri Net-Oriented Approach. Cooperative Information Systems series. MIT Press, Cambridge (2011)

4. van der Aalst, W.M.P., Weske, M., Grünbauer, D.: Case handling: a new paradigm for business process support. Data Knowl. Eng. **53**(2), 129–162 (2005)

5. Abdulla, P.A., Aiswarya, C., Atig, M.F., Montali, M., Rezine, O.: Recency-bounded verification of dynamic database-driven systems. In: Proceedings of PODS. ACM Press (2016)

6. Abiteboul, S., Hull, R., Vianu, V.: Foundations of Databases. Addison Wesley, Redwood City (1995)

7. Abiteboul, S., Segoufin, L., Vianu, V.: Static analysis of active XML systems. ACM Trans. Database Syst. **34**(4), 23 (2009)

8. Badouel, E., Hélouët, L., Morvan, C.: Petri nets with semi-structured data. In: Proceedings of PN, LNCS. Springer (2015)

9. Bagheri Hariri, B., Calvanese, D., De Giacomo, G., Deutsch, A., Montali, M.: Verification of relational data-centric dynamic systems with external services. In: Proceedings of PODS, pp. 163–174. ACM (2013)

10. Bagheri Hariri, B., Calvanese, D., Deutsch, A., Montali, M.: State boundedness in data-aware dynamic systems. In: Proceedings of KR (2014)

11. Calvanese, D., De Giacomo, G., Montali, M.: Foundations of data aware process analysis: a database theory perspective. In: Proceedings of PODS (2013)

12. Calvanese, D., Giacomo, G., Montali, M., Patrizi, F.: Verification and synthesis in description logic based dynamic systems. In: Faber, W., Lembo, D. (eds.) RR 2013. LNCS, vol. 7994, pp. 50–64. Springer, Heidelberg (2013). doi:10.1007/978-3-642-39666-3_5

13. Calvanese, D., Delzanno, G., Montali, M.: Verification of relational multiagent systems with data types. In: Proceedings of AAAI (2015)

14. Calvanese, D., Montali, M., Syamsiyah, A., Aalst, W.M.P.: Ontology-driven extraction of event logs from relational databases. In: Reichert, M., Reijers, H.A. (eds.) BPM 2015. LNBIP, vol. 256, pp. 140–153. Springer, Cham (2016). doi:10.1007/978-3-319-42887-1_12

15. Cohn, D., Hull, R.: Business artifacts: a data-centric approach to modeling business operations and processes. IEEE Data Eng. Bull. **32**(3), 3–9 (2009)

16. Damaggio, E., Hull, R., Vaculín, R.: On the equivalence of incremental and fixpoint semantics for business artifacts with guard-stage-milestone lifecycles. Inf. Syst. **38**(4), 561–584 (2013)

17. De Masellis, R., Di Francescomarino, C., Ghidini, C., Montali, M., Tessaris, S.: Add data into business process verification: bridging the gap between theory and practice. In: Singh, S.P., Markovitch, S. (eds.) Proceedings of AAAI, pp. 1091–1099 (2017)

18. Deutsch, A., Hull, R., Patrizi, F., Vianu, V.: Automatic verification of data-centric business processes. In: Proceedings of ICDT, pp. 252–267 (2009)

19. Dumas, M.: On the convergence of data and process engineering. In: Eder, J., Bielikova, M., Tjoa, A.M. (eds.) ADBIS 2011. LNCS, vol. 6909, pp. 19–26. Springer, Heidelberg (2011). doi:10.1007/978-3-642-23737-9_2

20. Hidders, J., Kwasnikowska, N., Sroka, J., Tyszkiewicz, J., Van den Bussche, J.: Dfl: a dataflow language based on petri nets and nested relational calculus. Inf. Syst. **33**(3), 261–284 (2008)
21. Hull, R.: Artifact-centric business process models: brief survey of research results and challenges. In: Proceedings of ODBASE, pp. 1152–1163 (2008)
22. Jensen, K., Kristensen, L.M.: Coloured Petri Nets - Modelling and Validation of Concurrent Systems. Springer, Heidelberg (2009). doi:10.1007/b95112
23. Künzle, V., Weber, B., Reichert, M.: Object-aware business processes: fundamental requirements and their support in existing approaches. Int. J. Inf. Syst. Model. Des. **2**(2), 19–46 (2011)
24. Lanti, D., Rezk, M., Xiao, G., Calvanese, D.: The NPD benchmark: Reality check for OBDA systems. In: Proceedings of EDBT, pp. 617–628 (2015). OpenProceedings.org
25. Lasota, S.: Decidability border for petri nets with data: WQO dichotomy conjecture. In: Kordon, F., Moldt, D. (eds.) PETRI NETS 2016. LNCS, vol. 9698, pp. 20–36. Springer, Cham (2016). doi:10.1007/978-3-319-39086-4_3
26. Libkin, L.: Elements of Finite Model Theory, LNCS, vol. 7360, chap. Fixed Point Logics and Complexity Classes. Springer (2004)
27. Lohmann, N.: Compliance by design for artifact-centric business processes. Inf. Syst. **38**(4), 606–618 (2013)
28. Montali, M., Calvanese, D.: Soundness of data-aware, case-centric processes. Int. J. Software Tools Technol. Transf. **18**, 535–558 (2016)
29. Montali, M., Rivkin, A.: Model checking petri nets with names using data-centric dynamic systems. Formal Aspects Comput. **28**(4), 615–641 (2016)
30. Reichert, M.: Process and data: two sides of the same coin? In: Meersman, R., Panetto, H., Dillon, T., Rinderle-Ma, S., Dadam, P., Zhou, X., Pearson, S., Ferscha, A., Bergamaschi, S., Cruz, I.F. (eds.) OTM 2012. LNCS, vol. 7565, pp. 2–19. Springer, Heidelberg (2012). doi:10.1007/978-3-642-33606-5_2
31. Richardson, C.: Warning: don't assume your business processes use master data. In: Hull, R., Mendling, J., Tai, S. (eds.) BPM 2010. LNCS, vol. 6336, pp. 11–12. Springer, Heidelberg (2010). doi:10.1007/978-3-642-15618-2_3
32. Rosa-Velardo, F., de Frutos-Escrig, D.: Decidability and complexity of petri nets with unordered data. Theor. Comput. Sci. **412**(34), 4439–4451 (2011)
33. Russell, N., Hofstede, A.H.M., Edmond, D., der Aalst, W.M.P.: Workflow data patterns: identification, representation and tool support. In: Delcambre, L., Kop, C., Mayr, H.C., Mylopoulos, J., Pastor, O. (eds.) ER 2005. LNCS, vol. 3716, pp. 353–368. Springer, Heidelberg (2005). doi:10.1007/11568322_23
34. Triebel, M., Sürmeli, J.: Homogeneous equations of algebraic petri nets. In: Proceedings of CONCUR, pp. 1–14. LNCS, Springer (2016)
35. Vianu, V.: Automatic verification of database-driven systems: a new frontier. In: Proceedings of ICDT, pp. 1–13 (2009)

Transition Systems Reduction:
Balancing Between Precision and Simplicity

Sergey A. Shershakov[✉], Anna A. Kalenkova, and Irina A. Lomazova

National Research University Higher School of Economics,
20 Myasnitskaya Street, 101000 Moscow, Russia
sshershakov@hse.ru
http://pais.hse.ru

Abstract. Transition systems are a powerful formalism, which is widely used for process model representation. A number of approaches were proposed in the process mining field to tackle the problem of constructing transition systems from event logs. Existing approaches discover transition systems that are either too large or too small. In this paper we propose an original approach to discover transition systems that perfectly fit event logs and whose size is adjustable depending on the user's need. The proposed approach allows the ability to achieve a required balance between simple and precise models.

Keywords: Transition systems · Process mining · Model reduction · Process model quality

1 Introduction

Process mining is a relatively new discipline, whose basic research and practical purpose is to extract process models from data given in the form of *event logs*, checking existing models for conforming to actual processes and improving them. *Transition systems* are extensively used to formalize processes extracted from event logs. A transition system can be constructed from an event log by using prefix-based techniques in a very natural way [3]. We consider several metrics that describe the model's quality [11]. Replay fitness quantifies the extent to which a process model can reproduce the behavior recorded in a log. Complexity of the model is estimated by simplicity and precision (the *metrics*, which shows how precise the model is in respect to the event log).

The major weakness of models constructed from real-life event logs is their size. Despite the fact that there are a number of approaches aimed to reduce the size of transition systems [3], application of the existing approaches results in either too large or too small models. In the former case the model size is too

This work is supported by the Basic Research Program at the National Research University Higher School of Economics in 2017 and the study was funded by RFBR and Moscow city Government according to the research project No. 15-37-70008 "mol_a_mos".

M. Koutny et al. (Eds.): ToPNoC XII, LNCS 10470, pp. 119–139, 2017.
DOI: 10.1007/978-3-662-55862-1_6

big to be readable. Beyond this point, it becomes difficult or even impossible to apply existing transition system analysis techniques that are sensitive to the size of input models. Despite the fact that there are polynomial synthesis algorithms for some classes of Petri nets, such as elementary nets [6], in general, the problem of synthesizing Petri nets is NP-complete [7]. Thus, the applicability of the state-based regions algorithm [12] is limited to fairly small models. In the latter case, due to states merging, a rather small model facilitates too much behavior that cannot be observed in the log, which makes the model less precise and thus less applicable.

A problem of a significant impact of the size of a transition system on the execution time of the regions algorithm was examined in detail in a number of papers, for example in [17,18]. Despite the fact that in this paper we do not immediately consider the task of synthesizing Petri nets from transition systems, such a task, however, is meant to be the final goal of this research. This paper is positioned as an intermediate step, which focuses precisely on the reduction of transition systems.

Several approaches for the reduction of transition systems were proposed previously. In this paper, we present an original reduction approach based on the frequency characteristics of traces. Unlike in the previous studies, efficiency of the proposed method is not estimated on the basis of the execution time of algorithms, but based on quality metrics obtained during the reduction. To this end, for calculating quality metrics of transition systems we propose new algorithms that have not previously been described.

The main goal of our study is to develop an approach for reducing the size of a transition system mined from an event log in a flexible manner. This paper describes an original 3-step algorithm achieving the goal by using a variable-size window based on a state frequency characteristic. The approach preserves the (perfect) fitness of a model and balances between its simplicity and precision by introducing a set of adjustable parameters.

Thus, the *main contributions* are as follows: (1) an original method for reducing transition systems and justification of its applicability; (2) a set of experimental results which show the advantages of the proposed approach as compared with existing methods; an openly available proof of the concept through implementation in a set of ProM plug-ins.

The remaining part of the paper is organized as follows. Section 2 gives an overview of related work in the context of inferring transition systems and their application in the process mining domain. Section 3 introduces basic concepts used further in this paper. A detailed description of the proposed algorithm is given in Sect. 4. A novel precision calculation algorithm, some significant implementation details, and experimental results are discussed in Sect. 5. Finally, Sect. 6 concludes the paper and discusses some directions for future work.

2   Related Work

A number of works concerning inferring transition systems from event traces exist. Biermann and Feldman in their work [10] proposed a k-tails algorithm which merges states of FSMs by basing on the similarity of behavior of the states. The algorithm falls into the class of prefix tree merging methods. Angluin [5] proposed a method of prefix tree states merging based on a notion of k-reversibility. In [15], Lorenzoli et al. proposed a GK-tail approach, an extension of the k-tail algorithm, dealing with parametrized finite state automata.

Cook and Wolf in their work [13] introduced *process discovery*, a new data analysis technique in the context of software engineering processes. They considered automatic generation of a formal model describing an ongoing process from captured event data. A new Markov method was developed specifically for this purpose. Moreover, two existing methods, the k-tail and RNet (based on neural networks) ones, were adopted for the process discovery technique.

Process discovery along with *conformance checking* and *process enhancement* form the basis of *process mining* [4], which deals with various types of process models including Petri nets, transition systems, fuzzy maps, C-nets, BPMN and others. In the context of process mining, transition systems are considered both a self-independent model and an intermediate model for building another type of model on this basis. In the latter case, one should mention region-based approaches discussed in [8,12,14,18].

The leading role of a transition system as an intermediate representation of a process is discussed in [3]. The paper considers a number of different strategies to construct a transition system that is more suitable to be a base for a resulting final Petri net model with respect to desirable metrics. Nevertheless, all discussed strategies are based on inferring algorithms with a fixed window.

Besides the strategies above, a number of other approaches for the transition system reduction were proposed. Most of them are based on merging of related states. In [17] authors consider an abstraction technique named *common final marking* (CFM). The technique involves merging all states without outgoing arcs (so-called *sink states*) into a single state.

In [18] authors propose an approach for compacting a transition system based on aggressive folding techniques. The proposed technique allows state space reduction through the detection of unfolded cycles in an acyclic transition system and its subsequent folding. Distinctive features of our approach are discussed in Sect. 5.3.

Another approach for the process discovery involves language-based methods which are applied directly to logs without constructing intermediate models [9, 20]. We do not consider these methods here.

3 Preliminaries

This section introduces basic concepts related to event logs, transition systems and some other notations that are needed for explaining the approach.

$\mathcal{B}(X)$ is the set of all multisets over some set X. For some multiset $b \in \mathcal{B}(X)$, $b(x)$ denotes the number of times element $x \in X$ appears in b. Thus, $x \in b$ iff $b(x) > 0$. By $b = [x_1, x_2^3, x_3^5]$ we denote that elements $x_1, x_2, x_3 \in X$ appear in b one, three and five times respectively. We say that $b' \subseteq b$ iff $\forall x \in X : b'(x) \leq b(x)$.

The size of a multiset b over set X is denoted by $|b|$ and defined as $|b| = \sum\limits_{x \in X} b(x)$.
For a given set Y, Y^+ is the set of all non-empty finite sequences over Y.

Definition 1 (Trace, Event Log). *Let A be a set of activities. A trace is a finite sequence $\sigma = \langle a_1, a_2, ..., a_i, ..., a_n \rangle \in A^+$. By $\sigma(i) = a_i$ we denote i-th element of the trace. The $[i, k]$-subtrace of trace σ ended at the i-th activity a_i is defined as*

$$\sigma[i, k] = \begin{cases} \langle \sigma(1), \sigma(2), ..., \sigma(i) \rangle, & if \ k > i; \\ \langle \sigma(i - k + 1), ..., \sigma(i) \rangle, & if \ 1 \leq k \leq i; \\ \langle \rangle, & if \ k = 0. \end{cases} \tag{1}$$

The complete subtrace of the trace σ ended at i-th event a_i is $\sigma[i] = \sigma[i, i]$. By $|\sigma|$ we denote trace length. For $k \leq i$, k denotes the length of the subtrace. $L \in \mathcal{B}(A^+)$, such that $|L| > 0$, is an event log. Here, $|L|$ is the number of all traces.

We assume, that event logs do not contain process states explicitly. This way, we need to deduce the desirable states from an event log based on some approach.

In [3], four approaches to determine the state in a log were proposed. They are *past, future, past and future* and *explicit knowledge*. In this paper we consider only the *past* approach, according to which a state is constructed based on the *prefix* of a trace. Then, the order of activities is important. Hence, we apply sequence policy [3] for determining a state.

Definition 2. *A labeled transition system is a tuple $TS = (S, E, T, s_0, AS)$, where S is a finite state space, E is a finite set of labels, $T \subseteq S \times E \times S$ is a set of transitions, $s_0 \in S$ is an initial state, and $AS \subseteq S$ is a set of accepting (final) states. We denote the set of output (input) transitions of a state $s \in S$ as $s\bullet = \{t = (s, e, s') \in T \mid e \in E, s' \in S\}$ ($\bullet s = \{t = (s', e, s) \in T \mid e \in E, s' \in S\}$).*

By $TS(L) = (S, E, T, s_0, AS)$, where $L \in \mathcal{B}(A^+)$ is an event log, we denote a transition system, such that $E = A$.

Let $\sigma = \langle a_1, ..., a_n \rangle$ be a trace ($\sigma \in L$) and $n = |\sigma|$. We say that trace σ can be *replayed* in the transition system $TS(L)$ if there is a sequence of states $\langle s_0, ..., s_n \rangle$ such that $\exists t_1 = (s_0, a_1, s_1), t_2 = (s_1, a_2, s_2), ..., t_n = (s_{n-1}, a_n, s_n)$, where $s_0, s_1, ..., s_n \in S, t_1, t_2, ..., t_n \in T$. We denote this as $s_0 \xrightarrow{a_1} s_1 \xrightarrow{a_2} ... \xrightarrow{a_n} s_n$. We say that trace σ can be *partially replayed* by its prefix in a transition system $TS(L)$ if $\exists k < n : s_0 \xrightarrow{a_1} s_1 \xrightarrow{a_2} ... \xrightarrow{a_k} s_k$ and $\nexists s_k \xrightarrow{a_{k+1}} s_{k+1} \xrightarrow{a_{k+2}} ... \xrightarrow{a_n} s_n$. We denote $\sigma^+(TS(L)) = \langle a_0, a_1, ..., a_k \rangle$ and $\sigma^-(TS(L)) = \langle a_{k+1}, ..., a_n \rangle$. Hence, $\sigma(TS(L)) = \sigma^+(TS(L)) + \sigma^-(TS(L))$ where $+$ denotes concatenation of two sequences.

Definition 3 (k-window transition system). *Let $L \in \mathcal{B}(A^+)$ be a log over set of activities A and let $k \in \mathbb{N}$ be a natural number called* window size. *$TS(L) = (S, E, T, s_0, AS)$ is a k-window (labeled) transition system built for log L and window size k, where $S = \{\sigma[i, k] \mid \sigma \in L, 0 \leq i \leq |\sigma|, k \leq i\}$, $s_0 = \sigma[0]^1$, $T = \{(\sigma[i-1, k], \sigma(i), \sigma[i, k]) \mid \sigma \in L, 1 \leq i \leq |\sigma|\}$, $AS = \{s \in S \mid s = \sigma[|\sigma|, k], \sigma \in L\}$.*

Definition 4 (Full transition system). *Let $L \in \mathcal{B}(A^+)$ be a log over set A of activities. The* full transition system *$TS(L) = (S, E, T, s_0, AS)$ for log L is a labeled transition system built for log L, where $S = \{\sigma[i] \mid \sigma \in L, 0 \leq i \leq |\sigma|\}$, $s_0 = \sigma[0]$, $T = \{(\sigma[i-1], \sigma(i), \sigma[i]) \mid \sigma \in L, 1 \leq i \leq |\sigma|\}$, $AS = \{s \in S \mid s = \sigma[|\sigma|], \sigma \in L\}$.*

To measure the quality of transition systems we consider three quality metrics. We based them primarily on the work [11], where metric definitions are given for *process trees*. In this paper we adopted them for *transition systems*. *Fitness* quantifies the extent to which a transition system can reproduce traces recorded in a log. *Simplicity* quantifies the complexity of a model. Simplicity is measured by comparing the size of a given transition system $TS(L)$ with the simplest possible transition system, which is the flower model (Fig. 1a). *Precision* compares the transition system $TS(L)$ with the full transition system built for log L, considering the latter to be the most precise. Such a comparison is done through a *simulation* of the full transition system by $TS(L)$ (for further details see Sect. 5.1).

Definition 5 (Metrics). *Let L be an event log and let $TS(L) = (S, E, T, s_0, AS)$ be a transition system built for L. Fitness is defined to be the ratio of the number of traces from log L that can be fully replayed in transition system $TS(L)$ to the total number of all traces. Log L perfectly fits transition system $TS(L)$ iff all traces of L can be fully replayed in $TS(L)$.*
Simplicity *of $TS(L)$ is:*

$$Simpl(TS(L)) = \frac{|E| + 1}{|T| + |S|}.$$

Precision *of $TS(L)$ is:*

$$Prec(TS(L)) = \frac{1}{|S|} \cdot \sum_{s \in S} Prec(s), \quad Prec(s) = \frac{1}{NoV(s)} \cdot \sum_{i=1}^{NoV(s)} \frac{|s \bullet| - |\widehat{s \bullet}_i|}{|s \bullet|},$$

where $Prec(s)$ is a partial precision for a state s, $NoV(s)$ is a number of all visits of state s during a simulation of the reference full transition system by $TS(L)$. $\widehat{s \bullet}_i$ is a set of such output transitions of state s that cannot be activated ("fired") during the i-th visit of state s. These transitions do not have active counterparts in the reference full transition system.

---

[1] Note, that $s_0 \in S$, since event log L contains at least one trace by Definition 1.

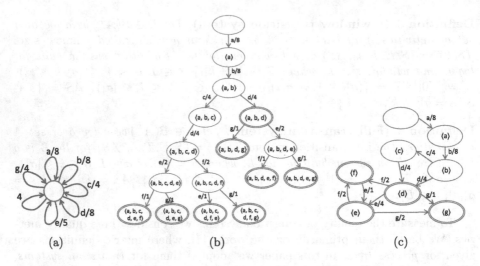

Fig. 1. (a) "Flower" model for log L_1; (b) $TS_1(L_1)$ built for log L_1; (c) transition system built for log L_1 with a fixed window of size 1. In the figures, each transition is labeled by an activity and its corresponding frequency characteristic (see. Definition 6)

4 Algorithm Description

For the clarification of the approach, the following motivating example is considered. Let L_1 be an event log that is defined as follows:

$$L_1 = [\langle a, b, c, d, e, f\rangle, \langle a, b, c, d, e, g\rangle, \langle a, b, c, d, f, e\rangle, \langle a, b, c, d, f, g\rangle, \qquad (2)$$
$$\langle a, b, d\rangle, \langle a, b, d, g\rangle, \langle a, b, d, e, f\rangle, \langle a, b, d, e, g\rangle]$$

In addition to the previously discussed flower model, one can build a number of other models that perfectly fit log L_1. A model built with unlimited window size is depicted in Fig. 1b. This model is a *full transition system* by the definition. Another model built by an algorithm with a fixed window of size 1 is depicted in Fig. 1c. Although all these models perfectly fit log L_1, none of them is satisfactory in simplicity and precision at the same time. Thus, we are interested in a trade off between these metrics.

The proposed approach incorporates a 3-steps algorithm sequentially building 3 transition systems. The first transition system, TS_1, is built from an event log. The second (TS_2) and the third (TS_3) transition systems are built from TS_1 and TS_2, respectively. Finally, TS_3 is considered as a desirable result.

The main point of the proposed approach is dynamic variation of the window used for deducing states. For this very purpose, two adjustable parameters are involved in the approach. The first one, *Threshold*, affects the size of the intermediate transition system (TS_2). The second one, *Vwsc*, is a linear factor used for the dynamic calculation of a variable window size while building the resulting model (TS_3). Each step of the algorithm along with both parameters is thoroughly discussed in the following sections.

4.1   Constructing a Full Transition System (Step 1)

The first step of the approach is to construct a full transition system and define a special labeling function mapping every transition to a natural number that determines its *frequency characteristic*.

Definition 6 (Frequency characteristic). *Let $L \in \mathcal{B}(A^+)$ be a log over set of activities A and let $TS(L) = (S, E, T, s_0, AS)$ be the full transition system for L. The frequency characteristic of $TS(L)$ is a function $f : T \to \mathbb{N}$ defined for $t = (\sigma[j-1], \sigma(j), \sigma[j])$ as $f(t) = |L'|$, where L' is the maximum multiset over A^*, such that $L' \subseteq L$ and $\forall \sigma' \in L'$ $\sigma'[j] = \sigma[j]$.*

Frequency characteristic determines for every transition t a number of traces in log L that start with prefixes $\sigma[j]$. The entire procedure of building a full transition system is presented in Algorithm 1.

From now on, we denote the full transition system for a given log L as $TS_1(L)$.

$TS_1(L_1)$ built for log L_1 with function f is depicted in Fig. 1b; it is a tree by construction. It is easy to see that fitness of the full transition system ($TS_1(L)$) is perfect (equals 1). This is inherent in the algorithm, since it builds for each trace in, a log a full chain of states following one after another, that corresponds to a sequence of activities in the trace.

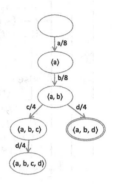

Fig. 2. $TS_2(L_1)$ (condensed) built from $TS_1(L_1)$ with $Threshold = 0.33$

4.2   Constructing a Condensed Transition System (Step 2)

The second step of our approach involves cutting some branches of the full transition system with frequency values which are less than a *cutting threshold* parameter. We refer to it as f_1. Once f_1 is set, all the states and transitions corresponding to a rarely observed behavior in the event log can be removed from the model. This results in simplifying the tree structure and reduction of the number of states and transitions.

Definition 7 (Condensed Transition System). *Let $TS_1(L) = (S_1, E_1, T_1, s_0, AS_1)$ be a full transition system constructed for log L and let f be a frequency characteristic. The Threshold is a real number from $[0; 1]$ determining a cutting threshold f_1 as follows: $f_1 = round(|L| \cdot Threshold) - 1$. The value $f_1 + 1 = round(|L| \cdot Threshold)$ is a minimum preserved frequency for $TS_1(L)$.*

A condensed transition system $TS_2(L)$ built for a $TS_1(L)$ with function f and a given cutting threshold f_1 is the transition system $TS_2(L) = (S_2, E_2, T_2, s_0, AS_2)$, where $S_2 \subseteq S_1$, $E_2 = E_1$, $T_2 \subseteq T_1$, $AS_2 \subseteq AS_1$ and $T_2 = \{t \mid t \in T_1 \wedge f(t) > f_1\}$, $S_2 = \{s_0\} \cup \{s \mid s \in S_1 \wedge \exists t = (s', a, s) \in T_2\}$, $AS_2 = AS_1 \cap S_2$.

Algorithm 1. Building a full transition system for a given log L	**Algorithm 2.** Building a condensed transition system $TS_2(L)$
Input : an event log L **Output** : a full transition system; $TS_1(L) = (S, E, T, s_0, AS)$; f is a frequency characteristic; **begin** $\quad S \leftarrow \{s_0\}$; $\quad$ **for** $\sigma \in L$ **do** $\quad\quad s \leftarrow s_0$; $\quad\quad$ **for** $i \leftarrow 1$ **to** $|\sigma|$ **do** $\quad\quad\quad s' \leftarrow \sigma[i]$; $\quad\quad\quad t \leftarrow (s, \sigma(i), s')$; $\quad\quad\quad$ **if** $t \notin T$ **then** $\quad\quad\quad\quad T \leftarrow T \cup \{t\}$; $\quad\quad\quad\quad f(t) \leftarrow 1$; $\quad\quad\quad$ **else** $\quad\quad\quad\quad f(t) \leftarrow f(t) + 1$; $\quad\quad\quad S \leftarrow S \cup \{s'\}$; $\quad\quad\quad E \leftarrow E \cup \{\sigma(i)\}$; $\quad\quad\quad$ **if** $i = |\sigma|$ **then** $\quad\quad\quad\quad AS \leftarrow AS \cup \{s\}$; $\quad\quad\quad s \leftarrow s'$;	**Input** : an event log L; a full transition system $TS_1(L) = (S_1, E_1, T_1, s_0, AS_1)$; f is a frequency characteristic; $Threshold$ is a real number determining a cutting threshold and a minimum preserved frequency; **Output** : $TS_2(L) =$ $\quad\quad (S_2, E_2, T_2, s_0, AS_2)$ is a condensed transition system; **begin** $\quad f_1 = round(|L| \cdot Threshold) - 1$; $\quad$ **for** $t \in T_1$ **do** $\quad\quad$ **if** $f(t) > f_1$ **then** $\quad\quad\quad T_2 \leftarrow T_2 \cup \{t\}$; $\quad S_2 \leftarrow \{s_0\}$; $\quad$ **for** $t = (s, a, s') \in T_2$ **do** $\quad\quad S_2 \leftarrow S_2 \cup \{s'\}$; $\quad E_2 \leftarrow E_1$;

Note that the frequencies of transitions diminish on the way to the leaves of $TS_1(L)$ and $TS_2(L)$. Hence, the exclusion of transition t_k from $TS_1(L)$ implies the exclusion of a total subtree that has state s_k as a root. Thus, $TS_2(L)$ obtained as a result of cutting with a given threshold, cannot be disconnected.

The entire procedure of constructing a condensed transition system is presented in Algorithm 2. For log L_1 with the size $|L| = 8$ and $Threshold = 0.33$, we have $f_1 = 2$. A $TS_2(L)$ built for the log L_1 and $f_1 = 2$ is depicted in Fig. 2. It is easy to see that not all the traces from the log can be replayed on $TS_2(L)$ as its fitness is not perfect. Therefore, we cannot consider this model as a final result.

4.3 Constructing a Reduced Transition System (Step 3)

In this section, we propose an approach to convert $TS_2(L)$ to a model with perfect fitness and a size that is less than the size of $TS_1(L)$.

Our proposal is to construct a new transition system $TS_3(L) = (S_3, E_3, T_3, s_0, AS_3)$ based on $TS_2(L)$ by adding missing states and transitions in order to fully replay all the traces. Unlike building the full transition system, in this case we use partial subtrace $\sigma[i, k]$ for representing newly added states of $TS_3(L)$. The important point here is that parameter k, is proportional to the frequency of a corresponding input transition.

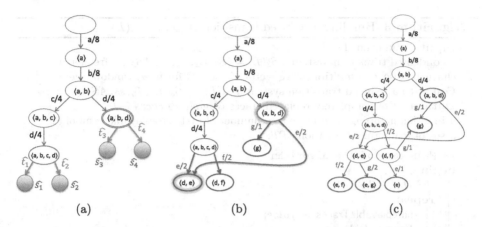

Fig. 3. (a) TS_3 under a restoring algorithm: temporary states and transitions after *the first stage*; (b) restored states and transitions after *the second stage* (c) $TS_3(L_1)$ (reduced) built from $TS_2(L_1)$ with *Threshold* = 0.33 for log L_1

The main part of the algorithm implementing the proposed approach is represented in Algorithm 3. In the beginning, we create a full copy of $TS_2(L)$, which is denoted as $TS_3(L)$. $TS_3(L)$ is a target transition system that is iteratively reconstructed by the following two stages of the algorithm.

At the *first stage*, implemented as function `ReplayTrace`, the algorithm tries to replay as many traces σ from event log L as possible. If all traces can be fully replayed, the algorithm successfully stops. Otherwise, if there is at least one trace that cannot be fully replayed, the *second stage* is performed. This stage is implemented as `RestateTS` procedure which tries to reconstruct the unreplayable parts of traces by adding new states and transitions to the target $TS_3(L)$.

The algorithm defines some auxiliary objects as follows. A special function ξ maps every trace σ onto number j that determines element $\sigma(j)$ splitting σ into σ^+ and σ^-, where $\sigma(j)$ is the first element of trace σ^-. A set TT of temporary transitions. A set of completely replayed traces $CompleteTraces \subseteq L$.

The stages of the algorithm are discussed below in more detail. For log L_1, we consider transition system $TS_3(L_1)$ copied from $TS_2(L_1)$ (Fig. 2). Then, the algorithm tries to replay log L_1 over $TS_3(L_1)$ and perform its transformation.

First stage (`ReplayTrace`). Let $\sigma = \langle a, b, c, d, e, f \rangle$. The longest prefix of σ that can be successfully replayed is $\sigma^+(TS_3(L_1)) = \langle a, b, c, d \rangle$. Correspondingly, the only suffix of σ that cannot be replayed is $\sigma^-(TS_3(L_1)) = \langle e, f \rangle$.

Algorithm 4 replays a single trace σ over transition system $TS_3(L)$ and also gets as its input a frequency characteristic f (discussed above). The algorithm starts with initial state s_0 as a current state s and the first element $\sigma(1)$ of a trace as a current element $\sigma(i)$. Then it tries to find an appropriate transition t starting with current state s and marked by symbol $\sigma(i)$.

Algorithm 3. Building a reduced transition system $TS_3(L)$

Input   : an event log L;
a condensed transition system $TS_2(L) = (S_2, E_2, T_2, s_0, AS_2)$; a frequency
characteristic f; a multiplicative factor $Vwsc \in \mathbb{R}$ for fixed window size;
Output : a reduced transition system $TS_3(L) = (S_3, E_3, T_3, s_0, AS_3)$;
Data: a set of completely replayed traces $CompleteTraces \subseteq L$;
a function mapping each trace to a number of first unreplayable symbol ξ;
a set of temporary transitions TT;

```
/* Main part of the algorithm                                      */
begin
    TS₃(L) ← TS₂(L);
    repeat
        unreplayableTraces ← false;
        for σ ∈ L do
            if ReplayTrace(σ, TS₃(L), f, CompleteTraces, ξ, TT) = false
            then
                unreplayableTraces ← true;

        if unreplayableTraces = true then
            RestateTS (L, TS₃(L), f, CompleteTraces, ξ, Vwsc, TT);

    until unreplayableTraces = false;
```

Figure 3 contains an example to illustrate the proposed approach. Next, there
are three possible cases. In the *first case* (for instance, during the replay $\sigma = \langle a, b, d \rangle$), transition $t = (s, \sigma(i), s')$ exists with some state $s' \in S_3$ and this is
a regular state ($t \notin TT$). In this case current state s is changed to s' and the
next element $\sigma(i + 1)$ is processed. In Fig. 3a, transition $t = (\langle a \rangle, b, \langle a, b \rangle)$ is an
example of such a case[2].

In the *second case* (if $\sigma = \langle a, b, d, g \rangle$), t does not exist. For that case a new
temporary transition $t = (s, \sigma(i), \widehat{s})$ is added to both the set of transitions T_3
and the set of temporary transitions TT. The end state $\widehat{s}$ is a special temporary
state, too. It is not marked by any substring and is unique for any temporary
transition. For the newly added transition t, the frequency characteristic f is
defined to be equal to 1; it means transition t "fired" only once. In Fig. 3a,
transition $t = \widehat{t_3} = (\langle a, b, d \rangle, g, \widehat{s_3})$ is an example of such a case.

In the *third case*, t exists and it is a temporary one ($t \in TT$). This is the case
when transition t "fires" one more time; hence, its frequency should be increased
by one.

In both the second and the third cases, replaying of the current trace σ is
broken and $\xi(\sigma)$ is set to the position of the first unreplayable element. This is
the reason why the temporary state $\widehat{s}$ cannot be marked with any subtrace by
this moment.

---

[2] To be precise, transition t is marked in the figure not only with activity b but also
with its frequency $b/8$.

Algorithm 4. Function ReplayTrace of the algorithm of building a reduced transition system $TS_3(L)$

Input : trace σ;
reduced transition system
$TS_3(L) = (S_3, E_3, T_3, s_0, AS_3)$;
frequency characteristic f; set of completely replayed traces $CompleteTraces \subseteq L$; function ξ mapping each trace to a number of the first unreplayable symbol ; set of temporary transitions TT;
Output : $true$, if a trace is replayed completely, $false$ otherwise

```
/* Replays a trace      */
Function ReplayTrace(σ,
  TS₃(L), f, CompleteTraces,
  ξ, TT): Boolean
  /* Already completed */
  if σ ∈ CompleteTraces
  then
    return true;
  s ← s₀;
  for i ← 1 to |σ| do
    if ∃s' : t =
      (s, σ(i), s') ∈ T₃ then
      if s' = ŝ then
        f(t) ← f(t) + 1;
        ξ(σ) = i;
        return false;
      s ← s';
    else
      S₃ ← S₃ ⋃ {ŝ};
      t ← (s, σ(i), ŝ);
      T₃ ← T₃ ⋃ {t};
      TT ← TT ⋃ {t};
      f(t) = 1;
      ξ(σ) = i;
      return false;
  /* Trace's complete  */
  ξ(σ) = |σ| + 1;
  return true;
```

Algorithm 5. Procedure RestateTS of the algorithm of building a reduced transition system $TS_3(L)$

Input : log L;
reduced transition system
$TS_3(L) = (S_3, E_3, T_3, s_0, AS_3)$; frequency characteristic f; set of completely replayed traces $CompleteTraces \subseteq L$; function ξ mapping each trace to a number of the first unreplayable symbol; multiplicative factor for fixed window size $Vwsc \in \mathbb{R}$; set of temporary transitions TT;

```
/* Converts temporaries      */
Procedure RestateTS(L, TS₃(L), f,
  CompleteTraces, ξ, Vwsc, TT)
  for σ ∈ L do
    i ← ξ(σ);
    /* If the trace is already
    complete                 */
    if i = |σ| + 1 then
      return ;
    s ← σ[i − 1];
    t ← (s, σ(i), ŝ);
    if t ∉ TT then
      return ;
    maxWndSize ← max(|σ|);
                  σ∈L
    wndSize ← round(maxWndSize ·
      f(t) · Vwsc ÷ |L|);
    /* a special 'trash' state */
    if wndSize = 0 then
      s' ← s₀ws;
    else
      s' ← σ[i, wndSize];
    t' ← (s, σ(i), s');
    /* Replace the temporary
    transition and the state by
    regular ones              */
    S₃ ← S₃ \ {ŝ} ∪ {s'};
    T₃ ← T₃ \ {t} ∪ {t'};
    TT ← TT \ {t};
    f(t') ← f(t);
    if i = |σ| then
      AS₃ ← AS₃ ∪ {s'};
  return ;
```

This way, at each iteration Algorithm 3 tries to replay as many traces from the log as possible. For each state the first unreplayable element is determined and a new temporary transition for the element, along with a temporary state, is built. $TS_3(L_1)$ with temporary transitions and states marked by symbols e, f, g and e are depicted in Fig. 3a. Note that the sum of the total frequencies for all temporary transitions is equal to the number of traces that could not be replayed in the first iteration.

Trace $\sigma_5 = \langle a, b, d \rangle$ from log L_1 is an example of a trace that can be replayed at the very first iteration. Once all the traces from the log can be replayed, the reconstruction of $TS_3(L)$ has successfully ended.

Second stage (RestateTS). As long as there is at least one temporary transition/state in $TS_3(L)$, it has to be converted to a regular one. This is done by Algorithm 5, which enumerates all uncompleted traces. For each such trace σ, the last regular state s, temporary transition t and temporary state $\widehat{s}$ are obtained; they correspond to the first unplayable element $\sigma(\xi(\sigma))$. Then state $\widehat{s}$ is converted to a regular state by being marked with subtrace $\sigma[\xi(\sigma), m]$ of trace σ ended by element $\sigma(\xi(\sigma))$ with length m that *is proportional to the frequency* of temporary transition t. In this way, such a state is marked with a *subtrace which is shorter* than that of the corresponding state in the full transition system. Note that temporary states and transitions are always converted to regular ones.

In Fig. 3b, transition $t = (\langle a, b, d \rangle, g, \langle g \rangle)$ is obtained from the former transition $\widehat{t_3}$. Unlike the original (full) transition system, the target state here is labeled by a shorter subtrace $\langle g \rangle$ instead of $\langle a, b, d, g \rangle$. It makes the state more "abstract" and facilitates the emergence of other states with the same label.

If a temporary state is marked with the same subtrace as one of the states existing in the model, both states are merged and the total number of states and transitions in the resulting transition system is decreased. Figure 3b shows how two states marked with subtrace $\langle d, e \rangle$ are merged to one state.

The frequency characteristic of some transitions can be relatively small for producing a window size equal to 0. In such situation the algorithm uses a dedicated state[3] s_{0ws}. This state accumulates all rare behavior patterns and prevents the appearance of unwanted states and transitions.

An important consequence of the presence of state s_{0ws} is that it is possible to obtain even *simpler* model than a model built with a fixed window of a size equal to 1 (Fig. 1c), and at the same time more *precise* one (see comparision in Sect. 5.3). Here, *simplicity* is achieved by removing a number of unimportant arcs and closing them as self-loops in state s_{0ws}. The maximum number of such self-loop arcs is limited by the number of all activities. A similar approach was applied in CFM method [17] by merging all sink states (states without outgoing arcs) into a single state s.

After the algorithm is finished, no temporary transitions and states are present in $TS_3(L)$ anymore. Moreover, all previously unreplayable elements in

---

[3] Formally, for a trace $\langle \rangle$, a state s_0 should be considered. Nevertheless, we explicitly distinguish the initial state s_0 and the rare-behavior state s_{0ws}.

the traces can now be replayed in $TS_3(L)$ as new states for them have been established. At the end of an iteration of the algorithm each trace from the log can be replayed at least by one more element than before the iteration. Since the length of each trace is finite, the number of iterations is also finite. Thus, the algorithm eventually stops. The resulting $TS_3(L_1)$ is depicted in Fig. 3c.

In Algorithm 3 $Vwsc$ is an additional parameter used to combine a varying window size approach with a classical fixed window size approach. It is a real value from $[0,1]$ determining a maximum size of a state window during the reconstruction phase of $TS_3(L)$.

Finally, considering the fitness of reduced transition system $TS_3(L)$, one can postulate the following proposition.

Theorem 1. *Let L be a log and let $TS_3(L)$ be a reduced transition system based on condensed transition system $TS_2(L)$. Then, $TS_3(L)$ perfectly fits L.*

Proof. Let $\sigma = \langle a_1, a_2, ..., a_n \rangle \in A^*$ be a trace of log L and $\sigma = \sigma^+(TS_2(L)) + \sigma^-(TS_2(L))$, where $\sigma^+(TS_2(L))$ is a trace prefix that can be "replayed" on $TS_2(L)$ and $\sigma^-(TS_2(L))$ is a trace suffix that cannot be "replayed" on $TS_2(L)$. $\sigma^+(TS_2(L))$ can be "replayed" on $TS_3(L)$ by the construction. Now we need to prove that the entire sequence σ can be "replayed" on $TS_3(L)$. We will prove that iteratively for sequences $\langle \sigma(1), ..., \sigma(i) \rangle$, where i varies from $|\sigma^+(TS_2(L))|$ to $|\sigma|$. Basis of induction: the proposition is valid for $i = |\sigma^+(TS_2(L))|$, since $\sigma^+(TS_2(L))$ can be "replayed" on $TS_3(L)$. Step of induction: the trace $\langle \sigma(1), ..., \sigma(i) \rangle$ can be "replayed". Now let us prove that the trace $\langle \sigma(1), ..., \sigma(i+1) \rangle$ can be "replayed" as well. According to Algorithms 4 and 5, we "replay" $\langle \sigma(1), ..., \sigma(i) \rangle$ and add a new state $\hat{s}$ (if it has not been added previously) and a new edge $t = (s, \sigma(i+1), \hat{s})$ correspondingly. Thus, trace $\langle \sigma(1), ..., \sigma(i+1) \rangle$ now can be replayed, and that proves the step of induction. $\square$

5   Evaluation and Discussion

In this section we evaluate the proposed approach as applied to real-life event logs. In the beginning of the section, an algorithm for precision calculation is introduced.

5.1   Metrics Calculation

Calculation of metrics for all three transition systems is performed throughout their building.

As we have shown above, *fitness* of $TS_1(L)$ and $TS_3(L)$ is perfect. Further, *simplicity* of a model is easily calculated on the basis of the number of model's elements.

We propose an algorithm calculating *precision* metrics for a given transition system $TS(L)$ based on an idea of simulation [16]. The algorithm assumes that $TS(L)$ perfectly fits log L. Suppose that $TS(L)$ can simulate $TS_1(L)$. The behavior which is present in $TS(L)$ but not observed in the log is penalized. Finally, a normalized total penalty forms the basis of a precision value.

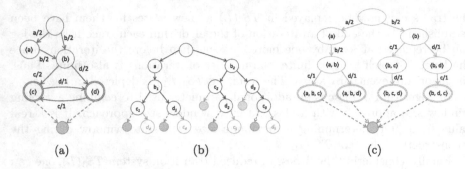

Fig. 4. Transition systems built for log L_2: (a) 1-window size (fixed) $TS_f(L_2)$; (b) unfolding graph obtained after $TS_f(L_2)$ simulated $TS_1(L_2)$; (c) full $TS_1(L_2)$

The approach for calculation of precision is described in Algorithm 6. The algorithm consists of two main steps. First, the algorithm iteratively calculates so-called *partial precisions* for every state in $TS(L)$ (Algorithm 9). Second, the algorithm sums partial precisions (Algorithm 7) and calculates the average over the number of states.

To get an illustration of this idea, consider the following log:

$$L_2 = [\langle a, b, c \rangle, \langle a, b, d \rangle, \langle b, c, d \rangle, \langle b, d, c \rangle]$$

Full transition system $TS_1(L_2)$ for the log is depicted in Fig. 4c. It is considered to be the *most precise reference model*. Transition system $TS_f(L_2)$ in Fig. 4a is built with a fixed window size (equal to 1). As a more general model than $TS_1(L_2)$ it allows more behavior than the reference model, which is *penalized* since it impacts precision.

The calculation of precision invokes a simulation routine implemented as a recursive procedure (Algorithm 8). For the example above, $TS(L) = TS_f(L_2)$ and $TS_1(L) = TS_1(L_2)$. Initially $s = s_0 \in TS(L)$ and $s_1 = s_{01} \in TS_1(l)$ are passed as parameters to the procedure. For each output transition of a current state s, the algorithm tries to find a transition labeled with the same event among output transitions of a current state s_1. Note, that all transition systems considered in the paper are deterministic by construction, i.e. it is not possible for a state to have more than one outgoing transition labeled by the same event.

For example, consider transition $(s_0, a, \langle a \rangle)$ in $TS_f(L_2)$. It has a matching transition $(s_0, a, \langle a \rangle)$ in $TS_1(L_2)$. The procedure is recursively called with parameters $s = \langle a \rangle$ and $s_1 = \langle a \rangle$. This step also produces an input edge to vertex a in an unfolding graph depicted in Fig. 4b. This step has to be repeated for transitions $(\langle a \rangle, b, \langle b \rangle)$ and $(\langle a \rangle, b, \langle a, b \rangle)$ (obtains b_1 in the unfolding graph) and transitions $(\langle b \rangle, c, \langle c \rangle)$ and $(\langle a, b \rangle, c, \langle a, b, c \rangle)$ (obtains c_1 in the unfolding graph). Here, $\langle c \rangle$ in $TS_f(L_2)$ is an accepting state; it contains a virtual output transition (depicted as a gray dashed arrow) to a virtual final state. Similarly, $\langle a, b, c \rangle$ from $TS_1(L_2)$ also has a virtual final transition, which maintains balance (depicted as a dashed output edge in the unfolding graph).

Together with that, $\langle c \rangle$ has transition $(\langle c \rangle, d, \langle d \rangle)$ to state $\langle d \rangle$, which has no counterpart in $TS_1(L_2)$ (edge (c_1, d_4) in the graph). The algorithm penalizes this extra transition and calculates partial precision for state $\langle c \rangle$ as a difference between the number of output transitions and the number of penalized output transitions divided by the total number of output transitions.

Since state $\langle a, b, c \rangle$ of $TS_1(L_2)$ does not allow any further moves, the algorithm leaves the current iteration of the procedure and, thereby, returns to a higher level, to state $\langle b \rangle$ of $TS_f(L_2)$ and $\langle a, b \rangle$ of $TS_1(L_2)$. Then, the algorithm repeats the same steps for all unvisited output transitions.

During its work, the algorithm can normally visit some states of a more general model ($TS_f(L_2)$ in the example) more than once. For each such visit a value of partial precision for the state is recalculated (Algorithm 9).

Finally, after all states of the reference model have been visited during the simulation, values of ultimate partial precision for each state of $TS(L)$ are represented by η. The last step is to calculate an average value (Algorithm 7), which is the required value of the model's precision.

Algorithm 6. Calculating precision for transition system $TS(L)$

Input   : general (perfectly fit) transition system $TS(L) = (S, E, T, s_0, AS)$ built for log L; reference full transition system $TS_1(L) = (S_1, E_1, T_1, s_{01}, AS_1)$;
Output : value of precision $Prec(TS(L))$ for $TS(L)$;
Data: partial function η mapping each state of $TS(L)$ to a real number determining the state's "partial precision"; partial function θ mapping each state $s \in TS(L)$ to a natural number determining how many times state s has been visited;

```
/* Main part of the algorithm     */
begin
    CalcStatePrecision (s_0, s_{01}, TS(L),
        TS_1(L), η, θ);
    Prec(TS(L)) ←SumPartialPrecisions
        (TS(L), η);
```

Algorithm 7. Function SumPartialPrecisions calculating total precision of $TS(L)$

Input   : general (perfectly fit) transition system $TS(L) = (S, E, T, s_0, AS)$ built for log L; function η mapping each state of $TS(L)$ to a real number determining state's "partial precision";
Output : value of precision $Prec(TS(L))$ for $TS(L)$;

Function
SumPartialPrecisions($TS(L)$, η):
    $Real$
    $sum \leftarrow 0$;
    for $s \in S$ **do**
        $sum \leftarrow sum + \eta(s)$;
    $res \leftarrow sum/|S|$;
    return res;

Algorithm 8. Procedure `CalcStatePrecision` calculating "partial precision for entire states" as function η

Input : current state s of $TS(L)$;
current state s_1 of $TS_1(L)$; general (perfectly fit) transition system
$TS(L) = (S, E, T, s_0, AS)$ built for log L; reference full transition system
$TS_1(L) = (S_1, E_1, T_1, s_{01}, AS_1)$; partial function η mapping each state of $TS(L)$
to a real number determining the state's "partial precision"; partial function θ
mapping each state $s \in TS(L)$ to a natural number determining how many
times state s has been visited;

Procedure `CalcStatePrecision`$(s, s_1, TS(L), TS_1(L), \eta, \theta)$

   $pen \leftarrow 0$;
   for $t = (s, a, s') \in s\bullet$ **do**
      /* If no matching trans.   */
      if $\exists t_1 = (s_1, a, s_1') \in TS_1(L)$ **then**
         `CalcStatePrecision` $(s', s_1', TS(L), TS_1(L), \eta)$;
      else
         $pen \leftarrow pen + 1$;

   /* Number of output trans-s   */
   $otn \leftarrow |s\bullet|$;
   if $s \in AS$ **then**
      $otn \leftarrow otn + 1$
      if $s_1 \notin AS_1$ **then**
         $pen \leftarrow pen + 1$;

   if $otn \neq 0$ **then**
      $partPartPrec = (otn - pen)/otn$;
      `RecalcStatePrecision` $(s, partPartPrec)$;

Algorithm 9. Procedure `RecalcStatePrecision` refines the value of a state's "partial precision"

Input : state $s \in S$ of $TS(L) = (S, E, T, s_0, AS)$;
function η mapping each state of $TS(L)$ to a real number determining the
state's "partial precision"; partial function θ mapping each state $s \in S$ to a
natural number determining how many times state s has been visited; new
state's partial precision $pprec$ for refining;

Procedure `RecalcStatePrecision`$(s, \eta, \theta, pprec)$

   /* If either η or θ is not defined for this state   */
   if $\eta(s)$ *is not defined* **then**
      $\eta(s) \leftarrow 0$;
   if $\theta(s)$ *is not defined* **then**
      $\theta(s) \leftarrow 0$;
   $stPrec \leftarrow \eta(s) \cdot \theta(s)$;
   $\theta(s) \leftarrow \theta(s) + 1$;
   $\eta(s) \leftarrow (stPrec + pprec)/\theta(s)$;

5.2   Implementation Details

To evaluate the proposed approach, we have developed a number of routines for the ProM toolkit [19]. The routines are implemented as plug-ins with several entry points intended for different sets of input parameters.

The "Build and reduce transition systems (xi)" plug-in combines routines for building $TS_1(L)$, $TS_2(L)$, $TS_3(L)$ for a given input log L, along with calculation metrics for each transition system built. In the simplest case, the plug-in obtains as its input only event log L and provides the ability to configure the settings as follows. (1) Specify a maximum window size for building $TS_1(L)$. The default size is unlimited (that is set at a value of -1). By setting the size to a natural number, one can make the algorithm act with a fixed window. We use this option for building reference models with fixed windows. (2) Specify the value of the *Threshold* parameter used for building $TS_2(L)$. (3) Specify the value of the multiplicative factor *Vwsc* used when building $TS_3(L)$.

Once successfully finished, the plug-in produces as its output *three transition systems*, and, what is the most important for analyzing the results, a *hierarchical report*. The report represents a set of characteristics organized in a tree structure. They include metrics for each built transition system and additional attributes calculated during the algorithm's operation. We created a special "view" plug-in for browsing such reports, which allows information to be exported as a JSON-structure or HTML-formatted text.

Both plug-ins are openly available to download on http://pais.hse.ru.

5.3   Experiments and Discussion

We evaluated our approach on a set of event logs, both artificial and real-life. In the following sections we consider "BPI challenge" logs [1] prepared for a Disco project [2] L3 (11 traces, 89 activities) and L4 (251 traces, 247 activities). Full transition systems built for the logs have the following frequency characteristics:

- $TS_1(L3)$: Maximum Window Size: 71;   514 states;   513 transitions;
- $TS_1(L4)$: Maximum Window Size: 83; 8088 states; 8087 transitions.

Our goal is to compare metrics of models built with an existing fixed window algorithm and models built with the algorithms proposed in this paper.

Table 1 shows metrics of condensed and reduced models constructed with unlimited window size. Metrics of k-window models for the logs are presented in Table 2. Comparing the results from both tables, one can consider the following outcome. By using a *fixed window* approach based on [3] the maximum reduction is reached for a parameter $k = 1$. This is the smallest model that can be built by any algorithm using h-*tail* approach [18]. Moreover, Table 2 shows that increasing window size (k) to a value greater than 7 does not significantly impact simplicity and precision.

In our algorithms, there are two parameters affecting model size: *Threshold* and *Vwsc*. Parameter *Threshold* has a limited impact on the model size. As it is shown in Table 1, dependence of the model size from *Threshold* is nonlinear in the entire domain of *Threshold*. For log *L*4, better simplicity results are in the vicinity of the points 0.2 and 0.8 and worse in the range ends. This is because in the case of negligibly small *Threshold* values, $TS_2(L)$ model is similar to $TS_1(L)$; so, the application area of a variable size window lies near the tree leaves. In this situation, a noticeable reduction of a model is achievable only for traces with similar suffixes.

Table 1. Dependence of model's metrics on parameters *Threshold* and *Vwsc* with an unlimited window size

Settings		TS₂(L3): Condensed				TS₃(L3): Reduced				TS₂(L4): Condensed				TS₃(L4): Reduced			
Threshold	VWSC	TThr	States #	Transs #	Act #	States #	Transs #	Simpl	Prec	TThr	States #	Transs #	Act #	States #	Transs #	Simpl	Prec
0	1	1	514	513	89	514	513	0,0876	1	0	8088	8087	247	8088	8087	0,0153	1
0,05	1	1	514	513	89	514	513	0,0876	1	13	37	36	20	320	1573	0,131	0,567
0,1	1	1	514	513	89	514	513	0,0876	1	25	12	11	10	327	1595	0,129	0,5482
0,25	1	3	11	10	9	470	478	0,0949	0,9911	63	9	8	8	320	1531	0,134	0,5585
0,33	1	4	9	8	8	464	474	0,0959	0,9905	83	9	8	8	320	1531	0,134	0,5585
0,5	1	6	7	6	6	470	478	0,0949	0,9911	126	6	5	5	308	1540	0,1342	0,5523
0,65	1	7	6	6	6	470	478	0,0949	0,9911	163	3	2	2	289	1490	0,1394	0,5595
0,75	1	8	7	6	6	470	478	0,0949	0,9911	188	3	2	2	289	1490	0,1394	0,5595
0,85	1	9	7	6	6	470	478	0,0949	0,9911	213	3	2	2	289	1490	0,1394	0,5595
0,95	1	10	7	6	6	470	478	0,0949	0,9911	238	2	1	1	308	1544	0,1339	0,5581
1	1	11	1	0	0	470	478	0,0949	0,9911	251	2	1	1	308	1544	0,1339	0,5581
0,25	0,5	3	11	10	9	397	438	0,1078	0,9505	63	9	8	8	173	992	0,2129	0,5514
0,33	0,5	4	9	8	8	395	438	0,108	0,9477	83	9	8	8	173	992	0,2129	0,5514
0,5	0,5	6	7	6	6	397	438	0,1078	0,9505	126	6	5	5	147	869	0,2441	0,556
0,75	0,5	8	7	6	6	397	438	0,1078	0,9505	188	3	2	2	141	866	0,2463	0,5809
0,25	0,25	3	11	10	9	312	403	0,1259	0,8764	63	9	8	8	73	645	0,3454	0,5116
0,33	0,25	4	9	8	8	311	405	0,1257	0,8739	83	9	8	8	73	645	0,3454	0,5116
0,5	0,25	6	7	6	6	309	400	0,1269	0,8771	126	6	5	5	78	639	0,3459	0,5387
0,75	0,25	8	7	6	6	309	400	0,1269	0,8771	188	3	2	2	86	709	0,3119	0,4843
0,33	0,12	4	9	8	8	139	320	0,1961	0,7012	83	9	8	8	59	565	0,3974	0,5333
0,33	0,05	4	9	8	8	55	201	0,3516	0,676	83	9	8	8	26	404	0,5767	0,5266

Table 2. Metrics of *k*-window models

k (wnd size)	L3				L4			
	States #	Transs #	Simpl	Prec	States #	Transs #	Simpl	Prec
1	90	273	0,2479	0,6117	248	1755	0,124	0,3791
2	274	371	0,1395	0,8574	1756	3602	0,046	0,7607
3	372	418	0,1139	0,9457	3603	4838	0,029	0,8892
4	419	437	0,1051	0,9828	4839	5600	0,024	0,946
5	438	451	0,1012	0,9882	5601	6129	0,021	0,9671
7	464	474	0,0959	0,9914	6515	6806	0,019	0,9836
10	492	497	0,091	0,9961	7228	7392	0,017	0,9929
15	508	508	0,0886	0,999	7840	7905	0,016	0,9968
20	513	513	0,0877	0,999	8037	8054	0,015	0,9991

When *Threshold* values come closer to 1, a smaller $TS_2(L)$ model is built. Consequently, at the stage of building $TS_3(L)$ model, most of it is to be reconstructed. Preliminary experiments show that selecting *Threshold* from a range $[0.2; 0.8]$ leads to better results; nevertheless, further elaboration of the parameter's impact is needed. We consider *Threshold* = 0.33 as a reference value. For such a value, only the states and transitions with frequencies that equal at least $1/3$ of the total number of traces are preserved in the condensed transition system. Hence, all other states are reconstructed in a more abstract manner. The results for *Threshold* = 0.33 are highlighted in blue in Table 1.

By decreasing the value of *Vwsc* parameter from 1 to 0, *significant reduction of a resulting model size* is achieved (last two rows of Table 1). For example, for log $L3$ and a value of $Vwsc = 0.05$ we have $Simpl(TS_3(L3)) = 0.3516$ and $Prec(TS_3(L3)) = 0.676$ versus $Simpl(TS_f(L3)) = 0.2479$ and $Prec(TS_f(L3)) = 0.6117$ for the case of one window size model. Generally, by adjusting the value of *Vwsc*, one can obtain a resulting model in a wide range of sizes. Unlike parameter *Threshold*, parameter *Vwsc* gives a linear dependence of the model size. Moreover, by varying both values *Threshold* and *Vwsc* it is possible to enhance the mutual influence of the parameters on each other. That allows flexible balancing between precision and simplicity.

Comparision with existing approaches to transition systems reduction. By comparing the proposed approach with existing approaches we can make the following conclusions. Most of the existing methods are based on different approaches used to determine a *state representation function* [4].

In this paper, we proposed an essentially new *adaptive* state representation function, which was not considered before. While inferring a transition system from an event log, the function takes into account the frequency of an individual event and varies the size of the window that determines the current state. Generally, the use of a *fixed window* allows improving *simplicity* of a model while the use of an unlimited window improves its *precision*. Our approach combines both and allows balancing between these two metrics in a flexible manner.

Intuitively, the bigger the number of events in a log corresponding to a state is, a more specific (and, correspondly, less abstract) the state is. The more specific state is marked by a longer subtrace, which reduces the probability of merging the state with another state. In contrast, a big number of states corresponding to rare behavior patterns can be easily merged, which dramatically impacts the size of the transition system (and, correspondly, increases its *simplicity*). The *precision* still slightly suffers.

The proposed approach implies an important corollary: the method is essentially insensitive to noise. This is a big advantage of the method over some existing methods, e.g. [18], where a comprehensive preprocessing of input logs is needed.

The experiments on both artificial and randomly chosen real-life logs supported the proposed approach.

6   Conclusion

This paper presented a new approach for reducing transition systems, based on an inference algorithm with a varied window size. In contrast to the existing approaches, the approach presented in this paper shows the advantage of allowing flexible adjustments of the size of the resulting model. The evaluation of a model's quality is made by measuring its metrics. For calculation of the *precision* metric, an original algorithm has been developed. This way, estimation of achievability of the main goal is made on the basis of numerical characteristics of resulting models. The experiments with artificial and real-life logs justified the proposed approach.

Future work is aimed at further investigation of impacts of various algorithm coefficients on time costs of the region-based algorithm applied to resulting transition systems obtained during more comprehensive experiments. Moreover, we plan to investigate the quality metrics of Petri nets synthesized from transition systems obtained as an outcome of the algorithm.

References

1. http://www.win.tue.nl/bpi/doku.php?id=2015:challenge&redirect=1id=2015/ challenge
2. http://fluxicon.com/blog/2015/05/bpi-challenge-2015/
3. van der Aalst, W.M.P., Rubin, V., Verbeek, H.M.W., Dongen, B.F., Kindler, E., Günther, C.W.: Process mining: a two-step approach to balance between underfitting and overfitting. Software Syst. Model. **9**(1), 87–111 (2008). http://dx.doi.org/10.1007/s10270-008-0106-z
4. van der Aalst, W.M.P.: Process Mining - Discovery, Conformance and Enhancement of Business Processes. Springer, Heidelberg (2011). doi:10.1007/ 978-3-642-19345-3
5. Angluin, D.: Inference of reversible languages. J. ACM **29**(3), 741–765 (1982). http://doi.acm.org/10.1145/322326.322334
6. Badouel, E., Bernardinello, L., Darondeau, P.: Polynomial algorithms for the synthesis of bounded nets. In: Mosses, P.D., Nielsen, M., Schwartzbach, M.I. (eds.) CAAP 1995. LNCS, vol. 915, pp. 364–378. Springer, Heidelberg (1995). doi:10. 1007/3-540-59293-8_207
7. Badouel, E., Bernardinello, L., Darondeau, P.: The synthesis problem for elementary net systems is NP-complete. Theoret. Comput. Sci. **186**, 107–134 (1997)
8. Badouel, E., Darondeau, P.: Theory of regions. In: Reisig, W., Rozenberg, G. (eds.) ACPN 1996. LNCS, vol. 1491, pp. 529–586. Springer, Heidelberg (1998). doi:10. 1007/3-540-65306-6_22
9. Bergenthum, R., Desel, J., Lorenz, R., Mauser, S.: Process mining based on regions of languages. In: Alonso, G., Dadam, P., Rosemann, M. (eds.) BPM 2007. LNCS, vol. 4714, pp. 375–383. Springer, Heidelberg (2007). doi:10.1007/ 978-3-540-75183-0_27
10. Biermann, A.W., Feldman, J.A.: On the synthesis of finite-state machines from samples of their behavior. IEEE Trans. Comput. **21**(6), 592–597 (1972)

11. Buijs, J.C.A.M., Dongen, B.F., van der Aalst, W.M.P.: On the role of fitness, precision, generalization and simplicity in process discovery. In: Meersman, R., Panetto, H., Dillon, T., Rinderle-Ma, S., Dadam, P., Zhou, X., Pearson, S., Ferscha, A., Bergamaschi, S., Cruz, I.F. (eds.) OTM 2012. LNCS, vol. 7565, pp. 305–322. Springer, Heidelberg (2012). doi:10.1007/978-3-642-33606-5_19
12. Carmona, J., Cortadella, J., Kishinevsky, M.: A region-based algorithm for discovering petri nets from event logs. In: Dumas, M., Reichert, M., Shan, M.-C. (eds.) BPM 2008. LNCS, vol. 5240, pp. 358–373. Springer, Heidelberg (2008). doi:10.1007/978-3-540-85758-7_26
13. Cook, J.E., Wolf, A.L.: Discovering models of software processes from event-based data. ACM Trans. Softw. Eng. Methodol. 7(3), 215–249 (1998). http://doi.acm.org/10.1145/287000.287001
14. Cortadella, J., Kishinevsky, M., Lavagno, L., Yakovlev, A.: Deriving petri nets from finite transition systems. IEEE Trans. Comput. 47(8), 859–882 (1998). http://dx.doi.org/10.1109/12.707587
15. Lorenzoli, D., Mariani, L., Pezzè, M.: Inferring state-based behavior models. In: 4th International Workshop on Dynamic Analysis (WODA 2006) co-located with the 28th International Conference on Software Engineering (ICSE 2006), pp. 25–32. ACM Press (2006)
16. Park, D.: Concurrency and automata on infinite sequences. In: Deussen, P. (ed.) GI-TCS 1981. LNCS, vol. 104, pp. 167–183. Springer, Heidelberg (1981). doi:10.1007/BFb0017309
17. Solé, M., Carmona, J.: Process mining from a basis of state regions. In: Lilius, J., Penczek, W. (eds.) PETRI NETS 2010. LNCS, vol. 6128, pp. 226–245. Springer, Heidelberg (2010). doi:10.1007/978-3-642-13675-7_14
18. Sole, M., Carmona, J.: Region-based foldings in process discovery. IEEE Trans. Knowl. Data Eng. 25(1), 192–205 (2013)
19. Verbeek, H., Buijs, J., Dongen, B., Aalst, W.: ProM 6: the process mining toolkit. In: Rosa, M.L. (ed.) Proceeding of BPM Demonstration Track 2010, CEUR Workshop Proceedings, vol. 615, pp. 34–39 (2010)
20. van der Werf, J.M.E.M., van Dongen, B.F., Hurkens, C.A.J., Serebrenik, A.: Process discovery using integer linear programming. In: van Hee, K.M., Valk, R. (eds.) PETRI NETS 2008. LNCS, vol. 5062, pp. 368–387. Springer, Heidelberg (2008). doi:10.1007/978-3-540-68746-7_24

Stubborn Set Intuition Explained

Antti Valmari and Henri Hansen[✉]

Tampere University of Technology, Mathematics,
P.O. Box 553, 33101 Tampere, Finland
{antti.valmari,henri.hansen}@tut.fi

Abstract. This study focuses on the differences between stubborn sets and other partial order methods. First a major problem with step graphs is pointed out with an example. Then the deadlock-preserving stubborn set method is compared to the deadlock-preserving ample set and persistent set methods. Next, conditions are discussed whose purpose is to ensure that the reduced state space preserves the ordering of visible transitions, that is, transitions that may change the truth values of the propositions that the formula under verification has been built from. Finally solutions to the ignoring problem are analysed both when the purpose is to preserve only safety properties and when also liveness properties are of interest.

1 Introduction

Ample sets [1,10,11], *persistent sets* [5,6], and *stubborn sets* [15,19] are methods for constructing reduced state spaces. In each found state, they compute a subset of transitions and only fire the enabled transitions in it to find more states. We call this subset an *aps set*.

The choice of aps sets depends on the properties under verification. Attempts to obtain good reduction for various classes of properties have led to the development of many different methods. Even when addressing the same class of properties, stubborn set methods often differ from other aps set methods. The present study focuses on these differences. The goal is to explain the intuition behind the choices made in stubborn set methods.

To get a concrete starting point, Sect. 2 presents a simple (and non-optimal) definition of stubborn sets for Petri nets that suffices for preserving all reachable deadlocks. The section also introduces the $\leadsto_M$-relation that underlies many algorithms for computing stubborn sets, and sketches one good algorithm. This relation and algorithm are one of the major differences between stubborn set and other aps set methods. The section also contains a small new result, namely an example showing that always choosing a singleton stubborn set if one is available does not necessarily guarantee best reduction results.

With Petri nets, it might seem natural to fire sets of transitions called steps, instead of individual transitions. Section 3 discusses why this is not necessarily a good idea. Ample and persistent sets are compared to stubborn sets in Sect. 4, in the context of deadlock-preservation. Furthermore, the difference between

© Springer-Verlag GmbH Germany 2017
M. Koutny et al. (Eds.): ToPNoC XII, LNCS 10470, pp. 140–165, 2017.
DOI: 10.1007/978-3-662-55862-1_7

weak and strong stubborn sets is explained. The verification of many properties relies on a distinction between *visible* and *invisible* transitions. This distinction is introduced in Sect. 5. Its ample and stubborn set versions are compared to each other.

Because of the so-called *ignoring problem*, deadlock-preserving aps set methods fail to preserve most other classes of properties. For many classes, it suffices to solve the ignoring problem in the terminal strong components of the reduced state space. To this end, two slightly different methods have been suggested. Section 6 first introduces them, and then presents and proves correct a novel idea that largely combines their best features.

The above-mentioned solutions to the ignoring problem do not suffice for so-called liveness properties. Section 7 discusses the stubborn set and ample set methods for liveness. A drawback in the most widely known implementation of the methods is pointed out. Section 8 discusses problems related to fairness. Aps set methods have never been able to appropriately deal with mainstream fairness assumptions. In this section we present some examples that illustrate the difficulties. They are from [22]. Section 9 concludes the study.

2   The Basic Idea of Stubborn Sets

In this section we illustrate the basic idea of stubborn sets and of one good algorithm for computing them.

We use T to denote the set of (all) transitions of a Petri net. Let M be a marking. The set of *enabled* transitions in M is denoted with $\mathrm{en}(M)$ and defined as $\{t \in T \mid M \,[t\rangle\}$. A *deadlock* is a marking that has no enabled transitions.

In Fig. 1 left, only firing t_1 in the initial marking leads to the loss of the deadlock that is reached by firing $t_3 t_2 t_3 t_1$. To find a subset of transitions that cannot lead to such losses, we first define a marking-dependent relation $\leadsto_M$ between Petri net transitions.

PNd. If $\neg(M \,[t\rangle)$, then choose $p_t \in {\bullet}t$ such that $M(p_t) < W(p_t, t)$ and declare $t \leadsto_M t'$ for every $t' \in {\bullet}p_t$ except t itself. (If many such p_t are available, only one is chosen. The correctness of what follows does not depend on the choice.)
PNe. If $M \,[t\rangle$, then declare $t \leadsto_M t'$ for every $t' \in ({\bullet}t){\bullet}$ except t itself.

On the right in Fig. 1, enabled transitions are shown with double circles, disabled transitions with single circles, and the $\leadsto_M$-relation with arrows.

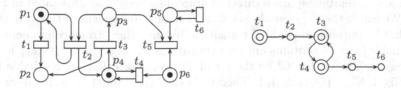

Fig. 1. A marked Petri net and its $\leadsto_M$-graph, with $p_{t_5} = p_5$.

For instance, t_4 is enabled, $\bullet t_4 = \{p_4, p_6\}$, and $\{p_4, p_6\}\bullet = \{t_3, t_4, t_5\}$, so **PNe** declares $t_4 \leadsto_M t_3$ and $t_4 \leadsto_M t_5$. Regarding t_5, **PNd** allows choosing $p_{t_5} = p_3$ or $p_{t_5} = p_5$. In the example p_5 was chosen, spanning the arrow $t_5 \leadsto_M t_6$.

Consider any $\leadsto_M$-*closed* set T_M of transitions, that is, for every t and t', if $t \in T_M$ and $t \leadsto_M t'$, then also $t' \in T_M$. Assume that $t \in T_M$, $t_i \notin T_M$ for $1 \le i \le n$, and $M [t_1 \cdots t_n\rangle M'$. **PNd** guarantees that if t is disabled in M, then t is disabled also in M'. This is because every transition that may increase the number of tokens in p_t is in T_M. **PNe** guarantees that if t is enabled in M, then there is M'' such that $M' [t\rangle M''$ and $M [tt_1 \cdots t_n\rangle M''$. This is because t does not consume tokens from the same places as $t_1 \cdots t_n$.

Let $\hat{M}$ be the initial marking of a Petri net. Let $\mathsf{stubb}(M)$ be a function that, for any marking M that is not a deadlock, returns an $\leadsto_M$-closed set of transitions that contains at least one enabled transition. This set is called *stubborn*. If M is a deadlock, then it does not matter what $\mathsf{stubb}(M)$ returns. Let the *reduced state space* be the triple $(S_r, \Delta_r, \hat{M})$, where S_r and Δ_r are the smallest sets such that (1) $\hat{M} \in S_r$ and (2) if $M \in S_r$, $t \in \mathsf{stubb}(M)$, and $M [t\rangle M'$, then $M' \in S_r$ and $(M, t, M') \in \Delta_r$. It can be constructed like the ordinary state space, except that only the enabled transitions in $\mathsf{stubb}(M)$ are fired in each constructed marking M. We have the following theorem.

Theorem 1. *The set S_r contains all deadlocks that are reachable from $\hat{M}$.*

Proof. The proof proceeds by induction. Let $M \in S_r$ and $M [t_1 \cdots t_n\rangle M_d$, where M_d is a deadlock. If $n = 0$, then $M_d = M \in S_r$.

If $n > 0$, then $M [t_1\rangle$. So M is not a deadlock and $\mathsf{stubb}(M)$ contains an enabled transition t. If none of t_i is in $\mathsf{stubb}(M)$, then **PNe** implies that t is enabled at M_d, contradicting the assumption that M_d is a deadlock. So there is i such that $t_i \in \mathsf{stubb}(M)$ but $t_j \notin \mathsf{stubb}(M)$ for $1 \le j < i$. Let M_{i-1} and M_i be the markings such that $M [t_1 \cdots t_{i-1}\rangle M_{i-1} [t_i\rangle M_i [t_{i+1} \cdots t_n\rangle M_d$. **PNd** implies that $t_i \in \mathsf{en}(M)$, because otherwise t_i would be disabled in M_{i-1}. So **PNe** implies $M [t_i t_1 \cdots t_{i-1}\rangle M_i [t_{i+1} \cdots t_n\rangle M_d$. Let M' be the marking such that $M [t_i\rangle M'$. Then $M' \in S_r$ and there is the path $M' [t_1 \cdots t_{i-1} t_{i+1} \cdots t_n\rangle M_d$ of length $n - 1$ from M' to M_d. By induction, $M_d \in S_r$.   □

The next question is how to compute stubborn sets. Clearly only the enabled transitions in $\mathsf{stubb}(M)$ affect the reduced state space. Therefore, we define $T_1 \sqsubseteq_M T_2$ if and only if $T_1 \cap \mathsf{en}(M) \subseteq T_2 \cap \mathsf{en}(M)$. If $\mathsf{stubb}_1(M) \sqsubseteq_M \mathsf{stubb}_2(M)$ for every reachable marking M, then stubb_1 yields a smaller or the same reduced state space as stubb_2. So we would like to use $\sqsubseteq_M$-minimal stubborn sets.

Each $\leadsto_M$-relation spans a directed graph $(T, \text{``}\leadsto_M\text{''})$ as illustrated in Fig. 1 right. We call it the $\leadsto_M$-*graph*. Let C be a strong component of the $\leadsto_M$-graph such that it contains an enabled transition, but no other strong component that is reachable from C contains enabled transitions. In Fig. 1, $C = \{t_3, t_4\}$ is such a strong component. Let C' be the set of all transitions that are reachable from C. In Fig. 1, $C' = \{t_3, t_4, t_5, t_6\}$. Then C' is an $\sqsubseteq_M$-minimal $\leadsto_M$-closed set that contains an enabled transition. That is, we can choose $\mathsf{stubb}(M) = C'$.

A fast algorithm that is based on this idea was presented in [15, 19, 26], among others. It uses Tarjan's strong component algorithm [14] (see [3] for an improved version). It has been implemented in the ASSET tool [21] (although not for Petri nets). Its running time is linear in the size of the part of the $\leadsto_M$-graph that it investigates. For instance, if it happens to start at t_2 in Fig. 1, then it does not investigate t_1 and its output arrow. Although in this example the resulting savings are small, they are often significant.

The algorithm performs one or more depth-first searches in the $\leadsto_M$-graph, until a search finds an enabled transition or all transitions have been tried. The description above leaves open the order in which transitions are used as the starting points of the searches. The same holds on the order in which the output arrows of each transition are investigated. For instance, when in t_4 in Fig. 1, the algorithm may follow the arrow $t_4 \leadsto t_5$ before or after the arrow $t_4 \leadsto t_3$. Therefore, the result of the algorithm may depend on implementation details. Furthermore, it may also depend on the choice of p_t if there are more than one alternatives. This is why we sometimes say that the method *may* produce some result, instead of saying that it *does* produce it.

The conditions **PNd** and **PNe** are not the best possible. For instance, $t \leadsto_M t'$ need not be declared in **PNd**, if $W(p_t, t') \geq W(t', p_t)$. Extreme optimization of the $\leadsto_M$-relation yields very complicated conditions, as can be seen in [15, 19]. A similar claim holds also with formalisms other than Petri nets. For this reason, and also to make the theory less dependent on the formalism used for modelling systems, aps set methods are usually developed in terms of more abstract conditions than **PNd** and **PNe**. We will do so in Sect. 4.

To analyse more properties than just deadlocks, additional conditions on the choice of stubborn sets are needed. Many of them will be discussed in Sects. 5, 6, and 7.

Until the end of Sect. 5 it will be obvious that if $\mathsf{stubb}_1(M) \sqsubseteq_M \mathsf{stubb}_2(M)$, then $\mathsf{stubb}_1(M)$ never yields worse but may yield better reduction results than $\mathsf{stubb}_2(M)$. In Sects. 6 and 7, the choices of $\mathsf{stubb}(M)$ with different M may interfere with each other, making the issue less trivial.

Even in the present section, it is not obvious which one to choose when $\mathsf{stubb}_1(M) \not\sqsubseteq_M \mathsf{stubb}_2(M)$ and $\mathsf{stubb}_2(M) \not\sqsubseteq_M \mathsf{stubb}_1(M)$. It was pointed out already in [16] that choosing the smallest number of enabled transitions does not necessarily guarantee best reduction results. In the remainder of this section we demonstrate that always favouring a set with precisely one enabled transition does not guarantee a minimal result. This strengthened observation is new.

A Petri net is *1-safe* if and only if no place contains more than one token in any reachable marking. For simplicity, we express a marking of a 1-safe Petri net by listing the marked places within { and }.

Consider the 1-safe Petri net in Fig. 2. Initially the only possibility is to fire t_1 and t_2, yielding $\{2, 8\}$ and $\{3, 8\}$. In $\{2, 8\}$, both $\{t_3, t_4\}$ and $\{t_9\}$ are stubborn. In $\{3, 8\}$, both $\{t_5, t_6\}$ and $\{t_9\}$ are stubborn. We now show that $\{t_3, t_4\}$ and $\{t_5, t_6\}$ yield better reduction than $\{t_9\}$.

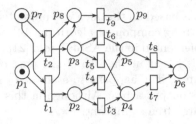

Fig. 2. A stubborn set with one enabled transition is not always the best choice.

If $\{t_3, t_4\}$ is chosen in $\{2, 8\}$ or $\{t_5, t_6\}$ is chosen in $\{3, 8\}$, then $\{4, 8\}$ and $\{5, 8\}$ are obtained. From them, $\{t_7\}$ and $\{t_8\}$ yield $\{6, 8\}$, from which $\{t_9\}$ leads to $\{6, 9\}$ which is a deadlock. Altogether seven markings and nine edges are constructed.

If $\{t_9\}$ is chosen in $\{2, 8\}$ and $\{3, 8\}$, then $\{2, 9\}$ and $\{3, 9\}$ are obtained. Then $\{t_3, t_4\}$ or $\{t_5, t_6\}$ yields $\{4, 9\}$ and $\{5, 9\}$, from which $\{t_7\}$ and $\{t_8\}$ produce $\{6, 9\}$. Altogether eight markings and ten edges are constructed.

3   Why Not Steps?

Before comparing aps set methods to each other, in this section we compare them to step graphs. For simplicity, we restrict ourselves to executions that lead to deadlocks. That is, the goal is to find all reachable deadlocks and for each of them at least one path that leads to it.

A *step* is any nonempty subset $\{t_1, \ldots, t_n\}$ of Petri net transitions. It is *enabled* at M if and only if $M(p) \geq \sum_{i=1}^{n} W(p, t_i)$ for every place p. Then there is M' such that $M\ [\pi\rangle\ M'$ for every permutation π of $t_1 \cdots t_n$. The idea of a *step graph* is to fire steps instead of individual transitions. Unlike the traditional state space, the order of firing of the transitions within the step is not represented, and intermediate markings between the firings of two successive transitions in π are not constructed. This is expected to yield a memory-efficient representation of the behaviour of the Petri net.

To maximize the savings, the steps should be as big as possible. Unfortunately, the following example shows that only firing maximal steps is not correct. By firing $t_3 t_2 t_3 t_1$ in Fig. 1, a deadlock is reached where $M(p_2) = 3$. The maximal steps in the initial marking are $\{t_1, t_3\}$ and $\{t_1, t_4\}$. If only they are fired in the initial marking, no deadlock with $M(p_2) > 2$ is reached.

This problem can be fixed by also firing a sufficient collection of non-maximal steps. If $\{t_1, t_3\}$, $\{t_1, t_4\}$, $\{t_3\}$, and $\{t_4\}$ are fired in the initial marking of our example, then no deadlock is lost although the marking M that satisfies $\hat{M}\ [t_1\rangle\ M$ is not constructed. However, another problem may arise even when it suffices to fire only maximal steps. We will now discuss it.

Consider the Petri net that consists of the black places, transitions, and arcs in Fig. 3 left. It models a system of n concurrent processes. It has $n!2^n$ different executions, yielding a state space with 3^n markings and $2n3^{n-1}$ edges. Its initial

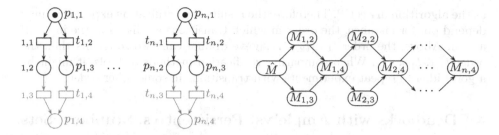

Fig. 3. An example of firing steps vs. aps sets.

marking has 2^n different steps of size n, consisting of one transition from each process. They yield a step graph with $2^n + 1$ markings and 2^n edges.

Any reasonable implementation of any aps set method investigates one process at a time in this example. That is, the implementation picks some i such that $M(p_{i,1}) = 1$, and chooses $\mathsf{aps}(M) = \{t_{i,1}, t_{i,2}\}$. If there is no such i, then $\mathsf{aps}(M) = \emptyset$. This yields $1 + 2 + 4 + 8 + \ldots + 2^n = 2^{n+1} - 1$ markings and $2^{n+1} - 2$ edges.

We see that both methods yield a significant saving over the full state space, and step graphs yield approximately 50 % additional saving over aps sets. Step graphs construct strictly as few markings and edges as necessary in this example.

Assume now that the grey places, transitions, and arcs are added. The step graph now has $2^n + 2$ markings and 2^{n+1} edges.

Aps sets may yield many different results depending on what $\mathsf{aps}(M)$ returns for each M. Assume that the algorithm in Sect. 2 is used and transitions are tried as the starting points of depth-first searches in the order $t_{1,1}$, $t_{1,2}$, $t_{1,3}$, $t_{1,4}$, $t_{2,1}$, $t_{2,2}$, $\ldots$. Then $\mathsf{aps}(M)$ is either $\{t_{i,1}, t_{i,2}\}$, $\{t_{i,3}\}$, or $\{t_{i,4}\}$, where i is the smallest index such that either $M(p_{i,1}) = 1$, $M(p_{i,2}) = 1$, or $M(p_{i,3}) = 1$. (If there is no such i, then $\mathsf{aps}(M) = \emptyset$.) In that case, the reduced state space shown at right in Fig. 3 is obtained. In $M_{i,j}$, $M(p_{k,4}) = 1$ for $1 \le k < i$, $M(p_{i,j}) = 1$, $M(p_{k,1}) = 1$ for $i < k \le n$, and the remaining places are empty. That is, only $3n + 1$ markings and $4n$ edges are constructed. This is tremendously better than the result with step graphs.

There is no guarantee that aps sets yield this nice result. If transitions are tried in the order $t_{1,1}$, $t_{2,1}$, $\ldots$, $t_{n,1}$, $t_{1,2}$, $t_{2,2}$, $\ldots$, then $3 \cdot 2^n - 2$ markings and $2^{n+2} - 4$ edges are obtained.

The point is that in this example, it is *guaranteed* that step graphs do not yield a good result, while aps sets *may* yield a very good result.

Another issue worth noticing in this example is that when aps sets failed to reduce well, they only generated approximately three times the markings and twice the edges that the step graphs generated. This is because where steps avoided many intermediate markings, aps sets investigated only one path through them and thus only generated a small number of them. For this reason, even when aps sets lose to step graphs, they tend not to lose much.

This example brings forward a problem with comparing different methods. Most of the methods in this research field are nondeterministic in the same sense as the algorithm in Sect. 2. Therefore, the results of a verification experiment may depend on, for instance, the order in which transitions are listed in the input of a tool. Above, the order $t_{1,1}$, $t_{2,1}$, ... gave dramatically worse results than the order $t_{1,1}$, $t_{1,2}$, ... When comparing verification methods or tools, it might be a good idea to repeat experiments with transitions in some other order.

4   Deadlocks with Ample vs. Persistent vs. Stubborn Sets

In this section we relate the ample set, persistent set, strong stubborn set, and weak stubborn set methods to each other when the goal is to preserve all deadlocks. Details of each method vary in the literature. We use the variant of ample sets described in [1], persistent sets in [6], and stubborn sets in [19]. These versions of the methods are mature and widely used.

We will use familiar or obvious notation for states, transitions, and so forth. A *set of states* is typically denoted with S, a *set of transitions* with T, and an *initial state* with $\hat{s}$. Transitions refer to *structural transitions* such as Petri net transitions or atomic statements of a program. Transition t is *deterministic*, if and only if for every s, t, s_1, and s_2, $s \xrightarrow{t} s_1$ and $s \xrightarrow{t} s_2$ imply $s_1 = s_2$.

Ample, persistent, and stubborn set methods compute an aps set $\mathsf{aps}(s)$ in each state s that they encounter. They construct a reduced state space by only firing the enabled transitions in each $\mathsf{aps}(s)$. It is the triple $(S_r, \Delta_r, \hat{s})$, where S_r and Δ_r are the smallest sets such that (1) $\hat{s} \in S_r$ and (2) if $s \in S_r$, $t \in \mathsf{aps}(s)$, and $s \xrightarrow{t} s'$, then $s' \in S_r$ and $(s, t, s') \in \Delta_r$. The full state space $(S, \Delta, \hat{s})$ is obtained by always choosing $\mathsf{aps}(s) = T$. Obviously $\hat{s} \in S_r \subseteq S$ and $\Delta_r \subseteq \Delta$.

The **ample set method** relies on the notion of *independence* between transitions. It is usually defined as any binary relation on transitions that has the following property:

Independence. If transitions t_1 and t_2 are independent of each other, $s \xrightarrow{t_1} s_1$, and $s \xrightarrow{t_2} s_2$, then there is s' such that $s_1 \xrightarrow{t_2} s'$ and $s_2 \xrightarrow{t_1} s'$.

Independence is not defined as the largest relation with this property, because it may be difficult to find out whether the property holds for some pair of transitions. In such a situation, the pair may be declared as dependent. Doing so does not jeopardize the correctness of the reduced state space, but may increase its size. This issue is similar to the use of non-optimal $\leadsto_M$-relations in Sect. 2.

Obviously transitions that do not access any variable (or Petri net place) in common can be declared as independent. (Here also the program counter or local state of a process is treated as a variable.) Two transitions that both increment the value of a variable by 42 without testing its value in their enabling conditions can be declared as independent, if they do not access other variables in common. A similar claim holds if they both assign 63 to the variable. Reading from a fifo queue and writing to it can be declared as independent, as can two transitions that are never simultaneously enabled.

An *ample set for deadlocks* in state s_0 is any subset of transitions that are enabled at s_0 that satisfies the following two conditions:

C0. If $\mathsf{en}(s_0) \neq \emptyset$, then $\mathsf{ample}(s_0) \neq \emptyset$.

C1. If $s_0 \xrightarrow{t_1\cdots t_n}$ and none of $t_1, \ldots, t_n$ is in $\mathsf{ample}(s_0)$, then each one of $t_1, \ldots, t_n$ is independent of all transitions in $\mathsf{ample}(s_0)$.

We show next that every deadlock of the full state space is present also in the reduced state space.

Theorem 2. *Assume that transitions are deterministic, $s \in S_r$, s_d is a deadlock, and $s \xrightarrow{t_1\cdots t_n} s_d$ in the full state space. If **C0** and **C1** are obeyed, then there is a permutation $t'_1 \cdots t'_n$ of $t_1 \cdots t_n$ such that $s \xrightarrow{t'_1\cdots t'_n} s_d$ in the reduced state space.*

Proof. We only present the parts where the proof differs from the proof of Theorem 1. If $n > 0$, then $\mathsf{ample}(s)$ contains an enabled transition t by **C0** and $\mathsf{ample}(s) \subseteq \mathsf{en}(s)$. If none of $t_1, \ldots, t_n$ is in $\mathsf{ample}(s)$, then $s_d \xrightarrow{t}$ by **C1**, contradicting the assumption that s_d is a deadlock. So there is a smallest i such that $t_i \in \mathsf{ample}(s)$. Let s_{i-1} and s_i be the states such that $s \xrightarrow{t_1\cdots t_{i-1}} s_{i-1} \xrightarrow{t_i} s_i$. Since $\mathsf{ample}(s) \subseteq \mathsf{en}(s)$, there is s' such that $s \xrightarrow{t_i} s'$. By **C1**, applying independence $i-1$ times, there is s'_i such that $s' \xrightarrow{t_1\cdots t_{i-1}} s'_i$ and $s_{i-1} \xrightarrow{t_i} s'_i$. Because transitions are deterministic, $s'_i = s_i$. As a consequence, $s \xrightarrow{t_i} s' \xrightarrow{t_1\cdots t_{i-1}} s_i \xrightarrow{t_{i+1}\cdots t_n} s_d$. $\square$

Strong stubborn sets are defined such that they may contain both enabled and disabled transitions. Deadlock-preserving strong stubborn sets satisfy the following three conditions. **D0** is essentially the same as **C0**. **D1** and **D2** will be motivated and related to **C1** after the definition.

D0. If $\mathsf{en}(s_0) \neq \emptyset$, then $\mathsf{stubb}(s_0) \cap \mathsf{en}(s_0) \neq \emptyset$.

D1. If $t \in \mathsf{stubb}(s_0)$, $t_i \notin \mathsf{stubb}(s_0)$ for $1 \leq i \leq n$, and $s_0 \xrightarrow{t_1\cdots t_n t} s'_n$, then $s_0 \xrightarrow{t t_1\cdots t_n} s'_n$.

D2. If $t \in \mathsf{stubb}(s_0)$, $t_i \notin \mathsf{stubb}(s_0)$ for $1 \leq i \leq n$, $s_0 \xrightarrow{t_1\cdots t_n} s_n$, and $s_0 \xrightarrow{t}$, then $s_n \xrightarrow{t}$.

This formulation was suggested by Marko Rauhamaa [12]. The most important reason for its use is that **D1** works well even if transitions are not necessarily deterministic. (For deadlocks, also **D2** can be used as such.) This is important for applying stubborn sets to process algebras, please see, e.g., [18,23,26]. In the proof of Theorem 2, the assumption that transitions are deterministic was explicitly used. Already the definition of independence relies on determinism. This issue makes ample and persistent set theories difficult to apply to process algebras.

Second, **D1** can be used as such and **D2** with a small change in the definition of weak stubborn sets towards the end of this section.

Third, **D1** and **D2** are slightly easier to use in proofs than **C1**. Let $s = s_0 \xrightarrow{t_1} s_1 \xrightarrow{t_2} \cdots \xrightarrow{t_n} s_n = s_d$. **D0** and **D2** yield an i such that $t_i \in \mathsf{stubb}(s)$ and $t_j \notin \mathsf{stubb}(s)$ for $1 \leq j < i$. Then the existence of s' such that $s \xrightarrow{t_i} s' \xrightarrow{t_1\cdots t_{i-1}} s_i$ is immediate by **D1**. This last piece of reasoning is repeated frequently in stubborn set theory, so it is handy that **D1** gives it as a ready-made step. We have proven the following generalization of Theorem 2.

Theorem 3. *Theorem 2 remains valid, if **D0**, **D1**, and **D2** replace **C0** and **C1**. Then transitions need not be deterministic.*

This is a generalization, because it applies to also nondeterministic transitions, and because, as will be seen in Theorem 5, in the case of deterministic transitions **C0** and **C1** imply **D0**, **D1**, and **D2**.

In the case of deterministic transitions, **D1** and **D2** have the following equivalent formulation:

Dd. If $t \in \mathsf{stubb}(s_0)$, $\neg(s_0 \xrightarrow{t})$, $t_i \notin \mathsf{stubb}(s_0)$ for $1 \leq i \leq n$, and $s_0 \xrightarrow{t_1 \cdots t_n} s_n$, then $\neg(s_n \xrightarrow{t})$.

De. If $t \in \mathsf{stubb}(s_0)$, $s_0 \xrightarrow{t} s_0'$, $t_i \notin \mathsf{stubb}(s_0)$ for $1 \leq i \leq n$, and $s_0 \xrightarrow{t_1 \cdots t_n} s_n$, then there is s_n' such that $s_n \xrightarrow{t} s_n'$ and $s_0' \xrightarrow{t_1 \cdots t_n} s_n'$.

Dd says that disabled transitions in the stubborn set remain disabled, while outside transitions occur. **De** says that enabled transitions in the stubborn set commute with sequences of outside transitions. It is immediately obvious that **PNd** and **PNe** imply **Dd** and **De**. Let us show that for deterministic transitions, this formulation indeed is equivalent to **D1** and **D2**.

Theorem 4. *If transitions are deterministic, then **D1** ∧ **D2** is equivalent to **Dd** ∧ **De**.*

Proof. Assume first that **D1** and **D2** hold. Then **Dd** follows immediately from **D1**. If $s_0 \xrightarrow{t} s_0'$ and $s_0 \xrightarrow{t_1 \cdots t_n} s_n$, then **D2** yields an s_n' such that $s_n \xrightarrow{t} s_n'$, after which **D1** yields an s_0'' such that $s_0 \xrightarrow{t} s_0'' \xrightarrow{t_1 \cdots t_n} s_n'$. Because transitions are deterministic, $s_0'' = s_0'$, so **De** is obtained.

Assume now that **Dd** and **De** hold. Then **D2** follows immediately from **De**. If $s_0 \xrightarrow{t_1 \cdots t_n} s_n \xrightarrow{t} s_n'$, then **Dd** yields an s_0' such that $s_0 \xrightarrow{t} s_0'$, after which **De** yields an s_0'' such that $s_0' \xrightarrow{t_1 \cdots t_n} s_n''$ and $s_n \xrightarrow{t} s_n''$. Because transitions are deterministic, $s_n'' = s_n'$, so **D1** is obtained. □

Similarly to the $\rightsquigarrow_M$-relation in Sect. 2, $\rightsquigarrow_s$-relations can be defined for Petri nets and other formalisms such that they guarantee **D1** and **D2**. Please see e.g., [19,24,26] for more information. This means that the stubborn set construction algorithm in Sect. 2 can be applied to many formalisms. Indeed, its implementation in ASSET is unaware of the formalism. It only has access to the $\rightsquigarrow_s$-relation and to the enabling status of each transition.

It would not be easy to describe this algorithm without allowing disabled transitions in the aps set. Indeed, instead of this algorithm, publications on ample and persistent sets suggest straightforward algorithms that test whether some obviously $\rightsquigarrow_s$-closed set is available and if not, revert to the set of all enabled transitions. This means that they waste reduction potential. The running time is not an important issue here, because, as experiments with ASSET have demonstrated [20, 21, 26], the algorithm is very fast.

The first publications on stubborn sets (such as [15]) used formalism-specific conditions resembling **PNd** and **PNe** instead of abstract conditions such as **D1** and **D2**.

It is now easy to show that every ample set is strongly stubborn.

Theorem 5. *If transitions are deterministic,* $\mathsf{ample}(s_0) \subseteq \mathsf{en}(s_0)$*, and* $\mathsf{ample}(s_0)$ *satisfies **C0** and **C1**, then* $\mathsf{ample}(s_0)$ *satisfies **D0**, **D1**, and **D2**.*

Proof. Clearly **C0** implies **D0**. **Dd** follows trivially from $\mathsf{ample}(s_0) \subseteq \mathsf{en}(s_0)$, and **De** follows immediately from **C1**. Now Theorem 4 gives the claim. ☐

Fig. 4. An example where $\{t\}$ satisfies **D0**, **D1**, and **D2**, but not **C1**.

Figure 4 demonstrates that the opposite does not hold. Clearly $\{t\}$ satisfies **D0** in 21. The only enabled sequences of transitions not containing t are ε and t_1. Checking them both reveals that $\{t\}$ also satisfies **D1** and **D2** in 21. However, $\{t\}$ does not satisfy **C1**, because t is not independent of t_1 because of 11.

To relate strong stubborn sets to persistent sets, the following theorem is useful.

Theorem 6. *Let* s_0 *be a state and* $\mathsf{stubb}(s_0)$ *be a set of transitions. If* $\mathsf{stubb}(s_0)$ *obeys **D0**, **D1**, and **D2** in* s_0*, then also* $\mathsf{stubb}(s_0) \cap \mathsf{en}(s_0)$ *obeys them in* s_0*.*

Proof. That $\mathsf{stubb}(s_0) \cap \mathsf{en}(s_0)$ obeys **D0** is immediate from **D0** for $\mathsf{stubb}(s_0)$.

Assume that $s_0 \xrightarrow{t_1 \cdots t_n}$, where $t_i \notin \mathsf{stubb}(s_0) \cap \mathsf{en}(s_0)$ for $1 \leq i \leq n$. We prove that no t_i is in $\mathsf{stubb}(s_0)$. To derive a contradiction, let i be the smallest such that $t_i \in \mathsf{stubb}(s_0)$. So $t_i \in \mathsf{stubb}(s_0)$, $t_i \notin \mathsf{en}(s_0)$, $s_0 \xrightarrow{t_1 \cdots t_{i-1} t_i}$, and $t_j \notin \mathsf{stubb}(s_0)$ for $1 \leq j < i$. This contradicts **D1** for $\mathsf{stubb}(s_0)$.

If the if-part of **D1** holds for $\mathsf{stubb}(s_0) \cap \mathsf{en}(s_0)$, then by the above, the if-part of **D1** holds also for $\mathsf{stubb}(s_0)$. So the then-part for $\mathsf{stubb}(s_0)$ holds, which is the same as the then-part for $\mathsf{stubb}(s_0) \cap \mathsf{en}(s_0)$. Similar reasoning applies to **D2**. ☐

Persistent sets also assume that transitions are deterministic. They rely on *independence in a state*. If t and t' are independent in s, then the following hold [6, Def. 3.17]:

1. If $s \xrightarrow{t}$ and $s \xrightarrow{t'}$, then there is s' such that $s \xrightarrow{tt'} s'$ and $s \xrightarrow{t't} s'$.
2. If $s \xrightarrow{tt'}$, then $s \xrightarrow{t'}$.

3. If $s \xrightarrow{t't}$, then $s \xrightarrow{t}$.

A set $\mathsf{pers}(s_0)$ is *persistent* in s_0 if and only if $\mathsf{pers}(s_0) \subseteq \mathsf{en}(s_0)$ and for every $t_1, \ldots, t_n$ and $s_1, \ldots, s_n$ such that $s_0 \xrightarrow{t_1} s_1 \xrightarrow{t_2} \cdots \xrightarrow{t_n} s_n$ and $t_i \notin \mathsf{pers}(s_0)$ for $1 \leq i \leq n$, it holds that every element of $\mathsf{pers}(s_0)$ is independent of t_i in s_{i-1} [6, Definition 4.1].

It is worth noticing that the concept of persistency would not change if items 2 and 3 were removed from the definition of independence in a state. Let $t \in \mathsf{pers}(s_0)$, and let s_0' be such that $s_0 \xrightarrow{t} s_0'$. Repeated application of item 1 yields $s_1', \ldots, s_n'$ such that $s_0' \xrightarrow{t_1} s_1' \xrightarrow{t_2} \cdots \xrightarrow{t_n} s_n'$ and $s_i \xrightarrow{t} s_i'$ for $1 \leq i \leq n$. Because for $1 \leq i \leq n$, both t and t_i are enabled in s_{i-1}, the then-parts of items 2 and 3 hold, and thus the items as a whole hold. That is, items 2 and 3 can be proven for the states s_{i-1}, so they need not be assumed. It seems plausible that items 2 and 3 were originally adopted by analogy to the independence relation in Mazurkiewicz traces [9].

The next theorem, from [27, Lemma 4.14], says that persistent sets are equivalent to strong stubborn sets restricted to deterministic transitions.

Theorem 7. *Assume that transitions are deterministic. Every nonempty persistent set satisfies **D0**, **D1**, and **D2**. If a set satisfies **D1** and **D2**, then its set of enabled transitions is persistent.*

Proof. Persistency immediately implies **De**. Because $\mathsf{pers}(s_0) \subseteq \mathsf{en}(s_0)$, it also implies **Dd**. These yield **D1** and **D2** by Theorem 4. If a persistent set is not empty, then it trivially satisfies **D0**.

Assume that $\mathsf{stubb}(s_0)$ satisfies **D1** and **D2**. Let $\mathsf{pers}(s_0) = \mathsf{stubb}(s_0) \cap \mathsf{en}(s_0)$. By Theorems 4 and 6, $\mathsf{pers}(s_0)$ satisfies **De**. Let $t \in \mathsf{pers}(s_0)$, s_0' be the state such that $s_0 \xrightarrow{t} s_0'$, $s_0 \xrightarrow{t_1} s_1 \xrightarrow{t_2} \cdots \xrightarrow{t_n} s_n$, and $t_i \notin \mathsf{pers}(s_0)$ for $1 \leq i \leq n$. **De** implies $s_0' \xrightarrow{t_1 \cdots t_n}$. Let $s_1', \ldots, s_n'$ be the states such that $s_0' \xrightarrow{t_1} s_1' \xrightarrow{t_2} \cdots \xrightarrow{t_n} s_n'$. Let $1 \leq i \leq n$. By giving **De** $t_1 \cdots t_i$ in the place of $t_1 \cdots t_n$ we see that **De** implies $s_i \xrightarrow{t} s_i'$ for $1 \leq i \leq n$. As a consequence, **De** implies for $1 \leq i \leq n$ that t is independent of t_i in s_{i-1}. This means that $\mathsf{pers}(s_0)$ is persistent. □

Deadlock-preserving **weak stubborn sets** use **D1** and the following condition **D2w**, that replaces both **D0** and **D2**.

D2w. If $\mathsf{en}(s_0) \neq \emptyset$, then there is $t_k \in \mathsf{stubb}(s_0)$ such that if $t_i \notin \mathsf{stubb}(s_0)$ for $1 \leq i \leq n$ and $s_0 \xrightarrow{t_1 \cdots t_n} s_n$, then $s_n \xrightarrow{t_k}$.

By choosing $n = 0$ we see that $s_0 \xrightarrow{t_k}$. That is, instead of requiring that all enabled transitions in a stubborn set remain enabled while outside transitions occur, **D2w** requires that one of them exists and remains enabled. This one is called *key transition* and denoted above with t_k.

Every strong stubborn set is also weak but not necessarily vice versa. Therefore, weak stubborn sets have potential for better reduction results. The first publication on stubborn sets [15] used weak stubborn sets. The added reduction potential of weak stubborn sets has only recently found its way to tools [4,7,8]. The proof of Theorem 3 goes through with **D2w** instead of **D2** and **D0**. Indeed, weak stubborn sets preserve many, but not necessarily all of the properties that strong stubborn sets preserve.

Excluding a situation that does not occur with most verification tools, if the system has infinite executions, then all methods in this section preserve at least one. The nondeterministic case of this theorem is new or at least little known.

Theorem 8. *Assume that $s_0 \in S_r$ and $s_0 \xrightarrow{t_1} s_1 \xrightarrow{t_2} \ldots$. If transitions are deterministic or the reduced state space is finitely branching, then there are t_1', t_2', $\ldots$ such that $s_0 \xrightarrow{t_1' t_2' \cdots}$ in the reduced state space.*

Proof. If any of the t_i is in $\mathsf{stubb}(s_0)$, then, for the smallest such i, by **D1**, there is s_0' such that $s_0 \xrightarrow{t_i} s_0' \xrightarrow{t_1 \cdots t_{i-1} t_{i+1} \cdots}$. Otherwise, by **D2w**, for every $j \in \mathbb{N}$ there is s_j' such that $s_j \xrightarrow{t_k} s_j'$. If transitions are deterministic, then **D1** yields $s_0' \xrightarrow{t_1} s_1' \xrightarrow{t_2} \cdots$. This argument can be repeated at s_0' and so on without limit, yielding the claim.

If transitions are not necessarily deterministic, then, for every $n \in \mathbb{N}$, **D1** can be applied to $s_0 \xrightarrow{t_1 \cdots t_n}$ or to $s_0 \xrightarrow{t_1 \cdots t_n t_k}$. This can be repeated n times, yielding an execution of length n in the reduced state space starting at s_0. If the reduced state space is finitely branching, then König's Lemma type of reasoning yields the claim. □

Consider a Petri net with two transitions and no places. Any reasonable implementation of the deadlock-preserving aps set method fires initially one transition, notices that it introduced a self-loop adjacent to the initial state, and terminates without ever trying the other transition. Let t be the fired and t' the other transition. In terms of Theorem 8, the infinite execution $\hat{s} \xrightarrow{t' t' t' \cdots}$ became represented by $\hat{s} \xrightarrow{ttt \cdots}$. So it is possible that $\{t_1, t_2, \ldots\} \cap \{t_1', t_2', \ldots\} = \emptyset$ in Theorem 8. More generally, if an original execution does not lead to a deadlock, then it is often the case that its representative in the reduced state space does not consist of precisely the same transitions. As a consequence, in the opinion of the present authors, when trying to understand aps set methods, Mazurkiewicz traces [9] and partial orders of transition occurrences are not a good starting point.

5   Visible and Invisible Transitions

Figure 5 shows a 1-safe Petri net, the directed graph that the $\leadsto_M$-relation spans in the shown marking $\{1, 4, 9\}$, and the similar graph for the marking $\{1, 6, 9\}$ that is obtained by firing t_3. Please ignore the grey p_{12} and t_7 until Sect. 6. Please ignore the dashed arrows for the moment. They will be explained soon.

Assume that we want to check whether always at least one of p_1 and p_8 is empty. We denote this property with $\square((M(p_1) = 0) \vee (M(p_8) = 0))$. It does not hold, as can be seen by firing $t_3 t_4 t_5$.

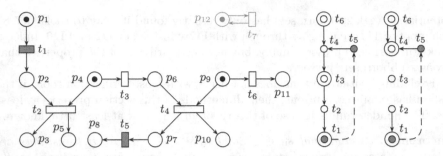

Fig. 5. A Petri net with two visible transitions and its $\leadsto_{\{1,4,9\}}$- and $\leadsto_{\{1,6,9\}}$-graphs. In the latter, p_2 is chosen as p_{t_2}. The dashed arrows arise from **V**.

According to the theory developed this far, $\{t_1\}$ is stubborn. Therefore, it suffices to fire just t_1 in the initial marking. After firing it, p_1 is permanently empty. As a consequence, no counterexample to $\Box((M(p_1) = 0) \vee (M(p_8) = 0))$ is found. We see that the basic strong stubborn set method does not preserve the validity of this kind of properties.

This problem can be solved in two steps. The second step will be described in Sects. 6 and 7, where systems that may exhibit cyclic behaviour are discussed. The first step consists of classifying transitions as *visible* and *invisible*, and adopting an additional requirement. The *atomic propositions* of $\Box((M(p_1) = 0) \vee (M(p_8) = 0))$ are $M(p_1) = 0$ and $M(p_8) = 0$. If a transition is known not to change the truth value of any atomic proposition in any reachable marking, it is classified as invisible. If the transition is known to change the truth value in at least one reachable marking or it is not known whether it can change it, then it is classified as visible. The additional requirement is the following.

V. If stubb(s_0) contains an enabled visible transition, then it contains all visible transitions (also disabled ones).

In the example, the grey transitions are visible and the rest are invisible. **V** adds the dashed arrows to the $\leadsto_M$-graphs in Fig. 5.

Assume **V**. Consider **D1**. Its t is enabled because $s_0 \xrightarrow{tt_1 \cdots t_n}$. Consider the sequence of visible transitions within $tt_1 \cdots t_n$, that is, the projection of $tt_1 \cdots t_n$ on visible transitions. If t is invisible, then it is obviously the same as the projection of $t_1 \cdots t_n t$. If t is visible, then **V** implies that $t_1, \ldots, t_n$ are invisible, because they are not in stubb(s_0) by the assumption in **D1**. So again the projections are the same. This means that when $t_1 \cdots t_n$ and $t'_1 \cdots t'_n$ are like in Theorems 2 and 3, the projection of $t_1 \cdots t_n$ is the same as the projection of $t'_1 \cdots t'_n$.

With Theorem 8, the projection of $t_1 t_2 \cdots$ is a prefix of the projection of $t'_1 t'_2 \cdots$ or vice versa. Sections 6 and 7 tell how they can be made the same.

For instance, $t_3 t_4 t_5 t_1$ leads to a deadlock in Fig. 5. In it, t_5 occurs before t_1. **V** guarantees that t_5 occurs before t_1 also in the permutation of $t_3 t_4 t_5 t_1$ whose existence Theorem 3 promises. By executing the permutation to a point where

t_5 has but t_1 has not yet occurred, a state in the reduced state space is found that violates $\Box((M(p_1) = 0) \vee (M(p_8) = 0))$. In this way $\mathbf{V}$ makes it possible to check many kinds of properties from the reduced state space.

Indeed, with the dashed arrow, the $\leadsto_M$-graph in Fig. 5 middle yields two stubborn sets: $\{t_1, \ldots, t_5\}$ and T. In both cases, t_3 is in the stubborn set. By firing t_3, the marking $\{1, 6, 9\}$ is obtained whose $\leadsto_M$-graph is shown in Fig. 5 right. This graph yields the stubborn sets $\{t_4, t_6\}$, $\{t_1, t_4, t_5, t_6\}$, and some others that have the same enabled transitions as one of these, such as $\{t_3, t_4, t_5, t_6\}$. All of them contain t_4. After firing it, each stubborn set contains t_1, t_5, and possibly some disabled transitions. So the sequence $t_3 t_4 t_5$ is fired in the reduced state space (after which t_1 is fired).

In the ample set theory, instead of $\mathbf{V}$ there is the following condition:

C2. If ample(s_0) contains a visible transition, then make ample(s_0) = en(s_0).

This condition is stronger than $\mathbf{V}$ in the sense that $\mathbf{C2}$ always forces at least the same enabled transitions to be taken as $\mathbf{V}$, but not necessarily vice versa. In particular, although $\{t_1, \ldots, t_5\}$ obeys $\mathbf{V}$ in the initial marking of our example, its set of enabled transitions (that is, $\{t_1, t_3\}$) does not obey $\mathbf{C2}$. Indeed, $\mathbf{C2}$ commands to fire all enabled transitions in $\{1, 4, 9\}$, including also t_6. Therefore, ample sets yield worse reduction in this example than stubborn sets.

It is difficult to formulate $\mathbf{V}$ without talking about disabled transitions in the stubborn set. For instance, consider "if the stubborn set contains an enabled visible transition, then it contains all enabled visible transitions". It allows to choose $\{t_1\}$ in $\{1, 4, 9\}$. However, we already saw that $\{t_1\}$ loses all counterexamples to the property. The ability to formulate better conditions than $\mathbf{C2}$ is an example of the advantages of allowing disabled transitions in stubborn sets.

The basis of the running example of this section (but not most of the details) is from [26].

6   The Ignoring Problem, Part 1: Finite Executions

Assume that the initially marked place p_{12}, transition t_7, and arcs between them are added to the Petri net in Fig. 5. Before the addition, the state space of the net is acyclic and has the deadlocks $\{3, 5, 11\}$, $\{2, 8, 10\}$, and $\{2, 6, 11\}$. The addition adds number 12 and the self-loop $M \xrightarrow{t_7} M$ to each reachable marking. It adds the stubborn set $\{t_7\}$ to each reachable marking and otherwise keeps the $\sqsubseteq_M$-minimal stubborn sets the same.

If t_7 is investigated first in the initial marking $\{1, 4, 9, 12\}$, then the stubborn set $\{t_7\}$ is chosen. Firing t_7 leads back to the initial marking. Therefore, the method only constructs the initial marking and its self-loop—that is, one marking and one edge. This is correct, because like the full state space, this reduced state space has no deadlocks but has an infinite execution. As a matter of fact, from the point of view of checking these two properties, the obtained reduction is ideal.

On the other hand, this reduced state space is clearly invalid for disproving the formula $\Box((M(p_1) = 0) \vee (M(p_8) = 0))$. This problem is known as the *ignoring problem*. After finding out that t_7 causes a self-loop in every reachable marking, the method stopped and ignored the rest of the Petri net.

Let $s \xrightarrow{\text{key}} s'$ denote that there are $s_0, \ldots, s_n$ and $t_1, \ldots, t_n$ such that $s = s_0 \xrightarrow{t_1} s_1 \xrightarrow{t_2} \cdots \xrightarrow{t_n} s_n = s'$ and t_i is a key transition of $\text{stubb}(s_{i-1})$ for $1 \leq i \leq n$. In [17,18], the ignoring problem was solved with the following condition **Sen**, and in [18] also with **SV**:

Sen. For every $t \in \text{en}(s_0)$ there is s_t such that $s_0 \xrightarrow{\text{key}} s_t$ and $t \in \text{stubb}(s_t)$.

SV. For every visible t there is s_t such that $s_0 \xrightarrow{\text{key}} s_t$ and $t \in \text{stubb}(s_t)$.

With deterministic transitions, **D1**, **D2w**, and **Sen** guarantee that if $s \in S_r$ and $s \xrightarrow{t_1 \cdots t_n}$, then there are $t'_1, \ldots, t'_m$ such that $s \xrightarrow{\pi}$ in the reduced state space for some permutation π of $t_1 \cdots t_n t'_1 \cdots t'_m$. This facilitates the verification of many properties. For instance, a transition is Petri net live (that is, from every reachable state, a state can be reached where it is enabled) if and only if it is Petri net live in the reduced state space. With deterministic transitions, **D1**, **D2w**, **V**, and **SV** guarantee that if $s \in S_r$ and $s \xrightarrow{t_1 \cdots t_n}$, then there is some transition sequence π such that $s \xrightarrow{\pi}$ in the reduced state space and the projection of π on the visible transitions is the same as the projection of $t_1 \cdots t_n$.

With deterministic transitions and strong stubborn sets, **Sen** can be implemented efficiently as follows [17,19]. Terminal strong components of the reduced state space can be recognized efficiently on-the-fly with Tarjan's algorithm [3,14]. (This resembles the algorithm in Sect. 2, but the directed graph in question is different.) If some transition is enabled in some state of a terminal strong component but does not occur in the component, then it is enabled in every state of the component by **D2** and **D1**. When the algorithm is about to backtrack from the component, it checks whether there are such transitions. If there are, it expands the stubborn set of the current state (called the *root* of the component) so that it contains at least one such transition. The expanded set must satisfy **D1** and **D2**. To avoid adding unnecessary enabled transitions, it is reasonable to compute it using the algorithm in Sect. 2 (without entering the transitions in the original stubborn set).

SV can be implemented similarly, except that the algorithm checks whether each visible transition is in some stubborn set used in the terminal strong component [26]. By **V**, this is certainly the case if any visible transition occurs in the component. Let $\text{CV}(M)$ denote the $\leadsto_M$-closure of the set of visible transitions. In the negative case, the algorithm expands the stubborn set of the root of the component with some subset of $\text{CV}(M)$ maintaining **D1**, **D2**, and **V**. This is continued until for each terminal strong component, either a visible transition occurs in it or the stubborn set of its root is a superset of $\text{CV}(M)$.

In the latter case it is certain that no visible transition can occur in the future, and the analysis may be terminated even if some enabled transitions were never investigated. This reasoning is valid also in the deadlocks of the reduced state space. In particular, if $\mathsf{CV}(M)$ contains no enabled transitions, then no transitions need to be fired, even if that violates **D0**. As a consequence, it is correct (and good for reduction results) to only use subsets of $\mathsf{CV}(M)$ as stubborn sets.

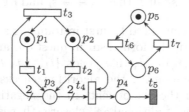

Fig. 6. Illustrating the nonoptimality of **Sen** and **SV**.

SV is nonoptimal in the sense that expanding the stubborn set with $\mathsf{CV}(M)$ may require the addition of enabled transitions that **Sen** and **V** together do not add. Figure 6 illustrates this. In it, the task is to find out whether t_5 can ever fire. It cannot, because t_4 is always disabled in a nontrivial way. We cannot assume that the stubborn set construction algorithm can detect that t_4 is always disabled, because detecting such a thing is **PSPACE**-hard in general. To be realistic, we instead assume that the stubborn set construction algorithm just uses **PNd** and **PNe** like in Sect. 2. In any reachable M, **PNd** declares either $t_4 \leadsto_M t_1$ and $t_4 \leadsto_M t_2$ or $t_4 \leadsto_M t_3$.

Assume that transitions are tried in the order of their indices as the starting points of the construction of stubborn sets. The stubborn set method first uses $\mathsf{stubb}(\hat{M}) = \{t_1\}$. So it fires t_1 yielding M_1. We have $t_1 \leadsto_{M_1} t_3 \leadsto_{M_1} t_1$, $t_3 \leadsto_{M_1} t_2 \leadsto_{M_1} t_4 \leadsto_{M_1} t_1$, and $t_4 \leadsto_{M_1} t_2$ (the last two via p_3). So the method uses $\mathsf{stubb}(M_1) = \{t_1, t_2, t_3, t_4\}$ and fires t_2 yielding M_2. Next it fires t_3 closing a cycle, using $\mathsf{stubb}(M_2) = \{t_3, t_4\}$, because $t_3 \leadsto_{M_2} t_4 \leadsto_{M_2} t_3$ (the latter via p_2). Because t_5 is visible and is not in any of these stubborn sets, the algorithm expands the root of the terminal strong component, that is, $\hat{M}$. The algorithm is cunning enough to avoid t_6, since $t_5 \not\leadsto^*_{\hat{M}} t_6$. On the other hand, $t_5 \leadsto_{\hat{M}} t_4 \leadsto_{\hat{M}} t_2$. So the algorithm fires t_2 at $\hat{M}$, making the size of the reduced state space grow.

Also **Sen** and **V** together guarantee that projections on visible transitions are preserved. Indeed, they were used in [18]. They do not add t_2 to $\mathsf{stubb}(\hat{M})$ in Fig. 6, because $t_2 \in \mathsf{stubb}(M_1)$. Unfortunately, they are nonoptimal in the sense that they unnecessarily solve the ignoring problem also for the invisible transitions. In Fig. 6, they add t_6 to $\mathsf{stubb}(\hat{M})$.

We now present and prove correct a novel condition that is free from both of these problems. We first rewrite **Dd** using T' in the place of $\mathsf{stubb}(s_0)$.

Dd. If $t \in T'$, $\neg(s_0 \xrightarrow{t})$, $t_i \notin T'$ for $1 \leq i \leq n$, and $s_0 \xrightarrow{t_1 \cdots t_n} s_n$, then $\neg(s_n \xrightarrow{t})$.

Let $T_i \subseteq T$ be any set of transitions. Typical examples of T_i are the set of visible transitions and the set of all transitions. We call its elements *the interesting transitions*. The following condition solves the ignoring problem.

S. There is $T' \subseteq T$ such that $T_i \subseteq T'$, T' satisfies **Dd** in s_0, and for every $t \in T' \cap \text{en}(s_0)$ there is s_t such that $s_0 \xrightarrow{\text{key}} s_t$ and $t \in \text{stubb}(s_t)$.

An often good T' can be computed by first introducing a $\leadsto'_s$-relation only using **PNd** or its counterpart in the formalism in question, and then computing the $\leadsto'_s$-closure of T_i. In Fig. 6 in $\hat{M}$, this yields $\{t_1, t_2, t_4, t_5\}$. For each root s of each terminal strong component, the algorithm checks that each element of $T' \cap \text{en}(s)$ occurs within the component. In the negative case, the algorithm expands $\text{stubb}(s)$ with the traditional $\leadsto_s$-closure (that is, the one that uses the counterparts of both **PNd** and **PNe**) of some missing element of $T' \cap \text{en}(s)$. To obtain an $\sqsubseteq_M$-minimal result, Tarjan's algorithm is used similarly to Sect. 2 also during this step. In Fig. 6 in $\hat{M}$, we have $T' \cap \text{en}(\hat{M}) = \{t_1, t_2\}$. Because $t_1 \in \text{stubb}(\hat{M})$ and $t_2 \in \text{stubb}(M_1)$, **S** holds. The algorithm terminates, without expanding $\text{stubb}(\hat{M})$ and without ever trying t_6.

By choosing $T_i = T$ we get $T' = T$ and see that **Sen** implies **S**. Together with the example in Fig. 6, this shows that **S** is strictly better than **Sen**.

The comparison of **S** to **SV** is more difficult. Therefore, we only compare their implementations described above. Let T_i be the set of visible transitions. If no visible transition can be made enabled in the future, then the algorithm for **SV** ultimately expands the stubborn set $\text{stubb}(s)$ of the root s of the terminal strong component with $\text{CV}(s)$. The word "ultimately" refers to the fact that the algorithm may try subsets of $\text{CV}(s)$ before trying $\text{CV}(s)$ as a whole, and, as a consequence, new states may be generated such that the component ceases from being terminal or s ceases from being its root.

In the same situation, the algorithm for **S** obtains $T' \cap \text{en}(s)$ by computing the $\leadsto'_s$-closure of T_i and picking the enabled transitions in it. If none of these transitions occurs in the component, then the **S** algorithm ultimately expands $\text{stubb}(s)$ with them. When doing so it computes their $\leadsto_s$-closures, to satisfy **D1**, **D2**, and **V**. The union of the computed sets is $\text{CV}(s)$. So in this case, the **S** algorithm makes the same expansion as the **SV** algorithm. On the other hand, if any of these transitions does occur in the component, then the **S** algorithm does not use it for expanding $\text{stubb}(s)$. Then the **S** algorithm is better than the **SV** algorithm. This is what happened with t_2 in Fig. 6.

We now prove that **S** is correct.

Lemma 9. *If transitions are deterministic, $s_0 \in S_r$, $\text{stubb}(s_0)$ obeys **S**, $\text{stubb}(s)$ obeys **D2w** in every $s \in S_r$, and $s_0 \xrightarrow{t_1 \cdots t_n} s_n$ where $t_n \in T_i$, then there are s'_0, ..., s'_m and $t^1_k, \ldots, t^m_k$ such that $s'_0 = s_0$, $s'_0 \xrightarrow{t^1_k} s'_1 \xrightarrow{t^2_k} \cdots \xrightarrow{t^m_k} s'_m$, t^{i+1}_k is a key transition of $\text{stubb}(s'_i)$ and $\{t_1, \ldots, t_n\} \cap \text{stubb}(s'_i) = \emptyset$ for $0 \leq i < m$, and $\{t_1, \ldots, t_n\} \cap \text{stubb}(s'_m) \neq \emptyset$.*

Proof. Because $t_n \in T_i \subseteq T'$, there is $1 \leq i \leq n$ such that $t_i \in T'$ but $t_j \notin T'$ for $1 \leq j < i$. By **Dd** $t_i \in \text{en}(s_0)$. By **S** there is s_{t_i} such that $t_i \in \text{stubb}(s_{t_i})$

and $s_0 \xrightarrow{\text{key}} s_{t_i}$. Let the states along this path be called $s'_0, \ldots, s'_h$. So $s'_0 = s_0$, $s'_h = s_{t_i}$ and $t_i \in \{t_1, \ldots, t_n\} \cap \text{stubb}(s'_h)$. Thus there is the smallest m such that $\{t_1, \ldots, t_n\} \cap \text{stubb}(s'_m) \neq \emptyset$, completing the proof. □

Theorem 10. *Assume that transitions are deterministic and* $\text{stubb}(s)$ *obeys* **D1**, **D2w**, *and* **S** *in every* $s \in S_r$. *Let* $s_0 \in S_r$ *and* $s_0 \xrightarrow{t_1} s_1 \xrightarrow{t_2} \cdots \xrightarrow{t_n} s_n$. *There are* $t'_1, \ldots, t'_m$, *and* s_m *such that* $s_0 \xrightarrow{t'_1 \cdots t'_m} s_m$ *in the reduced state space and each* $t \in T_i$ *occurs in* $t'_1 \cdots t'_m$ *at least as many times as it occurs in* $t_1 \cdots t_n$. *Furthermore,*

- *If* $T_i = T$, *then there are* $t_{n+1}, \ldots, t_m$ *such that* $s_n \xrightarrow{t_{n+1} \cdots t_m} s_m$ *and* $t'_1 \cdots t'_m$ *is a permutation of* $t_1 \cdots t_m$.
- *If* T_i *is the set of visible transitions and* $\text{stubb}(s)$ *obeys* **V** *in every* $s \in S_r$, *then the projections of* $t_1 \cdots t_n$ *and* $t'_1 \cdots t'_m$ *on* T_i *are the same.*

Proof. If none of $t_1, \ldots, t_n$ is in T_i, the first claim holds vacuously with $m = 0$. Otherwise let $1 \leq n' \leq n$ be the biggest such that $t_{n'} \in T_i$. Lemma 9 yields s' and $t^1_k, \ldots, t^{m'}_k$ such that $s_0 \xrightarrow{t^1_k \cdots t^{m'}_k} s'$ and $\{t_1, \ldots, t_{n'}\} \cap \text{stubb}(s') \neq \emptyset$. Applying **D2w**, **D1**, and determinism m' times yields s'' such that $s' \xrightarrow{t_1 \cdots t_{n'}} s''$ and $s_{n'} \xrightarrow{t^1_k \cdots t^{m'}_k} s''$. **D1** produces from $s' \xrightarrow{t_1 \cdots t_{n'}} s''$ a transition occurrence in the reduced state space that consumes one of $t_1, \ldots, t_{n'}$. The first claim follows by induction.

If $T_i = T$, then always $n' = n$. The $t^1_k, \ldots, t^{m'}_k$ introduced in each application of Lemma 9 are the $t_{n+1}, \ldots, t_m$.

In the case of the last claim, each key transition is invisible, because otherwise $t_{n'}$ would be in the stubborn set of the key transition by **V**, contradicting Lemma 9. Therefore, the applications of **D2w** neither add visible transitions nor change the order of the visible transitions. By **V**, the same holds for the applications of **D1**. □

In the literature, **S** may refer to any condition that plays the role of **Sen**, **SV**, or (from now on) the **S** of the present study. This is because there is usually no need to talk about more than one version of the condition in the same publication. The name **S** refers to "safety properties", which is the class of properties whose counterexamples are finite (not necessarily deadlocking) executions.

In [20,22] it was pointed out that it is often possible and perhaps even desirable to modify the model such that from every reachable state, a deadlock is reachable. Reduction with deterministic transitions, **D0**, **D1**, and **D2** preserves this property. Two efficient algorithms were given for checking from the reduced state space that this property holds. Such systems trivially satisfy **S**. This solution to the ignoring problem is simple. As far it is known, it gives good reduction results. (Little is known on the relative performance of alternative solutions to the ignoring problem.)

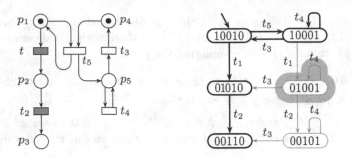

Fig. 7. Terminal strong components vs. cycles.

7 The Ignoring Problem, Part 2: Diverging Executions

Figure 7 demonstrates that **S** does not always suffice to preserve a property. Consider $\Diamond\Box(M(p_2) = 0)$, that is, from some point on, p_2 remains empty. It fails because of $t_5 t_1 t_4 t_4 t_4 \cdots$. However, the figure shows a reduced state space that obeys **D0**, **D1**, **D2**, **V**, and **S**, but contains no counterexample.

This problem only arises with *diverging* counterexamples, that is, those which end with an infinite sequence of invisible transitions. A state is called *diverging* if and only if there exists an infinite sequence of invisible transitions from it. When finite counterexamples apply, the methods in Sect. 6 suffice. If the reduced state spaces are finite (as they usually are with practical computer tools), they suffice also for counterexamples that contain an infinite number of visible transitions. This is because the methods preserve every finite prefix of the projection on visible transitions, from which König's Lemma type of reasoning proves that also the infinite projection is preserved.

With stubborn sets, this problem has been solved by two conditions that together replace **S**:

I. If $\mathsf{en}(s_0)$ contains an invisible transition, then $\mathsf{stubb}(s_0)$ contains an invisible key transition.

L. For every visible transition t, every cycle in the reduced state space (which is assumed to be finite) contains a state s such that $t \in \mathsf{stubb}(s)$.

Let $t_1 t_2 \cdots$ be such that $s_0 \xrightarrow{t_1 t_2 \cdots}$ and only a finite number of the t_i are visible. Assume that $t_1 t_2 \cdots$ contains at least one visible transition t_v. Similarly to the proof of Theorem 10, key transitions and **D2w** are used to go to a state whose stubborn set contains some t_i, and then **D1** is used to move a transition occurrence from the sequence to the reduced state space. At most $|S_r| - 1$ applications of **D2w** and **D1** may be needed before some t_i such that $i \leq v$ is consumed, because otherwise the reduced state space would contain a cycle without t_v in any of its stubborn sets, violating **L**. As a consequence, each visible transition of $t_1 t_2 \cdots$ is eventually consumed.

When that has happened, **I** ensures that the reduced state space gets an infinite invisible suffix. Without **I**, it could happen that only visible transitions are fired immediately after consuming the last t_v, spoiling the counterexample.

A diverging execution ξ is minimal if and only if there is no infinite execution whose projection on visible transitions is a proper prefix of the projection of ξ. Minimal diverging counterexamples are preserved even without **L** and **S**. This implies that if the reduced state space is finite, then **D1**, **V**, **I**, and a variant of **D2w** preserve [18, 23] the failures–divergences semantics in CSP theory [13]. **D2w** is replaced by a variant, because CSP uses nondeterministic transitions.

With deterministic transitions **D1** and **D2w** also give an interesting result for diverging executions, one that is worth commenting here.

Theorem 11. *Assume that transitions are deterministic and* stubb(s) *obeys* **D1** *and* **D2w** *in every* $s \in S_r$. *Assume further that* $s_0 \xrightarrow{t_1} s_1 \xrightarrow{t_2} \cdots \xrightarrow{t_m} s_0$ *are invisible key transitions. If* $s_0 \xrightarrow{u_1 \cdots u_n} s_0'$ *is a sequence in the full state space such that* $\{u_1, \ldots, u_n\} \cap \bigcup_{i=0}^{m-1}(\text{stubb}(s_i) \cap \text{en}(s_i)) = \emptyset$, *then* s_0' *is diverging in the full state space.*

Proof. Proof is by induction on m. $s_0 \xrightarrow{u_1 \cdots u_n} s_0'$ holds as the base case. Assume as inductive hypothesis that there is some s_i' such that $s_i \xrightarrow{u_1 \cdots u_n} s_i'$ and $s_0' \xrightarrow{t_1 \cdots t_i} s_i'$. $u_j \notin \text{stubb}(s_i) \cap \text{en}(s_i)$ for each $1 \leq j \leq n$. Because u_1, if it exists, is enabled at s_i, it must be that $u_1 \notin \text{stubb}(s_i)$, and applying **D1** to $j = 2, \ldots, n$ we get that $u_j \notin \text{stubb}(s_i)$ for each $1 \leq j \leq n$. Because t_{i+1} is a key transition, **D2w** guarantees $s_i' \xrightarrow{t_{i+1}} s_{i+1}'$ for some state s_{i+1}' and $s_{i+1} \xrightarrow{u_1 \cdots u_n} s_{i+1}'$ is guaranteed by **D1**. Because $s_{m-1} \xrightarrow{t_m} s_0$, deterministic transitions guarantee that $s_m' = s_0'$. ∎

Note that when **D2** or **De** is used instead of **D2w**, every enabled transition in any stubborn set is a key transition, so the theorem can be restated so that if a state is diverging in the reduced state space, then all states reachable by firing transitions that were ignored in the cycle are likewise diverging.

The theorem works to reinforce the intuition behind **L**. Consider Fig. 7. In the state in the upper right corner, $\{t_3, t_4\}$ is a stubborn set, and the state is diverging. According to the theorem, t_1 will lead to a diverging state, but nothing is guaranteed about the divergence in the part where t_3 has been fired. Theorem 11 can be used to make the reduced state space smaller, by not stipulating **I** when the presence of a divergence can be obtained with the theorem. More information on this is in [23].

Ample sets do not mention **I**, because it follows from **C0**, **C2**, and the fact that all transitions in an ample set are key transitions by **C1**. Instead of **L**, ample sets use the following condition.

C3. For every t and every cycle in the reduced state space, if t is enabled in some state of the cycle, then the cycle contains a state s such that $t \in \text{ample}(s)$.

The relation of **L** to **C3** resembles the relation of **SV** to **Sen**. This suggests that an improvement on **C3** could be developed similarly to how **S** improves **Sen**. We leave this for future research.

The recommended implementation of **C3'** is called **C3'** in [1]. It assumes that the reduced state space is constructed in depth-first order. It also implements **L**.

C3'. If $\mathsf{ample}(s) \neq \mathsf{en}(s)$, then for every $t \in \mathsf{ample}(s)$ and every s' such that $s \xrightarrow{t} s'$, s' is not in the depth-first stack.

Figure 8 illustrates that **C3'** sometimes leads to the construction of unnecessarily many states. In it, all reachable states are constructed, although the processes do not interact at all. Better results are obtained if the component (either $\{t_1, t_2, t_3\}$ or $\{t_4, t_5, t_6\}$) is preferred to which the most recent transition belongs. Then the sequence $t_1 t_2 t_4 t_5 t_3 t_1$ is fired, after which both t_2 and t_6 are fired. This improved idea fails badly with the three-dimensional version of the example. In [2, Sect. 4, Fig. 4], the bad performance of **C3'** was illustrated with a different example.

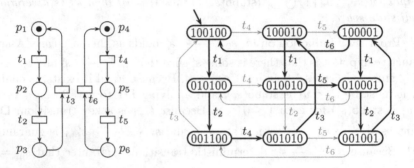

Fig. 8. Transitions are tried in the order of their indices until one is found that does not close a cycle. If such a transition is not found, then all transitions are taken.

C3' fully expands the last state of the cycle it closes. If the first state of the cycle is expanded instead and if the component is remembered, then the leftmost column and topmost row of Fig. 8 right are constructed. (Expanding the first or the last state is correct, but other states are not necessarily safe [23, Lemma 15].) This is better than with **C3'**, and works well also in the three-dimensional example, as well as for the example in [2]. There has been very little research on the performance of cycle conditions besides [2], although the problem is clearly important.

8   Trouble with Fairness

Fairness refers to assumptions about infinite executions that are used to root out certain nonsensical counterexamples. For example in Fig. 9, there is an infinite execution $(t_1 t_2)^\omega$ where t_5 is never fired, even though it is constantly enabled. *Weak fairness* is an assumption that if a transition is constantly enabled, it will eventually be fired. This can be understood, for example, so that in a concurrent

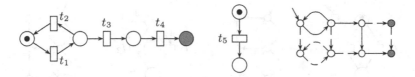

Fig. 9. All weakly fair non-progress cycles may be lost.

execution of several processes, each process gets processor time, making it a reasonable assumption to discuss. *Strong fairness* is a stronger assumption that if a transition is enabled infinitely often (though it may be disabled infinitely often also), then it is eventually fired. That is, we say that a cycle $s_0 \xrightarrow{t_1 \cdots t_n} s_n$ such that $s_0 = s_n$ is

- *weakly fair* if and only if for every $t \in T$, either there is some i such that $t_i = t$ or $t \notin \mathsf{en}(s_i)$, and
- *strongly fair* if and only if for every $t \in T$, either there is some i such that $t_i = t$ or $t \notin \mathsf{en}(s_j)$ for every $1 \leq j \leq n$.

In Fig. 9 we see a situation where weak fairness and stubborn sets encounter a problem. The set $\{t_1\}$ is an aps set in the initial state that satisfies all the conditions this far. In the second state $\{t_2, t_3\}$ satisfies all except **C3** and **C3'**. In particular, it satisfies **L**.

The cycle in the reduced state space, indicated by the solid arrows, seems like a fair cycle in the reduced state space, but in the full state space it has a constantly enabled transition that is not fired along the cycle. A cycle that is fair in the reduced state space, but not necessarily in the full state space, is called a *seemingly fair* cycle. The full state space has a fair cycle, but this is not explored, only the seemingly fair cycle above it. The condition **C3** is sufficiently strong in this example, as it guarantees that t_5 is fired in at least one state of the seemingly fair cycle. The cycle remains seemingly fair, but the corresponding fair cycle is also explored.

One is tempted to explore a hypothesis that a seemingly fair cycle exists in the reduced state space if and only if a corresponding fair cycle exists in the full state space. In Fig. 10, we see that this hypothesis does not hold. The transition t_3 is constantly enabled, and the transition is fired in one of the states along the cycle, so that **L** is satisfied. The cycle itself is not fair, but it is seemingly fair. This happens even if **C3** is used.

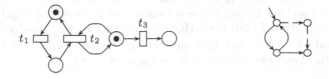

Fig. 10. A seemingly weakly fair non-progress cycle may be fake.

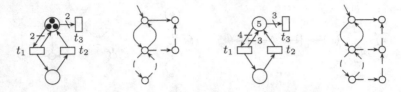

Fig. 11. Two Petri nets illustrating yet another weak fairness problem.

Again, we are tempted to form a hypothesis that some algorithm that makes use of book-keeping regarding transitions along a cycle could be used to determine whether a weakly fair cycle was lost or not. The example in Fig. 11 leaves little hope for the development of such methods. In the leftmost example, the first cycle is unfair, but becomes seemingly fair when reduced. The second cycle, consisting of the same transitions, is not explored and the initial state does have all the enabled transitions in the aps set, so that the reduction satisfies **C3**. The full state space has a fair cycle and the reduced state space has a seemingly fair cycle.

In the rightmost example in the same figure, exactly the same aps sets can be used. The reduced state space is the same as in the leftmost example, and the sets of enabled transitions are the same in all the states of the reduced state space. Now the full state space does not have a fair cycle, but the reduced state space still has a seemingly fair cycle.

The first state space contains a fair cycle in the unexplored part and the second does not. Unless a method can use information about the system structure beyond that expressed by the conditions seen this far, and the part of the state space that has been explored, it cannot distinguish between the two state spaces.

Fig. 12. Illustrating a strong fairness problem.

None of the cycles in Fig. 11 is strongly fair, but a similarly discouraging example for preserving strong fairness exists, and is shown in Fig. 12. The full state space has a strongly fair cycle that is never explored by a reduction. Again, from the point of view of aps sets and the enabled transitions in the reduced state space, the Petri net is equivalent to the ones in Fig. 11.

9   Conclusions

The goal in the development of stubborn sets has been as good reduction as possible, while ample and persistent sets have favoured straightforward easily implementable conditions and algorithms. As a consequence, where stubborn set methods differ from other aps set methods, stubborn sets tend to be more difficult to implement but yield better reduction results. Very little is known on the differences of the reduction power between different methods. Reliable information is difficult to obtain experimentally, because in addition to the issue that is being experimented, the results may depend on the optimality of the chosen $\rightsquigarrow_s$- or independence relation, on the order in which the transitions are listed in the input file (Sect. 3), and other things.

Some stubborn set ideas are difficult to implement efficiently. For instance, no very fast algorithm is known that can utilize the freedom to choose any one from among the places that disable a transition (the p_t in Sect. 2). On the other hand, the likelihood of finding good ways of exploiting some reduction potential decreases significantly, if the existence of the potential is never pointed out.

The algorithm in Sect. 2 seems intuitively very good, and experiments with the ASSET tool strongly support this view [20,21,26]. The present authors believe that it deserves more attention than it has received.

The biggest immediate difference between stubborn sets and other aps set methods is the possibility of disabled transitions in the set. It is difficult to think of the above-mentioned algorithm without this possibility. Furthermore, in Sect. 5 it was shown how it facilitates an improvement to the visibility condition. It is also important that stubborn sets allow nondeterministic transitions.

Perhaps the most important area where more research is needed is the ignoring problem. The example in Fig. 8 may be extreme and thus not representative of the typical situation. Unfortunately, very little is known on what happens in the typical situation with each solution.

Acknowledgements. This study is an extended version of [25]. We thank the anonymous reviewers of both PNSE and ToPNoC for their comments.

References

1. Clarke, E.M., Grumberg, O., Peled, D.A.: Model Checking. MIT Press, Cambridge (1999). 314 p
2. Evangelista, S., Pajault, C.: Solving the ignoring problem for partial order reduction. Software Tools Technol. Transf. **12**(2), 155–170 (2010)
3. Eve, J., Kurki-Suonio, R.: On computing the transitive closure of a relation. Acta Informatica **8**(4), 303–314 (1977)
4. Gibson-Robinson, T., Hansen, H., Roscoe, A.W., Wang, X.: Practical partial order reduction for CSP. In: Havelund, K., Holzmann, G., Joshi, R. (eds.) NFM 2015. LNCS, vol. 9058, pp. 188–203. Springer, Cham (2015). doi:10.1007/978-3-319-17524-9_14

5. Godefroid, P.: Using partial orders to improve automatic verification methods. In: Clarke, E.M., Kurshan, R.P. (eds.) Computer-Aided Verification 1990, AMS-ACM DIMACS Series in Discrete Mathematics and Theoretical Computer Science, vol. 3, pp. 321–340 (1991)
6. Godefroid, P. (ed.): Partial-Order Methods for the Verification of Concurrent Systems. LNCS, vol. 1032. Springer, Heidelberg (1996)
7. Hansen, H., Lin, S.-W., Liu, Y., Nguyen, T.K., Sun, J.: Diamonds are a girl's best friend: partial order reduction for timed automata with abstractions. In: Biere, A., Bloem, R. (eds.) CAV 2014. LNCS, vol. 8559, pp. 391–406. Springer, Cham (2014). doi:10.1007/978-3-319-08867-9_26
8. Laarman, A., Pater, E., van de Pol, J., Weber, M.: Guard-based partial-order reduction. In: Bartocci, E., Ramakrishnan, C.R. (eds.) SPIN 2013. LNCS, vol. 7976, pp. 227–245. Springer, Heidelberg (2013). doi:10.1007/978-3-642-39176-7_15
9. Mazurkiewicz, A.: Trace theory. In: Brauer, W., Reisig, W., Rozenberg, G. (eds.) ACPN 1986. LNCS, vol. 255, pp. 278–324. Springer, Heidelberg (1987). doi:10. 1007/3-540-17906-2_30
10. Peled, D.: All from one, one for all: on model checking using representatives. In: Courcoubetis, C. (ed.) CAV 1993. LNCS, vol. 697, pp. 409–423. Springer, Heidelberg (1993). doi:10.1007/3-540-56922-7_34
11. Peled, D.: Ten years of partial order reduction. In: Hu, A.J., Vardi, M.Y. (eds.) CAV 1998. LNCS, vol. 1427, pp. 17–28. Springer, Heidelberg (1998). doi:10.1007/ BFb0028727
12. Rauhamaa, M.: A comparative study of methods for efficient reachability analysis. Lic. Technical Thesis, Helsinki University of Technology, Digital Systems Laboratory, Research Report A-14. Espoo, Finland (1990)
13. Roscoe, A.W.: Understanding Concurrent Systems. Springer, Heidelberg (2010). doi:10.1007/978-1-84882-258-0. 533 p.
14. Tarjan, R.E.: Depth-first search and linear graph algorithms. SIAM J. Comput. 1(2), 146–160 (1972)
15. Valmari, A.: Error detection by reduced reachability graph generation. In: Proceedings of the 9th European Workshop on Application and Theory of Petri Nets, pp. 95–122 (1988)
16. Valmari, A.: State Space Generation: Efficiency and Practicality. Dr. Technical Thesis, Tampere University of Technology Publications 55, Tampere (1988)
17. Valmari, A.: Stubborn sets for reduced state space generation. In: Rozenberg, G. (ed.) ICATPN 1989. LNCS, vol. 483, pp. 491–515. Springer, Heidelberg (1991). doi:10.1007/3-540-53863-1_36
18. Valmari, A.: Stubborn set methods for process algebras. In: Peled, D., Pratt, V., Holzmann, G. (eds.) Partial Order Methods in Verification, Proceedings of a DIMACS Workshop, DIMACS Series in Discrete Mathematics and Theoretical Computer Science vol. 29, pp. 213–231. American Mathematical Society (1997)
19. Valmari, A.: The state explosion problem. In: Reisig, W., Rozenberg, G. (eds.) ACPN 1996. LNCS, vol. 1491, pp. 429–528. Springer, Heidelberg (1998). doi:10. 1007/3-540-65306-6_21
20. Valmari, A.: Stop it, and be stubborn!. In: Haar, S., Meyer, R. (eds.) 15th International Conference on Application of Concurrency to System Design, pp. 10–19. IEEE Computer Society (2015)
21. Valmari, A.: A state space tool for concurrent system models expressed in C++. In: Nummenmaa, J., Sievi-Korte, O., Mäkinen, E. (eds.) CEUR Workshop Proceedings of SPLST 2015, Symposium on Programming Languages and Software Tools, vol. 1525, pp. 91–105 (2015)

22. Valmari, A.: Stop it, and be stubborn!. ACM Trans. Embed. Comput. Syst. **16**(2), 46:1–46:26 (2017)
23. Valmari, A.: More stubborn set methods for process algebras. In: Gibson-Robinson, T., Hopcroft, P., Lazić, R. (eds.) Concurrency, Security, and Puzzles. LNCS, vol. 10160, pp. 246–271. Springer, Cham (2017). doi:10.1007/978-3-319-51046-0_13
24. Valmari, A., Hansen, H.: Can stubborn sets be optimal? Fundam. Informaticae **113**(3–4), 377–397 (2011)
25. Valmari, A., Hansen, H.: Stubborn set intuition explained. In: Cabac, L., Kristensen, L.M., Rölke, H. (eds.) CEUR Workshop Proceedings of the International Workshop on Petri Nets and Software Engineering 2016, vol. 1591, pp. 213–232 (2016)
26. Valmari, A., Vogler, W.: Fair testing and stubborn sets. In: Bošnački, D., Wijs, A. (eds.) SPIN 2016. LNCS, vol. 9641, pp. 225–243. Springer, Cham (2016). doi:10.1007/978-3-319-32582-8_16
27. Varpaaniemi, K.: On the Stubborn Set Method in Reduced State Space Generation. Ph.D. Thesis, Helsinki University of Technology, Digital Systems Laboratory Research Report A-51, Espoo, Finland (1998)

Decomposed Replay Using Hiding
and Reduction as Abstraction

H.M.W. Verbeek[✉]

Department of Mathematics and Computer Science, Eindhoven University of
Technology, Eindhoven, The Netherlands
h.m.w.verbeek@tue.nl

Abstract. In the area of process mining, decomposed replay has been
proposed to be able to deal with nets and logs containing many different activities. The main assumption behind this decomposition is that
replaying many subnets and sublogs containing only some activities is
faster then replaying a single net and log containing many activities.
Although for many nets and logs this assumption does hold, there are
also nets and logs for which it does not hold. This paper shows an example net and log for which the decomposed replay may take way more time,
and provides an explanation why this is the case. Next, to mitigate this
problem, this paper proposes an alternative way to abstract the subnets
from the single net, and shows that the decomposed replay using this
alternative abstraction is faster than the monolithic replay even for the
problematic cases as identified earlier. However, the alternative abstraction often results in longer computation times for the decomposed replay
than the original abstraction. An advantage of the alternative abstraction
over the original abstraction is that its cost estimates are typically better.

1 Introduction

The area of *process mining* [1] is typically divided into *process discovery*, *process
conformance*, and *process enhancement*. In the context of *big data*, a decomposition approach [2] has been introduced that includes both process discovery
(decomposed discovery) and process conformance (decomposed replay). In this
paper, we take this decomposed replay for process conformance as a starting
point. The main assumptions for this decomposed replay are that (1) checking
conformance using a monolithic replay (that is, by replaying a single net and
log, which contain many different activities) takes prohibitively much time, and
that (2) checking conformance using a decomposed replay (that is, by replaying
a series of abstracted subnets and sublogs, which each contain far less different
activities than the single net and log) takes far less time. The decomposition
approach as introduced in [2] abstracts from a single Petri net a collection of
subnets with shared transitions on their borders, and guarantees that (1) the
result of the decomposed replay is perfect if and only if the result of the monolithic replay is perfect, and (2) the result of the decomposed replay provides a
lower bound for the result of the monolithic replay otherwise.

© Springer-Verlag GmbH Germany 2017
M. Koutny et al. (Eds.): ToPNoC XII, LNCS 10470, pp. 166–186, 2017.
DOI: 10.1007/978-3-662-55862-1_8

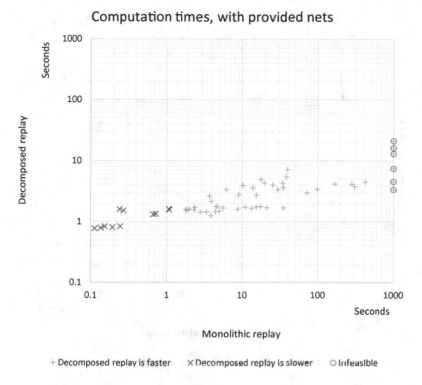

Fig. 1. Computation times for the monolithic and decomposed replay with the nets as provided by the data sets.

Figure 1 supports this assumption by showing typical computation times for the nets and logs as found in a number of data sets [7–9]. These data sets contain in total 59 cases of varying size, ranging from 12 to 429 activities, from 500 to 2000 traces, with varying numbers of mismatching traces (from 0% to 50%). This figure shows that if the monolithic replay would take more than a second, the decomposed replay would be faster. Furthermore, it shows that some replays do not finish within 10 min (see [9] why we use a timeout here of 10 min) using the monolithic replay, whereas all replays finish well within 10 min using the decomposed replay.

However, Fig. 2 paints a different picture. It shows the typical computation times for replaying the log as found in the data sets on the net *as discovered using the Inductive miner* [6] from that log. As for this replay we only require a log (and not a net), we included some additional data sets [4,5] for this figure. This figure shows that in some cases the decomposed replay actually requires much more time than the monolithic replay. For example, the monolithic replay requires less than 10 s for the *a22f0n05* case, where the decomposed replay takes more than 10 min.

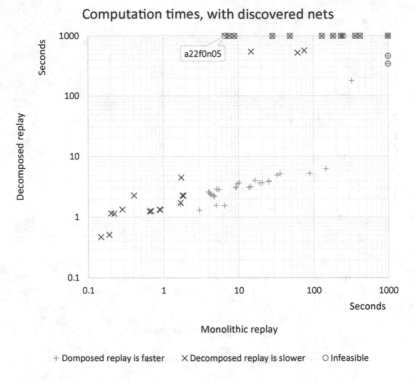

Fig. 2. Computation times for the monolithic and decomposed replay with the nets discovered using the *Inductive Miner* from the logs as provided by the data sets.

In this paper, we investigate the root cause of this problem. Based on these findings, we propose an *alternative abstraction* to mitigate the problem. This alternative abstraction is based on the well-known concepts of hiding transitions and reducing nets. We show that, in almost all cases that take more than 10 s for the monolithic replay the decomposed replay using this hide-and-reduce abstraction is indeed faster. However, we will also show that the original decomposed replay (that is, the decomposed replay using the original abstraction) is often faster than the hide-and-reduce decomposed replay (that is, the decomposed replay using the hide-and-reduce abstraction). But, whereas the original decomposed replay does take more time for some of the observed cases, the hide-and-reduce decomposed replay does not. Finally, we show that the hide-and-reduce decomposed replay has an extra advantage, as it may provide a better estimate for the replay costs than the original decomposed replay.

The remainder of this paper is organized as follows. First, Sect. 2 introduces the necessary concepts, like accepting Petri nets and alignments. Second, Sect. 3 shows that there is a possible problem with the original decomposed replay, and proposes the hide-and-reduce abstraction to mitigate this problem. Third, Sect. 4 evaluates the hide-and-reduce decomposed replay using the existing data sets, which shows that it can handle more cases than the monolithic and/or original decomposed replay, and that it returns a better lower bound for the costs as the original decomposed replay. Last, Sect. 5 concludes the paper.

2   Preliminaries

2.1   Logs

In this paper, we consider *activity logs*, which are an abstraction of the *event logs* as found in practice. An *activity log* is a collection of traces, where every trace is a sequence of *activities* [1]. Table 1 shows the example activity log L_1, which contains information about 20 cases, for example, 4 cases followed the trace $\langle a_1, a_2, a_4, a_5, a_8 \rangle$. In total, the log contains $13 + 17 + 9 + 2 \times 9 + 9 + 4 \times 5 + 9 + 9 + 5 + 5 + 17 + 3 \times 5 + 5 + 5 = 156$ activities.

Table 1. An example activity log L_1 in tabular form.

Trace	Frequency
$\langle a_1, a_2, a_4, a_5, a_6, a_2, a_4, a_5, a_6, a_4, a_2, a_5, a_7 \rangle$	1
$\langle a_1, a_2, a_4, a_5, a_6, a_3, a_4, a_5, a_6, a_4, a_3, a_5, a_6, a_2, a_4, a_5, a_7 \rangle$	1
$\langle a_1, a_2, a_4, a_5, a_6, a_3, a_4, a_5, a_7 \rangle$	1
$\langle a_1, a_2, a_4, a_5, a_6, a_3, a_4, a_5, a_8 \rangle$	2
$\langle a_1, a_2, a_4, a_5, a_6, a_4, a_3, a_5, a_7 \rangle$	1
$\langle a_1, a_2, a_4, a_5, a_8 \rangle$	4
$\langle a_1, a_3, a_4, a_5, a_6, a_4, a_3, a_5, a_7 \rangle$	1
$\langle a_1, a_3, a_4, a_5, a_6, a_4, a_3, a_5, a_8 \rangle$	1
$\langle a_1, a_3, a_4, a_5, a_8 \rangle$	1
$\langle a_1, a_4, a_2, a_5, a_6, a_4, a_2, a_5, a_6, a_3, a_4, a_5, a_6, a_2, a_4, a_5, a_8 \rangle$	1
$\langle a_1, a_4, a_2, a_5, a_7 \rangle$	3
$\langle a_1, a_4, a_2, a_5, a_8 \rangle$	1
$\langle a_1, a_4, a_3, a_5, a_7 \rangle$	1
$\langle a_1, a_4, a_3, a_5, a_8 \rangle$	1

Definition 1 (Universe of activities). *The set $\mathcal{A}$ denotes the universe of activities.*

To capture an activity log, we use multi-sets. If S is a set of objects, then $\mathcal{B}(S)$ is a multi-set of objects, that is, if $B \in \mathcal{B}(S)$ and $o \in S$, then object o occurs $B(o)$ times in multi-set B.

Definition 2 (Activity log). *Let $A \subseteq \mathcal{A}$ be a set of activities. An activity log L over A is a multi-set of activity traces over A, that is, $L \in \mathcal{B}(A^*)$.*

2.2 Nets

In this paper, we assume that a net is an accepting Petri net, that is, a labeled Petri net with an initial marking and a set of final markings. The transition labels are used to denote the activity a transition corresponds to. Transitions that do not correspond to an activity are labeled τ, and are henceforth called invisible. The other (activity-labeled) transitions are henceforth called visible transitions. The initial marking and final markings are needed for the replay, which needs to start at the initial marking and needs to end in a final marking.

Definition 3 (Petri net). *A Petri net is a 3-tuple (P, T, F) where P is a set of places, T is a set of transitions such that $P \cap T = \emptyset$, and $F \subseteq (P \times T) \cup (T \times P)$ is a set of arcs.*

Definition 4 (Accepting Petri net). *Let $A \subseteq \mathcal{A}$ be a set of activities. An accepting Petri net over the set of activities A is a 6-tuple (P, T, F, l, I, O) where (P, T, F) is a Petri net, $l \in T \rightarrow (A \cup \{\tau\})$ is a labeling function that links every transition onto an activity (possibly the dummy activity τ), $I \in \mathcal{B}(P)$ is an initial marking, and $O \subseteq \mathcal{B}(P)$ is a set of final markings.*

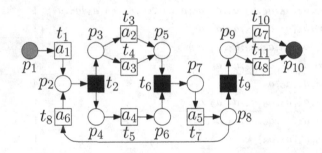

Fig. 3. An accepting Petri net N_1. (Color figure online)

Figure 3 shows an accepting Petri net containing 10 places $\{p_1, \ldots, p_{10}\}$, 11 transitions $\{t_1, \ldots, t_{11}\}$ of which 8 labeled with activities $\{a_1, \ldots, a_8\}$ and 3 invisible, and 24 arcs. The initial marking consists of a single token in place p_1 (indicated by the light green color), and the only final marking consists of a single token in place p_{10} (indicated by the darker red color). Please note that, although this example does not show this, multiple transitions can be labeled by the same activity.

2.3 Alignments

Assume that on the example net N_1 we want to replay the trace $\langle a_1, a_2, a_3, a_4, a_5, a_6, a_7, a_8 \rangle$, that is, we want to find the *best* transition sequence that starts in the initial marking, ends in a final marking, and that has the given trace as *activity sequence*. Basically, the activity sequence corresponds to the transitions sequence which every transitions replaced by its label and all τ labels removed afterwards. Finding the best transition sequence is done by first finding a transition sequence, and second to impose some notion of costs to every found transition sequence. By keeping these costs minimal while finding a transition sequence, we then obtain the best transition sequence.

To find a transition sequence, the replayer [3] creates a number of possible *moves*, and assigns *costs* to every move. A move can be a synchronous move, a log move, a visible model move, or an invisible model move. A synchronous move consists of a transitions and its label, that is, its corresponding activity. As an example, the move (t_3, a_2) is a synchronous move for net N_1, indicating that transition t_3 was fired which matched activity a_2 in the trace. A log move consists of a dummy transition (indicated by $\gg$) and an activity. As an example, the move $(\gg, a_2)$ is a log move for net N_1, indicating that activity a_2 could not be matched to any enabled transition. A visible model move consists of a visible transition and a dummy activity (also indicated by $\gg$). As an example, the move $(t_3, \gg)$ is a visible model move for net N_1, indicating that visible transition t_3 was fired but could not be matched to any activity in the trace. An invisible model move consists of an invisible transition and the τ label. As an example, the move (t_2, τ) is an invisible model move for net N_1, indicating that invisible transition t_2 was fired.

Definition 5 (Legal moves). *Let $A \subseteq \mathcal{A}$ be a set of activities, let $\sigma \in A^*$ be an activity trace over A, and let $N = (P, T, F, l, I, O)$ be an accepting Petri net over A. The set of legal moves of A and N is the union of the sets $\{(a, t) | a \in A \wedge t \in T \wedge l(t) = a\}$ (synchronous moves), $\{(a, \gg) | a \in A\}$ (log moves), $\{(\gg, t) | t \in T \wedge l(t) \in A\}$ (visible model moves), and $\{(\tau, t) | t \in T \wedge l(t) = \tau\}$ (invisible model moves).*

Log moves and visible model moves hint at mismatches, as these indicate that either some activity could not be matched by a proper enabled transition, or that the firing of the transition could not be matched to its activity in the trace. For this reason, the costs of these moves are typically set to positive values, whereas the costs for the other moves are set to 0. For sake of completeness, we mention that in this paper we have used costs 10 for every log move and costs 4 for every visible model move. Although these values are quite arbitrary, they were inspired by (1) the fact that by default the monolithic replay uses costs 5 for every log move and costs 2 for visible model move, and (2) the fact that the decomposed replay needs to divide the costs over multiple (often one or two) subnets. So, we kept the ratio 5:2, but used even numbers[1].

Definition 6 (Costs structure). *Let $A \subseteq \mathcal{A}$ be a set of activities, and let $N = (P, T, F, l, I, O)$ be an accepting Petri net over A. A cost structure \$ for A*

---

[1] A complicating factor here is that the current implementation of the monolithic replayer takes costs with an integer value. As a result, we cannot evenly split the costs 5 of a model move over two subnets. Therefore, we initially set out with costs 10 and 4. Later on, we implemented a more elaborate scheme to have the decomposed replayer support a costs divided by any number of subnets.

and N is a function that maps every legal move of A and N onto a (non-negative) natural number.

Using these moves and these costs, the question for the replayer is then to find a sequence of moves such that (1) the activities correspond to the given activity sequence, (2) the transitions correspond to a possible transition sequence in the net that starts in the initial marking and ends in the final marking, and (3) has minimal costs. This sequence of moves is henceforth called an *optimal trace alignment*.

Definition 7 (Trace alignment). *Let $A \subseteq \mathcal{A}$ be a set of activities, let $\sigma \in A^*$ be an activity trace over A, and let $N = (P, T, F, l, I, O)$ be an accepting Petri net over A. A trace alignment h for trace σ on net N is a sequence of legal moves $(a, t) \in ((A \cup \{\tau, \gg\}) \times (T \cup \{\gg\}))$ such that:*

- *$\sigma = h\lceil_A^1$ and*
- *For some $o \in O$ it holds that $I[h\lceil_T^2 \rangle o$,*

where

$$h\lceil_A^1 = \begin{cases} \langle \rangle & \text{if } h = \langle \rangle; \\ \langle a \rangle \cdot \overline{h}\lceil_A^1 & \text{if } h = \langle (a, t) \rangle \cdot \overline{h} \text{ and } a \in A; \\ \overline{h}\lceil_A^1 & \text{if } h = \langle (a, t) \rangle \cdot \overline{h} \text{ and } a \notin A \end{cases}$$

and

$$h\lceil_T^2 = \begin{cases} \langle \rangle & \text{if } h = \langle \rangle; \\ \langle t \rangle \cdot \overline{h}\lceil_T^2 & \text{if } h = \langle (a, t) \rangle \cdot \overline{h} \text{ and } t \in T; \\ \overline{h}\lceil_T^2 & \text{if } h = \langle (a, t) \rangle \cdot \overline{h} \text{ and } t \notin T. \end{cases}$$

Definition 8 (Costs of trace alignment). *Let $A \subseteq \mathcal{A}$ be a set of activities, let $\sigma \in A^*$ be an activity trace over A, let $N = (P, T, F, l, I, O)$ be an accepting Petri net over A, let $h = \langle (a_1, t_1), \ldots, (a_n, t_n) \rangle$ be a trace alignment (of length n) for σ and N, and let $\$$ be a cost structure for A and N. The costs of trace alignment h, denoted $\$h$, is defined as the sum of the costs of all legal moves in the alignment, that is, $\$h = \sum_{i \in \{1, \ldots, n\}} \$(a_i, t_i)$.*

Definition 9 (Optimal trace alignment). *Let $A \subseteq \mathcal{A}$ be a set of activities, let $\sigma \in A^*$ be an activity trace over A, let $N = (P, T, F, l, I, O)$ be an accepting Petri net over A, let h be a trace alignment for σ and N, and let $\$$ be a cost structure for A and N. The trace alignment h is called optimal if there exists no other trace alignment h' such that $\$h' < \$h$.*

Figure 4 shows an optimal trace alignment for the trace $\langle a_1, \ldots, a_8 \rangle$ and net N_1. Please note that an optimal trace alignment may not be unique. In the example, we could also have chosen to do a synchronous move on a_3 and a log move on a_2. The resulting alignment would also be optimal.

a_1	τ	a_2	a_3	a_4	τ	a_5	a_6	τ	a_7	a_8
t_1	t_2	t_3	$\gg$	t_5	t_6	t_7	$\gg$	t_9	t_{10}	$\gg$
0	0	0	10	0	0	0	10	0	0	10

Fig. 4. A trace alignment for the trace $\langle a_1,\ldots,a_8\rangle$ and net N_1. Every column corresponds to a move, where the top row contains the activities, the middle row the transitions, and the bottom row the costs of every move.

2.4 Decomposed Replay

For small number of activities (like 8 as in the example), computing an optimal trace alignment on the entire net may be possible within 10 min, but for larger numbers (say 200 or more), the replay will take considerable more time. To alleviate this, decomposed replay has been proposed in [2]. In decomposed replay, we first decompose the net into subnets, where the following restrictions are taken into account:

– Every place ends up in a single subnet.
– Every invisible transition ends up in a single subnet.
– Every arc ends up in a single subnet.
– If multiple visible transitions share the same label, then these transitions end up in a single subnet.

As a result, only visible transitions that have a unique label can be distributed over the subnets. Figure 5 shows how the example net N_1 can be decomposed into 5 subnets.

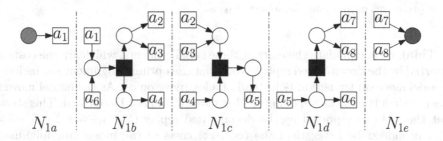

Fig. 5. The decomposed nets obtained by decomposing the net N_1. Subnets N_{1b}, N_{1c}, N_{1d}, and N_{1e} have the empty marking as initial marking, while the subnets N_{1a}, N_{1b}, N_{1c}, and N_{1d} have the empty marking as the only final marking.

The costs associated to the various moves are also decomposed (see also [2]). For example, the activity a_1 appears in two subnets (N_{1a} and N_{1b}). As a result, a log move on a_1 in N_{1a} costs $10/2 = 5$ and a log move on a_1 in N_{1b} costs 5 as well. Note that, by coincidence, all activities appear in two subnets, therefore, all log moves in all subnets now cost 5. If some activity would have appeared in three subnets, then the costs for a log move for every subnet would be 10/3. As a result of this decomposition, if all subalignments in the decomposed replay agree on a log move for a_1, then the costs are identical to a log move in the monolithic replay. Likewise, a visible model move on transition t_1 in N_{1a} costs $4/2 = 2$ and a visible model move in N_{1b} costs 2 as well. In theory, the costs for the synchronous moves and invisible model moves are also decomposed in a similar way, but as both are typically 0, we typically ignore them.

Second, we decompose the trace into subtraces, and replay every subtrace on the corresponding subnet. Figure 6 shows the resulting subalignments.

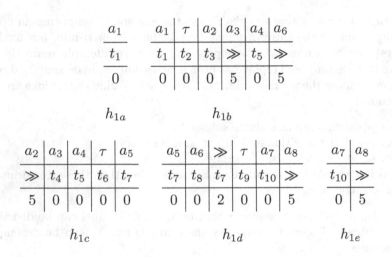

Fig. 6. Possible optimal decomposed alignments. h_{1b} is an optimal alignment for sub-trace $\langle a_1, a_2, a_3, a_4, a_6 \rangle$ and the subnet N_{1b}, etc.

Third, we accumulate the costs of these subalignments, which are the costs as reported by the decomposed replay. Note that the optimal alignment h_{1d} includes a model move on transition t_7 instead of a log move on a_7. As the model move is cheaper than the log move, doing the log move would not be optimal. This shows that the costs as reported by the decomposed replay ($5 + 5 + 5 + 2 + 5 + 5 = 27$) can indeed be lower than the (correct) costs of the monolithic alignment ($10 + 10 + 10 = 30$).

As indicated in the Introduction, the decomposed replay is often much faster than the monolithic replay. Because of the formal guarantees as provided by [2], we know that the decomposed replay only returns costs 0 if and only if the monolithic replay returns costs 0, and that otherwise the decomposed replay returns less costs than the monolithic replay (that is, the decomposed replay provides a lower bound for the correct costs of the monolithic replay). As such, we can use the decomposed replay as a fast way to check whether there are any costs involved, and to obtain a lower bound for the correct costs.

3   Hide and Reduce

In the Introduction, we have shown that for some cases, the decomposed replay actually takes way more time than the monolithic replay. As an example, if we take the log from the *a22f0n05* case [7], discover a net for it using the *Inductive Miner*, and replay the log on the discovered net, then the monolithic replay requires less than 10 s, whereas the decomposed replay fails to finish within 10 min. In this section, we use the *a22f0n05* case to find the root cause of this problem. After having found that root cause, this section proposes an alternative way of abstracting subnets from the single net for the decomposed replay to mitigate this root cause.

Figure 7 shows the net as discovered by the *Inductive Miner* from the *a22f0n05* log. This net can be decomposed into 9 subnets. Two of these subnets contain a single activity (*S+complete*, *E+complete*), 6 contain two activities, and the last subnet contains 20 activities (only the activities *S+complete* and *t+complete* are not included in this subnet). The time to replay the first 8

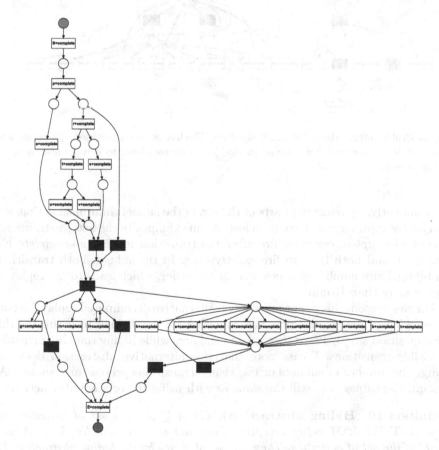

Fig. 7. The net as discovered by the *Inductive Miner* from the *a22f0n05* log.

sublogs on the subnets range from 9 to 65 ms, but the replay on this last subnet turns out to require more than 10 min.

Figure 8 shows this problematic subnet, which immediately shows the root cause of the problem: This subnet contains five source transitions (transitions without incoming arcs), and a fair number (13) of places. Because the source transitions are always enabled, they can be fired at any possible reachable state. While checking for the optimal path through the search space of alignments, the replayer needs to investigate all enabled transitions in every state. For this subnet, the fact that 5 transitions are enabled in every state is too much for the replayer.

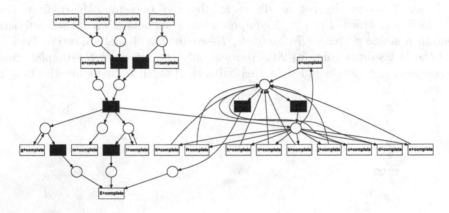

Fig. 8. Problematic subnet for *a22f0n05* case. The five source transitions (*a+complete*, *p+complete*, *s+complete*, *u+complete*, and *v+complete*) lead to a huge search space for the replay.

Apparently, by removing parts of the net in the subnet, information that was vital for the replayer may have been lost. As an example, in the net, the transition labeled *s+complete* can only fire after the transition labeled *p+complete* has been fired, and both have to fire exactly once. In the subnet, both transitions can be fired any number of times, and in any order, which leads to the replay to require more than 10 min.

For this reason, this paper presents an alternative decomposed replay. Instead of removing places, transitions, and arcs that do not belong to a subnet, this decomposition simply keeps these places and arcs while hiding (making invisible) all visible transitions. Please note that this alternative abstraction does not change the number of subnets or the visible transitions present in a subnet. As a result, the sublogs are still the same as with using the original abstraction.

Definition 10 (Hiding abstraction). *Let $A \subseteq \mathcal{A}$ be a set of activities, let $N = (P, T, F, l, I, O)$ be an accepting Petri net over A, and let $A_i \subseteq A$ be a subset of the set of activities. Then the net obtained by the hiding abstraction for*

N and A_i, denoted $N(A_i)$, is the accepting Petri net $(P, T, F, l(A_i), I, O)$ such that

$$l(A_i)(t) = \begin{cases} l(t) & \textit{if } l(t) \in A_i; \\ \tau & \textit{if } l(t) \notin A_i. \end{cases}$$

As a result, the structure of the otherwise-removed parts is maintained, and hence the inter-transition relations as described before are maintained.

We now first show that the optimal costs when using the hiding abstraction is a lower bound for the optimal monolithic costs. Second, we show that the optimal costs when using the original abstraction is a lower bound for the optimal costs when using the hiding abstraction. Third, we conclude that optimal costs when using the hiding abstraction offers a *better lower bound* for the optimal monolithic costs.

Theorem 1 (Hiding abstraction preserves trace alignments). *Let $A \subseteq \mathcal{A}$ be a set of activities, let $N = (P, T, F, l, I, O)$ be an accepting Petri net over A, let $\sigma \in A^*$, let h be a (monolithic) trace alignment for σ and N, and let $A_i \subseteq A$ be a subset of the set of activities. Then $h\restriction_{A_i}$ is a (decomposed) trace alignment for $\sigma\restriction_{A_i}$ and $N(A_i)$, where*

$$h\restriction_{A'} = \begin{cases} \langle\rangle & \textit{if } h = \langle\rangle; \\ \langle(a', t)\rangle \cdot \overline{h}\restriction_{A'} & \textit{if } h = \langle(a', t)\rangle \cdot \overline{h} \textit{ and } a' \in A'; \\ \langle(\gg, t)\rangle \cdot \overline{h}\restriction_{A'} & \textit{if } h = \langle(a', t)\rangle \cdot \overline{h} \textit{ and } a' \notin A'. \end{cases}$$

and

$$\sigma\restriction_{A'} = \begin{cases} \langle\rangle & \textit{if } h = \langle\rangle; \\ \langle a'\rangle \cdot \overline{\sigma}\restriction_{A'} & \textit{if } h = \langle a'\rangle \cdot \overline{h} \textit{ and } a' \in A'; \\ \overline{\sigma}\restriction_{A'} & \textit{if } h = \langle a'\rangle \cdot \overline{h} \textit{ and } a' \notin A'. \end{cases}$$

Proof. By construction. By applying the hiding abstraction, visible transitions not contained in A_i are made invisible, while the rest remains as-is. Hence the moves in the monolithic trace alignment become invisible model moves in the decomposed trace alignment.

Corollary 1 (The optimal decomposed costs when using the hiding abstraction is a lower bound for the optimal monolithic costs). *If we assume that only log moves and visible model moves have non-zero costs, then the optimal decomposed costs when using the hiding abstraction is a lower bound for the optimal monolithic costs.*

Proof. For every subnet, a decomposed trace alignment can be constructed from the optimal monolithic trace alignment. The combined costs of these constructed decomposed trace alignments for all subnets is identical to the costs of the monolithic trace alignment. The costs for an *optimal* decomposed trace alignment of all subnets is a lower bound for these decomposed costs, and hence for the monolithic costs.

Theorem 2 (Original abstraction preserves trace alignments). *Let $A \subseteq \mathcal{A}$ be a set of activities, let $N = (P, T, F, l, I, O)$ be an accepting Petri net over A, let $\sigma \in A^*$, let $A_i \subseteq A$ be a subset of the set of activities, let h be an (alternative decomposed) trace alignment for $\sigma \restriction_{A_i}$ and $N(A_i)$, and let $N' = (P', T', F', l', I', O')$ be the subnet obtained from N for A_i by using the original abstraction. Then $h \restriction_{T'}$ is an (original decomposed) trace alignment for $\sigma \restriction_{A_i}$ and N', where*

$$
h \restriction_{T'} = \begin{cases} \langle \rangle & \text{if } h = \langle \rangle; \\ \langle (a, t') \rangle \cdot \overline{h} \restriction_{T'} & \text{if } h = \langle (a, t') \rangle \cdot \overline{h} \text{ and } t' \in T'; \\ \overline{h} \restriction_{T'} & \text{if } h = \langle (a, t') \rangle \cdot \overline{h} \text{ and } t' \notin T'. \end{cases}
$$

Proof. By construction. The net N' is a subnet of net $R(A_i)$, and on the interface between N' and $N(A_i)$ there are only visible transitions. As a result, the behavior of $R(A_i)$ is more restrictive than the behavior of N'.

Corollary 2 (The optimal decomposed costs using the original abstraction is a lower bound for the optimal costs using the hiding abstraction). *If we assume that only log moves and visible model moves have non-zero costs, then the optimal decomposed costs when using the original abstraction is a lower bound for the optimal costs when using the hiding abstraction.*

Proof. If we have an optimal decomposed trace alignment using the hiding abstraction, we can construct a trace alignment using the original abstraction. These trace alignments have identical costs, as all transitions present in $N(A_i)$ but not present in N' are invisible. The costs for an *optimal* decomposed trace alignment when using the original abstraction is a lower bound for the costs of the constructed trace alignment, and hence for the costs of the optimal decomposed trace alignment using the hiding abstraction.

As a result of both Corollaries, if we assume that only log moves and visible model moves have non-zero costs, than the decomposed costs using the hiding abstraction offers a *better lower bound* for the monolithic costs than the decomposed costs using the original abstraction.

Corollary 3 (Hiding abstraction preserves costs 0). *An optimal monolithic trace alignment has costs 0 if and only if the optimal decomposed trace alignment using the hiding abstraction has costs 0.*

Proof. ($\Rightarrow$) If the optimal monolithic trace alignment has costs 0, then the optimal decomposed trace alignment using the hiding abstraction also has costs 0, as it is a lower bound. ($\Leftarrow$) From [2] we know that the original abstraction preserves costs 0. Hence, if the optimal monolithic trace alignment has costs >0, then the decomposed trace alignment using the original abstraction has costs >0. As the costs of the optimal decomposed trace alignment using the original abstraction is a lower bound for the costs of the optimal decomposed trace alignment using the hiding abstraction, these latter costs also have to be >0.

This hiding abstraction step is then optionally followed by a reducing abstraction step using well-known Petri-net-reduction rules [10]. This makes the net as small as possible for the replayer. Figure 9 shows an overview of these reduction rules when applied to accepting Petri nets. From this figure, it is clear that these rules preserve the branching activity behavior of the net:

- The rules cannot remove any visible transition.
- The FPT rule can only remove an invisible transition if there exists another invisible transition.

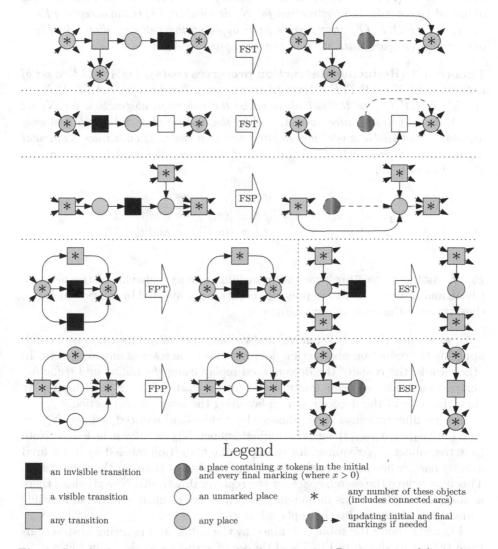

Legend

- ■ an invisible transition
- □ a visible transition
- ▨ any transition
- ◗ a place containing x tokens in the initial and every final marking (where $x > 0$)
- ○ an unmarked place
- ◯ any place
- ＊ any number of these objects (includes connected arcs)
- ◖▶ updating initial and final markings if needed

Fig. 9. Standard reduction rules extended for accepting Petri nets, and limited to preserve the branching activity behavior.

- The FPP rule can only remove an unmarked place (that is, a place not involved in the initial or any final marking) if there exists another unmarked place.
- The ESP rule can only remove a marked place which has x tokens in the initial and every final marking, where $x > 0$.
- If a marked place is removed, the initial and final markings are updated accordingly.

Definition 11 (Reducing abstraction). *Let $A \subseteq \mathcal{A}$ be a set of activities, and let $N = (P, T, F, l, I, O)$ be an accepting Petri net over A. Then the net obtained by the reducing abstraction for N, denoted $R(N)$, is the accepting Petri net (P', T', F', l, I', O') that results from applying the rules as shown in Fig. 9 over and over again until no rule can be applied anymore.*

Theorem 3 (Reducing abstraction preserves costs). *Let $A \subseteq \mathcal{A}$ be a set of activities, let $N = (P, T, F, l, I, O)$ be an accepting Petri net over A, let $R(N) = (P', T', F', l, I', O')$ be the net obtained by the reduction abstraction for N, let $\sigma \in A^*$ be an activity trace over A, and let the cost function $\$$ be such that only log moves and visible model moves have non-zero costs. Then a trace alignment h for σ and N has costs X if and only if the trace alignment $h \restriction_{T'}$ for σ and $R(N)$ has costs X, where*

$$
h \restriction_{T'} = \begin{cases} \langle \rangle & \text{if } h = \langle \rangle; \\ \langle (a, t') \rangle \cdot \overline{h} \restriction_{T'} & \text{if } h = \langle (a, t') \rangle \cdot \overline{h} \text{ and } t' \in T'; \\ \overline{h} \restriction_{T'} & \text{if } h = \langle (a, t') \rangle \cdot \overline{h} \text{ and } t' \notin T'. \end{cases}
$$

Proof. As these rules preserve the branching activity behavior of the net (see Fig. 9, and as moves that have non-zero costs are not affected by these reductions, they preserve the costs of any alignment.

If we assume that only log moves and visible model moves have non-zero costs, applying the reduction abstraction does not affect the costs of any alignment. In other words, the costs of the decomposed replay using *the hiding and reduction* abstraction is also a *better lower bound* for the costs of the monolithic replay than the costs of the decomposed replay using the *original* abstraction.

As an illustration, Fig. 10 shows the hidden-and-reduced subnet $N'_{1b} = R(N(\{a_1, a_2, a_3, a_4, a_6\}))$ for the original subnet N_{1b} as shown in Fig. 5. Note that the subnet N'_{1b} requires, for example, the transition labeled a_1 to be fired exactly once, whereas it could be fired any number of times in the subnet N_{1b}. This may reduce the search space for the replayer drastically. Nevertheless, there is also a downside, as this hiding-and-reducing may result in additional invisible transitions, which need to be replayed as well.

Figure 11 shows the subnet obtained by the hiding and reducing abstractions from the net as shown in Fig. 7 and the set of activities as shown in Fig. 8.

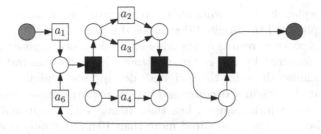

Fig. 10. Hidden-and-reduced subnet $N'_{1b} = R(N(\{a_1, a_2, a_3, a_4, a_6\}))$.

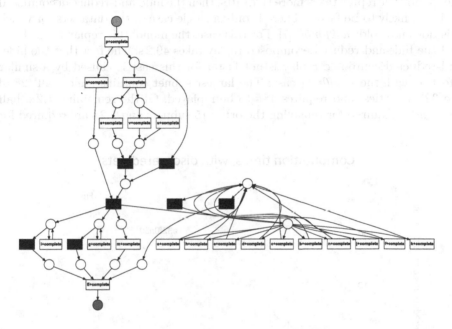

Fig. 11. Hidden-and-reduced subnet for *a22f0n05* case.

We expect this *hide-and-reduce* decomposed replay (that is, the decomposed replay using the hide-and-reduce abstractions) to be faster than the monolithic replay, and to provide a better (higher) lower bound for the correct replay costs as the *original* decomposed replay. In the next section, we will evaluate these assumptions.

4   Evaluation

We have evaluated the hide-and-reduce decomposed replay on the same data sets as we used in the Introduction. First, this section will evaluate the computation times of the hide-and-reduce decomposed replay by comparing them to the computation times of the monolithic replay. Second, it will evaluate the lower bounds for the correct replays costs as obtained by the hide-and-reduce decomposed replay by comparing them to the costs as obtained by both the monolithic replay and the original decomposed replay.

Figure 12 shows the results of the hide-and-reduce decomposed replay using the nets as discovered by the *inductive Miner*. Note the contrast with Fig. 2, which shows similar times for the (original) decomposed replay.

Recall that the original decomposed replay requires more than 10 min for a number of cases which required less than 10 min with the monolithic replay. The hide-and-reduce replay required more than 10 min for only one single case (*prFm6* [9]), which also requires more than 10 min with the monolithic replay. If the monolithic replay takes more than 10 s, then the hide-and-reduce decomposed replay is likely to be faster. There is only a single case in the data sets for which this does not hold: *a32f0n50* [7]. For this case, the monolithic replay takes 49.1 s and the hide-and-reduce decomposed replay takes 49.2 s. The fact that the hide-and-reduce decomposed replay is not faster for this case is caused by a similar effect as with the *a22f0n05* case: The largest subnet contains almost all (28 of the 32) activities, and requires 48 s to be replayed. Of the remaining 1.2 s, half a second is required for replaying the other 15 subnets and 1.2 s are required for

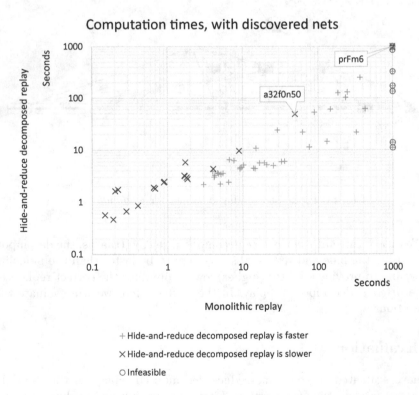

Fig. 12. Computation times for the monolithic and hide-and-reduce decomposed replay with the nets discovered using the *Inductive Miner* from the logs as provided by the data sets.

splitting the log and net and merging the alignments. In contrast, the original decomposed replay requires more than 10 min for this and 13 other cases, and takes way longer for another three.

As a result we conclude that for the nets as discovered by the *Inductive Miner*, the hide-and-reduce decomposed replay requires less than 10 min for more cases than the other two replays. As such, it is an improvement over these other replays. Furthermore, it is typically faster than the monolithic replay when the latter takes more than 10 s. As such, it is an improvement over this replay.

Figure 13 shows the results of the hide-and-reduce decomposed replay using the nets as provided by the data sets. Like the original decomposed replay, the hide-and-reduce decomposed replay requires less than 10 min for all data sets and it is typically faster than the monolithic replay. Exceptions to this are the *prAm6* and *prBm6* cases [9]. In both cases, the nets and logs are decomposed in more than 300 subnets and sublogs, the replay of these sublogs on these subnets requires only 2 s (where the monolithic replay requires almost 40 s), but the reduction step takes about 60 and 40 s. For the other five cases for which the hide-and-reduce decomposed replay takes more than 10 s, this reduction step is also the bottleneck. For all these cases, the replay requires at most 5 s, but the

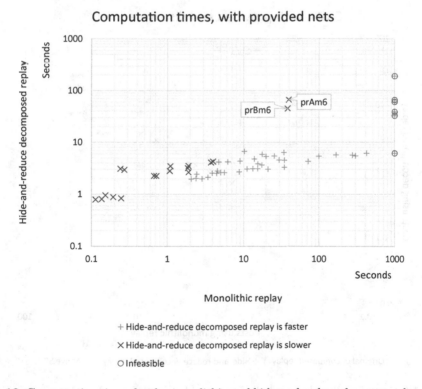

Fig. 13. Computation times for the monolithic and hide-and-reduce decomposed replay with the nets and logs as provided by the data sets.

reduction requires from 25 to 167 s. Apparently, the reduction step is a possible bottleneck for the hide-and-reduce decomposed replay.

With regard to the computation times, we can conclude that both the original and hide-and-reduce decomposed replays can handle more cases than the monolithic replay, that they are typically faster than the monolithic replay, and that the net at hand largely determines whether the original decomposed or the hide-and-reduce decomposed replay should be used. If every subnet contains only very few source transitions, then the original decomposed replay would be fastest, but this replay may take more than 10 min if some subnet contains more than a few source transitions. Therefore, in case one does not know whether some subnet contains more than a few source transitions, the prudent approach would be the hide-and-reduce decomposed replay.

Apart from evaluating the differences in computation times, we also need to evaluate the reported costs of the three replays. We know that the monolithic replay provides the correct costs, and that the hide-and-reduce decomposed replay provides a better lower bound than the original decomposed replay. Figure 14 shows the costs as reported by all replays on all nets (either provided or discovered) and all logs from the data sets. This figure shows that indeed the

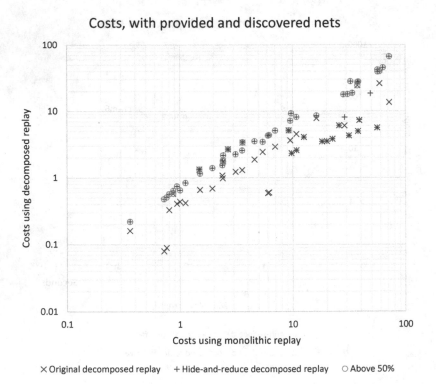

Fig. 14. Costs for all replays and all nets (provided or discovered) and logs as provided by the data sets.

costs as reported by hide-and-reduce decomposed replay (on average, 59% of the correct costs) are a better lower bound than the costs as reported by the original decomposed replay (on average, 38% of the correct costs). To emphasize this, we have highlighted in the figure those costs that are at least half (Above 50%) of the correct costs. Most of these highlighted costs are reported by the hide-and-reduce decomposed replay, only a few by the original decomposed replay.

5   Conclusions

In this paper, we have shown that, for some cases, the (original) decomposed replay [2] may take longer than the monolithic replay. Although for many nets this is typically not the case, it may very well be the case for nets that result in subnets having more than a few source transitions and more than a few places. As such, a user who wants to check conformance on a log and an unknown net may want to think twice to use the original decomposed replay, as the monolithic replay may be faster (less than 10 s) while providing correct costs, while the original decomposed replay may take longer (more than 10 min) while only providing a lower bound for the correct costs.

We have also shown that a root cause of this problem of the original decomposed replay is the fact that the decomposition may result in a subnet with a fair amount of places and more than a few source transitions. As a result of the fair amount of places, the state space will contain a fair amount of states as well. As a result of the more than a few source transitions, the replayer needs to investigate from every reachable state at least all source transitions, which may all lead to new states that again need to be investigated. We have shown that the replay of a subnet with 13 places and 5 source transitions may require more than 10 min for the original decomposed replayer.

To mitigate this problem with the source transitions, we have proposed a *hide-and-reduce* decomposed replay, which uses the same collection of sublogs but maintains the structure of the original net in the subnets, and hence does not introduce source transitions. We have shown that this new replay requires less than 10 min for all-but-one of the cases in the data sets used, and that this case required more than 10 min for the monolithic and original decomposed replays as well. As such, the hide-and-reduce decomposed replay offers a replay that can handle more situations than either of the other replays can. For this reason, if it is possible that the net at hand results in some subnet that contains a fair amount of places and more than a few source transitions, then using the new hide-and-reduce decomposed replay is the best approach. Granted, it may be slower than the original decomposed replay, but chances are that the case at hand simply requires more than 10 min for the original decomposed replay.

Furthermore, we have shown that the costs as reported by the hide-and-reduce decomposed replay are at least as good as the costs as reported by the original decomposed replay, but possibly better. Therefore, if it is important to the user to have an as-good-as-possible estimate for the correct costs, then using the hide-and-reduce decomposed replay is better than using the original decomposed replay.

Finally, we have shown that in some cases the required reduction step in the hide-and-reduce replay is the bottleneck of the entire replay. Whereas the entire replay on the subnets would take only 2 s, the required reduction of these subnets may have taken 60 s. As a result of this bottleneck, the hide-and-reduce replay is sometimes slower than the monolithic replay. For this reason, we aim to improve in the near future on the reduction rules [10] as used by the hide-and-reduce replay. Possibly, the rules may be simplified as they only need to preserve the costs of any trace replayed on the net, and not the entire behavior.

References

1. van der Aalst, W.M.P.: Process Mining: Discovery, Conformance and Enhancement of Business Processes, 1st edn. Springer, Heidelberg (2011). doi:10.1007/978-3-642-19345-3
2. van der Aalst, W.M.P.: Decomposing Petri nets for process mining: a generic approach. Distrib. Parallel Dat. 31(4), 471–507 (2013)
3. van der Aalst, W.M.P., Adriansyah, A., van Dongen, B.F.: Replaying history on process models for conformance checking and performance analysis. Data Min. Knowl. Disc. 2(2), 182–192 (2012)
4. van Dongen, B.F.: BPI challenge 2012 data set (2012). doi:10.4121/uuid: 3926db30-f712-4394-aebc-75976070e91f
5. van Dongen, B.F.: BPI challenge 2015 data set (2015). doi:10.4121/uuid: 31a308ef-c844-48da-948c-305d167a0ec1
6. Leemans, S.J.J., Fahland, D., van der Aalst, W.M.P.: Discovering block-structured process models from event logs - a constructive approach. In: Colom, J.-M., Desel, J. (eds.) PETRI NETS 2013. LNCS, vol. 7927, pp. 311–329. Springer, Heidelberg (2013). doi:10.1007/978-3-642-38697-8_17
7. Maruster, L., Weijters, A.J.M.M., van der Aalst, W.M.P., van der Bosch, A.: A rule-based approach for process discovery: dealing with noise and imbalance in process logs. Data Min. Knowl. Disc. 13(1), 67–87 (2006)
8. Munoz-Gama, J., Carmona, J., van der Aalst, W.M.P.: Conformance checking in the large: partitioning and topology. In: Daniel, F., Wang, J., Weber, B. (eds.) BPM 2013. LNCS, vol. 8094, pp. 130–145. Springer, Heidelberg (2013). doi:10. 1007/978-3-642-40176-3_11
9. Munoz-Gama, J., Carmona, J., van der Aalst, W.M.P.: Single-entry single-exit decomposed conformance checking. Inf. Syst. 46, 102–122 (2014)
10. Murata, T.: Petri nets: properties, analysis and applications. P. IEEE 77(4), 541–580 (1989)

Multiplicative Transition Systems

Józef Winkowski[✉]

Institute of Computer Science of the Polish Academy of Sciences,
ul. Jana Kazimierza 5, 01-248 Warszawa, Poland
wink@ipipan.waw.pl

Abstract. The paper is concerned with algebras whose elements can be used to represent runs of a system. These algebras, called multiplicative transition systems, are partial categories with respect to a partial binary operation called multiplication. They can be characterized by axioms such that their elements and operations can be represented by partially ordered multisets of a certain type and operations on such multisets. The representation can be obtained without assuming a discrete nature of represented elements. In particular, it remains valid for systems with elements which can represent continuous and partially continuous runs.

1 Introduction

This paper is an attempt to develop a universal framework for describing systems that may exhibit arbitrary combinations of discrete and continuous behaviours.

There are reasons for which we need such a universal framework.

First, in order to describe and analyse systems including computer components, which operate in discrete steps, and real-world components, which operate in a continuous way, we need a framework including ideas from both computer science and control theory (cf. [4]). Consequently, we need a simple language to describe in the same way and to relate behaviours of systems of any nature, including discrete, continuous, and hybrid systems. Second, we need basic axioms valid for systems of any nature such that every particular subclass of systems could be characterized by only adding to the list of basic axioms the respective specific axioms. Third, we need a representation theorem resulting in a representation of system runs by well defined mathematical structures and in a representation of the composition of system runs by a composition of such structures. In particular, we need runs of discrete, continuous, and hybrid systems to be represented by structures of the same type. This will allow us to avoid inventing a special representation in every particular case.

Our idea of a universal framework for describing systems consists in a generalization of the concept of a transition system.

Transition systems are models of systems which operate in discrete indivisible steps called transitions (cf. [7–10]). They specify system states and transitions. Consequently, they have means to represent implicitly partial and complete system runs viewed as sequences of successive transitions, including one-element sequences representing states. They can be provided in a natural way with a

© Springer-Verlag GmbH Germany 2017
M. Koutny et al. (Eds.): ToPNoC XII, LNCS 10470, pp. 187–215, 2017.
DOI: 10.1007/978-3-662-55862-1_9

composition of runs of which one starts from the final state of the other, and this results in the structure of a partial category.

Models more precise than simple transition systems are needed to reflect that some system steps can be executed in parallel (parallel independent steps) or in arbitrary order (sequentially independent steps). Consequently, the corresponding simple transition systems must be provided with information reflecting the independence of transitions and the fact that some sequences of transitions may represent the same run.

Finally, together with runs of entire system also runs of subsystems can be considered and partially ordered by inclusion. Consequently, the corresponding transition systems can be provided with a partial order.

In the case of systems with continuous behaviour runs cannot be viewed as sequences of discrete indivisible steps. Nevertheless, the concept of a run still makes sense, and there is a natural composition of runs of which one starts from the resulting state of the other. Then the continuity reflects in an infinite divisibility of runs with respect to such a composition, and the existing independence of transitions can be defined using the composition.

Moreover, together with runs of entire system also runs of subsystems can be considered and partially ordered by inclusion. Consequently, a partially ordered partial category of states and runs of the possible subsystems is obtained, called a transition structure.

Thus the partial category consisting of system runs and of the respective composition is a good candidate for a universal structure allowing one to represent both discrete and continuous behaviour. We call it a multiplicative transition system and call system runs represented in it transitions.

Note that the concept of a multiplicative transition system generalizes the standard concept of a transition system in the sense that every usual transition system can be regarded as the set of generators of the multiplicative transition system of the respective runs.

The paper is organized as follows. In Sect. 2 we present formal tools exploited in the paper. In Sect. 3 we introduce multiplicative transition systems. In Sect. 4 we define regions. In Sect. 5 we represent transitions as labelled posets. In Sect. 6 we represent multiplicative transition systems as a partial category of pomsets. In Sect. 7 we describe a partial order of transitions. The paper is an essential extension of [13]. In the paper we exploit the concepts and properties of processes and operations on processes described in [11,12,14].

2 Preliminaries

In this section we represent the necessary tools related to partial categories and labelled partially ordered sets exploited in the paper.

Transitions of a system such that one transition starts from the final state of the other can be concatenated with a result which can also be regarded as a transition. If also transitions without an initial or a final state are considered then the resulting structure looks like a category which is partial in the sense that some arrows are lacking a source or a target (cf. example at the end of section).

Formally, a partial category can be defined in exactly the same way as an arrows-only category in the sense of [6], except that sources and targets may be not defined for some arrows that are not identities, and that it may restrict the composability of arrows.

Let $\mathbf{A} = (A, ;)$ be a partial algebra with a binary partial operation $(\alpha, \beta) \mapsto \alpha; \beta$ called *composition*, where $\alpha; \beta$ is written also as $\alpha\beta$. An element $\iota \in A$ is called an *identity* if $\iota\phi = \phi$ whenever $\iota\phi$ is defined and $\psi\iota = \psi$ whenever $\psi\iota$ is defined. We call elements of A *arrows* or *morphisms* and say that $\mathbf{A}$ is a *partial category* if the following conditions are satisfied:

(1) For every α, β, and γ in A, if $\alpha\beta$ and $\beta\gamma$ are defined then $\alpha(\beta\gamma)$ and $(\alpha\beta)\gamma$ are defined and $\alpha(\beta\gamma) = (\alpha\beta)\gamma$; if $\alpha(\beta\gamma)$ is defined then $\alpha\beta$ is defined; if $(\alpha\beta)\gamma$ is defined then $\beta\gamma$ is defined.
(2) For every identity $\iota \in A$, $\iota\iota$ is defined.

The conditions (1) and (2) imply the following properties.

(3) For every $\alpha \in A$, there exists at most one identity $\iota \in A$, called the *source* or the *domain* of α and written as $dom(\alpha)$, such that $\iota\alpha$ is defined, and at most one identity $\kappa \in A$, called the *target* or the *codomain* of α and written as $cod(\alpha)$, such that $\alpha\kappa$ is defined.
(4) For every α and β in A, $\alpha\beta$ is defined if and only if $cod(\alpha) = dom(\beta)$. If $\alpha\beta$ is defined then $dom(\alpha\beta) = dom(\alpha)$ and $cod(\alpha\beta) = cod(\beta)$.

A morphism α with the source $dom(\alpha) = s$ and the target $cod(\alpha) = t$ is represented in the form $s \xrightarrow{\alpha} t$, and it is said to be *closed*.

Note that $\alpha \mapsto dom(\alpha)$ and $\alpha \mapsto cod(\alpha)$ are definable partial operations assigning to a morphism α respectively the source and the target of this morphism, if such a source or a target exists.

Dealing with arrows-only categories rather than with categories in the usual sense is sometimes more convenient since it allows us to avoid two sorted structures and more complicated denotations.

Given a morphism α, a morphism β such that $\alpha = \gamma\beta\varepsilon$ or $\alpha = \beta\varepsilon$ or $\alpha = \gamma\beta$ is called a *segment* of α. If $\alpha = \gamma\beta\varepsilon$ then β is said to be a *closed* segment of α. A segment of a segment β of α is said to be a *subsegment* of α.

Given a partial category $\mathbf{A} = (A, ;)$, let A' be the set of quadruples $(\alpha, \sigma, \tau, \beta)$ where $\sigma\alpha\tau$ is defined and $\sigma\alpha\tau = \beta$, or $dom(\alpha)$ and σ are not defined and $\alpha\tau$ is defined and $\alpha\tau = \beta$, or $cod(\alpha)$ and τ are not defined and $\sigma\alpha$ is defined and $\sigma\alpha = \beta$, or $dom(\alpha)$ and $cod(\alpha)$ are not defined and $\alpha = \beta$. The set A' thus defined and the partial operation

$$((\alpha, \sigma, \tau, \beta), (\beta, \sigma', \tau', \gamma)) \mapsto (\alpha, \sigma'\sigma, \tau\tau', \gamma)$$

form a category $occ(\mathbf{A})$, called the *category of occurrences of morphisms in morphisms* of $\mathbf{A}$.

Given a partial category $\mathbf{A} = (A, ;)$ and its morphism α, let A'_α be the set of triples (ξ_1, δ, ξ_2) such that $\xi_1\delta\xi_2 = \alpha$. The set A'_α thus defined and the partial operation

$$((\eta_1, \delta, \varepsilon\eta_2), (\eta_1\delta, \varepsilon, \eta_2)) \mapsto (\eta_1, \delta\varepsilon, \eta_2)$$

form a category dec_α, called the *category of decompositions* of α. In this category each triple (ξ_1, δ, ξ_2) in which δ is an identity, and thus $\delta = cod(\xi_1) = dom(\xi_2)$, is essentially a decomposition of α into a pair (ξ_1, ξ_2) such that $\xi_1\xi_2 = \alpha$ and it can be identified with this decomposition.

Given partial categories $\mathbf{A} = (A, ;)$ and $\mathbf{A}' = (A', ;')$, a mapping $f : A \to A'$ such that $f(\alpha);' f(\beta)$ is defined and $f(\alpha);' f(\beta) = f(\alpha\beta)$ for every α and β such that $\alpha\beta$ is defined, and $f(\iota)$ is an identity for every identity ι, is called a *morphism* or a *functor* from $\mathbf{A}$ to $\mathbf{A}'$. Note that such a morphism becomes a functor in the usual sense if $\mathbf{A}$ and $\mathbf{A}'$ are categories.

Diagrams, limits and colimits in partial categories can be defined as in usual categories.

A *direct system* is a diagram $(a_i \overset{\alpha_{ij}}{\to} a_j : i \le j, i, j \in I)$, where $(I, \le)$ is a directed poset, α_{ii} is identity for every $i \in I$, and $\alpha_{ij}\alpha_{jk} = \alpha_{ik}$ for all $i \le j \le k$. The *inductive limit* of such a system is its colimit, i.e. a family $(a_i \overset{\alpha_i}{\to} a : i, j \in I)$ such that $\alpha_i = \alpha_{ij}\alpha_j$ for all $i \in I$ and for every family $(a_i \overset{\beta_i}{\to} b : i, j \in I)$ such that $\beta_i = \alpha_{ij}\beta_j$ for all $i \in I$ there exists a unique $a \overset{\beta}{\to} b$ such that $\beta_i = \alpha_i\beta$ for all $i \in I$.

A *projective system* is a diagram $(a_i \overset{\alpha_{ij}}{\leftarrow} a_j : i \le j, i, j \in I)$, where $(I, \le)$ is a directed poset, α_{ii} is identity for every $i \in I$, and $\alpha_{ij}\alpha_{jk} = \alpha_{ik}$ for all $i \le j \le k$. The *projective limit* of such a system is its limit, i.e. a family $(a_i \overset{\alpha_i}{\leftarrow} a : i, j \in I)$ such that $\alpha_i = \alpha_j\alpha_{ij}$ for all $i \in I$ and for every family $(a_i \overset{\beta_i}{\leftarrow} b : i, j \in I)$ such that $\beta_i = \beta_j\alpha_{ij}$ for all $i \in I$ there exists a unique $a \overset{\beta}{\leftarrow} b$ such that $\beta_i = \beta\alpha_i$ for all $i \in I$.

A *bicartesian square* is a diagram $(v \overset{\alpha_1}{\leftarrow} u \overset{\alpha_2}{\to} w, v \overset{\alpha_2'}{\to} u' \overset{\alpha_1'}{\leftarrow} w)$ such that $v \overset{\alpha_2'}{\to} u' \overset{\alpha_1'}{\leftarrow} w$ is a pushout of $v \overset{\alpha_1}{\leftarrow} u \overset{\alpha_2}{\to} w$ and $v \overset{\alpha_1}{\leftarrow} u \overset{\alpha_2}{\to} w$ is a pullback of $v \overset{\alpha_2'}{\to} u' \overset{\alpha_1'}{\leftarrow} w$, i.e. such that for every $v \overset{\beta_1}{\to} u'' \overset{\beta_2}{\leftarrow} w$ such that $\alpha_1\beta_1 = \alpha_2\beta_2$ there exists a unique $u' \overset{\beta}{\to} u''$ such that $\beta_1 = \alpha_2'\beta$ and $\beta_2 = \alpha_1'\beta$, and for every $v \overset{\gamma_1}{\leftarrow} t \overset{\gamma_2}{\to} w$ such that $\gamma_1\alpha_2' = \gamma_2\alpha_1'$ there exists a unique $u \overset{\gamma}{\leftarrow} t$ such that $\gamma_1 = \gamma\alpha_1$ and $\gamma_2 = \gamma\alpha_2$.

As transitions of a system need not to be indecomposable, they have a natural internal structure which can be reflected in a representation of a transition by a labelled partially ordered set. Hence the partial categories of transitions are related to some partial categories of isomorphism classes of labelled partially ordered sets (cf. example at the end of section).

Formally, a partial order on a set X is a binary relation $\le$ between elements of X that is reflexive, anti-symmetric and transitive.

Given a partial order $\le$ on a set X, the pair $P = (X, \le)$ is called a *partially ordered set*, or briefly a *poset*. Given a partial order $\le$ on a set X and a function $l : X \to W$ that assigns to every $x \in X$ a label $l(x)$ from a set W, the triple $L = (X, \le, l)$ is called a *labelled partially ordered set*, or briefly an *lposet*. A subset $Y \subseteq X$ is said to be *downwards-closed* iff $x \le y$ for some $y \in Y$ implies $x \in Y$, *upwards-closed* iff $y \le x$ for some $y \in Y$ implies $x \in Y$, *bounded* iff it has an upper bound, i.e. an element $z \in X$ such that $y \leq z$ for all $y \in Y$, *directed* iff for every $x, y \in Y$ there exists in Y an upper bound z of $\{x, y\}$, a *chain* iff $x \leq y$ or $y \leq x$ for all $x, y \in Y$, an *antichain* iff $x < y$ does not hold for any $x, y \in Y$, and L is said to be *directed complete* or a *directed complete partial order* (a DCPO) iff every of its directed subsets has a unique least upper bound. A Scott topology on the underlying set X of L is the topology in which a subset $U \subseteq X$ is open iff it is upwards-closed and does not contain the least upper bound of any directed subset of $X - U$.

A *cross-section* of L is a maximal antichain Z of $P = (X, \leq)$ such that, for every $x, y \in X$ for which $x \leq y$ and $x \leq z'$ and $z'' \leq y$ with some $z', z'' \in Z$, there exists $z \in Z$ such that $x \leq z \leq y$.

The concept of a cross-section is defined independently of the properties of partially ordered sets called N-density and K-density (cf. [8]). Its main role is to reflect how a partial order on L consists of the partial orders on parts of L.

More precisely, if Z is a cross-section of L then the relation $\leq$ is the transitive closure of the union of the restrictions of the relation $\leq$ to the subsets $Z^- = \{x \in X : x \leq z$ for some $z \in Z\}$ and $Z^+ = \{x \in X : z \leq x$ for some $z \in Z\}$.

A cross-section Z' is said to *precede* a cross-section Z'', written as $Z' \preceq Z''$, iff $Z'^- \subseteq Z''^-$. The relation $\preceq$ is a partial order on the set of cross-sections of L.

For every two cross-sections Z' and Z'' of L there exist the greatest lower bound $Z' \wedge Z''$ and the least upper bound $Z' \vee Z''$ of Z' and Z'' with respect to $\preceq$, where

$$Z' \wedge Z'' = \{z \in Z' \cup Z'' : z \leq z' \text{ and } z \leq z'' \text{ for some } z' \in Z' \text{ and } z'' \in Z''\},$$

$$Z' \vee Z'' = \{z \in Z' \cup Z'' : z' \leq z \text{ and } z'' \leq z \text{ for some } z' \in Z' \text{ and } z'' \in Z''\}.$$

Moreover, the set of cross-sections of L with the operations thus defined is a distributive lattice.

A partially ordered subset K of L such that K is the restriction $L|[Z', Z'']$ of L to subset $[Z', Z''] = Z''^- - Z'^-$ for some cross-sections Z' and Z'' such that $Z' \preceq Z''$, or the restriction $L|Z^-$ to the subset Z^- for a cross-section Z, or to the restriction $L|Z^+$ to the subset Z^+ for a cross-section Z, is said to be a *segment* of L. A segment $L|Z^-$ (resp.: $L|Z^+$) is said to be *initial* (resp.: *final*). If $K = L|[Z', Z'']$ then it is said to be a *closed* segment of L. A segment of a segment K of L is said to be a *subsegment* of L. Given a function f defined on L, an *initial segment* of f is defined as the restriction of f to an initial segment of L.

Given a cross-section c of L, the restrictions of L to the subsets $c^- = \{x \in X : x \leq z$ for some $z \in c\}$ and $c^+ = \{x \in X : z \leq x$ for some $z \in c\}$ are called respectively the *head* and the *tail* of L with respect to c, and written respectively as $head(L, c)$ and $tail(L, c)$.

The *sequential decomposition* of L at a cross-section c is the pair $s(c) = (head(L, c), tail(L, c))$ and L is said to *consist* of $head(L, c)$ *followed by* $tail(L, c)$.

A *splitting* of L is a pair $p = (p^F, p^S)$ of disjoint subsets p^F and p^S of X such that $p^F \cup p^S = X$ and $x' \leq x''$ only if x' and x'' are both in one of these subsets.

Given a splitting $p = (p^F, p^S)$ of L, the restrictions of L to the subsets p^F and p^S are called respectively the *first component* and the *second component* of

L with respect to p, they are written respectively as $first(L, p)$ and $second(L, p)$, and called *independent components* of L. The pair $(first(L, p), second(L, p))$ is called the *parallel decomposition* of L corresponding to the splitting p, and L is said to *consist of parallel* $first(L, p)$ and $second(L, p)$.

Note that L itself is an independent component of L.

A *fragment* or a *component* of L is an independent component C of a segment S of L such that the set of minimal elements of C is a cross-section of C and it is contained in the cross-section of P that consists of minimal elements of S.

An lposet L' is said to *occur* in L if it is a fragment of L.

If the set of elements of $L = (X, \leq, l)$ that are minimal (resp., maximal) with respect to $\leq$ is a cross-section of L then we call the restriction of L to this set the *origin* (resp., the *end*) of L, write it as $origin(L)$ (resp., as $end(L)$). If $origin(L)$ and $end(L)$ exist then L is said to be *closed*.

By **LPOSETS** we denote the category of lposets and their morphisms, where a *morphism* from an lposet $L = (X, \leq, l)$ to an lposet $L' = (X', \leq', l')$ is defined as a mapping $b : X \rightarrow X'$ such that, for all x and y, $x \leq y$ iff $b(x) \leq' b(y)$, and, for all x, $l(x) = l'(b(x))$. In the category **LPOSETS** a morphism from $L = (X, \leq, l)$ to $L' = (X', \leq', l')$ is an *isomorphism* iff it is bijective, and it is an *automorphism* iff it is bijective and $L = L'$. If there exists an isomorphism from an lposet L to an lposet L' then we say that L and L' are *isomorphic*. A *partially ordered multiset*, or briefly a *pomset*, is defined as an isomorphism class ξ of lposets. Each lposet that belongs to such a class ξ is called an *instance* of ξ. The pomset corresponding to an lposet L is written as $[L]$.

A pomset γ is said to *consist* of a pomset α *followed* by a pomset β, written as $\gamma = \alpha; \beta$, iff γ has an instance G with a cross-section c and a sequential decomposition of this instance at c into $G_1 \in \alpha$ and $G_2 \in \beta$.

A pomset γ is said to *consist* of two *parallel* pomsets: a pomset α and a pomset β, written as $\gamma = \alpha \parallel \beta$, iff γ has an instance G with a parallel decomposition into $G_1 \in \alpha$ and $G_2 \in \beta$.

Example 2.1. Define a transition system without a distinguished initial state as $M = (S, E, T)$ such that S is a set of states, E is a set of events, and $T \subseteq S \times E \times S$ is a set of transitions, where $(s, e, s') \in T$ stands for the transition from the state s to the state s' due to the event e. Assume that E contains a distinguished element $*$ standing for "no event", and assume that for every state $s \in S$ the set T contains an idle transition $(s, *, s)$ standing for "stay in s". Then M can be represented by the structure $G(M) = (T, dom, cod)$, where $dom(s, e, s') = (s, *, s)$ and $cod(s, e, s') = (s', *, s')$ for every $(s, e, s') \in T$.

Write $s \xrightarrow{e} s'$ to indicate that $(s, e, s') \in T$. Denote by Lts the set of finite and infinite sequences $\alpha = ..., t_1, t_2, ..., t_m, ...$ of elements of T such that for every subsequence t_i, t_{i+1} the final state of t_i is the initial state of t_{i+1}. Define $dom(\alpha) = dom(t_1)$ for $\alpha = t_1, ...$ and $cod(\alpha) = cod(t_j)$ for $\alpha = ..., t_j$. For $\alpha_1 = ..., t_1, ..., t_i$ and $\alpha_2 = t_j, t_{j+1}, ...$ such that the final state of t_i is the initial state of t_j define the result of composing α_1 and α_2 as $\alpha_1 \alpha_2 = ..., t_1, ..., t_i, t_j, t_{j+1}, ...$

The set Lts with the composition thus defined is a partial category $LTS(M)$. In this partial category every arrow α has the natural linear order and $(v \overset{\alpha_1}{\leftarrow} u \overset{\alpha_2}{\to} w, v \overset{\alpha'_2}{\to} u' \overset{\alpha'_1}{\leftarrow} w)$ is a bicartesian square iff α_1 and α'_1 are identities or α_2 and α'_2 are identities.

Consider the transition system M, a symmetric irreflexive relation $I \subseteq (E - \{*\})^2$ in M, called an independence relation, and the least equivalence relation $\|_I$ between elements of Lts such that words $uabv$ and $ubav$ are equivalent whenever $(a, b) \in I$. The equivalence classes of such a relation are known in the literature as Mazurkiewicz traces with respect to I (see [5]). Denote by Ts the set of classes of equivalent elements of Lts replaced by the corresponding traces with respect to I. Define dom and cod and the composition as before, but with the concatenation of sequences replaced by the induced concatenation of traces.

The set Ts with the composition thus defined is a partial category $TS(M, I)$, and that this partial category is a homomorphic image of the partial category $LTS(M)$. However, in this partial category there exist non-trivial bicartesian squares, namely, the squares $(v \overset{\alpha_1}{\leftarrow} u \overset{\alpha_2}{\to} w, v \overset{\alpha'_2}{\to} u' \overset{\alpha'_1}{\leftarrow} w)$ such that $\alpha_1 = u \overset{x_1}{\to} v$, $\alpha_2 = u \overset{x_2}{\to} w$, $\alpha'_1 = w \overset{x_1}{\to} u'$, $\alpha'_2 = v \overset{x_2}{\to} u'$ with $(a, b) \in I$ for all (a, b) such that a occurs in x_1 and b occurs in x_2.   ♯

3   Basic Notions

Basic axioms characterizing multiplicative transition systems can be formulated regarding transitions as abstract entities and expressing their properties with the aid of a partial operation of composing transitions, called *multiplication*.

Let A be the set of transitions representing runs of a system, some transitions possibly without an initial or a final state. Then $\mathbf{A} = (A, ;)$ is a partial algebra that consists of the set A and of the multiplication $(\alpha, \beta) \mapsto \alpha\beta$, where $\alpha\beta$ denotes $\alpha; \beta$. It is reasonable to assume that this algebra is a partial category and that it enjoys some natural properties.

First, it is natural to expect that the multiplication satisfies the following cancellation laws.

(A1) If α is closed then $\sigma\alpha = \sigma'\alpha$ implies $\sigma = \sigma'$.
(A2) If β is closed then $\beta\tau = \beta\tau'$ implies $\tau = \tau'$.

Second, identities are expected to represent states and to be indecomposable into transitions which do not represent states.

(A3) If $\sigma\tau$ is an identity then σ and τ are also identities.

Third, transitions which are not identities are expected to be essentially different from their proper segments.

(A4) If $\sigma\alpha\tau$ is defined, it has a source and a target, and the category $dec_{\sigma\alpha\tau}$ of decompositions of $\sigma\alpha\tau$ is isomorphic to the category dec_α of decompositions of α then σ and τ are identities.

Fourth, the independence of transitions α_1 and α_2, transitions α_1 and α_2', and transitions α_2 and α_1' is expected to be represented by the existence of a bicartesian square $(v \xleftarrow{\alpha_1} u \xrightarrow{\alpha_2} w, v \xrightarrow{\alpha_2'} u' \xleftarrow{\alpha_1'} w)$, and it is expected to imply the independence of transitions represented by segments of α_1 and α_2.

(A5) If $(v \xleftarrow{\alpha_1} u \xrightarrow{\alpha_2} w, v \xrightarrow{\alpha_2'} u' \xleftarrow{\alpha_1'} w)$ is a bicartesian square then for every decomposition $u \xrightarrow{\alpha_1} v = u \xrightarrow{\alpha_{11}} v_1 \xrightarrow{\alpha_{12}} v$ (resp. $w \xrightarrow{\alpha_1'} u' = w \xrightarrow{\alpha_{11}'} w_1 \xrightarrow{\alpha_{12}'} u'$) there exist a unique decomposition $w \xrightarrow{\alpha_1'} u' = w \xrightarrow{\alpha_{11}'} w_1 \xrightarrow{\alpha_{12}'} u'$ (resp. $u \xrightarrow{\alpha_1} v = u \xrightarrow{\alpha_{11}} v_1 \xrightarrow{\alpha_{12}} v$), and a unique $v_1 \xrightarrow{\alpha_2''} w_1$, such that $(v_1 \xleftarrow{\alpha_{11}} u \xrightarrow{\alpha_2} w, v_1 \xrightarrow{\alpha_2''} w_1 \xleftarrow{\alpha_{11}'} w)$ and $(v \xleftarrow{\alpha_{12}} v_1 \xrightarrow{\alpha_2''} w_1, v \xrightarrow{\alpha_2'} u' \xleftarrow{\alpha_{12}'} w_1)$ are bicartesian squares.

Fifth, the independence of segments of a transition is expected to be the only reason of a representation of such a transition by two different expressions.

(A6) For all ξ_1, ξ_2, η_1, η_2 such that $\xi_1\xi_2 = \eta_1\eta_2$ there exist unique σ_1, σ_2, and a unique bicartesian square $(v \xleftarrow{\alpha_1} u \xrightarrow{\alpha_2} w, v \xrightarrow{\alpha_2'} u' \xleftarrow{\alpha_1'} w)$, such that $\xi_1 = \sigma_1\alpha_1$, $\xi_2 = \alpha_2'\sigma_2$, $\eta_1 = \sigma_1\alpha_2$, $\eta_2 = \alpha_1'\sigma_2$.

Finally, every transition is expected to be an inductive limit of its closed segments.

(A7) Every direct system D in the category $occ(\mathbf{A})$ of occurrences of morphisms in morphisms in $\mathbf{A}$ such that elements of D are closed in the sense that they possess sources and targets has an inductive limit (a colimit).

(A8) Every $\alpha \in A$ is the inductive limit of the direct system of its closed segments.

Thus we have come to the following definition.

Definition 3.1. *A multiplicative transition system, or briefly an MTS, is a partial category* $\mathbf{A} = (A, ;)$ *with a set A of morphisms and with a composition* $(\alpha_1, \alpha_2) \mapsto \alpha_1; \alpha_2$ *such that the axioms (A1)–(A8) hold.*   ♯

In $\mathbf{A}$ two partial unary operations $\alpha \mapsto dom(\alpha)$ and $\alpha \mapsto cod(\alpha)$ are definable that assign to an element a source and a target, if they exist.

An element α of A is said to be a *atom* of $\mathbf{A}$ iff it is not an identity, has a source and a target, and for every $\alpha_1 \in A$ and $\alpha_2 \in A$ the equality $\alpha = \alpha_1\alpha_2$ implies that either α_1 is an identity and $\alpha_2 = \alpha$ or α_2 is an identity and $\alpha_1 = \alpha$.

We say that $\mathbf{A}$ is *discrete* if every $\alpha \in A$ that is not an identity can be represented in the form $\alpha = \alpha_1...\alpha_n$, where $\alpha_1,...,\alpha_n$ are atoms.

Note that if $\mathbf{A}$ is discrete then its every element has a source and a target and thus $\mathbf{A}$ is a category.

By a *cut* of $\alpha \in A$ we mean a pair (α_1, α_2) such that $\alpha_1\alpha_2 = \alpha$.

Cuts of every $\alpha \in A$ are partially ordered by the relation $\sqsubseteq_\alpha$, where $x \sqsubseteq_\alpha y$ with $x = (\xi_1, \xi_2)$ and $y = (\eta_1, \eta_2)$ means that $\eta_1 = \xi_1\delta$ with some δ. Due to

(A1)–(A2) for $x = (\xi_1, \xi_2)$ and $y = (\eta_1, \eta_2)$ such that $x \sqsubseteq_\alpha y$ there exists a unique δ such that $\eta_1 = \xi_1 \delta$, written as $x \to y$.

The partial order $\sqsubseteq_\alpha$ makes the set of cuts of α a lattice LT_α.

Indeed, let $\alpha = \xi_1 \xi_2 = \eta_1 \eta_2$, $\xi_1 = \sigma_1 \alpha_1$, $\xi_2 = \alpha_2' \sigma_2$, $\eta_1 = \sigma_1 \alpha_2$, $\eta_2 = \alpha_1' \sigma_2$ with $\alpha_1, \alpha_1', \alpha_2, \alpha_2', \sigma_1, \sigma_2$ as in (A6). The least upper bound of $x = (\xi_1, \xi_2)$ and $y = (\eta_1, \eta_2)$ can be defined as $z = (\xi_1 \alpha_2', \sigma_2) = (\eta_1 \alpha_1', \sigma_2)$. To see this consider any $u = (\zeta_1, \zeta_2)$ such that $x \sqsubseteq_\alpha u$ and $y \sqsubseteq_\alpha u$. Then $\zeta_1 = \xi_1 \delta$ and $\zeta_1 = \eta_1 \epsilon$ for some δ and ϵ. As α_1' and α_2' form a pushout of α_1 and α_2, there exists a unique φ such that $\delta = \alpha_2' \varphi$ and $\epsilon = \alpha_1' \varphi$. Hence $\zeta_1 = \xi_1 \alpha_2' \varphi = \eta_1 \alpha_1' \varphi$ and, consequently, $z \sqsubseteq_\alpha u$.

Similarly, due to the fact that α_1 and α_2 form a pullback of α_1' and α_2', we obtain that $t = (\sigma_1, \alpha_1 \alpha_2' \sigma_2)$ is the greatest lower bound of x and y.

The lattice LT_α is obviously an MTS.

Given two cuts x and y, by $x \sqcup_\alpha y$ and $x \sqcap_\alpha y$ we denote respectively the least upper bound and the greatest lower bound of x and y. From (A6) it follows that $(x \leftarrow x \sqcap_\alpha y \to y, x \to x \sqcup_\alpha y \leftarrow y)$ is a bicartesian square.

Given $\alpha \in A$ and its cuts $x = (\xi_1, \xi_2)$ and $y = (\eta_1, \eta_2)$ such that $x \sqsubseteq_\alpha y$, by a *segment* of α from x to y we mean $\beta \in A$ such that $\xi_2 = \beta \eta_2$ and $\eta_1 = \xi_1 \beta$, written as $\alpha|[x, y]$. A segment $\alpha|[x', y']$ of α such that $x \sqsubseteq_\alpha x' \sqsubseteq_\alpha y' \sqsubseteq_\alpha y$ is called a *subsegment* of $\alpha|[x, y]$. If $x = x'$ (resp. if $y = y'$) then we call it an *initial* (resp. a *final*) subsegment of $\alpha|[x, y]$. An initial segment ι of α is called also a *prefix* of α, written as ι *pref* α.

In the set $A_{s-closed}$ of those $\alpha \in A$ which are semiclosed in the sense that they have a source $dom(\alpha)$, one can define as follows a relation $\sqsubseteq$, where $\alpha \sqsubseteq \beta$ whenever every prefix of α is a prefix of β, and this relation is a partial order, i.e. $(A_{s-closed}, \sqsubseteq)$ is a poset.

Elements of A are called *transitions* of **A**. Transitions of **A** which are identities of **A** are called *states* of **A**. Transitions which are atomic identities are called *atomic states*. A transition α is said to be *closed* if it has the source $dom(\alpha)$ and the target $cod(\alpha)$. For every closed transition α, the existing states $u = dom(\alpha)$ and $v = cod(\alpha)$ are called respectively the *initial state* and the *final state* of α.

Partial categories described in Example 2.1 are multiplicative transition systems. Some interesting multiplicative transition systems are described in the following example.

Example 3.2. Imagine a tank v to keep a liquid. Imagine transitions of the level of liquid in intervals of real time. Suppose that the flow of real time cannot be observed. Then only the flow of intrinsic time that can be derived from what happens in the tank is available. Consequently, a concrete transition during which the level of liquid at a moment t in an interval $[t', t'']$ of real time is $f(t)$ must be represented by a modified version $s \mapsto \widehat{f}(s)$ of the correspondence $t \mapsto f(t)$, where $\widehat{f}(s)$ is the variation of f in the interval $[t', t]$, and where the variation of f in the interval $[u', u'']$, $var(f; u', u'')$, is defined as the least upper bound of the set of quantities $|f(t_1) - f(t_0)| + ... + |f(t_n) - f(t_{n-1})|$, each quantity corresponding to a partition $t_0 = u' < t_1 < ... < t_n = u''$ of the interval $[u', u'']$. Such a transition can be represented by the labelled ordered set $P =$

$(X_P, \leq_P, l_P)$, where $X_P = \{v\} \times domain(\hat{f})$, $(v, s) \leq_P (v, s')$ iff $s \leq s'$, and $l_P(v, s) = \hat{f}(s)$. When considered up to isomorphism and then called an abstract transition it can be represented by the isomorphism class $[P]$ that contains P. An abstract transition $\pi = [P]$ in v and an abstract transition $\rho = [R]$ in another tank v' are illustrated in Fig. 1.

Let A_v be the set of abstract transitions in v of this kind. The composition of abstract transitions in v is a partial operation $(\pi_1, \pi_2) \mapsto \pi_1;_v \pi_2$ where $\pi_1;_v \pi_2$ is defined as $[P]$ for a concrete transition P that consists of a segment $P_1 \in [P_1] = \pi_1$ and a segment $P_2 \in [P_2] = \pi_2$ such that the maximal element of P_1 is the minimal element of P_2. The partial category $\mathbf{A}_v = (A_v, ;_v)$ is a multiplicative transition system.

In the case of the system of two tanks v and v' such that there is no pouring of liquid from v to v' or from v' to v the set of abstract transitions, $A_{v,v'}$, consists of the sets A_v and $A_{v'}$ of abstract transitions in v and v', and of the set of abstract transitions τ where τ is defined as $[T] = \pi \parallel \rho$ for a concrete transition T that consists of two parallel concrete transitions: a concrete transition $P \in [P] = \pi \in A_v$ and a concrete transition $R \in [R] = \rho \in A_{v'}$. The composition is the partial operation $(\tau_1, \tau_2) \mapsto \tau_1;_{v.v'} \tau_2$ where $(\tau_1, \tau_2) \mapsto \tau_1;_{v.v'} \tau_2$ is $(\tau_1, \tau_2) \mapsto \tau_1;_v \tau_2$ if $\tau_1, \tau_2 \in A_v$, $(\tau_1, \tau_2) \mapsto \tau_1;_{v.v'} \tau_2$ is $(\tau_1, \tau_2) \mapsto \tau_1;_{v'} \tau_2$ if $\tau_1, \tau_2 \in A_{v'}$, and $(\tau_1, \tau_2) \mapsto \tau_1;_{v.v'} \tau_2 = [T]$ for a concrete transition T that consists of two parallel concrete transitions: a concrete transition $P \in [P] \in [P_1]; [P_2]$ and a concrete transition $R \in [R] \in [R_1]; [R_2]$ if $\tau_1, \tau_2 \in A_{v,v'}$, $\tau_1 = [T_1]$ with T_1 consisting of two parallel concrete transitions $P_1 \in [P_1] \in A_v$ and $R_1 \in [R_1] \in A_{v'}$, and $\tau_2 = [T_2]$ with T_2 consisting of two parallel concrete transitions $P_2 \in [P_2] \in A_v$ and $R_2 \in [R_2] \in A_{v'}$. The partial category $\mathbf{A}_{v,v'} = (A_{v,v'}, ;_{v,v'})$ is a multiplicative transition system.

In the case of the system of two tanks v and v' such that from time to time a quantity of liquid is poured from v to v' the set of abstract transitions, $A'_{v,v'}$, consists of the sets A_v and $A_{v'}$ of abstract transitions in v and v', of the set $A_{v,v'}$ of abstract transitions of the system of v and v' running independently, and of the set of abstract transitions corresponding concrete transitions $K = (X_K, \leq_K, l_K)$, each K consisting of a sequence $..., T_1, S_1, T_2, S_2, ...$ of segments $..., T_1, T_2, ...$ and $..., S_1, S_2, ...$ such that x is a maximal element of T_i iff it is a minimal element of S_i and y is a maximal element of S_i iff it is a minimal element of T_{i+1}, where each S_i is a concrete pouring of an amount m of liquid represented by an lposet $S = (X_S, \leq, l_S)$ with $X_S = \{x_1, x_2, x_3, x_4\}$, $x_1 <_S x_3$, $x_1 <_S x_4$, $x_2 <_S x_3$, $x_2 <_S x_4$, $l_S(x_1) = (d, r)$, $l_S(x_2) = (p, q)$, $l_S(x_3) = (d, r+m)$, $l_S(x_4) = (p, q-m)$.

Abstract transitions corresponding to segments of a concrete transition K are illustrated in Fig. 2. The abstract transition corresponding to a concrete transition K is illustrated in Fig. 3.

The composition is the extension $(\kappa_1, \kappa_2) \mapsto \kappa_1;'_{v,v'} \kappa_2$ of $(\kappa_1, \kappa_2) \mapsto \kappa_1;_{v.v'} \kappa_2$ such that $\kappa_1;'_{v,v'} \kappa_2$ is defined as $[K]$ with a concrete transition K that consists of $K_1 \in \kappa_1$ followed by $K_2 \in \kappa_2$. The partial category $\mathbf{A}'_{v,v'} = (A'_{v,v'}, ;'_{v,v'})$ is a multiplicative transition system. In this system an abstract transition which corresponds to a concrete transition K, where K consists of $S' = S_1$ followed by T and followed by $S'' = S_2$, where T consists of parallel P and R, can be represented as $\sigma';''(\pi \parallel \rho);''\sigma''$, where $\sigma' = [S']$, $\pi = [P]$, $\rho = [R]$, and $\sigma'' = [S'']$. ♯

The concept of a bicartesian square can be used to define a sequential and a parallel independence of transitions similar to the concepts introduced in [3].

Definition 3.3. *Transitions* $u \overset{\alpha_1}{\to} v$ *and* $u \overset{\alpha_2}{\to} w$ *are said to be* parallel independent *iff there exist unique transition* $v \overset{\alpha_2'}{\to} u'$ *and* $w \overset{\alpha_1'}{\to} u'$ *such that* $(v \overset{\alpha_1}{\leftarrow} u \overset{\alpha_2}{\to} w, v \overset{\alpha_2'}{\to} u' \overset{\alpha_1'}{\leftarrow} w)$ *is a bicartesian square.* ♯

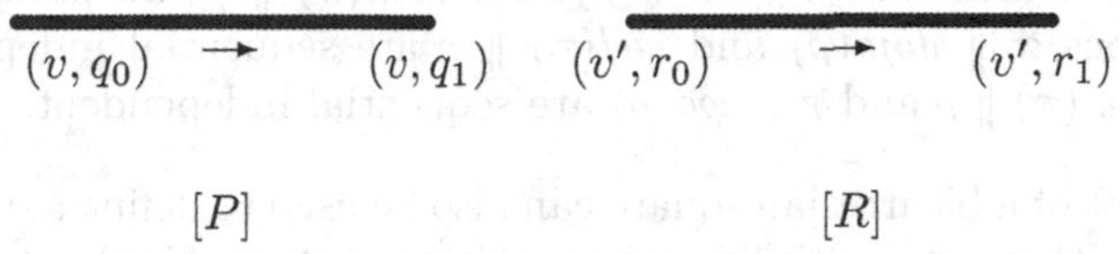

$(v, q_0) \quad \rightarrow \quad (v, q_1) \qquad (v', r_0) \quad \rightarrow \quad (v', r_1)$

$$[P] \qquad\qquad\qquad\qquad [R]$$

Fig. 1. The abstract transitions $\pi = [P]$ and $\rho = [R]$

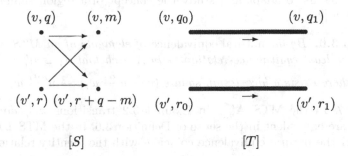

Fig. 2. The abstract transitions $\sigma = [S]$ and $\tau = [T]$

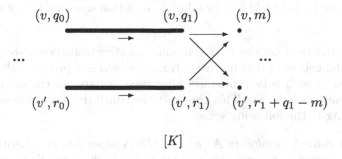

Fig. 3. The abstract transition $\kappa = [K]$

Definition 3.4. *Transitions* $u \overset{\alpha_1}{\to} v$ *and* $v \overset{\alpha_2'}{\to} u'$ *are said to be* sequential independent *iff there exist unique transition* $u \overset{\alpha_2}{\to} w$ *and* $w \overset{\alpha_1'}{\to} u'$ *such that* $(v \overset{\alpha_1}{\leftarrow} u \overset{\alpha_2}{\to} w, v \overset{\alpha_2'}{\to} u' \overset{\alpha_1'}{\leftarrow} w)$ *is a bicartesian square.* ♯

Example 3.5. In the MTS $LTS(M)$ in Example 2.1 transitions $u \overset{\alpha_1}{\to} v$ and $u \overset{\alpha_2}{\to} w$ are *parallel independent* only if one of them is an identity. Similarly, transitions $u \overset{\alpha_1}{\to} v$ and $v \overset{\alpha_2'}{\to} u'$ are sequential independent only if one of them is an identity. In the MTS $TS(M)$ in Example 2.1 transitions $u \overset{\alpha_1}{\to} v$ and $u \overset{\alpha_2}{\to} w$ are *parallel independent* iff $(a, b) \in I$ for all a occurring in α_1 and all b occurring in α_2. Similarly, transitions $u \overset{\alpha_1}{\to} v$ and $v \overset{\alpha_2'}{\to} u'$ are sequential independent iff $(a, b) \in I$ for all (a, b) such that a occurs in α_1 and b occurs in α_2'. In the MTS $\mathbf{A}'_{v,v'}$ in Example 3.2 transitions $\pi \parallel dom(\rho)$ and $dom(\pi) \parallel \rho$ are parallel independent, transitions $\pi \parallel dom(\rho)$ and $cod(\pi) \parallel \rho$ are sequential independent, and transitions $dom(\pi) \parallel \rho$ and $\pi \parallel cod(\rho)$ are sequential independent. ♯

The concept of a bicartesian square can also be used to define a natural equivalence of transitions of multiplicative transition systems similar to the equivalence of transitions in transition systems with independence considered in [15]. This will allow us to adapt and study the concept of a region similar to that introduced in [2].

Definition 3.6. *By the* natural equivalence *of elements of an MTS* $\mathbf{A} = (A, ;)$ *we mean the least equivalence relation* $\equiv$ *in* A *such that* $\alpha_1 \equiv \alpha_1'$ *whenever in this MTS there exists a bicartesian square* $(v \overset{\alpha_1}{\leftarrow} u \overset{\alpha_2}{\to} w, v \overset{\alpha_2'}{\to} u' \overset{\alpha_1'}{\leftarrow} w)$. ♯

Example 3.7. In the MTS $\mathbf{A}'_{v,v'}$ in Example 3.2 transitions $\pi \parallel dom(\rho)$ and $cod(\rho) \parallel \pi$ are equivalent in the sense of Definition 3.6. In the MTS $LTS(M)$ in Example 2.1 the natural equivalence coincides with the identity relation. In the MTS $TS(M)$ in Example 2.1 we have $\alpha_1 \equiv \alpha_1'$ whenever $(v \overset{\alpha_1}{\leftarrow} u \overset{\alpha_2}{\to} w, v \overset{\alpha_2'}{\to} u' \overset{\alpha_1'}{\leftarrow} w)$ with α_1 and α_1' representing the same trace t_1, and α_2 and α_2' representing the same trace t_2, for $(a, b) \in I$ for all (a, b) such that a occurs in t_1 and b occurs in t_2. ♯

The definitions of notions related to multiplicative transition systems are adequate in subalgebras of multiplicative transition systems provided that bicartesian squares in such subalgebras are bicartesian squares in the original multiplicative transition systems. This appears to be true if the respective subalgebras are inheriting in the following sense.

Definition 3.8. *A subalgebra* $\mathbf{A}'$ *of an MTS* $\mathbf{A}$ *is said to be* inheriting *if it is closed with respect to components of its elements in the sense that arrows* α *and* β *of* $\mathbf{A}$ *are also arrows of* $\mathbf{A}'$ *whenever* $\alpha\beta$ *is an arrow of* $\mathbf{A}'$. ♯

The following proposition reflects the crucial property of inheriting subalgebras of multiplicative transition systems.

Proposition 3.9. *If* $\mathbf{A}'$ *is an inheriting subalgebra of an MTS* $\mathbf{A}$ *then:*

(1) each bicartesian square of $\mathbf{A}$ *whose arrows are in* $\mathbf{A}'$ *is a bicartesian square in* $\mathbf{A}'$,

(2) each bicartesian square in $\mathbf{A}'$ *is a bicartesian square in* $\mathbf{A}$. ♯

Proof. The first part of this proposition is immediate. For the second part it suffices to exploit the property (A6) of $\mathbf{A}$ and the fact that $\mathbf{A}'$ is an inheriting subalgebra of $\mathbf{A}$. ♯

Multiplicative transition systems are richer models of concurrent system than usual transition systems in the sense that they specify not only states, indecomposable transitions, and independence of indecomposable transitions of the modelled systems, but also their runs which may be continuous, and how runs compose. Moreover, the independence becomes a definable notion, and it can be defined not only for indecomposable transitions, but also for compound transitions.

4 Regions

The existence in multiplicative transition systems of the natural equivalence of transitions allows us to adapt and exploit the concept of a region similar to those introduced in [2] and exploited in the context of Petri nets and automata in [1]. The fact that such an equivalence is closely related to the algebraic structure of partial categories is an essential novelty of our approach that makes this approach different from the others.

Definition 4.1. *By a* region *of an MTS* $\mathbf{A} = (A, ;)$ *we mean a nonempty subset* r *of the set of states of* $\mathbf{A}$ *such that:*

$$dom(\alpha) \in r \text{ and } cod(\alpha) \notin r \text{ and } \alpha' \equiv \alpha$$
$$\text{implies } dom(\alpha') \in r \text{ and } cod(\alpha') \notin r,$$

$$dom(\alpha) \notin r \text{ and } cod(\alpha) \in r \text{ and } \alpha' \equiv \alpha$$
$$\text{implies } dom(\alpha') \notin r \text{ and } cod(\alpha') \in r.$$ ♯

Example 4.2. Consider the MTS $\mathbf{A}'_{v,v'}$ in Example 3.2. In this MTS the sets $[(v,q)] = \{(v,q)\} \cup (\{v'\} \times [0,+\infty))$ with $q \geq 0$, the sets $[(v',r)] = \{(v',r)\} \cup (\{v\} \times [0,+\infty))$ with $r \geq 0$, and disjoint unions of such sets are regions. ♯

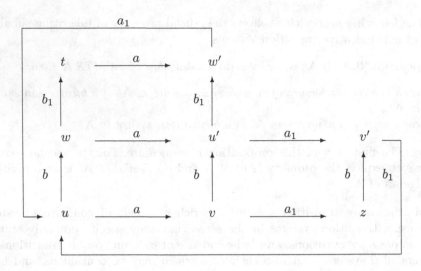

$$M'$$

Fig. 4. The transition system M'

Example 4.3. Consider the transition system M' in Fig. 4.

Consider the independence relation $I' = \{(a,b), (a,b_1), (a_1,b), (a_1,b_1)\}$ and the MTS $TS(M', I')$. In this MTS we have transitions

$$\alpha = u \xrightarrow{[a]} v, \beta = u \xrightarrow{[b]} w, \alpha' = w \xrightarrow{[a]} u', \beta' = v \xrightarrow{[b]} u' \alpha'' = t \xrightarrow{[a]} w',$$

$$\beta'' = z \xrightarrow{[b]} v', \alpha_1 = u' \xrightarrow{[a_1]} v', \beta_1 = u' \xrightarrow{[b_1]} w', \alpha_1' = w' \xrightarrow{[a_1]} u, \beta_1' = v' \xrightarrow{[b_1]} u$$

$$\alpha_1'' = v \xrightarrow{[a_1]} z, \beta_1'' = w \xrightarrow{[b_1]} t,$$

where $[a], [a_1], [b], [b_1]$ are traces corresponding to a, a_1, b, b_1, and compositions of these transitions. For example,

$$\alpha\beta' = \beta\alpha' = \gamma = u \xrightarrow{[ab]} u', \alpha_1\beta_1' = \beta_1\alpha_1' = \gamma_1 = u' \xrightarrow{[a_1 b_1]} u,$$

transitions α, α' are equivalent, transitions β, β' are equivalent, and we have regions

$$E = \{u, w, t, v', z\}, F = \{u, v, z, t, w'\}, G = \{v, u', w'\},$$
$$H = \{w, u', v'\}, E \cup G, F \cup H, \text{ and } \{u, v, w, z, t, u', v', w'\}. \qquad \sharp$$

From the definition of a region we obtain the following proposition.

Proposition 4.4. *If* $\mathbf{A} = (A, ;)$ *is an MTS,* r *is a region of* $\mathbf{A}$, *and* $(v \xleftarrow{\alpha_1} u \xrightarrow{\alpha_2} w, v \xrightarrow{\alpha_2'} u' \xleftarrow{\alpha_1'} w)$ *is a bicartesian square in* $\mathbf{A}$, *then* $v \in r$ *implies that* $u \in r$ *or* $u' \in r$. $\qquad \sharp$

Due to the property (A5) of multiplicative transition systems we obtain the following proposition.

Proposition 4.5. *If* $\mathbf{A} = (A, ;)$ *is an MTS, r is a region of $\mathbf{A}$, and $(v \xleftarrow{\alpha_1} u \xrightarrow{\alpha_2} w, v \xrightarrow{\alpha'_2} u' \xleftarrow{\alpha'_1} w)$ is a bicartesian square in $\mathbf{A}$ with morphisms which are not identities, then for every decomposition $u \xrightarrow{\alpha_1} v = u \xrightarrow{\alpha_{11}} v_1 \xrightarrow{\alpha_{12}} v$ such that $u, v \in r$ we have $v_1 \in r$, and for every decomposition $w \xrightarrow{\alpha'_1} u' = w \xrightarrow{\alpha'_{11}} w_1 \xrightarrow{\alpha'_{12}} u'$ such that $w, u' \in r$ we have $w_1 \in r$.* ♮

The following three propositions follow from the definition of a region.

Proposition 4.6. *The set of all states of $\mathbf{A}$ is a region of $\mathbf{A}$.* ♮

Proposition 4.7. *If p and q are disjoint regions of $\mathbf{A}$ then $p \cup q$ is a region of $\mathbf{A}$.* ♮

Proposition 4.8. *If p and q are different regions of $\mathbf{A}$ such that $p \subseteq q$ then $q - p$ is a region of $\mathbf{A}$.* ♮

Moreover, we are also able to prove the following proposition.

Proposition 4.9. *Every state of a region of $\mathbf{A}$ belongs to a minimal region.* ♮

Proof. Let r be a region of $\mathbf{A}$ and let x be an element of r. Given a chain $(r_i : i \in I)$ of regions of $\mathbf{A}$ that are contained in r and contain x, for $r' = \bigcap(r_i : i \in I)$ and a transition α such that $dom(\alpha) \in r'$ and $cod(\alpha) \notin r'$, there exists $i_0 \in I$ such that $dom(\alpha) \in r_i$ and $cod(\alpha) \notin r_i$ for $i > i_0$. Consequently, for every transition α' such that $\alpha' \equiv \alpha$ we have $dom(\alpha') \in r_i$ and $cod(\alpha') \notin r_i$ for $i > i_0$, and thus $dom(\alpha') \in r'$ and $cod(\alpha') \notin r'$. Similarly, for α such that $dom(\alpha) \notin r'$ and $cod(\alpha) \in r'$ and for $\alpha' \equiv \alpha$. So, r' is a region. Consequently, according to the Lemma of Zorn and Kuratowski (cf. [16]), in the set of regions that are contained in r and contain x there exists a minimal region. ♮

The Propositions 4.8 and 4.9 imply the following properties.

Proposition 4.10. *Every region of $\mathbf{A}$ contains a minimal region.* ♮

Proposition 4.11. *If a state s of $\mathbf{A}$ does not belong to a region r then there exists a minimal region r' such that $r \cap r' = \emptyset$ and s belongs to r'.* ♮

Proposition 4.12. *Every region of $\mathbf{A}$ can be represented as a disjoint union of minimal regions.* ♮

Proof. Let m be the disjoint union of a family M of minimal regions of $\mathbf{A}$. Then m is a region of $\mathbf{A}$ and if it does not cover A then $A - m$ is a region of $\mathbf{A}$ and the family M can be extended by a minimal region of $\mathbf{A}$ that contains a given element of $A - m$ as in the proof of Proposition 4.9. Consequently, a family of disjoint minimal regions of $\mathbf{A}$ can be defined such that its union covers A. ♮

5 Transitions as Labelled Posets

Now we shall show that elements of multiplicative transition systems can be interpreted as posets.

Let $\mathbf{A} = (A, ;)$ be an MTS.

Definition 5.1. *Given $\alpha \in A$ and a cut $x = (\xi_1, \xi_2)$ of α, by a state corresponding to such a cut x we mean $cod(\xi_1) = dom(\xi_2)$, and we write such a state as $state_\alpha(x)$.* ♯

It is easy to see that the lattice LT_α of cuts of α viewed as a category is an MTS and that the obvious extension of the correspondence $x \mapsto state_\alpha(x)$ to the mapping mp_α from LT_α to $\mathbf{A}$ preserves the composition. Given two cuts x and y, by $x \sqcup_\alpha y$ and $x \sqcap_\alpha y$ we denote respectively the least upper bound and the greatest lower bound of x and y. The diagram $(x \leftarrow x \sqcap_\alpha y \rightarrow y, x \rightarrow x \sqcup_\alpha y \leftarrow y)$ is a bicartesian square in LT_α. From (A6) it follows that the image under the mapping mp_α of such a diagram is a bicartesian square in $\mathbf{A}$.

Example 5.2. Consider the MTS $\mathbf{A}'_{v,v'}$ in Example 3.2. For the transition $\kappa = \sigma'(\pi \parallel \rho)\sigma''$ of this MTS we have the MTS LT_κ shown in Fig. 5 and its minimal regions

$$i = \{(u, \kappa)\},$$
$$j = \{(\sigma', (\pi \parallel \rho)\sigma''), ..., (\sigma'(\pi \parallel dom(\rho)), (cod(\pi) \parallel \rho)\sigma'')\}, ...,$$
$$j' = \{(\sigma'(dom(\pi) \parallel \rho), (\pi \parallel cod(\rho))\sigma''), ..., (\sigma'(\pi \parallel \rho), \sigma'')\}, ...,$$
$$k = \{(\sigma', (\pi \parallel \rho)\sigma''), ..., (\sigma'(dom(\pi) \parallel \rho), (\pi \parallel cod(\rho))\sigma'')\}, ...,$$
$$k' = \{(\sigma'(\pi \parallel dom(\rho)), (cod(\pi) \parallel \rho)\sigma''), ..., (\sigma'(\pi \parallel \rho), \sigma'')\},$$
$$l = \{(\kappa, u)\}.$$
♯

Example 5.3. Consider the MTS $TS(M', I')$ in Example 4.3. For the transition $\delta = \gamma\gamma_1 = \alpha\beta'\alpha_1\beta_1'$ of this system we have the MTS LT_δ shown in Fig. 6 and its minimal regions

$$(\sigma'(dom(\pi) \parallel \rho), (\pi \parallel cod(\rho))\sigma'') \; \longrightarrow \; \cdots \; \longrightarrow \qquad (\sigma'(\pi \parallel \rho), \sigma'') \; \longrightarrow \; (\kappa, u)$$

$$\uparrow \qquad\qquad\qquad\qquad\qquad\qquad\qquad\qquad\qquad\qquad\qquad \uparrow$$

$$(u, \kappa) \longrightarrow (\sigma', (\pi \parallel \rho)\sigma'') \qquad \longrightarrow \quad \cdots \quad \longrightarrow \qquad (\sigma'(\pi \parallel dom(\rho)), (cod(\pi) \parallel \rho)\sigma'')$$

$$LT_\kappa$$

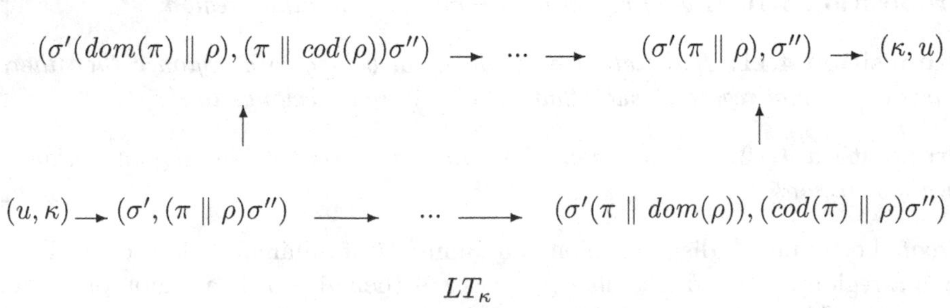

Fig. 5. The lattice LT_κ

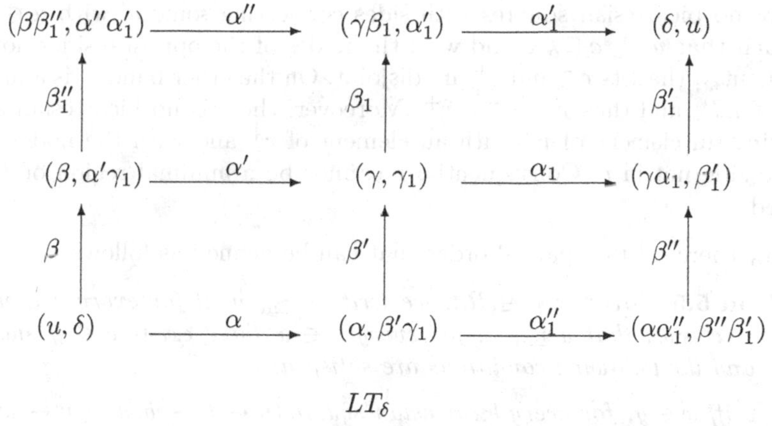

$$(\beta\beta_1'', \alpha''\alpha_1') \xrightarrow{\quad \alpha'' \quad} (\gamma\beta_1, \alpha_1') \xrightarrow{\quad \alpha_1' \quad} (\delta, u)$$

$$(\beta, \alpha'\gamma_1) \xrightarrow{\quad \alpha' \quad} (\gamma, \gamma_1) \xrightarrow{\quad \alpha_1 \quad} (\gamma\alpha_1, \beta_1')$$

$$(u, \delta) \xrightarrow{\quad \alpha \quad} (\alpha, \beta'\gamma_1) \xrightarrow{\quad \alpha_1'' \quad} (\alpha\alpha_1'', \beta''\beta_1')$$

$$LT_\delta$$

Fig. 6. The lattice LT_δ

$$e = \{(u, \delta), (\beta, \alpha'\gamma_1), (\beta\beta_1'', \alpha''\alpha_1')\}, g = \{(\alpha, \beta'\gamma_1), (\gamma, \gamma_1), (\gamma\beta_1, \alpha_1')\},$$
$$e' = \{(\alpha\alpha_1'', \beta''\beta_1'), (\gamma\alpha_1, \beta_1'), (\delta, u)\}, f = \{(u, \delta), (\alpha, \beta'\gamma_1), (\alpha\alpha_1'', \beta''\beta_1')\},$$
$$h = \{(\beta, \alpha'\gamma_1), (\gamma, \gamma_1), (\gamma\alpha_1, \beta_1')\}, f' = \{(\beta\beta_1'', \alpha''\alpha_1'), (\gamma\beta_1, \alpha_1'), (\delta, u)\}. \qquad \sharp$$

Let $\mathbf{A} = (A, ;)$ be an arbitrary MTS.

Given an element α of $\mathbf{A}$, by R_α we denote the set of minimal regions of the multiplicative transition system LT_α.

Using regions of $\mathbf{A}$ we want to assign to each transition α of $\mathbf{A}$ a labelled partially ordered set (an lposet) $L_\alpha = (X_\alpha, \leq_\alpha, l_\alpha)$. Each element $x \in X_\alpha$ is supposed to play the role of an occurrence in α of a minimal region $l_\alpha(x)$ of $\mathbf{A}$. The partial order $\leq_\alpha$ is supposed to reflect how occurrences of minimal regions arise from other minimal occurrences.

The underlying set X_α of L_α is supposed to be defined referring to the set R_α of minimal regions of the MTS LT_α and to a relation $\vdash_\alpha$ between minimal regions of LT_α and minimal regions of $\mathbf{A}$.

We are going to show how to define the respective lposet L_α for every element of $\mathbf{A}$.

Proposition 5.4. *Every minimal region $r \in R_\alpha$ is convex in the sense that $w \in r$ for every w such that $u \sqsubseteq_\alpha w \sqsubseteq_\alpha v$ for some $u \in r$ and $v \in r$.* $\qquad \sharp$

Proof. Suppose that $r \in R_\alpha$ and $a \sqsubseteq_\alpha c \sqsubseteq_\alpha b$ for $a, b \in r$ and $c \notin r$. Define r^- to be the set of $u \in r$ such that $u \sqsubseteq_\alpha c$ or $u' \sqsubseteq_\alpha c$ for some u' that can be connected with u by a side of a bicartesian square with the nodes of the opposite side not in r. Define r^+ to be the set of $u \in r$ such that $c \sqsubseteq_\alpha u$ or $c \sqsubseteq_\alpha u'$ for some u' that can be connected with u by a side of a bicartesian square with the nodes of the opposite side not in r. There is no bicartesian square with a side connecting some $u \in r$ and $v \in r$ such that $u \sqsubseteq_\alpha c \sqsubseteq_\alpha v$ and with the nodes of the opposite side not in r because by (A5) it would imply $c \in r$. By (A5) there are no bicartesian squares with sides connecting some u' with $u \in r$ and $v \in r$ such that $u \sqsubseteq_\alpha c \sqsubseteq_\alpha v$ and with the nodes of the opposite sides not in r. Consequently, the sets r^- and r^+ are disjoint. On the other hand, r is a minimal region of LT_α and thus $r \subseteq r^- \cup r^+$. Moreover, there is no bicartesian square connecting an element of r^- with an element of r^+ and with the nodes of the opposite side not in r. Consequently, r cannot be a minimal region of LT_α as supposed.   ♯

In R_α there exists a partial order that can be defined as follows.

Definition 5.5. *Given $x, y \in R_\alpha$, we write $x \preceq_\alpha y$ iff for every $v \in y$ there exists $u \in x$ such that $u \sqsubseteq_\alpha v$, for every $u \in x$ there exists $v \in y$ such that $u \sqsubseteq_\alpha v$, and the following conditions are satisfied:*

(1) $t \in x$ iff $w \in y$, for every bicartesian square $(u \leftarrow t \rightarrow w, u \rightarrow v \leftarrow w)$ with $u \in x$ and $v \in y$,

(2) $t' \in x$ iff $w' \in y$, for every bicartesian square $(t' \leftarrow u \rightarrow v, t' \rightarrow w' \leftarrow v)$ with $u \in x$ and $v \in y$.   ♯

Proposition 5.6. *If minimal regions $x, y \in R_\alpha$ are not disjoint and different then neither $x \preceq_\alpha y$ nor $y \preceq_\alpha x$.*   ♯

Proof. Suppose that x and y are different minimal regions of LT_α such that $x \cap y \neq \emptyset$. Then $x - y$ and $y - x$ are nonempty and there exist $u \in x - y$, $v \in y - x$, and $w, z \in x \cap y$ such that u and w are adjacent nodes of a bicartesian square U, z and v are adjacent nodes of a bicartesian square V, and the nodes of the bicartesian square $W = (w \leftarrow w \sqcap_\alpha z \rightarrow z, w \rightarrow w \sqcup_\alpha z \leftarrow z)$ are in $x \cap y$.

Consider the case in which $w = u \sqcup_\alpha u'$ for some u' not in x and $z = v \sqcap_\alpha v'$ for some v' not in y, as it is depicted in Fig. 11. Then $u' \in y$, $v' \in x$, and the condition (1) is not satisfied for $z \sqsubseteq_\alpha v$ and the bicartesian square $(v \leftarrow z \rightarrow v', v \rightarrow v \sqcup_\alpha v' \leftarrow v')$. Consequently, $x \preceq_\alpha y$ does not hold.

Similarly, in the other possible cases we come to the conclusion that neither $x \preceq_\alpha y$ nor $y \preceq_\alpha x$ (Fig. 7).   ♯

Proposition 5.7. *If minimal regions $x, y \in R_\alpha$ are disjoint then either $x \preceq_\alpha y$ or $y \preceq_\alpha x$.*   ♯

Proof. It is impossible that u and v are incomparable for all $u \in x$ and $v \in y$ since one of the regions x or y contains $u \sqcap_\alpha v$ or $u \sqcup_\alpha v$.

Suppose that $u \sqsubseteq_\alpha v$ for $u \in x$ and $v \in y$. As x and y are disjoint and convex, it suffices to prove that every element of y has a predecessor in x. Consider $w \in y$. If $v \sqsubseteq_\alpha w$ then $u \sqsubseteq_\alpha w$. If $w \sqsubseteq_\alpha v$ then $u' \sqsubseteq_\alpha w$ for $u' = u \sqcap_\alpha w$ and by considering the bicartesian square $(u \leftarrow u' \rightarrow w, u \rightarrow w' \leftarrow w)$ we obtain that $w' \in y$ because y is convex. Hence $u' \in x$. If w and v are incomparable then either $v \sqcap_\alpha w \in y$ and we may replace w by $v \sqcap_\alpha w$ and proceed as in the previous case, or $v \sqcup_\alpha w \in y$ and we may replace v by $v \sqcup_\alpha w \in y$ and proceed as in the previous case. On the other hand, $u \sqsubseteq_\alpha v$ for $u \in x$ and $v \in y$ excludes $v' \sqsubseteq_\alpha u'$ for $u' \in x$ and $v' \in y$ since x and y are convex. Hence $x \preceq_\alpha y$.

Similarly, in the case $v \sqsubseteq_\alpha u$ we obtain $y \preceq_\alpha x$.   ♯

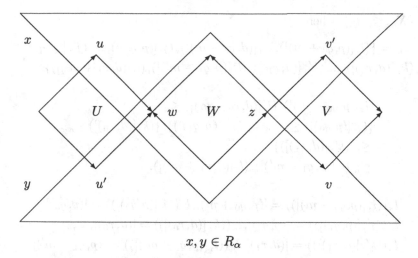

$$x, y \in R_\alpha$$

Fig. 7. Two minimal regions $x, y \in R_\alpha$

Proposition 5.8. *The relation $\preceq_\alpha$ is a partial order on R_α.*   ♯

Proof. The transitivity of the relation $\preceq_\alpha$ follows from the definition of this relation. The antisymmetry follows from the transitivity and from the Propositions 5.6 and 5.7.   ♯

The relation $\vdash_\alpha$ between minimal regions of LT_α and minimal regions of **A** can be defined as follows.

Proposition 5.9. *For every minimal region m of LT_α there exists a minimal region r of **A** such that the set $state_\alpha(m) = \{state_\alpha(u) : u \in m\}$ is contained in r, and we write $m \vdash_\alpha r$.*   ♯

Proof. Given a minimal region m of LT_α, let r be a minimal element of the set of regions of **A** containing the set $state_\alpha(m)$. As the image of every bicartesian square of LT_α under the mapping mp_α from LT_α to **A** is a bicartesian square in **A**, and for every partition of m into two disjoint nonempty subsets m' and m'' there exists in LT_α a bicartesian square connecting m' and m'', the same holds true for r. Consequently, r is a minimal region of **A**.   ♯

Finally, the lposet $L_\alpha = (X_\alpha, \leq_\alpha, l_\alpha)$ can be defined by defining X_α as the set of pairs (m, r) such that $m \in R_\alpha$ and $m \vdash_\alpha r$, the relation $\leq_\alpha$ as the partial order on X_α such that $x \leq_\alpha x'$ for $x = (m, r)$ and $x' = (m', r')$ whenever $m \preceq_\alpha m'$, and $l_\alpha(x)$ as r for $x = (m, r) \in X_\alpha$.

Example 5.10. Consider the MTS $\mathbf{A}'_{v,v'}$ described in Example 3.2, its minimal regions $[(v, q)]$, $[(v', r)]$ described in Example 5.2, and the minimal regions $i, j, ..., j', k, ..., k', l$ of LT_κ for $\kappa = \sigma'(\pi \parallel \rho)\sigma''$ as in Example 5.2. We obtain

$L_\kappa = (X_\kappa, \leq_\kappa, l_\kappa)$, where

$$X_\kappa = \{(i, [(p, q_0 + m)]), (i, [(d, r_0 - m)]), (j, [(p, q_0)]), ..., (j', [(p, q_1)]),$$
$$(k, [(d, r_0)]), ..., (k', [(d, r_1)]), (l, [(p, q_1 - m')]), (l, [(d, r_1 + m')])\},$$

$$(i, [(p, q_0 + m)]), (i, [(d, r_0 - m)]) \leq_\kappa$$
$$\{(j, [(p, q_0)]) \leq_\kappa \cdots \leq_\kappa (j', [(p, q_1)])\}, \{(k, [(d, r_0)]) \leq_\kappa \cdots$$
$$\leq_\kappa (k', [(d, r_1)])\}$$
$$\leq_\kappa (l, [(p, q_1 - m')]), (l, [(d, r_1 + m')]),$$

$$l_\kappa((i, [(p, q_0 + m)])) = [(p, q_0 + m)], l_\kappa((j, [(p, q_0)])) = [(p, q_0)],$$
$$l_\kappa((j', [(p, q_1)])) = [(p, q_1)], l_\kappa((k, [(d, r_0)])) = [(d, r_0)], ...,$$
$$l_\kappa((k', [(d, r_1)])) = [(d, r_1)], l_\kappa((l, [(p, q_1 - m')])) = [(p, q_1 - m')],$$
$$l_\kappa((l, [(d, r_1 + m')])) = [(d, r_1 + m')].$$

The corresponding $[L_\kappa]$ is essentially as that in Fig. 3.   ♯

Example 5.11. Consider the MTS $TS(M', I')$ described in Example 4.3, its minimal regions E, F, G, H, and the minimal regions e, g, e', f, h, f' of LT_δ for $\delta = \gamma\gamma_1 = \alpha\beta'\alpha_1\beta_1'$ as in Example 5.3. We obtain $L_\delta = (X_\delta, \leq_\delta, l_\delta)$, where

$$X_\delta = \{(e, E), (g, G), (e', E), (f, F), (h, H), (f', F)\},$$
$$(e, E) \leq_\delta (g, G) \leq_\delta (e', E), (f, F) \leq_\delta (h, H) \leq_\delta (f', F),$$
$$l_\delta((e, E)) = l_\delta((e', E) = E, l_\delta((g, G)) = G,$$
$$l_\delta((f, F)) = l_\delta((f', F)) = F, l_\delta((h, H)) = H.$$

Note that (e, E) and (e', E) are different instances of E, and (f, F) and (f', F) are different instances of F. The corresponding $[L_\delta]$ is presented in Fig. 8.   ♯

Proposition 5.12. *For every element u of LT_α, and for every $x, y \in R_\alpha$ such that $x \preceq_\alpha y$, and $x \preceq_\alpha x'$ for some $x' \in X_\alpha$ such that $u \in x'$, and $y' \preceq_\alpha y$ for some $y' \in X_\alpha$ such that $u \in y'$, there exists $z \in X_\alpha$ such that $u \in z$, and $x \preceq_\alpha z$, and $z \preceq_\alpha y$.*   ♯

Proof. For $x' = x$ it suffices to define z as x. For $y' = y$ it suffices to define z as y. Consider the case in which $x' \neq x$ and $y' \neq y$. By Proposition 5.6 in this case x and y are disjoint, x' and x are disjoint, and y' and y are disjoint. Consequently, u does not belong to x, u does not belong to y, and, by Proposition 4.11, there exists $z \in X_\alpha$ that is disjoint both with x and with y, as required.   ♯

Crucial for a representation of behaviour-oriented partial categories are the properties of **A** described in Proposition 5.12 and in the following propositions.

Proposition 5.13. *Every two different minimal regions x and y of LT_α such that $x \vdash_\alpha r$ and $y \vdash_\alpha r$ for a minimal region r of **A** are disjoint.*   ♯

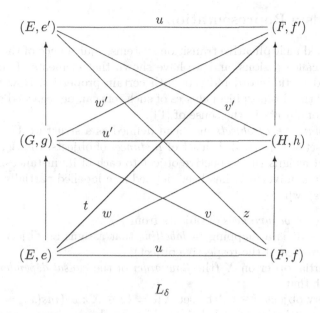

$$L_\delta$$

Fig. 8. The labelled partially ordered set L_δ

Proof. The correspondence between $u \xrightarrow{\delta} v$ such that $u = (\xi_1, \xi_2)$, $v = (\eta_1, \eta_2)$, $\eta_1 = \xi_1 \delta$, $\xi_2 = \delta \eta_2$ and $mp_\alpha(u) \xrightarrow{\delta} mp_\alpha(v)$ is a functor F_α from LT_α to $\mathbf{A}$. Due to (A6) this functor preserves bicartesian squares and, consequently, $mp_\alpha^{-1}(r)$ is a region in LT_α. Indeed, the image of a bicartesian square $D = (v \leftarrow t \rightarrow w, v \rightarrow u \leftarrow w)$ of LT_α under F_α is a bicartesian square $E = (v' \leftarrow t' \rightarrow w', v' \rightarrow u' \leftarrow w')$ of $\mathbf{A}$ since otherwise due to (A5) there would be a bicartesian square $E' = (v' \leftarrow t'' \rightarrow w', v' \rightarrow u'' \leftarrow w')$ that would be the image of a diagram $D' = (v \leftarrow \bar{t} \rightarrow w, v \rightarrow \bar{u} \leftarrow w)$ with $\bar{t} \neq t$ or $\bar{u} \neq u$, what is impossible in LT_α.

Say that elements $u, v \in mp_\alpha^{-1}(r)$ are connected if in LT_α there exists a bicartesian square S with one side with the vertices u and v and with the opposite side with the images of vertices under F_α not in r. Divide $mp_\alpha^{-1}(r)$ into parts such that different parts have no connected vertices and consider maximal decreasing chains of parts thus obtained. Each part is a region of LT_α and for every element x of this part the intersection of a chain of regions contained in this part and containing x is a region as in the proof of Proposition 4.9. Consequently, there exists a minimal region of LT_α that is contained in the considered part and contains x. Consequently, $mp_\alpha^{-1}(r)$ can be represented in a unique way as the union of disjoint minimal regions of LT_α. As these are the only minimal regions contained in $mp_\alpha^{-1}(r)$, the required conclusion follows. ♯

Proposition 5.14. *For every α in $\mathbf{A}$ and for $x, y \in X_\alpha$, the equality $l_\alpha(x) = l_\alpha(y)$ implies $x \leq_\alpha y$ or $y \leq_\alpha x$.* ♯

Proof. It suffices to take into account Propositions 5.7 and 5.13. ♯

6   Towards a Representation

We have defined multiplicative transition systems, equivalence of their elements, their subsets called regions, and we have shown that elements of such systems define labelled partially ordered sets with certain properties. Now we are prepared to show that isomorphism classes of such sets can be regarded as processes in a universe of objects in the sense of [14].

In [14] a *universe of objects* has been defined as a structure $\mathbf{U} = (V, W, ob)$ where V is a set of *objects*, W is a set of *instances* of objects from V, and ob is a mappings that assigns the respective object to each of its instances. A *concrete process* in such a universe $\mathbf{U}$ has been defined as a labelled partially ordered set $L = (X, \leq, ins)$, where

(1) X is a set (of *occurrences* of objects from V),
(2) $ins : X \to W$ is a mapping (a *labelling* that assigns an object instance to each occurrence of the respective object),
(3) $\leq$ is a partial order on X (the *flow order* or the *causal dependency relation* of L) such that
(3.1) for every object $v \in V$, the set $X|v = \{x \in X : ob(ins(x)) = v\}$ is either empty or it is a maximal chain and has an element in every cross-section,
(3.2) every element of X belongs to a cross-section,
(3.3) no segment of L is isomorphic to one of its proper subsegments.

and an *abstract process* has been defined as an isomorphism class of concrete processes. In [11,14] it has been shown that for every abstract processes α and β such that the source of β is the target of α there exists exactly one abstract process γ such that $\alpha; \beta$ defined as γ *consist* of α *followed* by β, and that the set of processes in $\mathbf{U}$ with the operation $(\alpha, \beta) \mapsto \alpha; \beta$ is a partial category (a *behaviour oriented partial category*). It has been shown that for every abstract processes α and β in disjoint sets of objects there exists exactly one abstract process γ such that $\alpha \parallel \beta$ defined as γ consists of parallel abstract processes α and β.

The construction of the labelled poset $L_\alpha = (X_\alpha, \leq_\alpha, l_\alpha)$ for every element α of an MTS $\mathbf{A}$ is such that due to the properties (A1)–(A4) of $\mathbf{A}$ we obtain that no segment of L_α is isomorphic to its subsegment. This suggests that elements of MTSs represent processes in a universe of objects in the sense of [14].

To see this, consider the universe $U(\mathbf{A}) = (V(\mathbf{A}), W(\mathbf{A}), ob(\mathbf{A}))$ of objects, where $V(\mathbf{A})$ is the set of decompositions of the set of states of $\mathbf{A}$ into disjoint unions of minimal regions of $\mathbf{A}$, $W(\mathbf{A})$ is the set of pairs $w = (v, r)$ consisting of a decomposition v of the set of states of $\mathbf{A}$ into a disjoint union of minimal regions of $\mathbf{A}$ and of a minimal region $r \in v$, and $(ob(\mathbf{A}))(w) = v$ for every $w = (v, r) \in W(\mathbf{A})$. Due to Proposition 4.12 the sets $V(\mathbf{A})$ and $W(\mathbf{A})$ are nonempty. Given $\alpha \in A$, consider the lposet $L_\alpha^* = (X_\alpha^*, \leq_\alpha^*, l_\alpha^*)$, where X_α^* is the set of triples (m, v, r) such that such that $m \in R_\alpha$ and $m \vdash_\alpha r$ and $(v, r) \in W(\mathbf{A})$, the relation $\leq_\alpha^*$ is the partial order on X_α^* such that $x \leq_\alpha^* x'$ for $x = (m, r, v)$ and $x' = (m', r', v')$ whenever $m \preceq_\alpha m'$ and $r = r'$ implies $v = v'$ and $m = m'$ implies $r = r'$, and $l_\alpha^*(x) = (v, r)$ for $x = (m, r, v) \in X_\alpha^*$. As the minimal regions of every decomposition $v \in V(\mathbf{A})$ are disjoint, due to Propositions 4.6, 4.12, 5.6 and 5.7 we obtain that the set $X_\alpha^* | v = \{x \in X_\alpha^* : (ob(\mathbf{A}))(l_\alpha^*(x)) = v\}$ is a chain and has an element in every cross-section of L_α^*. Moreover, $X_\alpha^* | v$ is a maximal chain since otherwise every $x = (m, r, v) \in X_\alpha^* | v$ would be comparable with $x' = (m', r', v')$ for some $v' \neq v$ and, consequently, there would be $r = r'$ for every $x = (m, r, v) \in X_\alpha^* | v$ and this would imply $v = v'$. Hence, taking into account (A4), we obtain that L_α^* is a concrete process in $U(\mathbf{A})$.

Thus we obtain the following proposition.

Proposition 6.1. *Given a multiplicative transition system* $\mathbf{A}$, *the correspondence* $\alpha \mapsto [L_\alpha^*] = [(X_\alpha^*, \leq_\alpha^*, l_\alpha^*)]$ *between elements of* $\mathbf{A}$ *and pomsets is a mapping from* $\mathbf{A}$ *to the partial category of processes in the universe* $U(\mathbf{A}) = (V(\mathbf{A}), W(\mathbf{A}), ob(\mathbf{A}))$ *in the sense of [14].* ♯

Example 6.2. Consider the MTS represented by the diagram in Fig. 9, where $\alpha\beta' = \beta\alpha' \neq \varphi$. In this diagram $(q \xleftarrow{\alpha} p \xrightarrow{\beta} r, q \xrightarrow{\beta'} s \xleftarrow{\alpha'} r)$ is a bicartesian square, the sets $pq = \{p, q\}$, $pr = \{p, r\}$, $qs = \{q, s\}$, $rs = \{r, s\}$ are minimal regions, and $X = \{pq, rs\}$, $Y = \{pr, qs\}$ are decompositions of the set of states into disjoint unions of minimal regions. For the transition φ the lattice LT_φ of decompositions of this transition consists of the least element $a = (p, \varphi)$ and the greatest element $b = (\varphi, s)$. Consequently, L_φ^* is a transition as shown in Fig. 10 and it is identical with L_φ^{**}. ♯

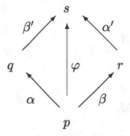

Fig. 9. A diagram

Note that the correspondence $\alpha \mapsto [L_\alpha^*] = [(X_\alpha^*, \leq_\alpha^*, l_\alpha^*)]$ need not be a homomorphism. To see this, it suffices to consider a MTS $\mathbf{A}$ that is the reduct of an algebra of transitions, and in this MTS a transition $\gamma = \alpha\beta$, where $\alpha = dom(\varphi) \parallel \psi$ and $\beta = \varphi \parallel cod(\psi)$. It is easy to see that $[L_\gamma^*] \neq [L_\alpha^*][L_\beta^*]$.

However, every transition L_α^* can be transformed into a process L_α^{**} such that the correspondence $\alpha \mapsto [L_\alpha^{**}]$ is a homomorphism. This can be done as follows.

The fact that all $(m, r, v) \in X_\alpha^*$ with the same r and v form a chain implies the following proposition.

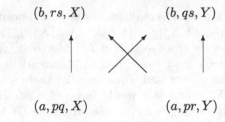

Fig. 10. The transition L_φ^*

Proposition 6.3. *The following relation between elements of X_α^* is an equivalence relation: $(m, r, v) \simeq_\alpha (m', r', v')$ iff $v' = v$, $r' = r$, $m \vdash_\alpha r$, $m' \vdash_\alpha r$, and $m'' \vdash_\alpha r$ for all m'' such that $m \sqsubseteq_\alpha m'' \sqsubseteq_\alpha m'$ or $m' \sqsubseteq_\alpha m'' \sqsubseteq_\alpha m$.*   ♮

Due to this proposition we obtain the following proposition.

Proposition 6.4. *The triple $L_\alpha^{**} = (X_\alpha^{**}, \leq_\alpha^{**}, l_\alpha^{**})$ with $X_\alpha^{**} = X_\alpha^*/\simeq_\alpha$, $x \leq_\alpha^{**}$ x' iff $(m, r, v) \leq_\alpha^* (m', r', v')$ for all $(m, r, v) \in x$ and $(m', r', v') \in x'$, and $l_\alpha^{**}(x) = l_\alpha^*(m, r, v)$ for $(m, r, v) \in x$, is a concrete process in $U(\mathbf{A})$.*   ♮

Example 6.5. Consider a system M consisting of machines M_1 and M_2 which work independently as shown in Fig. 11 and execute jointly an action γ that is not shown in Fig. 11 and leads M_1 to the state a and M_2 to the state c if M_1 comes to the state b and M_2 comes to the state d.

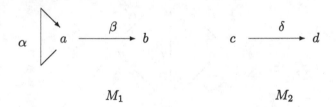

Fig. 11. Machines M_1 and M_2

In this system we have among others the following transitions:

- a, b, c, d are transitions reducing to their initial (and final) states,
- $a \parallel c$, $a \parallel d$, $b \parallel c$, $b \parallel d$ are transitions identical with their initial and final states,
- α is an atomic transition with the initial state a and the final state a,
- β is an atomic transition with the initial state a and the final state b,
- γ is an atomic transition with the initial state $b \parallel c$ and the final state $a \parallel d$,
- δ is an atomic transition with the initial state c and the final state d,
- $\alpha \parallel \delta$ is a transition with the initial state $a \parallel c$ and the final state $a \parallel d$ that consists of parallel transitions α and δ,

- an execution of α twice is a transition with the initial state a and the final state a that consists of α followed by α,
- an infinite repetition of α that begins but never ends is a transition with the initial state a and no final state, etc.

In particular, we have transitions $a \parallel c$, $a \parallel d$, $b \parallel c$, $b \parallel d$, $\alpha_c = \alpha \parallel c$, $\alpha_d = \alpha \parallel d$, $\beta_c = \beta \parallel c$, $\beta_d = \beta \parallel d$, γ, $\delta_a = \delta \parallel a$, $\delta_b = \delta \parallel b$,

The system is an MTS with bicartesian squares

$$(a \parallel c \overset{\alpha_c^m}{\leftarrow} a \parallel c \overset{\delta_a}{\to} a \parallel d, a \parallel c \overset{\delta_a}{\to} a \parallel d \overset{\alpha_d^m}{\leftarrow} a \parallel d),$$

$$(b \parallel c \overset{\beta_c}{\leftarrow} a \parallel c \overset{\delta_a}{\to} a \parallel d, b \parallel c \overset{\delta_b}{\to} b \parallel d \overset{\beta_d}{\leftarrow} a \parallel d),$$

minimal regions

$$A = \{a \parallel c, a \parallel d\}, B = \{b \parallel c, b \parallel d\}, C = \{a \parallel c, b \parallel c\}, D = \{a \parallel d, b \parallel d\},$$

and decompositions $P = \{A, B\}$, $Q = \{C, D\}$ of the set of states into disjoint unions of minimal regions.

The respective universe of objects is $\mathbf{U}(\mathbf{A_1}) = (V(\mathbf{A_1}), W(\mathbf{A_1}), ob(\mathbf{A_1}))$, where $W(\mathbf{A_1}) = \{A, B, C, D\}$, $V(\mathbf{A_1}) = \{P, Q\}$, $(ob(\mathbf{A_1}))(A) = (ob(\mathbf{A_1}))(B) = P$, $(ob(\mathbf{A_1}))(C) = (ob(\mathbf{A_1}))(D) = Q$.

For every transition π of we have the corresponding lattice LT_π of decompositions of π, the corresponding set R_π of minimal regions of this lattice, the corresponding partial order $\preceq_\pi$ on R_π, and the corresponding transition L_π^* in $\mathbf{U_1}$. For example, for $\pi = \alpha_c \beta_c \delta_b \gamma \beta_c$ we have the lattice of decompositions of π shown in Fig. 12 and we have the set

$$R_\pi = \{x, y, z, p, q, r, s\} \text{ of minimal regions, where}$$

$$x = \{(a \parallel c, \pi)\} \vdash_\pi A, C,$$

$$y = \{(\alpha_c, \beta_c \delta_b \gamma \beta_c), (\alpha_c \delta_a, \beta_d \gamma \beta_c)\} \vdash_\pi A$$

$$z = \{(\alpha_c \beta_c, \delta_b \gamma \beta_c), (\alpha_c \beta_c \delta_b, \gamma \beta_c)\} \vdash_\pi B$$

$$p = \{(\alpha_c, \beta_c \delta_b \gamma \beta_c), (\alpha_c \beta_c, \delta_b \gamma \beta_c)\} \vdash_\pi C$$

$$q = \{(\alpha_c \delta_a, \beta_d \gamma \beta_c), (\alpha_c \beta_c \delta_b, \gamma \beta_c)\} \vdash_\pi D$$

$$r = \{(\alpha_c \beta_c \delta_b \gamma, \beta_c)\} \vdash_\pi A, C$$

$$s = \{(\pi, b \parallel c)\} \vdash_\pi B, C$$

the process L_π^* in $\mathbf{U_1}$ shown in Fig. 13, and the corresponding process L_π^{**} in $\mathbf{U_1}$ shown in Fig. 14.   ♯

Now we want to prove that the correspondence $\alpha \mapsto [L_\alpha^{**}] = [(X_\alpha^{**}, \leq_\alpha^{**}, l_\alpha^{**})]$ between elements of an MTS $\mathbf{A}$ and processes in the universe $U(\mathbf{A}) = (V(\mathbf{A}), W(\mathbf{A}), ob(\mathbf{A}))$ of objects enjoys the following property.

Proposition 6.6. *If $\gamma = \alpha\beta$ with $cod(\alpha) = dom(\beta) = c$ then L_γ^{**} is the pushout object in the category* **LPOSETS** *of the injections of L_c^{**} in L_α^{**} and in L_β^{**}.* ♯

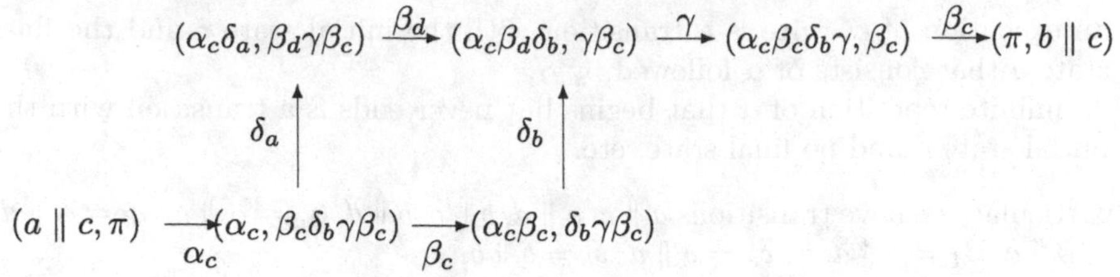

$$(\alpha_c\delta_a, \beta_d\gamma\beta_c) \xrightarrow{\beta_d} (\alpha_c\beta_d\delta_b, \gamma\beta_c) \xrightarrow{\gamma} (\alpha_c\beta_c\delta_b\gamma, \beta_c) \xrightarrow{\beta_c} (\pi, b \parallel c)$$

$$\delta_a \uparrow \qquad\qquad \delta_b \uparrow$$

$$(a \parallel c, \pi) \xrightarrow[\alpha_c]{} (\alpha_c, \beta_c\delta_b\gamma\beta_c) \xrightarrow[\beta_c]{} (\alpha_c\beta_c, \delta_b\gamma\beta_c)$$

Fig. 12. The lattice of decompositions of π

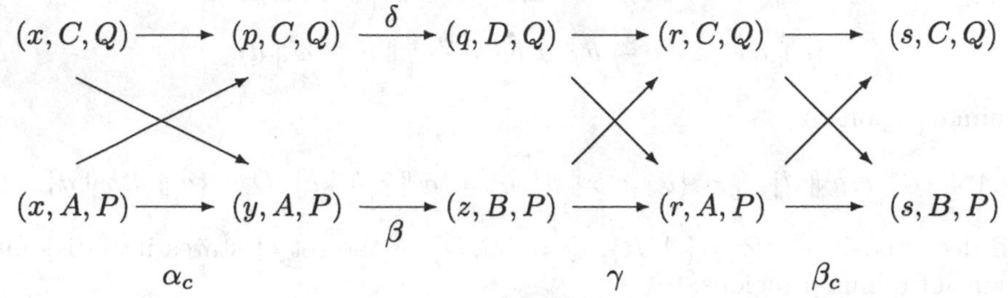

Fig. 13. The transition L_π^*

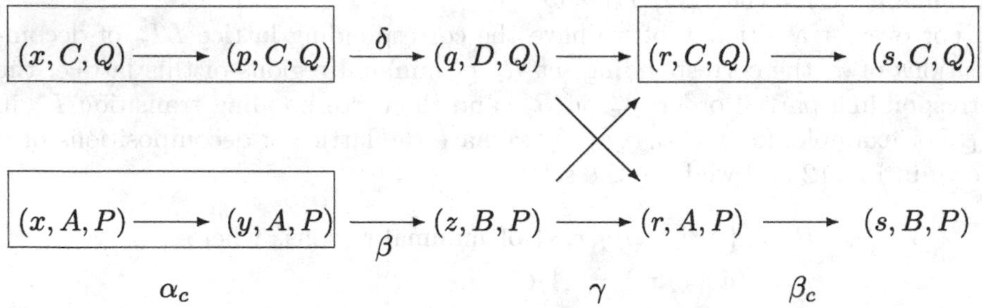

Fig. 14. The corresponding process L_π^{**}

Proof. Let $d \in LT_\gamma$ be the cut (α, β) of γ. The correspondence $i_\alpha : (\alpha_1, \alpha_2) \mapsto (\alpha_1, \alpha_2\beta)$ is an isomorphism between the lattice LT_α and the sublattice $LT_{\gamma,\alpha}$ of LT_γ consisting of the cuts between $(dom(\gamma), \gamma)$ and (α, β). Similarly, the correspondence $i_\beta : (\beta_1, \beta_2) \mapsto (\alpha\beta_1, \beta_2)$ is an isomorphism between the lattice LT_β and the sublattice $LT_{\gamma,\beta}$ of LT_γ consisting of the cuts between (α, β) and $(\gamma, cod(\gamma))$.

Let r be a region of LT_γ and let r_α and r_β be respectively the part of r in $LT_{\gamma,\alpha}$ and the part of r in $LT_{\gamma,\beta}$. Every bicartesian square that is contained in $LT_{\gamma,\alpha}$ and has a side outside of r_α must be disjoint with r_α or must have the entire opposite side in r_α. Consequently, r_α is a region of $LT_{\gamma,\alpha}$. Similarly, r_β is a region of $LT_{\gamma,\beta}$.

Due to (A6) every bicartesian square that is contained in LT_γ and has a side in r_α and the opposite side disjoint with r can be decomposed into two bicartesian squares of which one has a side in r_α and the opposite side disjoint with r_α. Consequently, r_α is a minimal region of $LT_{\gamma,\alpha}$ whenever r is a minimal region of LT_γ, and $r_\alpha \subseteq m$ for every minimal region of LT_γ that contains m. Similarly, every bicartesian square that is contained in LT_γ and has a side in r_β and the opposite side disjoint with r can be decomposed into two bicartesian squares of which one has a side in r_β and the opposite side disjoint with r_β. Consequently, r_β is a minimal region of $LT_{\gamma,\beta}$ whenever r is a minimal region of LT_γ, and $r_\alpha \subseteq n$ for every minimal region of LT_γ that contains n.

Thus every minimal region r of LT_γ has a part r_α in $LT_{\gamma,\alpha}$ and a part r_β in $LT_{\gamma,\beta}$, these parts are minimal regions of $LT_{\gamma,\alpha}$ and $LT_{\gamma,\beta}$, respectively, and they determine r uniquely. Moreover, if both r_α and r_β are nonempty then, due to the convexity of minimal regions of LT_γ, the cut $d = (\alpha,\beta)$ belongs to r.

Exploiting these facts we can verify that $(L_\alpha^{**} \xrightarrow{k_{\gamma,\alpha}} L_\gamma^{**} \xleftarrow{k_{\gamma,\beta}} L_\beta^{**})$ is a pushout of $(L_\alpha^{**} \xleftarrow{j_{\alpha,c}} L_c^{**} \xrightarrow{j_{\beta,c}} L_\beta^{**})$ with

$j_{\alpha,c} : [m,r,v] \mapsto [m',r,v]$ for m containing (c,c) and m' containing (α,c)

$j_{\beta,c} : [m,r,v] \mapsto [m',r,v]$ for m containing (c,c) and m' containing (c,β)

$k_{\gamma,\alpha} : [m,r,v] \mapsto [m',r,v]$ for m containing (α_1,α_2) and m' containing $(\alpha_1,\alpha_2\beta)$

$k_{\gamma,\beta} : [m,r,v] \mapsto [m',r,v]$ for m containing (β_1,β_2) and m' containing $(\alpha\beta_1,\beta_2)$.

♯

Consequently, we obtain the following result.

Proposition 6.7. *Given a multiplicative transition system* **A**, *the correspondence* $\alpha \mapsto [L_\alpha^{**}] = [(X_\alpha^{**}, \leq_\alpha^{**}, l_\alpha^{**})]$ *between elements of* **A** *and processes in the universe* $U(\mathbf{A}) = (V(\mathbf{A}), W(\mathbf{A}), ob(\mathbf{A}))$ *of objects is a homomorphism from* **A** *to the partial category of processes in* $U(\mathbf{A})$. ♯

This proposition is the main result of the paper. It tells that every algebraic structure which satisfies the axioms characterizing multiplicative transition systems is essentially the partial category of processes in a universe of objects in the sense of [14]. Put in another way, such processes and their partial categories seem to be the most natural models of concurrent systems and their runs.

7   Partial Order of Transitions

The representation of each transition α of a multiplicative transition system **A** by an lposet $L_\alpha^* = (X_\alpha^*, \leq_\alpha^*, l_\alpha^*)$ can be exploited as a basis of a formal definition of the parallel composition of transitions and of the corresponding partial order of transitions. To this end it suffices to define the parallel composition of abstract transitions in disjoint sets of objects from $V(\mathbf{A})$ as the partial operation $(\alpha,\beta) \mapsto$

$\alpha \parallel \beta$, where $\alpha \parallel \beta$ consists of parallel pomsets α and β. Then the inclusion of an abstract transition α in an abstract transition β can be defined as the relation $\ll$ that is satisfied iff α is an independent component of β. Due to 5.14 the relation $\ll$ is a partial order such that

(1) there exists the least element 0,
(2) every two elements α and β have a greatest lower bound $\alpha \bigtriangleup \beta$,
(3) some elements α and β have a least upper bound $\alpha \bigtriangledown \beta$,
(4) the partial operations $(\alpha, \beta) \mapsto \alpha \bigtriangleup \beta$ and $(\alpha, \beta) \mapsto \alpha \bigtriangledown \beta$ are commutative and associative (the latter as it is defined for partial operations),
(5) $\alpha \bigtriangleup (\beta \bigtriangledown \gamma) = (\alpha \bigtriangleup \beta) \bigtriangledown (\alpha \bigtriangleup \gamma)$ whenever either side is defined,
(6) for every α_1, α_2, β_1, β_2 such that $\alpha_1; \alpha_2$ and $\beta_1; \beta_2$ are defined also $(\alpha_1 \bigtriangleup \beta_1); (\alpha_2 \bigtriangleup \beta_2)$ is defined and $(\alpha_1; \alpha_2) \bigtriangleup (\beta_1; \beta_2) = (\alpha_1 \bigtriangleup \beta_1); (\alpha_2 \bigtriangleup \beta_2)$,
(7) the least upper bound $\alpha \bigtriangledown \beta$ exists iff α and β have segments α' and β' such that α' and β' have the least upper bound $\alpha' \bigtriangledown \beta'$.

Moreover, if in a multiplicative transition system $\mathbf{A}$ there exists a partial order $\ll$ which enjoys the properties (1)–(7) then $\alpha \parallel \beta$ can be defined as $\alpha \bigtriangledown \beta$ for α and β such that $\alpha \bigtriangleup \beta = 0$.

The possibility of studying an MTS $\mathbf{A}$ together with is partial order $\ll$ is important because together with runs of entire represented systems also runs of subsystems of such systems can be considered.

8   Concluding Remarks

Making use of the fact that runs of a system and a composition of such runs form a partial algebra satisfying a set of axioms, we have defined a multiplicative transition system, MTS, as an arbitrary partial algebra satisfying this set of axioms, and we have shown that every MTS can be viewed as a partial category of processes in a universe of objects. As elements of an MTS may represent decomposable runs, algebras of this type become a universal framework for describing systems that may exhibit any combination of discrete and continuous behaviour. As every MTS can be viewed as a partial category of processes in a universe of objects, such processes become universal basic structures for representing arbitrary system runs.

The fact that every MTS is an algebraic structure has also practical consequences. Using the concept of homomorphism it is possible to relate easily systems which simulate one another, to define a refinement of a system, and to verify system properties.

Acknowledgements. The author is grateful to the referees for their remarks which helped to improve the final version of the paper.

References

1. Badouel, E., Darondeau, P.: Trace nets and process automata. Acta Inform. **32**, 647–679 (1995)
2. Ehrenfeucht, A., Rozenberg, G.: Partial 2-structures. Acta Inform. **27**, 315–368 (1990)
3. Ehrig, H., Kreowski, H.-J.: Parallelism of manipulations in multidimensional information structures. In: Mazurkiewicz, A. (ed.) MFCS 1976. LNCS, vol. 45, pp. 284–293. Springer, Heidelberg (1976). doi:10.1007/3-540-07854-1_188
4. Lynch, N., Segala, R., Vaandrager, F.: Hybrid i/o automata. Inf. Comput. **185**(1), 105–157 (2003)
5. Mazurkiewicz, A.: Basic notions of trace theory. In: de Bakker, J.W., de Roever, W.-P., Rozenberg, G. (eds.) REX 1988. LNCS, vol. 354, pp. 285–363. Springer, Heidelberg (1989). doi:10.1007/BFb0013025
6. Mac Lane, S.: Categories for the Working Mathematician. Springer, New York (1971). doi:10.1007/978-1-4757-4721-8
7. Nielsen, M., Rozenberg, G., Thiagarajan, P.S.: Elementary transition systems. Theor. Comput. Sci. **96**, 3–33 (1992)
8. Petri, C.A.: Introduction to general net theory. In: Brauer, W. (ed.) Net Theory and Applications. LNCS, vol. 84, pp. 1–19. Springer, Heidelberg (1980). doi:10.1007/3-540-10001-6_21
9. Rozenberg, G., Thiagarajan, P.S.: Petri nets: basic notions, structure, behaviour. In: de Bakker, J.W., de Roever, W.-P., Rozenberg, G. (eds.) Current Trends in Concurrency. LNCS, vol. 224, pp. 585–668. Springer, Heidelberg (1986). doi:10.1007/BFb0027048
10. Winkowski, J.: An algebraic characterization of independence of petri net processes. Inf. Process. Lett. **88**, 73–81 (2003)
11. Winkowski, J.: An algebraic framework for defining behaviours of concurrent systems. Part 1: the constructive presentation. Fundamenta Informaticae **97**, 235–273 (2009)
12. Winkowski, J.: An algebraic framework for defining behaviours of concurrent systems. Part 2: the axiomatic presentation. Fundamenta Informaticae **97**, 439–470 (2009)
13. Winkowski, J.: Multiplicative transition systems. Fundamenta Informaticae **109**(2), 201–222 (2011). http://www.ipipan.waw.pl/~wink/winkowski.htm
14. Winkowski, J.: An Algebraic Framework for Concurrent Systems. Monograph 2 in Monograph Series. Institute of Computer Science of the Polish Academy of Sciences, Warsaw (2014)
15. Winskel, G., Nielsen, M.: Models for concurrency. In: Abramsky, S., Gabbay, D.M., Maibaum, T.S.E. (eds.) Handbook of Logic in Computer Science, vol. 4, pp. 1–148 (1995)
16. Zorn, M.: A remark on method in transfinite algebra. Bull. Am. Math. Soc. **41**, 667–670 (1935)

Author Index

Barylska, Kamila   1
Best, Eike   1

Carmona, Josep   43

De Koninck, Pieter   19
de la Houssaye, Jordan   70
De Weerdt, Jochen   19
Deniel, Philippe   70

Hansen, Henri   140
Holderer, Julius   43

Kalenkova, Anna A.   119

Lomazova, Irina A.   119

Montali, Marco   91
Müller, Günter   43

Pommereau, Franck   70

Rivkin, Andrey   91

Schlachter, Uli   1
Shershakov, Sergey A.   119
Spreckels, Valentin   1

Taymouri, Farbod   43

Valmari, Antti   140
Verbeek, H.M.W.   166

Winkowski, Józef   187

Printed in the United States
by Bookmasters

Printed in the United States
By Bookmasters